# The Psalms from a Christian Perspective
## Rev. Dr. George L. Earnshaw, Ph. D.

Edited by
Stanford Erickson
Jane Weise

WESTBOW
PRESS®
A DIVISION OF THOMAS NELSON
& ZONDERVAN

WestBow Press books may be ordered through booksellers or by contacting:

WestBow Press
A Division of Thomas Nelson & Zondervan
1663 Liberty Drive
Bloomington, IN 47403
www.westbowpress.com
1 (866) 928-1240

Scripture taken from the King James Version of the Bible.

Scripture quotations marked (NLT) are taken from the Holy Bible, New Living Translation, copyright © 1996, 2004, 2007 by Tyndale House Foundation. Used by permission of Tyndale House Publishers, Inc., Carol Stream, Illinois 60188. All rights reserved.

ISBN: 978-1-9736-6600-4 (sc)
ISBN: 978-1-9736-6599-1 (hc)
ISBN: 978-1-9736-6601-1 (e)

Library of Congress Control Number: 2019943814

Print information available on the last page.

WestBow Press rev. date: 7/15/2019

Dedicated to my beloved wife Virginia Earnshaw and the First
Presbyterian Men's Christian Fellowship in Vero Beach, Florida.

# FOREWORD
## Rev. Dr. J. Andrew Dearman

In the fourth century AD, the esteemed Bishop of Alexandria in Egypt wrote a classical letter on the interpretation of the Psalms. The Psalms, said Athanasius, reveal all aspects of the human soul. Reading them is like looking into a mirror and seeing oneself revealed in all the human emotions known to us. The Psalms, furthermore, are inspired guidelines for connecting the spiritual life to its source in God.

I don't know whether Dr. George Earnshaw ever read Athanasius' *Letter to Marcellinus on the Interpretation of the Psalms,* but I do know that he read and meditated on those hymns and prayers in the Bible's largest book for decades, following a classical pattern of discipline. He does describe reading the Psalms as like looking in a mirror and finding a window to God. And he and Athanasius (and many, many others) are surely right in this regard. There is nothing new in this perspective on the life of faith, but it stands the test of time.

Although I didn't meet Dr. Earnshaw until late in his distinguished life, I learned quickly from observing him and from listening to those who loved him that he had been a faithful Christian pastor and a wise soul in matters related to the Christian life. You need not take my word for it, however. Just take the time to read various psalms and then the brief, but discerning comments that he offers on each of them. Yes, it will be like looking in a mirror, where the psalmist's words help you see yourself and the human condition before God. And when you read his judicious comments, which draw in various parts of Holy Scripture for a Christian interpretation, they will seem like a window pointing you to the grace and transforming presence of the Lord.

J. Andrew Dearman, PhD, ThD
Professor of Old Testament, Fuller Theological Seminary

# REV. DR. GEORGE EARNSHAW
## By Stanford Erickson

An outside observer might say that Rev. Dr. George Earnshaw, Ph. D. was lucky in his upbringing. His father, George "Moose" Earnshaw, was one of the greatest minor and major league pitchers of organized baseball. In 1929, his second year in the big leagues, his 24 victories against 8 losses was best in the major leagues, and his 149 strikeouts were second only to teammate Lefty Grove in the American League. In a nine-year major league career, he won four World Series games.

But to Dr. George, his father was "not very kind," difficult for his mother and him, and "a constant embarrassment because of his drunkenness." Moose Earnshaw was known to pass out at times in the bullpen while waiting his turn to pitch.

Although the family was Episcopalian, Dr. George generally was the only one who attended church because he enjoyed singing in the choir. "I never read the Bible until later in life," he said.

Dr. George was raised in Swarthmore, Pa., a Quaker town famous for Swarthmore College, where his father was renowned as an athlete and his uncle provided a major endowment. Dr. George, however, chose to attend Penn State. But that was 1941. When the Untied States declared war on Japan after the infamous Pearl Harbor Attack December 7, 1941, Dr. George was drafted in the U.S. Army in 1942. For the next four years, Dr. George was an infantryman, carrying an M 1 rifle, while fighting the Japanese in the Pacific. When the war over, he remained stationed in Japan with the U.S. Army for the next year.

"That's when my life began to change," he said. He was befriended by Neisa Kawa, a Japanese Christian who was a conscientious objector in Japan during the war. "Neisa began proselytizing me. He was so profound. What he said was so over my head at the time, but somehow it touched my spirit."

Mustered out of the Army, Dr. George returned to finish his undergraduate degree at Penn State. Again, a major change occurred in his life. The Baptist Chaplain at Penn State, Rev. Robert Eades, began inviting him over to dinner each Friday night. In 1948, Rev. Eades baptized him by emersion. "It dawned on me then that Neisa Kawa, translated in English, means *west river*. As I was being baptized, the Spirit brought that to my mind."

During this time, Dr. George married Clare and over the next several years four daughters were born. With Rev. Eades' encouragement, he attended seminary at Colgate Rochester Crozer Divinity School, in Rochester, NY. Soon he was a Chaplain at University of Wisconsin followed by being a Chaplain at Syracuse University, where he also received a Ph.D. in psychology.

About this time he wrote *Serving Each Other in Love*, a book he and other ministers provide to those who plan to be married. "Like most deep understanding of things, my book came about with the help of sadness and misfortune. My own marriage did not survive," he said. "God often permits sadness and misfortune to school us in understanding what it takes to have joy."

Before agreeing to serve as Visitation Pastor at First Presbyterian Church in Vero Beach, Fl, where I first became acquainted with him, two other major events occurred for Dr. George. His daughter Helen introduced him to Virginia, a widow with four sons. Soon he and Jinny were married. She was an Elder at Sebastian Presbyterian in Sebastian, Fl, a town next to Vero Beach. "Jinny is what you call a *doer*. She is in charge of the food pantry and works in the garden of the church. Jinny is the epitome of joy in my life. A true blessing of God."

Dr. George also spent five years as an instructor in small group ministry for Rev. Dr. Billy Graham, at his conference center in Ashville, N.C. "At the time, I thought that was sort of the culmination of my career. What I failed to realize is that it just further prepared me to be useful to the congregation of First Presbyterian Church."

When Dr. George was not meeting or visiting with those in need, he was filling in for Rev. Dr. G. Timothy Womack when he was traveling by teaching classes and giving Sunday sermons, and singing in the choir. Dr. George's last sermon, titled "There Is Healing in Humor," unexpectedly for him, received a standing ovation from the congregation.

But that is not all. Dr. George for the last twenty years had been writing a book on "a human understanding" of each of the 150 Psalms. "Jesus in his short three-year ministry quotes the Psalms more than any other part of the Bible," Dr. George said. "I think that's because most of the Psalms are about Jesus and He helped write them through His Spirit. Easy to recall what you've helped write and when you are God."

Dr. George began sharing some of his commentaries on the psalms with me, asking me to review and perhaps edit them because of my long history as a journalist, writer and author. Over the next year or so, I edited all 150 of his commentaries on the psalms. Since he had not saved his commentaries on his computer, Dr. George enlisted Carol Bradley, a parishioner at First Presbyterian Church, to retype them with my edits. Unfortunately Dr. George died July 4, 2014. He was 90 years of age.

Over the last four years, I have reviewed and edited again, and attempted to check every reference cited by Dr. George to assure myself they were accurate. Also, when Dr. George began writing his commentaries, he first began using the *Living Bible*. Later, he used the *New Living Translation*. Jinny Earnshaw provided me with all of her husband's notes and I systematically made certain in almost every case that his commentaries relied on the *New Living Translation* for the sake of consistency. Finally when I was satisfied with my editing, I had Jane Weise, a talented former teacher of English, review and improve my editing.

November 2018

# COMMENTS BY JANE WEISE

## who provided the final edit of *The Psalms from a Christian Perspective.*

It is with relief and gratitude that I have finished the editing of Dr. Earnshaw's manuscript. I have learned so much in reading the text while editing. Dr. George has written a major work in interpreting the Psalms, acquainting the reader with Jewish History and the life David, translating Judaism for Christians, bridging the gap from the Old Testament to the New Testament, and adding much enrichment with songs and poetry. I can envision this book being used by pastors for sermons and teaching, but also for the Christian reader for learning and enjoying this amazing poetry and emotionally engaging text. I hope this book can get published either in one large work or in smaller works.

# INTRODUCTION TO THE PSALMS
## By Rev. Dr. George L. Earnshaw, Ph.D.

Christianity owes its beginnings to Judaism. The Lord Jesus was from the lineage of King David and God chose Him to be our Savior and Messiah of the world.

The Psalms are the Scriptural basis for much of the praise and prayers of the Christian church. The words and thoughts of the Psalms have been used for responsive readings, invocations and inspiration in the writing of many hymns. Over the years, countless Christians have been inspired as they turned to the Psalms for personal meditation and private devotions, being uplifted spiritually by the marvelous words of trust in God.

The title of this book, *The Psalms from a Christian Perspective*, is an attempt to do two things. (1) To critically analyze each of the individual 150 Psalms, without going into too much background, but enough to help the reader better understand the setting and the reasons for its writing. When necessary, certain Hebrew words will be explained and English alternatives given. (2) A concerted effort is made to interpret each Psalm from the distinctive perspective of the Christian faith. It is my assumption that those reading this work will be, mainly, Christians who want to know and better understand the Psalms, and who will want to see how the Psalms fit in with traditional Christianity.

God has given us Christians these Psalms to read and ponder. They run the gamut of various emotions and cover many diverse subject matters. It is surprising how many of the same problems the Psalmists deal with we also face today. As we read them, we must always bring our Christian faith to bear. We need always to read and interpret them through the eyes of the Lord Jesus Christ. Many of the Psalmists' words are quoted in the New Testament. They constitute a worthy foundation upon which New

Testament writers built. I assume the Apostle Paul had memorized many Psalms. They came readily to mind as he wrote his epistles to the converts of Christianity.

For the neophyte Christian, with little or no background of the Psalms, I offer the following as a brief overview.

The Psalms were considered the "song book" of the Jewish people. They are poems written by talented authors, telling about the work of God in creation, and His loving purpose for His chosen people. Many were written to be sung or recited as part of the liturgy of the annual Festivals held in the Temple. All of Israel's history is contained in the Psalms. Psalms 1-72 seem to deal with the earliest time of the Nation's beginning, specifically the great days of David and Solomon. Psalms 73-150 reflect the later time, when the mighty prophets of the 8th, 7th and 6th century B.C. were active. During this time: the ten Hebrew tribes of the Northern Kingdom were demolished in 722 B. C.; there was a revival of faith in Judah in the days of King Josiah; the fateful destruction of Jerusalem in 587 B.C.; and, the exile of the Jews to Babylon. Later Psalms include the exile's return to Judah and the rebuilding of Jerusalem and the Temple. Also, certain Psalms are considered "Messianic," anticipating and describing the redeeming Savior not only for the Hebrews but of all people. In the New Testament, Jesus actually refers to and quotes the Psalms more than any other book in the Old Testament.

Every writer of the Psalms was conscious of the fact that God had revealed Himself to Israel by what He did and how He acted. In the early days, God revealed Himself to Abraham. Later, He sent Moses to Egypt to expedite the freeing of the Hebrew people from slavery, with His miraculous help. Then, camping around Mount Sinai, God gave his people the law (the Torah), the first five books of the Old Testament. He also made a covenant (an agreement) with His chosen people (Exodus 19:3-6). He promised He would be their God if they would *obey me and keep my covenant*. If they would agree, then they would be God's special treasure among all the nations.

The *New Living Translation* of the Bible sets the Psalms in the idiom of poetry. My commentary refers to the *The New Livng Translation*. When we Christians read the English version of the *NLT*, we are reading the words and meaning that I believe are reflective of the original authors' intent. *The Living Bible* was first published in 1971. It was a paraphrase of the original words in an attempt to have a translation that more clearly portrayed the intent and meaning of the original authors. The *NLT* is a revision of *The Living Bible*. It attempts to make the closest equivalent of the message expressed by the original language text—both in meaning and in style.

The *NLT* is also a "thought-for-thought" as contrasted with a "word-for-word" translation. In making a thought-for-thought translation, the translators sought to enter into the thought pattern of the ancient writers. To guard against personal biases, the *NLT* was created by a group of scholars who could "check and balance" each other's work. One of the most difficult problems for them was to choose the closest meaning of the words written by the original authors. Each Hebrew word has a variety of English equivalents. For instance, the important Hebrew word *("Checed")* can mean "love," "mercy," "grace," "kindness," "faithfulness" and "loyalty." Which is right? What does the context call for? Another difficulty is found in the Hebrew metaphorical language. For instance, in the *Song of Songs* 1:15, the ancient poet writes *"Your eyes are doves."* In order to help the modern reader, the *NLT* scholars added, "soft like." "Your eyes are soft like doves." The NLT uppercases *"LORD"* when the text refers to the tetragrammaton "YHWH" and uses the lower case *"Lord"* when the text refers to *"Adonai."*

Most of the Biblical verses in this commentary come from the *NLT.* In a few instances, I have resorted to using the *Living Bible* translation because I have concluded it more readily expresses the purpose of the psalm. In addition, I often rely on a translation of specific Psalms by Eugene H. Peterson from his book titled *The Message.* He has a unique ability not only to capture the inherent meaning of the Psalms but his creative use of modern-day language and often slang capture the vibrancy of the original author. I believe Peterson is particularly good in doing that with the Psalms of David.

The Psalms cover a multitude of subjects. Many of them tell the reader to remember the *"mighty acts"* of the Lord. All of the poems either address God directly, or speak about His miracles indirectly. The Psalmists call upon the Lord to bless or heal them, or ask God to go with them with His" *"strong right hand"* to support them in battle. Many Psalms are complaints (laments). Some are confessions of sin. There are Psalms composed on sick beds in anticipation of death. Many focus around the king, and there are Psalms that admire the beauty and significance of the Holy City of Jerusalem. A number of them deal with God's concern for righteousness and His negativity toward wickedness. Several joyously declare the reign of God.

There is a belief among many Christian circles today that only spontaneous, unlearned prayers are authentic. God has placed a prayer book—the Psalms—in our hands. The Psalms are at the heart of the Bible and they are not to just inform us how the people of ancient times prayed, but they are put in our hands by God to teach us how to pray today! Praying a lament psalm can be beneficial, even if we are not in distress. Why? Because it prepares us for a time of trouble that will surely come to us all. It makes us aware that suffering is a part of our human experience—it happens to the righteous as well as the wicked. These Psalms give us the assurance that God is in control and they provide us with strength and confidence in times of trouble. Secondly, praying the lament Psalms sensitizes us to have compassion toward other sufferers.

King David was a prolific writer of Psalms: 3-41 and 51-72. Most of these Psalms are individual prayers to God and songs of dependence and trust featuring the LORD as his refuge. Two other individuals, Korah and Asaph (and their sons and grandsons, all workers in the Temple), each have collections of Psalms attributable to them: Korahite 42-49 and Asaphites, 50, 73-85.

One final thought:

God's purpose with all people, and that includes why He inspired the writers of the Psalms and preserved them for all of us today, is that God wants to bring all of us into His fold. He saves us out of His sheer grace ("Yesha"). When He touches us with his "Yesha," (His salvation), we automatically become God's "junior partners." We are, thereby, called to bear this fruit of God's saving love. Since He created all us human beings in His image (see Genesis 1:26), we are given the potential of doing what God does. We are empowered to share God's "saving love" with others. When we approach another, our (Yesha") becomes ("Yeshu ah") (a feminine rather than the male use of (Yesha"). This divine "saving love" puts the other person in a spiritual condition where they are "open" to be receptive to "being right" with God.

Probably sometime after the Jews were allowed to return to Judah following their exile, the Psalms were gathered in their current form: 1 through 150 into five books or sections, each ending in a doxology thought. Book 1: Psalms 1-41; Book 2: Psalms 42-77; Book 3: Psalms 73-89; Book 4: Psalms 90-106; and Book 5: Psalms 107-150. It is best to use the *New Living Translataion* when reading my commentary.

The Psalms are a mirror of self and a window to God.

# PSALM 1
## Delight in Doing God's Will

The opening psalm of book 1 in the Psalter sets the tone for what is to follow. It is the gateway to the ancient collection of a group of Hebrew poetry. This particular poem was probably written after the Jews in exile were allowed to return to their homeland, under Ezra, and they became known as the people of the Law.

The Psalmist in this opening psalm underscores the dichotomy between two groups of Hebrew folks in how they respond to God's Law—those who do and those who do not. The dichotomy is not made based on nationality or geography but on the reaction to God's covenant. In the book of Exodus, God told Moses on Mount Sinai to tell the people that if they will obey him and keep their part of the agreement (the covenant), He will bless and prosper them. (See Exodus 19:5 and Deuteronomy 28:1.) But if they turn their backs on the demands of the covenant, then they will be cursed!

### Segment One – The Joys of Following God's Laws. Verses 1 - 3

Those who don't associate with sinners to the point of becoming influenced by them are joyful, the Psalmist says in verse 1. Rather, they do everything they can to please God, which means meticulously following and obeying God's will as it is written in the scriptures (V. 3). They spend their time thinking and praying about ways they can put God's instructions, His Torah, into positive actions in their life.

One can compare these godly individuals with trees planted along the riverbanks (V. 3). They can learn the way of the Lord through His Word and can store up God's will in their hearts so that living righteously will become

1

second nature to them. Therefore, in their journey through life (*derek* in Hebrew), they will be able to bear fruit each season without fail (*V. 3*).

## Segment Two – The Wicked Are in Deep Trouble. Verses 4 - 3

The wicked Hebrews, because of their self-centered ways, find themselves cut off from God's covenant people! Metaphorically, the wind blows these me-first people away, separating them like worthless chaff (*V. 4*). They will not be included with the godly but will be condemned to judgment (*V. 5*).

## Segment Three – The LORD Watches over the Godly. Verse 6

Psalm 1 is a comfort for those who honestly try to be obedient to God's revealed way of life in His Torah, for they know God will bless them (*V. 6*). Some critics of Psalm 1 say it is too black and white; it eliminates all nuances. However, it makes its point! From a Christian perspective, God's word, the Law, is much broader. It means *all* of God's revelation, and specifically for us, it means God's revelation in Jesus Christ!

We Christians have to associate with sinners to win them, but as Psalm 1 warns, we don't dare allow the wicked to influence us, or we will become like them. Jesus told parables similar to Psalm 1, such as "The Wheat and the Tares" (*Matthew 13:37–43*) and "The Sheep and the Goats" (*Matthew 25:31–46*). Jesus spoke about discipleship and how we Christians have to choose between God and mammon (*Matthew 6:19–24*) and the broad and narrow way (*Matthew 7:13*).

# PSALM 2

## The Lord's Anointed

Psalms 1 and 2 are a paired introduction to the Psalter, the songbook of the Jewish people. When the Hebrews returned after seventy years exiled in Babylon, they rebuilt the temple, and many years after that, they were able to reassemble the Psalter that had been destroyed by the troops of King Nebuchadnezzar. Psalm 1 orients the reader to receive instruction from the scriptures, and Psalm 2 makes known the message that the Lord reigns! Some would say we ought to read these two psalms together. Also, this psalm has been labeled a Messianic psalm by Christians, referring to Jesus Christ.

### Segment One — A Plot to Overthrow God's Authority. Verses 1 - 3

The narrator introduces the rebellious would-be rulers of the world and asks why the nations rage *(V. 1)*. Why are they trying to do something as foolish and stupid as opposing the mighty God of the universe and His anointed king? Because they feel they are enslaved by the Lord of the universe *(V. 3)*.

### Segment Two — Heaven Responds. Verses 4 - 6

The speaker is God the Father in heaven, and His reaction to the haughty words of these rebellious kings is to *laugh at them (V. 4)*! It is a laugh of derision. Finally He has had enough, and with anger, He rebukes them and terrifies them *(V. 5)*. The Lord then declares He has placed His chosen king on the throne in Jerusalem *(V. 6)*.

## Segment Three – The LORD's Decrees. Verses 7 - 9

In verse 7, the LORD proclaims that the Jewish king is His son. The words in this section go back to 1,000 BC when God made a sacred promise to King David that he was specially chosen to guide and shepherd the Lord's chosen people. Furthermore, God promised David that his dynasty was to govern his people forever! (See 2 Samuel 2:7.) Some secular scholars see Psalm 2 as a coronation for a Jewish king, and they take the words of verse 7 to mean a symbolic adoption of the Jewish king by God. We Christians, on the other hand, see the "Son" as the Lord Jesus Christ. Not once but twice during Jesus's earthly ministry these words from verse 7 were applied to him: at his baptism and at his transfiguration. (See Matthew 3:17 and 17:5.) The Jewish scholar Paul of Tarsus says the second psalm is talking about Jesus, God's own Son *(Acts 13:33)*.

In verses 8 and 9, this Jewish king will be given the nations of the world as an inheritance to do what he wants with them. Verses 8 and 9, from a Christian perspective, are a great missionary challenge to the Christian church. We need to go to the ends of the earth to make Jesus known among the nations and to proclaim his rule as God's Messiah!

## Segment Four – The Holy Spirit Speaks. Verses 10 - 12

The narrator speaks words of warning to all those who have yet to bow their knees before God's Son *(V. 10)*. Serve the LORD with reverent fear *(V. 11)*. Submit yourself to God's royal Son, and receive his joy *(V. 12)*. The Holy Spirit is the One who draws us to Jesus, so we might say that He is the narrator. Usually we think of the Third Person of the Trinity as a gentle, loving, and tender voice. In this segment, the Holy Spirit is saying to all of us rebellious human beings that we would be wise to serve the Lord with fear and trembling. But what joy for all who find protection in Him!

The apostle Paul, a Jew by birth and a great intellectual scholar, says in his letter to the Romans that a true Jew is not one who was born of Jewish parents or a man who has gone through the Jewish ceremony of circumcision but one whose heart is right with God. That is true circumcision *(Romans 2:29)*. By these criteria, we can all call ourselves Jewish Christians.

# PSALM 3

## But You, LORD, Are a Shield around Me

The superscription of Psalm 3 says it is written by David and concerns the time when David had to flee from his son Absalom. The story of David's escape from Jerusalem with his entire household plus fighting men loyal to him is found in 2 Samuel 15–18.

It seems that while David was routinely absorbed with matters of governing, his son Absalom was gathering support around Judea for his own kingship. Finally, in the neighboring city of Hebron, he declared himself king of Israel. Absalom raised an army and marched on his father in order to occupy the capital city of Jerusalem. Taken unaware, David had no recourse other than fleeing for safety and heading into the wilderness. Psalm 3 probably was written by David during the rebellion.

This poem can be organized into four segments (or stanzas). The first (verses 1–2) is David's expression of the crisis that has come into his life as his son's army is out to destroy him. The second segment (verses 3–4) indicates his confidence that God will not forsake him or allow his enemies to prevail. The third is composed of two strophes (verses 5–6). In Jewish poetry, a strophe is made up of two approximately equal verses. In the last part (verses 7–8), David is expressing his certainty that God has heard his plea for help and will provide the needed deliverance.

### Segment One – David's Crisis due to Absalom's Invasion. Verses 1 - 2

The psalm begins with a sorrowful prayer to the LORD lamenting that David fully realizes he has so many enemies and so many of his subjects now oppose his being their king (*V. 1*). His son and his son's troops are giving him the message that he (as the king) has forfeited the right to receive divine assistance *(V. 2)*. Although David does not write it into this composition, we know from reading 2 Samuel that he takes the Ark of the Covenant (the symbol of God's presence) with him in his flight from the city initially. However, he changes his mind and sends it back to Jerusalem so that God can radiate his influence from his holy city.

## Segment Two – David's Trust and Confidence in God. Verses 3 - 4

David puts God first in his life and trusts Him. One of his favorite metaphors is God being his "shield" and giving him protection *(V. 3)*. He also says God is "my glory," which takes the place of the slanderous words coming from his foes *(V.3)*. When someone back then came before the king to ask for a favor, he would prostrate before the king. If the king granted his request, he would lift the person up by the chin.

David, referring to this common practice, says God (the divine King) is the One who lifts David's head up high. *(V.3)* There is no question about it; David had a personal relationship with the spiritual presence of the LORD. He was, indeed, a man after His (the LORD's) own heart. (*1 Samuel 13:14*) However, David did believe that God resided in Mount Zion, and that is why he sent the Ark back to Jerusalem, and that is also why he says in verse 4 that God answers his prayer from his holy mountain.

## Segment Three – David's Confident Assurance. Verses 5 - 6

David's confident faith allows him to have a good night's rest. As a result, he wakes up the next morning confident, knowing that God is His dependable support. David doesn't dwell on the dangers surrounding him. That would be depressing. Instead, he keeps his thoughts on the greatness of God. He is positive that the LORD is watching over him. *(V.5)* When we concentrate and turn our attention on God's presence, rather than upon our difficulties, God is seen in His true and great stature and our problems shrink to manageable proportions.

David is saying the same thing. He is not afraid even though thousands of enemies are drawing down on him because he believes God is his shield! *(V.6)* A more contemporary example is the way Martin Luther felt when summoned by the Roman Catholic Pope to come and defend his faith at the Council of Worms. Yes, Luther was promised safe conduct, but that was iffy.

Like David, Luther put his faith and trust in God's grace and went undaunted. It was at the Diet of Worms where the Church Fathers commanded Luther to renounce his faith and repudiate what he had written as being untrue. Here is what Luther replied. It is a classic! *"Unless I can be persuaded by the words of Scripture and sound reason, I cannot and will not recant. Here I stand. I can do no other, God help me. Amen."*

### Segment Four – David's War Cry. Verses 7 - 8

David gets aggressive here and asks God to slap all of David's enemies in the face. *(V.7)* Absalom took some bad advice and did not pursue David right away, allowing his father to regroup and get prepared. When the two forces met in battle in the forest of Ephraim, Scriptures tells us that 20,000 soldiers were killed – including Absalom! David was victorious and continued to reign for many years. David closed his psalm by reiterating his faith in Jehovah God (the LORD). *(V.8)*

As we Christians read psalms like this one, we can learn valuable lessons from David. Not about warfare and fighting, for that was the nature of their culture. David was a warrior and a child of his time, but from his early years he developed an absolute dependence on God. He put God first and turned to Him in every aspect of his life. This is something we can emulate.

We Christians have a loving relationship with the Spirit of Jesus who is available to indwell us. The Apostle Paul knew this and prayed that the Ephesians would begin to understand, through the power of the Holy Spirit, how wide, how long, how high and how deep is God's love for them (and us). *(Ephesians 3.14-19)*

We can learn a lot from David, for he sincerely and fervently loved the LORD and put Him first in his life. This gave him a positive perspective so he could face disasters and not let them overwhelm him.

A wonderful Biblical example in the Old Testament is where Moses sent out twelve spies to explore the land of Canaan. They were gone for many weeks and when they returned and gave a report of their observations, ten of the spies were flabbergasted by the strength and size of the Canaanites. Unfortunately, the report of the majority of the spies was negative. They said they felt like grasshoppers next to the Canaanites. *(Numbers 13:27-33)* The two groups of spies witnessed the same things. What was the difference that allowed Joshua and Caleb to tell Moses that they should go in and possess the land? Joshua and Caleb kept their eyes on God – and the Giants appeared small!

# PSALM 4
## Contentment, Come What May

In this psalm, David is the target of many false accusations, even though his life does not appear to be threatened. This is different from Psalm 3 where his life was in serious danger.

This short psalm (8 verses) can be organized as follows: One, David's Prayerful Plea to the God for Help Him; Two, David Deals with His Accusers; and Three, David's Final Feelings of Joy.

### Segment One – David's Prayerful Plea to the God for Help. Verse 1

Most people when they are upset and have troubles will go to a friend for sympathy and encouragement. Not David. He goes to "God"("Elohiym"), the plural name for God in Hebrew. God is David's source of protection and solace. He prays to God and lays before Him his inner feelings. He says that God declares him innocent. The Hebrew word for "innocent" is ("Tsedeq") and it means "right with God." It's a Hebrew word that is synonymous with truth.

### Segment Two – David Deals with His Accusers. Verses 2 - 5

After challenging those who want to ruin his reputation (V.2), David tells them that there is one thing for sure that the LORD has set aside those considered godly for Himself. (V.3) When we put God first in our lives, it is then that we know we are in Covenant with Him. Being His Covenant people, we can depend on God to care for us, and protect us and we can know firsthand His unfailing love. David says to those wanting to ruin his reputation to think about it overnight and keep quiet. *(V.4)* Also, offer proper sacrifices but mainly trust in the LORD. *(V.5)*

## Segment Three – David's Final Feelings of Joy. Verses 6 - 8

Many people around us cannot see God at work in our lives; they see only our past failures. But as we seek God and, with His help, make changes, our success in recovery will allow others to see God's power. True joy comes from God – a joy that is greater than all the gladness the world can produce. Nothing will bring us more peaceful nights of sleep than the knowledge that God is with us and helping us to progress in recovery.

Many folks live as practical atheists, that is, they live as if God is not a part of their lives. David was the opposite. He consulted God at every turn. His prayer in verse 6 came after he wondered about the future. Will better times be coming? *(V.6)* Then at once he recalls the wonderful blessing Moses gave to Aaron and his sons. That the LORD protect you, smile on you, be gracious to you, show you favor and give you peace. *(Numbers 6:24-26)* With this inspiring thought, he relaxes and praises God, telling Him that the gladness of His spiritual blessing is far greater than abundant harvest and wine. *(V.7)*

What wonderful thoughts! David realizes that God has blessed him in the past because God is a merciful and loving Father. He knows God can be counted on in the future to surround him with kindness and unfailing love. Therefore he is totally at peace and secure. *(V.8)*

This is one of the loveliest psalms written by the talented David. In the New Testament, our Lord Jesus spoke similar teachings in His Sermon on the Mount. He tells us that our heavenly Father knows we need food and clothing, and He will make sure we will have them. *(Matthew 6:33-34)*

Hearing David's words, as he lectures his accusers in this psalm, makes us Christians realize that God is the same with us. He hasn't changed. The New Testament writer, John, says we should love one another and anyone who does not love does not know God. *(1 John 4:7-8)* To love God was tremendously important to David and also is for us Christians. The Apostle John goes on to say that God showed how much he loved us by sending His own Son into the world to die for us. *(1 John 4:9-10)* Imagine!

There is another similarity between David and we born-again Christians. David knew inwardly that God had set him apart (chosen him) when he was anointed by the Prophet Samuel (see 1 Samuel 16:11-12). Because of his godly demeanor, David is confident that God would respond to his prayers, as He had in the past. (V.3) He speaks to his accusers (his enemies) in verse 4 telling them that he can't stop them from being angry with him, but they shouldn't allow their anger to gain control over them. When we Christians allow God's Spirit in Jesus to come into our lives, some amazing miracles take place. His presence in us helps us control our unholy desires, impure thoughts, the envy and jealousies that cause so much hurt in our relationships. But with our inner eyes centered on Jesus, we are able to do what is loving and kind, and our outlook (our attitude) will be the same Jesus had!

# PSALM 5
## Approaching a Holy God

This psalm of David was used in the Sanctuary as a morning song. According to the superscription (added later), it was sung and orchestrated by the choir director and accompanied by flutes. Long before David's son, Solomon, built the Temple, David appointed a choir of Levites who also were skilled players of harps, lyres and percussion.

There are five stanzas in this psalm of 12 verses. In the first, third, and fifth stanzas, David is dealing with a holy God, face-to-face. In the other two stanzas, he is reflecting and contrasting the wicked of the world with the righteous interactions of the LORD. In this psalm, David is not only seeking protection from a myriad of evil persons around him, but he doesn't want any of their influence to seep into his character. This poem is a model of how we should approach a holy God.

### Segment One – Listen to My Voice in the Morning, LORD. Verses 1 - 3

There are three kinds of communication or prayers in this segment. The first are <u>words.</u> (V.3) David communicates with God by using his voice. The second way he prays is through his groaning. This is when he knows what he wants to say, but can't find words, so he uses "sighing." Essentially he is resorting to a non-verbal means of communicating. The third way he prays is by <u>cries.</u> (V.2) Cries are when he wants to add emotion and let God know it's important to him.

All of us have doubts whether we are approaching God correctly. In what spirit ought we to be going to God? David suggests three ways: First is a <u>spirit of urgency.</u> (V.2) David was no dilettante; he was serious and urgent

11

in his righteous dealings with God. James, in the New Testament, says the prayers of a righteous person have great power. (*James 5:16*)

The second way to approach a holy God suggested by David is with a spirit of persistence. If he prays and God doesn't seem to respond, David repeats his request. (*V.3*) Jesus reinforces this when He told the parable of the unjust Judge. In this illustration, the woman wants the judge to do her a favor and she persists until finally the judge accedes to her wishes. Jesus then says if an evil judge will provide justice if you persist don't you think God who loves you will provide justice for you if you persist. (*Luke 18:6-7*)

The third spirit to embrace as you bring your requests to God that David recommends is one of expectancy. (*V.3*) Again James in the new Testament is our expert. He tells us if we seek wisdom we not only have to ask but we have to expect him to respond to our request. True faith is in expecting God's response. (*James 1.5-6*)

### Segment Two – God Detects Evil. Verses 4 - 6

In this Segment, David describes God's relationship with the ungodly. The following words tell how God sees sin: wickedness (*V.4*), the proud (*V.5*), those who do evil (*V.5*), liars (*V.6*), murderers (*V.6*) and deceivers. (*V.6*)

David is telling us in this section that we dare not take sin lightly. In Psalm 66, it says that if I had not confessed my sin with a sincere heart God would not have listened. (*Psalm 66:18-19*) We cannot come into God's presence involved with evil, as verse 4 says. As we draw close to God, we become increasingly sensitive to sin, and that is why we must keep our eye on the Lord at all times. God is a holy God who hates sin, as verse 5 says. Specially David says God will destroy those who tell lies, are murders and deceivers. (*V.6*) A profound corollary to this is the fact that we Christians will never be able to understand why Jesus had to go to the cross until we accept the fact that a God of love must hate sin!

### Segment Three – Lead Me in the Right Path, O LORD. Verses 7 - 8

In this section, David says to the Covenant community that because of God's "unfailing love" (*"Checed"*), He accepts individuals in spite of their past unacceptable behavior. (*V.7*) To have this happen, they have to indicate by their actions that they are willing to humble themselves and join the community in corporate worship. *(V.7)* God's forgiving love goes out to those who are sincerely traveling in the right path toward God and not away from Him. *(V.8)* God wants to redeem evil-minded sinners, and that is why Jesus, in His Sermon on the Mount, says God sends rain to the justice and unjust. *(Matthew 5:45)* He exhibits His patient-love, even when He detests murders and deceivers *(V.6)*, so they can hopefully be back in the fold. David as the king leads by example. He humbles himself and, with deepest awe, participates in worship held in the Tent of Meeting.

## Segment Four – Drive My Enemies from Me. Verses 9 - 10

When you lead a nation composed of people with differing economic, political and social points of view, you are bound to have opposition. David was a strong-willed individual not afraid to make decisions. Therefore, he had enemies – even in his court, including some in his own family! To David's face they flattered him, but, as he says, they don't speak a single truthful word. *(V.9)* So David goes to God in prayer and tells Him everything he feels – both good and bad. The LORD listens and understands how upset David was. David wasn't afraid to express his anger. *(V.10)*

We Christians have a different slant on things because of Jesus and His teachings. He teaches us to love our enemies and to pray for them (see Matthew 5:43-44). David wasn't a Christian. He was a Jewish man living under the Law of Moses. David demanded God's justice.

## Segment Five – Protect and Bless the Godly. Verses 11- 12

What a joyful and optimistic closing! David is telling us readers to stay close to the Lord and sing praises forever. *(V.11)* Very good advice. When we come into the Lord's presence on a daily basis, we will be filled with the Lord's happiness, and what is more – we will be protected by God's love for us. *(V.12)*

Reading Psalm Five from a Christian perspective, we see David, a man who fervently believed in a higher power, was able to direct not only his own individual pathway, but influenced and controlled the destiny of his nation. This was a wonderful foundational position of faith for David. It gave him a way to believe in a power beyond himself that kept his ego in check and provided him with a transcendent way to view the world! With this faith in hand, he lived life to its fullest.

David and the Jews of his day looked forward to a time when God would send a Messiah. In the meantime, God made a promise to David telling him that his kingdom would be established forever. God kept His word. He chose a descendant of David named Jesus to be the world's Messiah. Jesus was God's Son and He walked the earth teaching, preaching and healing. He was condemned to die by the Jews, but God raised Him from the dead and sent His Spirit to earth to indwell Christians and lead them from within. God converted another great Jew named Paul of Tarsus, who took the Christian message all over the world. (*Romans 5:8-11*)

# PSALM 6

## A Psalm of Sickness

This psalm of David has been designated throughout the centuries of Christian history as the first of the penitential psalms. This classification is given to psalms where the writer confesses his sins and asks God to forgive him. The other penitential psalms are 32, 38, 51, 102, 130 and 143.

But Psalm 6 is not a strict penitential psalm because there is no confession of sin (although it is implied) and no repentance. It is more of a Psalm of Sickness.

A heading accompanied this psalm, which was probably given to it in post-exile days, says this psalm should be accomplied with stringed instruments, a "sheminith." The Hebrew word *("sheminith")* means eight, but its meaning for this poem can be confusing and not clear. The *New Living Translation*, which I prefer to use, translates the heading in the following way (which would appear to make more sense) as a psalm of David accompanied by an eight-stringed instrument.

Psalm 6 can be divided into three segments: (1) David's Pleas for Healing; (2) A Description of His Physical Grief; and (3) God's Answer to David's Pleas.

### Segment One – David's Pleas for Healing. Verses 1 - 5

David is feeling a sense of God's disapproval and anger toward him. We don't know the exact cause of his anguish—whether he had committed some sin, or was simply depressed by the outward circumstances of his physical illness. We know that he is feeling overwhelmed by what is happening and so he appeals to God asking Him not to rebuke him in His anger. (*V.1*)

We do know that depression is usually the aftermath of sin, and David would naturally feel that God is chastising him because of his sin, or that his depression was the result of God's judgment (punishment). At any rate, by his own admission, he is upset. A depressed state of mind we know could result from sickness of the body. In verse 2, he says he is weak and his body is in agony. He may be near death and he is begging the LORD to restore him. (V.3) David fervently prays to God imploring Him to rescue him because of God's unfailing love. (V.4) He pleads with God to heal him because he won't be able to praise God if he dies and goes to the "grave" ("Sh-ol"). (V.5)

This tells us something about the limited belief in the afterlife in ancient Jewish theology. Incidentally, David wrote something similar about death in Psalm 30. In Psalm 30 he pleads with God and reminds Him that David's dust cannot praise God from the grave. (Pslam 30:9-10)

Most Jews back then – David included – believed that when you died and went to the grave, there was nothing- -no remembrance, no memory, no nothing. Isn't it wonderful that we Christians know that when we die, we will go to heaven and will be with God and Jesus for all eternity! Halleluiah!

### Segment Two – A Description of David's Physical Grief. Verses 6 - 7

For most sufferers, it is in the night when silence and loneliness increase and the warmth of human companionship is absent that our pain and grief reach their darkest point. Many drag through the day having trouble functioning only to lay awake at night and sleep won't come. It is instructive to note that these words in Segment Two were written not by some unsuccessful person who had no resources but by King David, the mighty king of a great empire. He was a successful and powerful ruler, and, yet in his grief, he cried out that he was sobbing and his eyes were worn out by his enemies. (V.6-7)

These two words, "grief" and my "enemies" in this segment lead me to hypothesize that this psalm was written after David had been driven out of Jerusalem when his son, Absalom, threatened to usurp his kingship (see 2 Samuel 18-19). When Absalom and his army arrived in Jerusalem, he did not immediately pursue his father, giving David enough time to recruit and organize thousands of fighting men loyal to him.

Absalom and his army eventually marched out of the capital city with the intention of capturing or killing David. The two armies met in battle in the forest of Ephraim and, as 2 Samuel records, twenty thousand men died that day. (2 Samuel 18.7) During the horrible fighting, Absalom was killed.

2 Samuel records that King David went up to his room and burst into tears wishing he had died instead of his son. (*2 Samuel 18:33*)

## Segment Three — God Answers David's Pleas. Verses 8 - 10

If my reasoning is correct concerning David's grief over the death of his son, Absalom, then in this last section he sends away his loyal friends and supporters, saying they did evil because against his orders they killed his son (while he was dangling helplessly in a tree).

It is encouraging to see that the tone of the psalm suddenly changes. God has indeed heard David's prayer for deliverance. We also should note that his prayer for healing (back in verse 2) was not as a result of David's righteousness, but on the basis of God's "compassion," God's (*"Chanon"*). David's pleas had nothing to do with any personal merit. It is never wrong to ask for God's mercy on the basis of our emotional loss or weakness. David eventually calms down as his grief ran its course and he says the LORD heard my plea. (*V.8-9*) As he ruminates on how his fellow Jews had joined up with Absalom's abortive attempt to dislodge him as king, he utters this final prayer. Somewhat vindicative, David asks that his enemies be disgraced and shamed. (*V.10*)

We can learn a lot from David's discipline of praying. We need to call on the Lord as David did, asking for comfort and strength. God, after all, is our hope in life and death. He is the One who sent us His Son, Jesus to be our Savior, and the One who gives us eternal life!

# PSALM 7

## Maintaining Integrity Is Imperative!

The heading on this psalm of David says this is a Shiggaion of David that he sang concerning Cush, a Benjamite. A "Shiggaion" is a musical term long lost, and Cush is not mentioned in the text of this poem. We wonder where the post-exilic editors got their information?

There are five books in the Psalter, probably patterned after the five books of Moses (the Pentateuch). Book One is composed of Psalms 1-41, and, with the exception of the first two introductory psalms, most of the rest of Book One was written by David (or dedicated in his honor).

Psalm 3 is a short prayer for deliverance from David's military foes. Psalm 4 is a little longer (8 verses) and again it is a cry to God for help against false accusations. Psalm 5 is another short prayer to God given in the morning, reflecting on those in David's surroundings who he says are deceitful and dishonest. Psalm 6 finds the king in anguish at the death of his son, Absalom, killed in the ferocious battle over his attempt to usurp David's kingship.

This present composition, Psalm 7, is longer than the first four psalms but is in the same general approach and style. David took over the kingship after King Saul was killed in battle. At that time, Israel was composed of a loose federation of tribes. Saul came from the Tribe of Benjamin, and most of David's opposition came from the Benjaminites, who were jealous of David and who had previous loyalties to the former slain king. The problem addressed in Psalm 7 is that David was falsely accused of doing some evil or betraying a friendship (verse 4).

## Segment One – Presenting David's Case to the LORD. Verses 1 - 2

Feeling persecuted and threatened, and even with the possibility of being assassinated, David goes to God in prayer seeking protection. *(V.1)* If you do not rescue me, David cries out to the LORD my enemies like lions will tear me apart. *(V.2)* Warfare and violence were a way of life back then. David no sooner was crowned king when he led his army to battle the Jebusites and captured the fortress city of Jerusalem, making it his capitol. Then he fought the Philistines and recaptured the Ark of the Covenant and, amidst much fanfare, brought it to his capitol city (see 1 Chronicles 15). This went a long way to help unify the country. Now Jerusalem (the City of David) could become the political and religious center for Israel.

## Segment Two – David Protests His Innocence. Verses 3 - 5

To the charges against him that he betrayed a friend *(V.3-4)*, he tells God in his prayer that if he had done wrong then You would be justified to let the people trample me to the ground. *(V.5)*

## Segment Three – David Asks God for His Judgment. Verses 6 - 8

Now he challenges God, because he feels he is innocent! He demands that God wake up and bring him justice! *(V.6)* The Hebrew word for "justice" is *("Mispat")*. David is confident that if God would gather the nations together (as in a court of law) *(V.7)*, He would judge them and find his accusers guilty and then God would declare him righteous. *(V.8)* To be righteous in this context means to be in a right relationship with God, which David knew himself to be. It doesn't mean he felt self-righteous, that he was without sin. No. God's righteous ones are His forgiven ones, those who are in God's Covenant love. He is saying to God that if God will do this, then I will be justified publicly (vindicated).

## Segment Four – God is the Righteous Judge. Verses 9 - 11

In this section, David believes in a righteous God. *(V.9)* The Hebrew adjective for "righteousness" is *("Tsaddiyq")*, which means that God's nature is just. He will always fulfill His part of His Covenant that He made with

His People. God is also a perfectly fair judge. *(V.11)* The Hebrews believed that under a fair judge the righteousness will prevail and evil will be brought low. Psalm One says the LORD watches over the godly and the path of the unGodly leads to destruction. *(Psalm 1:6)* This will not necessarily happen immediately, but ultimately it will!

### Segment Five – The Consequence of Evil. Verses 12 - 16

God has chosen David to be His representative on earth and has consequently enlightened his mind so he is able to put in words the truths of God. In Psalm 7, David writes about the consequences of evil. If a person does not repent he will feel the sharp edge of God's sword. *(V.12-13)* David contends that God orders things so that evil people do things that ultimately destroy themselves. They make trouble, yes, but it backfires on them. *(V.14-16)*

### Segment Six – Thanksgiving for God's Righteousness. Verses 17

David is so optimistic that God will vindicate him that he breaks out in praise for the LORD's goodness and righteousness. He is so sure that God's will be done that he thanks Him ahead of time. *(V.17)* The lesson Psalm 7 teaches us is that it is better to maintain our integrity and continue to suffer injustice (if that is our lot) than to sell out to evil and join ranks with the ungodly. We must remember that goodness and integrity are their own rewards!

# PSALM 8

## A Hymn of Praise to the LORD of Creation

Psalm 8 is one of David's masterpieces. It is a hymn of praise to the Creator God. He begins with the celebration of the surpassing wonderment of God and mankind's place in the universe. This puts us human beings within the cosmic framework. David is saying that we will never be able to fully understand our fellow men and women until we see them as God's creatures, and recognize that we all have a special responsibility toward our heavenly Father's world.

### Segment One – Our Glorious Creator God. Verse 1

David's whole life was centered on his relationship with God and so he doesn't begin the psalm by extolling the beauty and grandeur of the earth, as you would expect. No, he declares O LORD "our Lord," which is the title for the God of the Covenant *("Adon")*, meaning that Israel has a special relationship with the Creator. Then, with awe and wonder, he extols God by saying God's glory is higher than the heavens. *(V.1)* David is implying that God's glory is most visible to those who see it with the eyes of faith.

### Segment Two – The Power of Children's Praise. Verse 2

With creative poetry in verse 2, our Psalmist says that God has established a stronghold against the wicked through the praise of innocent little children.

In the New Testament when Jesus and His disciples entered into Jerusalem, many in the crowd of His followers spread their coats and palm branches on the road ahead of Jesus as He entered the Holy city in triumph! Immediately, He went to the Temple and the blind and lame came to Him and He healed them. Those who opposed Jesus – the priests and Teachers of the Law – saw His wonderful miracles and heard the little children in the Temple shouting that Jesus was the son of David, an indication that He might be the long-awaited Messiah. *(Matthew 21:15)* The religious leaders were indignant and asked Jesus to stop the children's shoutings. *(Matthew 21:16)* Jesus's response was to ask the religious leaders if they had read the Scriptures. In Psalm 8 it points out that the children and infants will give praise to the Messiah. Jesus was indeed the son of David and the long-awaited Messiah. These enemies of Jesus were silenced by the praises of the children.

### Segment Three – Humans Are Crowned with Glory and Honor. Verses 3 - 8

David is like the little children who stand in awe of God's majesty. In humility, he writes that when he looks at the night sky he sees the work of God's fingers and is amazed that God should care for us mere mortals. *(V.3-4)* It is very interesting that the Hebrew word used here for "mortals" is *("Enowsh")* and not *("Adam")*, the more familiar word for human beings or mankind. *("Enowsh")*, Enosh in English, was a son of Seth. Genesis 4:26 says it was during Enosh's lifetime that for the first time people began to worship the LORD. David obviously wanted his poem to reflect a God-centeredness of Enosh, rather than the likes of his self-centered and violent brother Cain.

A little background may give a perspective from which to better understand Psalm 8. David undoubtedly knew the Book of Genesis and drew on its words as he thought about the grandeur of God's creation. In the first chapter of Genesis, it says that in the beginning God created the heavens and earth. Then He inhabited the earth with plants and fish and animals and finally the Lord created people in His own image, male and female. (Genesis 1:27). After this, God blessed them and told them to fill the earth with children and subdue the earth. *(Genesis 1:28)* Being created in God's image means that the Creator God gave us mortals the power to do what He does – to become God's instruments on earth to carry forth His creative activity in caring for His world.

In verse 5, David says that we were made only a little lower than God. O God, thank You for this wonderful recognition and privilege. We know with this honor goes <u>great</u> <u>responsibility.</u> Verse 6 re-emphasizes our obligation. We are to be in charge with everything that God made. But being in charge doesn't give us the right to exploit nature. We are to be good stewards of what God has created. *(V.7-8)*

There is a footnote in Segment Three in the *New Living Translation* on Verse 4. It parallels the *New International Version*. It says what is the Son of Man that we should care for him. The phrase that needs explanation is "the Son of Man" (the Hebrew is *("Ben Adam")*. "Son of Man" has two meanings. It literally means "a descendant of Adam" (the first man). It also can mean someone who represents all mankind, including males and females (humanity). Adam and Eve in Genesis are both Adam, i.e., they are representatives of mankind. In the Old Testament there are a number of books where this phrase is used, particularly the prophet Ezekiel, who frequently refers to himself as "Son of Man." For instance, in his prophesy of "the dry bones," Ezekiel is asked as the "Son of Man" if these bones can become living people again. *(Ezekiel 37:3)* Ezekiel is representing mankind here and elsewhere as he gives God's message to the people. Jesus, in the New Testament, often referred to Himself in His teachings as Son of Man. He saw Himself as a representative of a new humanity.

An interesting sidelight: In the *King James Bible*, published in 1611, Psalm 8 has verse 4 rendered, *"For Thou hast made him a little lower than the angels ..."* When the Old Testament was translated into the Greek language in 255 B.C. (Septuagint), the translators changed "God" to "angels." The King James translators used the Septuagint and changed God to "angels" also.

### Segment Four – The Majesty of Your Name Fills the Earth! Verse 9

Verses 1 and 9, in which David rejoices in the majesty of the LORD's name, is like God putting His arms around Psalm 8 and making it one of the most inspiring and meaningful of all the psalms.

# PSALM 9

## A Lesson About the LORD

In the past, the Greek translation of the Old Testament (the Septuagint) considered Psalms 9 and 10 as one unit. This was also the case with St. Jerome's Latin Vulgate, for years the main version of the Roman Catholic Church. Both Psalms 9 and 10 are acrostic psalms– each succeeding set of two verses begins with a consecutive letter of the Hebrew alphabet. The first eleven letters of the Hebrew alphabet occur in Psalm 9 and the final eleven letters of the Hebrew alphabet occur in Psalm 10. There is no heading for Psalm 10. This would tend to imply the two psalms were at one time together. Because the *New Living Translation* considers the two psalms separately, we shall analyze them accordingly.

These two psalms are a careful work of art. The first, Psalm 9, could have been written specifically for a school child who had died. This then gave a teacher an opportunity to raise questions about death and dying, and how each child still needed to keep their trust in God.

Verses 1 – 2 (*Aleph*)) The Teacher-Writer begins by thanking the LORD for all the marvelous things God had done. Verses 3 - 4. (*Beth*) The writer has personified his audience and speaks as if they were an individual--you are all part of God's covenant. When he speaks of his enemies, there is a solidarity in being an Israelite. It's wonderful to have God as our Judge. Verses 5 - 6 (*Gimel*) With much hyperbole the Psalmist says God has rebuked the nations and destroyed the wicked. (*V.5*) There's a feeling of pride being built up in the students as the writer recalls what the mighty God did in the past, how God has protected them. (*V.6*) Verses 7 - 8 (*Daleth* is missing) Two important words are put forth in verse 7: "judgment" (*"Mishpat"*) and "justice" (*"Tsedeq"*). God is a righteous Judge and the students need to know this. Verses 9-10 (*Waw*) The good news is the God who judges is also a refuge

24

in time of trouble. *(V.9)* This loving LORD will never abandon anyone so long as they search for God. *(V.10)* Verses 11 – 12 *(Zain)* Isn't it wonderful that we have a God who reigns forever? So let us sing praises to God. *(V.11)* He doesn't ignore those who cry for help. *(V.12)* Verses 13 - 14 *(Heth)* God's unfailing love will rescue individuals who are ill or near death. *(V.13)* The gates are where people congregated for public meetings, and it is here where they looked for justice. Verses 15 - 16 *(Teth)* The Psalmist proclaims that the LORD is justice. *(V.16)* God has arranged the world so that evil nations fall into the pits they dug for themslves. *(V.15-16)* Verses 17-18 *(Yond* and Kaph) Two truths are put forth: (1) Wicked nations will ceased to exist; *(V.17)* and (2) Those in need will never be forgotten by a righteous God. *(V.18)* Verses 19-20--this section doesn't use the next letter of the Hebrew alphabet, which probably means some later editor added this as a chorus to be sung. It was probably based on Numbers 10.35, which is a cry from Moses who shouted let your enemies be scattered. The Psalm ends with the congregation singing that they place their trust in the LORD. *(V.20)*

# PSALM 10

## Punishes the Wicked!

Psalm 9 and Psalm 10 in some versions of the Bible were together as one psalm. In the Greek translation (the Septuagint), and the Latin Vulgate translated by Jerome and for many years the official version of the Roman Catholic Church, both considered the two psalms as one.

Both Psalms are acrostic in pattern, which means that every other verse or stanza begins with the consecutive letters of the Hebrew alphabet. Psalm 9 contains verses beginning with the alphabet's first eleven letters, but omits *Daleth*. Psalm 10 includes the eleven letters of the second half of the Hebrew alphabet, beginning with the letter *Lameth,* with some irregularities and some reversals.

Even though Psalm 9 and Psalm 10 might have been one psalm at one time (the older Hebrew text has them as one), we will consider them as two and will analyze them accordingly. The two psalms are markedly different in content. Psalm 10 is considered a lament. The Psalmist (whomever that might be) is upset over the easy life of prosperity lived by the wicked and, therefore, he asks God to take them down a peg!

In one of the Gallup polls, it was reported that America was unusually religious. However, the same research reported that America's religious beliefs made little difference as to how Americans live and act. It was stated that 71% believed in life after death; 81% claimed to be "very religious;" and nearly every home had at least one Bible. Although 4 out of 5 said they were religious, research indicated only 1 out of 8 said religion made a significant difference in their lives! These statistics show Americans are mainly practical atheists.

Verses 1 - 2 (*Lamed*) Our Psalmist is upset because the LORD stands so far away. The Psalmist's concern is that wicked people oppress the poor and God seems to permit this. *(V.2)* Verses 3 – 4 *(Memo is missing)* Our Psalmist sees these wicked as proud, greedy and arrogant. God doesn't mean much to them. They act as if God is dead. *(V.4)* These wicked are practical atheists. They live and behave as if there is no God. Psalm 10 is concerned about what is happening to Judaism at the hands of these practical atheists. The author sees ungodly Jews persecuting and exploiting their weaker countrymen. These godless people of means have one goal: to get rich at the expense of others. Verses 5 - 6 *(Nun)* The sad fact is that these Godless people seem to succeed in all they do and are scornful of others. *(V.5)* God's judgment doesn't trouble them a bit. *(V.6)* Verses 7 - 8a *(Pe)* These uncouth individuals also are full of cusing, lies and threats. They are evil-filled and murder the innocent. *(V.8)* Verses 9 - 11 *(Ayin)* The Psalmist is appalled at the seemingly indifference of Yahweh God (the LORD) at how the poor are treated by these wicked individuals. These practical atheists brag about their evil desires, and never give a thought to any possible punishment. *(V.9)* Sad to say, the helpless are overwhelmed and collapse. Meanwhle the wicked whisper to themselves that God is not even watching us. *(V.11)* Verses – 12 - 13 *(Qoph)* Our Psalmist realizes that only God can right the horrible conditions brought about by the wicked, so he cries out to the Almighty for His aid. *(V.12)* Verse 14 *(Resh)* But the Psalmist upon reflection realizes that God is aware of the trouble and grief these practical atheists cause and will ultimately punish them and will take care of the orphans. Verses 15 - 16 *(Shin)* You, God, are the King of the universe and, therefore, You have the right to exercise judgment. I have utmost faith that You will side with the humble and that You will take action to alleviate their concerns, and that You will bring justice *("Shaphat")* to the orphan and the oppressed. Verses 17 - 18 *(Tau)* This last couplet probably was added and sung by the congregation. *(V.17)* The praise and worship ends with the affirmation that God will bring justice to the orphans and the oppressed. *(V.18)*

In the New Testament, the Apostle Paul paralleled many of the same experiences, as did our Psalmist in terms of godless men who acted immorally and self-interestedly. *(Romans 1:29-32)* But Paul had the same optimistic faith as the writer of Psalm 10. He knew that God would punish people for sins, and yet he looked out at the world and saw many godless folks apparently getting away with not being punished. *(Romans 2:3-8)*

God has given us Christians these psalms to read and ponder. They run the gamut of various emotions and cover many diverse subject matters. It is surprising how many of the same problems the Psalmists deal with that we face today. As we read them, we must always bring our Christian faith to bear and always we need to read and interpret them through the eyes of the Lord Jesus Christ.

# PSALM 11

## Faith's Response to Fear's Counsel

The heading on this short psalm says it if for the choir director and it is a psalm of David.

We live in precarious times. Morality is undermined. Evil people prey on the innocent. The Bible is under attack. Secularism is running rampant. The question is what can we do when everything around us seems to be falling apart? Run away? David's counsel in Psalm 11 is to take counsel in the LORD!

The crisis that led to the writing of this poem is not stated. The logical explanation for the predicament King David was facing would be when his rebellious son, Absalom, had raised an army and was marching on Jerusalem to overthrow his father and take over as king of Israel. (See 2 Samuel 15:10.)

In the midst of this crisis, some of David's fearful but well-meaning counselors ask, since law and order have collapsed, what can a righteous person do? (V.3) Others of his staff advised that the people need to head to the mountains for safety. (V.1)

We will examine Psalm 11 by dividing it into three parts.

### Segment One – Being Shot at from the Shadows. Verses 1 - 3

David is saying in this segment that it seems to him as if the world is populated with unscrupulous and wicked people. He feels alone and isolated with deceivers who lie and cheat. He probably felt like Elijah after his encounter with the priests of Baal on top of Mount Carmel. The wicked Queen Jezebel sent a message to Elijah saying by this time tomorrow I will kill you like those whom you killed. (1Kings 19:2) Elijah was afraid and fled for his life finally ending up alone in a cave on Mount Sinai. The LORD asked him what

29

he was doing hidding in the cave. Elijah defended himself by pointing out how zealous he had served God. Also, he said all the other prophets serving God have been killed. He alone is left and Queen Jezebel was trying to kill him, too. *(1 Kings 19:9-10)*

Elijah had it all wrong. God tells him there are 7,000 believers who had not bowed down to the gods of Baal—but it didn't change the way Elijah felt. We all have felt alone like that at times as if everyone was against us.

David's response when experiencing a similar situation is to put his faith and trust in God even though his counselors are advising him to flee to the mountains. *(V.1)* David acknowledges he's getting shot at from the shadows *(V.2)* and law and order has collapsed. *(V.3)* We know of David's commitment to the LORD from other psalms he's written. In earlier psalms, David acknowledges that the LORD is the light of his salavation so there was no need to be afraid. *(Psalm 27:1)* That God is his safe fortress where his enemies could not reach him. *(Psalm 31:2)* That the LORD is his shepherd. *(Psalm 23:1)* To the question what do the righteous do *(Psalm 11:3)*, he says we can all put our trust in God!

## Segment Two – God Still Rules from Heaven. Verses 4 - 6

God knows what's going on. David says He is in His holy temple. *(V.4)* It seems that David is thinking about God's covenant, where the LORD said He would care for, protect and bless all the righteous who were committed to obey God's commandments and were faithful to the covenant. This was at the heart of David's faith. He obviously sees the unprovoked attack by Absalom as a violation of God's covenant and, therefore, God will punish him. *(V.5)* God hates those who love violence. My son is being wicked. God will punish him. *(V.6)*

David realized that he is outnumbered and that if he remained in Jerusalem and tried to defend his capitol city many innocent women and children would be slaughtered. David and his bodyguards (plus 600 Gittites who had come from Gath) leave the city, crossing over the Jordan River into the wilderness.

With David's departure, Absalom and his troops march into the city unopposed and take control, without any bloodshed. Instead of pursuing David immediately, Absalom postpones following his father, content to bask in his newfound glory and self-righteous power. However, with his putting off following his father, he allowed David enough time to put out a call for his loyal fighting men. When Absalom finally decided to lead his troops against what he thought would be an easy engagement, he met his father's seasoned warriors in the forest of Ephraim. A bloody battle ensued with David's forces victorious. In the fighting, Absalom was killed. (See 2 Samual 18.) After a period of mourning his son's death, David eventually returned to Jerusalem and resumed his duties as king.

The LORD's promises are sure, because He is Sovereign. *(V.4)* He allows a good degree of freedom, which means He doesn't always step in and interfere with our day-to-day activities. But He is still in charge. We human beings are created in God's image (Genesis 1:27). God is a person like us. He loves and hates just like we do. The LORD hates sin and the "wicked" *("Rasha"). (V.6)*

It is interesting to note that many of the translations, including the *New International Version*, the *New Revised* Standard *Version*, and the *King James* Version, all treat verse 5 as follows: *"The LORD tests the righteous and wicked, and his soul hates the lover of violence."* There is no essential difference in meaning from the *NLT*, with the exception of the word *"soul."* The New Living *Translation* implies it. The Hebrew word for "soul" is *("Nephesh").* When applied to human beings, it means the whole person, mind, body and spirit. Persons are created in God's image, and by using "his soul," it implies that God is a person, which makes good theological sense.

When the Psalter was reassembled in its present form (after God's people were allowed to return from exile), the Priest-Editor who placed Psalm One at the beginning of the 150 psalms knew what he was doing because it set the tone for all that was to follow. The LORD watches over the godly, and the path of the ungodly leads to destruction. *(Psalm 1:6)*

We don't know when David composed this psalm. Perhaps he wrote the first two segments in stages, as a kind of question and answer style (as it is difficult to determine who was doing the speaking). Following the departure from the capitol city, we can only hypothesize that verse seven was added after his return as a kind of postlude.

### Segment Three – The LORD is Gracious. Verse 7

David writes the last verse calling God "righteous" *("Tsedeq").* By this he meant that God can be relied upon to do good and to care for those who

31

were faithful to His covenant. In another psalm authored by David, he says that the righteous God can look deep in the mind and heart of you and me. (*Psalm 7:9*)

In the second part of his postlude, David probably remembered Moses' words of blessing to the Hebrew people—that the LORD blessses and keeps them. (*Numbers 6:24-25*) So he borrows these words and write them in verse 7. What he meant was that faithful worshipers would sense the LORD's presence.

Today, we Christians can draw upon David's faith. While he didn't intend his words of seeing God's face to be more than a symbol or metaphor for intense worship, we today can read these words through the eyes of Christianity and can apply the words in John's Gospel where it says that God so loved the world that he gave us His Son so we can have eternal life. (*John 3:16*)

Everlasting life from a Christian understanding will include all those whose names are written in The Lamb's Book of Life, i.e., those who have committed their lives to following Jesus. When Christians die it is our belief that we will be given new spiritual bodies and go to heaven where we will be with God and Jesus for all eternity!

We don't know all the details, but John of Patmos tells us when we get to heaven God's curse will be gone and we will see Jesus's face and his name will be written on our foreheads. (*Revelation 22:3-5*)

# PSALM 12

## The Importance of Words

Psalm 12 is a psalm of David. It is about words and how words can be perverted and used wrongly. It is a lament written at a time of moral and spiritual bankruptcy. It is only eight verses.

### Segment One – David's Appeal for Help. Verses 1 - 4

As in the first three verses of Psalm 11, David is saying in verse 1 that it seems to him the world is populated with unscrupulous and wicked people. Modern life is full of double talk and language to deceive. For an example, some mortgage people and bankers of America distorted the truth to people purchasing new homes in the early part of the 21st century. "Home values will always go up," they said, and that was a lie! In New York City, it came to light that a man by the name of Bernard Madoff made huge profits in investments by deceiving customers and putting their money in his own pocket. Lying, flattering, and deceiving – there is no doubt about it that there were a lot of arrogant and ungodly people back in David's day. (V.2) But we have our share of them today! What we sow we shall reap. David prays that God will ultimately destroy those proud liars. David appeals to the LORD to silence their flattering tongues. (V.3) But their response is, "Who can stop us—our lips are our own." (V.4)

### Segment Two – God's Word of Promise. Verses 5 - 6

The LORD's promises are sure because He is Sovereign! He knows about the boasting and the hypocrisy in the world today, just as He did back in David's day. He allows freedom, which means He does not always step in and interfere with the day-to-day activities. But – He is still in charge!

33

The Psalmist reflects the Prophets in telling of the LORD's concern for the underdogs of society. Verse 5 tells us that when godless and self-centered people flaunt their freedom, cheat and lie, it is the poor and downtrodden of society, who cannot protect themselves, who usually end up being hurt. God's Word calls for justice! The Prophet Isaiah had similar words to Psalm 12 in Isaiah 1:17.

David says that God has heard the cries (groans) of the poor and He will rescue them. *(V.5)* The LORD's promises are pure and David says His promises are purified seven times over. *(V.6)* Seven in the Bible is a symbol for perfection so God's Word in this psalm is the perfect truth!

### Segment Three – An Appeal to God Renewed. Verses 7 - 8

We can depend on God's love and mercy to lead and care for us. *(V.7)* But there are evil individuals prowling and strutting about. *(V.8)* Self-centeredness is the essence of wickedness. As God's people, we try to keep our eyes on the Lord and, with the Spirit of Christ living in us, we do not choose to live by selfish standards. Our help is in the Lord, and we are His servants.

As Christians, we are now and probably always will be a minority in a secular society. We are resident aliens, which means we have one foot in heaven and the other foot in the world. We are in the world but not of it. *(Philippians 3:20)* Before He left this world, Jesus prayed for us as His disciples, asking the Father to make His disciples pure and holy. *(John 17:11-19)*

Jesus, died upon a cross. Romans 5:8
Rose again to save the lost. John 3:16
Forgive me of all my sin. 1 John 1:9
Be my Savior, Lord and friend. Romans 10:9
Change my life, make me new. 2 Corinthians 5:17
Help me, Lord, to live for You. Colossians 2:6

# PSALM 13
## Darkness and the Dawn

King Saul threatened to kill David and he meant it! The king was insanely jealous of the young and popular David. As a result, David had to flee for his very life! Nobody wanted to be near him for fear of Saul's wrath! This kept up for months, even years and most of the time David was in the wilderness alone. After a while, David began to be depressed, and you can't blame him. Without friends, he felt abandoned. This was the situation when David wrote Psalm 13. The worst part was that without friends, David felt that <u>even God had withdrawn from him.</u>

Before we discuss this psalm, let me make a few observations <u>about being abandoned.</u> It is much more common than most people think. A person feels forsaken by other people and, in time, he or she feels abandoned by God. When this happens, it becomes a spiritual problem. A lot of depression and false guilt get involved and form a deep gulf between the person and God, and it becomes a vicious cycle!

Although feelings of abandonment are quite common, many people are not willing to talk about how they feel. The reasons for their silence are to cover up their inner feelings, saying to themselves that it is too embarrassing. Even Christians hesitate to share. The wonderful part of Psalm 13 is that David does talk about it. He is not afraid to air his inner feelings and that is why he is such a good author. He feels abandoned by God and he says so! If David can talk about his feelings, so can we. We can learn from him. In this Psalm, he goes from despair to being able to trust God, <u>and so can we.</u>

### Segment One — David's Feelings of Abandonment. Verses 1 - 2

In these first two verses, David uses the words "how long" four times. He even uses the word "forever." He must have felt like an outlaw fleeing from

King Saul's soldiers. The *New International Version* translates verse 1b as God hiding His "face" from David. The "face of God" is a metaphor meaning an intimate oneness with the LORD, a special blessing. Back in Moses' time, he told Aaron to give a special blessing to the people of Israel asking that the LORD "smile" on the people. (*Numbers 6:25*) This beautiful blessing is what David felt was being withheld from him. Having God look the other way is another way of describing his anguish. (*V.1*) How long will Saul, his enemy, have the upper hand? (*V.2*) It was an interminable period – at least eight years! Can you imagine?

### Segment Two – David's Prayer for Spiritual Light. Verses 3 - 4

David is crying out to the LORD to answer him. (*V.3*) If they defeat him, he says, his enemies will gloat and rejoice. (*V.4*)

Life is never in a straight line. No, we all have our ups and downs. That is why we need to be in worship each week – to hear the Gospel preached and hear the message of Jesus and His love! If we are feeling low, we need to do what Jesus did. He prayed. We may not have an enemy like King Saul breathing down our necks, but if we are a disciple of Jesus then we have a serious enemy who is continually trying to tempt us into sin. The enemy, of course, is the Devil, our great enemy. He is the one the Apostle Peter says prowls around like a hungry lion trying to devour us. (*1 Peter 5:8-9*) He and his foul demons are always looking for ways to embarrass us by urging us to commit foolish sins.

### Segment Three – David's Renewed Trust in God. Verses 5 - 6

A major component of our faith is the word trust. It is our reliance and confidence upon God's omnipotence, His sovereignty, His all powerful love and care for us. All during those tortuous years that David had to escape from King Saul, he never wavered in his faith. Yes, he had times when things looked dark, but he always reaffirmed his dependence on Yahweh God.

In addition to being a talented warrior, David was also a marvelous musician. He played the harp and had a beautiful singing voice. Notice in verse 6, David sings to the LORD in gratitude for His blessings. We cannot be downcast and depressed if we are singing to the Lord! David says in verse 5 that we must trust in God's "unfailing love." The Hebrew word for "unfailing love" is *("Checed")*, and it is one of the most important words describing God's character in the Old Testament. It tells of the eternal principles that stem from God's very nature. *("Checed")* can be translated as "mercy," "grace," "loving kindness," and "loyalty". It is a Covenant word. God made an agreement (covenant) with Israel, saying, if they would remain loyal to Him and would obey His commandments, then He would bless them.

From agony to adoration, God's renewing presence by means of His unfailing love has moved David from being fearful, anxious and mindful of death to an inner condition of hope and optimism. His situation didn't change, but his inner self did, so he picked up his harp and began singing praises. *(V.6)*

Moses went up to Mount Sinai and met with God and was told to prepare two stone tablets, upon which God would write the Ten Commandments. Then the LORD descended in the form of a pillar of cloud and announced the meaning of His name—that He is merciful, slow to anger, full of unfailing love and forgiving of every sin. *(Exodus 34:6-7)* At this Moses fell down before the LORD and worshiped. Then God told him that He would make a covenant with Moses. Evidence of this covenant would be that Moses would perform wonders that had never been seen in the world before. Moses's responsibility was to obey *all* the commandments God gave to him. *(Exodus 34:10-11)*

We have to read the psalms through the insight of our Christian faith. Jesus is the definitive statement of God's mercy and unfailing love! David had faith and wrote psalms that are inspiring, like Psalm 23. However, David didn't know Jesus as we know Him. *(John 14:6, 10, 15-17)*

# PSALM 14

## Practical Atheism and Its Consequences

This psalm of David can be classified as Prophetical Liturgy. Some interpreters classify the first five verses as a Prophetic Oracle. The words of this song are repeated almost word-for-word in Psalm 53. Why? We don't know. Also, the most important part of Psalm 14 was taken by the Apostle Paul and inserted in his letter to the Romans *(Romans 3:10-13)* The subject matter concerns atheism, that no one is seeking to know God.

### Segment One – All Have Sinned. Verses 1 - 5

David begins by saying fools say there is no God. *(V.1a)* Then he classifies these fools as corrupt and their deeds evil. *(V.1b)* The question is why do these people deny the existence of God? Paul in his treatise to the Romans says they are fools because intellectually they know God exists but choose to deny it. *(Romans 1:18-20)*. Evidence of the divine, Paul concludes, is seen in the stars, the snowflakes, and in the flowers.

In verse 2, David says the LORD looks at the world of human beings to see if there is not even one who seeks God. A all have turned their *backs* on God. All are corrupt. *(V.3)*

Again Paul takes the words of David and says people everywhere suppress the truth about God because they don't like God's moral demands. This puts a crimp in their freedom. They don't like the fact that God is sovereign, and they aren't; that God is holy, and they are not; that God is all-wise, and by contrast, they are foolish. They don't want to acknowledge God because they don't want to be accountable and responsible to Him. On the Day of Judgment, Paul, says they will have no excuse for not knowing God. *(Romans 1:20b-22)*

38

Paul then quotes verse 3 of David's Psalm 14 in chapter three of Romans. After telling us that God in His anger will punish sin wherever it is found, he says that Scripture says that no one is good, not one. *(Romans 3:9-10)*

In verse 4, David is concerned about the ordinary people (the widows and the poor) who get oppressed by these so-called atheists. In verse 5, he warns these non-believers that the terror of God will grip them, implying that God is committed to care for the weak and defenseless people in society. God's judgment will fall upon those who flaunt His laws.

## Segment Two — Praying for Restoration. Verses 6 - 7

Verse 6 seems to be a re-statement of verse 5, put a little differently. David is clearly a one hundred percent believer in adhering to God's covenant. This is why he is so adamant that God's *("Checed")*, that is, God's faithfulness and His unfailing love, will be with and bless those who obey Him. And He will protect His people *(V.6)*, including the poor and downtrodden.

As Christians read this psalm through the perspective of the Gospel of Jesus Christ, we see how God's Holy Spirit was able to endow David with wonderful wisdom that transcended his day and is applicable to our time as well. Therefore, we need to see Paul's insights as he followed up on the words he borrows from David. In chapter three of Romans, Paul tells the world that all persons are sinners and that is why we need Jesus Christ to free us by taking away our sins on His own body on the cross. *(Romans 3:20-24)*

Psalm 14 Segment One (verses 1-5) is truly a Prophetic Oracle because it accurately predicts that all of us lack the necessary righteousness to be in complete communion with God, or as Paul says to be right (or complete) in the sight of God. Because all have sinned, our sins judge us guilty! Consequently, we deserve God's wrath and His punishment and this is bad news. However, the Good News of Christianity is that God sent Jesus to us and He took upon Himself the punishment for our sins so that we are declared not guilty! *(Romans 3:24-26) (Romans 5:1-2)*

David ends Psalm 14 by looking to the future saying God will rescue Isreal. *(V. 7)* Mighty God is transcendent. He is above our world – above Mount Zion, and on His throne in heaven. He has sent His Son, Jesus to rescue and save us all. He has made it possible, by faith, to have our sins forgiven and to have peace with God and with our fellow human beings. We all can rejoice and shout with joy when Israel and the rest of the world choose Jesus as their Savior.

# PSALM 15

## Who May Go into the Tabernacle?

After David became king of Israel, the first thing he did was to invade Jerusalem and set up his headquarters there. Soon afterwards, he brought the Ark of the Covenant to Jerusalem, which had become his capitol city. Now Jerusalem became not only the political center of Judaism, but the religious focal point also. Having done this, Jews from all over the countryside would make pilgrimages to attend the various Holy days that were celebrated in Jerusalem. With crews of folks flocking into the Holy City for worship, it raised the question of what were the righteous requirements of the law? The question was obviously in David's mind when he composed Psalm 15.

When proposing his question to the LORD, who is able to worship in your sanctury *(V.1)*, David was really asking what kind of character a person should have in order to be approved by God. In other words, how should people live if they wanted to be in union with the LORD of life? This is a fundamental question David asks and then gives us readers several representative answers.

Many years before on Mount Sinai, God gave the law to Moses and the just requirements are called the moral law. The moral law can be summed up in the Ten Commandments, as interpreted by the rest of the Scriptures. In the New Testament, Jesus sums up the moral law. He says the first and greatest commandment is that we must love the Lord our God with all our heart, soul and mind. But the second comment is equally important, Jesus adds, that we must love our neighbor as ourself. *(Matthew 22.37-40)* This is God's plumb line by which all else must be measured!

The question of who should go into the Tabernacle is about godly living and not about who will be right with God. They are related, of course, but they are two different questions. To know we are one with the Lord and are going to heaven with Him when we die are only achieved by putting our faith and trust in Jesus as our Lord and Savior! In gratitude for what Christ did for us on the cross, we will endeavor to do all we can to keep the moral law. However, we cannot be made right with God by merely keeping the law (which is also impossible to do).

The answers David gives us as to who should be able to find refuge and shelter in God's Tabernacle are certainly not all that can be said. David's moral statements are merely representative answers. Why do we say this? Because David gave other answers. In Psalm 24:3-4, David says we need hands and hearts that are pure, not worship idols and never tell lies. The Prophet Isaiah also had his opinions. In Isaiah 33:14-17 he says those who are honest and fair, reject making profit by fraud, don't take bribes and shut their eyes to evil. These answers cited are similar but not identical.

In verses 2 through 5, David lists a number of things that would qualify persons to be worthy to enter God's place of worship. We list four categories:

## THE WAY A PERSON ACTS
A person must lead a blameless life doing what's right. *(V.2)*
A person must keep their promises. *(V.4)*
A person must not accept bribes. *(V.5)*

## THE WAY A PERSON COMMUNICATES
A person must not slander others. *(V.3)*
A person must not speak evil of their friends. *(V.3)*
A person must speak truth from a sincere heart. *(V.2)*

## THE WAY A PERSON BEHAVES
A person must not harm their neighbors. *(V.3)*
A person must honor faithful followers of the LORD. *(V.4)*

## THE WAY A PERSON USES MONEY
Persons cannot charge interest on the money they lend. *(V.5)*

Another way to analyze David's words of those who are qualified or spiritually prepared for worship in God's House is to use a plus and minus category:

## POSITIVE NEGATIVE

| | |
|---|---|
| Blameless *(V.2)* | Doesn't slander *(V.3)* |
| Does what is right *(V.2)* | Doesn't harm neighbors *(V.3)* |
| Sincere *(V.2)* | Despises sinners *(V.4)* |
| Speaks the truth *(V.2)* | Doesn't gossip *(V.3)* |
| Keeps promises *(V.4)* | Doesn't take bribes *(V.5)* |
| Honor followers of the LORD *(V.4)* | Won't testify against the innocent *(V.5)* |

The words of David in Psalm 15 are worthy of imitation. As Christians, we should read the Psalter with appreciation. Many of the Psalmists' words are quoted in the New Testament. They constitute a worthy foundation upon which the New Testament writers build. The Apostle Paul was thoroughly grounded in the Psalms, and drew heavily upon them in his many epistles. Romans 12:3-11 mirror the spirit of David's Psalm 15.

# PSALM 16
## David's Beautiful Psalm of Trust

Psalm 16 is a meditation written by David on the joys that are his as a result of his oneness with God. Scholars describe it as a psalm of trust. Along the lines of the 23rd Psalm, it is an expression of David's serene confidence in the LORD. Psalm 16 is also considered a Messianic Psalm.

### Segment One —All the Good Things I Have Are from You. Verses 1 - 4

David begins why asking God to keep him safe. *(V.1)* He then confesses that God is his Master. *(V.2)* Everything he values in this life he attributes to the LORD. He tells us that the true heroes of the the land are godly people. *(V.3)* They support him when he associates with them and they have common values. He stays away from people who chase other Gods. *(V.4)* You, Yahweh God, are my Number One commitment in life!

### Segment Two – The LORD Gives Me a Wonderful Inheritance. Verses 5 - 6

David goes back in history to the Book of Joshua when God assigned the twelve tribes their portion of land. But David says the LORD alone is his inheritance. *(V.5)* He thinks about how God had the Prophet Samuel anoint him and how he is now the king of a great nation. God has been good to him. *(V.5)* He looks around and marvels at the brooks and meadows as he views the Judean countryside and acknowledges that is his inheritance as well. *(V.6)*

43

## Segment Three – David's Trust Is in the LORD. Verses 7 - 9

David's happiness is full and he wants to give a "blessing" to th LORD who "guides" him. (V.7) Isn't it interesting that David (and perhaps we) mere mortals can bless God Almighty. The Hebrew word for "bless" ("Barak") also can mean "praise," an "act of adoration." The Hebrew word ("Ya'ats") is translated as "guides." It also means "to counsel or advise." God counsels David at night through the still small voice of the Holy Spirit and this keeps him from straying. He says he is not fearful because the Spirit is beside him. (V.8) Because David's total self (his mind, spirit and body) is dedicated to the doing God's will, he is able to sleep at night and remains totally safe. He is joyful because of this. (V.9)

## Segment Four – Are David's Words a Prophecy? Verses 10 - 11

Verses 10-11 are what makes this a Messianic Psalm. David not only praises God for making him secure on a day-to-day basis, but his joy abounds in his confidence (his faith) that God will not leave his soul among the dead. (V.10) In the Hebrew mind there was nothing beyond death. When a person dies, his or her body was buried in ("Sheol"), "the Pit," and that was the end! David's declaration in verse 10 was a <u>hint of immortality.</u>

In verse 11, David expands on this thought. He thanks God for the joy of living with Him forever. What makes these two verses so profound is the fact that several New Testament leaders have picked up David's words and used them in their preaching in proclaiming the Good News of Jesus' resurrection! The Apostle Peter preached before a huge crowd in Jerusalem at Pentecost where he said that Jesus was the Messiah. He uses David's words in Psalm 16:10, of not leaving his soul among the dead, to explain the miracle of the resurrection. (Acts 2:24-27)

Later, when Paul and Barnabas were in Antioch, the Apostle Paul spoke in the Synagogue and told all who were gathered how Jesus was condemned to death and crucified and placed in a tomb. Then God raised Him from the dead and He appeared to His disciples. (Acts 13:32-39)

The question we raise is whether David really understood what he wrote in verse 10? Was he prophesizing the resurrection of Jesus as both Peter and Paul interpreted? He may have, but most contemporary scholars say no. Peter called David a prophet, but it is doubtful that David thought he was writing about Jesus. He did reason that if God loved him and protected him in this life, then God would keep him and bless him in the future life. He didn't spell this out.

As we read in Psalm 16, David puts his faith and trust completely in God's hands, and, consequently, he believed God would also take care of him in death (by the logic of faith). Whether David was thinking about the Messiah is a matter of conjecture. However, we Christians can learn from David, but ultimately we do not look to David, but to Jesus Christ as our Lord and savior. It was His victory on the cross that sealed our salvation!

# PSALM 17

## David's Cry for Vindication

It was said that David was a man after God's own heart. *(1 Samuel 13:14)* One of the reasons for this was that David was a man of prayer. Psalm 17 is a prayer by David asking God's protection and vindication for him.

### Segment One – Vindication and Innocence. Verses 1 - 5

Like Job, David asks God for justice. He is saying that his life is beyond reproach. *(V.1)* He wants God to declare him innocent. *(V.2)* At night when asleep and my defenses are down, David says, God will find nothing amiss. *(V.3)* I am doing my utmost to follow Your commands and I am not doing the bidding of cruel and evil people. *(V.4)* I have not wavered from following your path. *(V.5)* David is arguing with God in his prayer claiming he is innocent and righteous. How can that be?

We are all sinners and, as such, are unworthy before God. If we are able to stand before Him, it is only by His grace! (See Ephesians 2:5.) Paul quotes David's own written words in Psalm 14, which says, no one does good, not even one. *(V.3)*

So how can David claim he is innocent? Jesus taught Christians to pray to God asking Him to forgive us our sins. *(Matthew 6:12)* Apart from Jesus' death for us on the cross, we Christians are not innocent. However, in gratitude for what He did for us, we try with all our hearts to be beyond reproach. Even Isaiah in the Old Testament spoke against self – righteousness. *(Isaiah-59:1-2)* David had a wonderful relationship with God, but, in this instance, he needed to be more humble. It is true for all of us – if we don't humble ourselves and ask forgiveness, we put up a barrier.

An important part of prayer is <u>self examination</u> to determine whether or not we are free from sins that would prevent God from answering us. Paul told the Corinthian Christians to look inward and examine themselves before preparing for the Lord's Supper. (1 Corinthians 11:28)

## Segment Two – David Asks for God's Strong Love. Verses 6 - 9

David's appeal to the God of Might *("El")* on the basis of His Covenant-keeping love is a much more legitimate way for him to pray rather than claiming he is innocent. *(V.6)* God's "love" in Hebrew is translated as *("Checed")*, which has a variety of meanings, such as "loving-kindness," "mercy," "unfailing love," and it refers to the covenant between God and the Hebrews. This is the love that persuaded God to enter into a relationship with His chosen people – promising to bless them if the people would obey and follow Him. David asks God to show him God's unfailing love. *(V.7)* He asks God to protect him. *(V.8)* David borrows a metaphor from Moses in Dueteronomy 32:11 when he asks God to hide him in the shadow of God's wings. David also asks God to protect him like he was the apple of God's eye. *(V.8)*

With regard to the covenant, David knows God has pledged to keep His part of the bargain which includes helping Israel in her battles against her enemies and to protect her people against wicked people. *(V.9)* David feels he has kept his covenant obligations and this assures him that God will help him in the future. It is the same covenant-keeping love that God reaches out and saves us Christians through the death and resurrection of the Lord Jesus Christ.

## Segment Three – A Plea for Intervention. Verses 10 - 14

David's enemies are seriously threatening to close in on him. He reminds God that they are without pity. *(V.10)* He uses hyperbole in verses 11 and 12 to described how they might tear him apart like hunger young lions.

Much of David's life was full of controversy because he was a strong leader and not afraid to make decisions and so he had enemies who opposed him at every stage of his long career (including his son, Absalom). So he prays to God for deliverance. *(V.13)* It would not be a psalm attributed to David without his asking that his enemies and their children be punished. *(V.14)*

Prayer should not be used only as a parachute, that is, only in emergencies. We cannot accuse David of that because he communicated with the Almighty constantly. He does, however, ask God to fight his battles for him and uses imprecatory language—which means he frequently prays for God to curse and destroy his adversaries.

## Segment Four – Assurance of Vindication. Verse 15

In verse 14b, David asks God to not only punish his enemies, but he wants this wrathful judgment to extend to generations. This was the typical type of ask-for-violence toward enemies in David's day. He ends this psalm by saying God should do this because David has done what is right. *(V.15)* Then he concludes by saying that when he awakes he will be fully satisfied. *(V.15)* "Satisfied" is the Hebrew word *("Tsadaq")* which is the same word used in verse 1 when David asks God to hear his pleas for "justice." Other English words for *("Tsadaq")* are "to be right" *("Eous")*, "to be clean."

We must not read our Christian understanding of the afterlife and heaven into David's wording of being fully satisfied when he awakes. *(V.15)* Jewish thought had not fully developed into this realm of Christian thinking. Back then when someone died, they were buried and went to the place of the dead *("Sheol")* and that was the end.

Some of the Hebrew prophets spoke about the "Day of the LORD." Most of them agreed with Amos that the Day would be a time of darkness and disaster. *(Amos 5:18-20)* Another thought about the future was the idea that the Lord will dwell on Mount Zion as the King over the world and nations will come to worship Him. The Prophet Joel wrote that all the wicked warriors of the world will gather in the Valley of Jehoshaphat where the Lord will pronounce judgment on them. Then the Day of the LORD will come. *(Joel 3:16)*

Psalm 17 ends with David's prophesy that he will see God "face to face." *(V.15)* The Hebrew word here is *("T\*munah")*, which is a female noun meaning "a likeness," "an image." This may be wistful thinking on David's part because God is Spirit and cannot be seen by the human eye.

The wonderful part of our Christian faith is that God came down to earth in His Son, Jesus, so we can know God. *(John 14:6-9)* When God raised Jesus from the dead and brought Him up to heaven with Him to share His throne (see Hebrews 12:1-2), God set Jesus' Spirit free from the limitations of time and space and that means Jesus' Holy Spirit can come and indwell anyone who is open and has faith in Him. So we can only know God by having His Son live in our hearts!

Another inspirational passage of Scripture based on God's "unfailing love," is the 13th chapter of 1Corinthians. *(1 Corinthians 13:8-13)*

# PSALM 18
## The Living God Is David's Rock!

The superscription of Psalm 18 states that this is a psalm of David that he sang on the day the LORD rescued him from Saul and all of David's enemies.

Psalm 18 is a psalm of thanksgiving. It has 50 verses! It is David's recitation of God's many blessings for him. The superscription is the second longest in the Psalter. Turning to 2 Samuel 22, one finds that Psalm 18 is reproduced word-for-word (including the heading). It is not clear which came first. From the context in First and Second Samuel, it appears that the words of Psalm 18 were the final words written when David was an old man-- a kind of summary of all of God's deliverances throughout his life.

In the psalm are three categories of deliverances from the LORD:

1. Deliverance from King Saul. In the second half of First Samuel, we read how King Saul became insanely jealous of David because of the way everybody praised him. Saul tried numerous times to kill David. Consequently, David had to flee first to the land of the Philistines, and later to the cave in the wilderness called Adullam, and other wilderness areas. More than once, God had to intervene. At the end of First Samuel, we read that Saul died after a disastrous battle with the Philistines, and so David was crowned king.

2. As king, God delivers David during the years of fighting against Israel's enemies. God gave David many victories. These were the years when he conquered the Philistines, Moabites, Edomites, etc.

3. The third deliverance was against David's son, Absalom. The son plotted to take over David's kingdom and he did succeed in driving his father out of Jerusalem, as David fled to the wilderness with his army. Later, there was a huge battle between the two forces and

Absalom was killed. God delivered David once again, but David was saddened at the son's death. This leads to 2 Samuel, where Psalm 18 is reproduced. *(2 Samuel 1-51)*

In this psalm, David gives his thanks to the LORD for protection during all those dangerous years.

## Segment One – The Introduction. Verses 1 - 3

David begins by proclaiming his love for the LORD. *(V.1)* He then goes on to affirm that the LORD protected and sustained him over the years. David replies on various metaphors to describe God's protection of those who put their trust in Him. The first kind has to do with David's military victories. The LORD is his shield. *(V.2)* A second set of metaphors signifies how God protected him from his enemies. These images picture God as a rock, a fortress, and a savior. *(V.2)* Probably the most powerful metaphor is the word rock, an image of protection and shade. While hiding from Saul and his troops, David knew every secret hiding place in the rocky wilderness. The psalm invokes an image of David perched on a high rock overlooking his enemies, saved by God many times. *(V.3)* Another way that rock is used was as a solid foundation underneath one's feet.

Jesus used this image at the end of the Sermon on the Mount, when he contrasted a person who builds a house on sand – as compared with the person who builds on solid rock! The person who builds a house on sand suffers the loss of everything when a storm hits; but the person's house built on rock, stands firm! *(Matthew 5:24-27)*

David gives his testimony to God's faithfulness, that the LORD is rock solid and a protecting fortress. *(V.2)* We Christians have the same security as we put our faith in God's Son, Jesus Christ!

## Segment Two – What the LORD Did for David. Verses 4 - 19

In this second segment, David is explaining what God did for him. Though David is surrounded by ropes of death *(V.4-5)* the LORD heard his cries. *(V.6)* Then in beautiful poetic language, David describes how God descended to earth amidst earthquakes, thunder and lightning and riding on an angel shoots arrows to scatter David's enemies. *(V.7-14)* At David's weakest moment, the LORD rescues him from powerful enemies as if drawing him up from the deepest waters. *(V.15-18)* Why? Because He delights in me! *(V.19)*

## Segment Three — The Reason David Was Delivered. Verses 20 - 24

For his part, David says, he has always done what was right *(V.20)*, kept the ways the the LORD *(V.21)*, never abandoned His principles *(V.22)*, kept himself from sin *(V.23)*, and in his heart followed the LORD's decrees. *(V.24)* Since this psalm was written late in David's life, his words raise a serious question of how he would write these words in the light of his sin against Bathsheba and her husband Uriah. How could he claim to be blameless and had kept himself from sin? If we could somehow confront David, I suppose he would readily agree that he had sinned. In fact, he writes about this in Psalm 51, where he asks God to blot out his sins. *(Psalm 51:1)* Obviously, God had forgiven David, although he had to suffer the consequences of what his sin did to his family and kingdom.

## Segment Four — An Important Principle. Verses 25 - 35

In this section, David comments on the ways God deals with folks in general. His insight here is that merciful folks are able to see the mercy of God toward them, and the pure in heart see purity around them (as Jesus pointed out in Matthew 5:8). David says if you are going to be faithful to the LORD you must be: faithful to the faithful *(V.25)*; pure to the pure *(V.26)*; and rescue the humble. *(V.27)* God permitted David to act like this because God provided light for him when he was in darkness and all God's promises to him proved to be true. *(V.28-29)* God also made his way safe *(V.32)*, made him surfooted as a deer *(V.33)*, gave him the strength to draw a bow of bronze *(V.34)* and was his shield of protection. *(V.35)*

As David says in Psalm 14, all have sinned. No one is uncorrupted, not even one. *(Psalm 14:.2-3)* All of us have stumbled into sin many times; some of us have stumbled dreadfully! But when we come to the end of our life and look back (as David is doing in Psalm 18), and confess our many failings and weaknesses, we can say with conviction that God has never failed us!

We, who stand on the Victory side of the cross, can appreciate David and his life. He really was a man after God's own heart. *(1Samuel 13:14)* He wasn't perfect as none of us are perfect. David looked forward to the coming of the Messiah, but we Christians know that, in Jesus Christ, the <u>MESSIAH HAS COME!</u> And, as we bring the Lord Jesus into our hearts, we are safe and secure in His loving arms. *(John 15:1-4)* Our task in life as Christians is to live in Jesus and let Him live in us. Then we will be fruitful and filled with His joy. Jesus tells us we must not worry day to day. That the Father will take care of us if we live for Him. *(Matthew 6:31-34)*

## Segment Five — Conclusions. Verses 36 - 50

In verses 36 to 46, David again recites how God has made him a successful king of Israel. He was able to conquer his enemies in battles *(V.37)*, he destroyed all those who hated him *(V.40)*, he was appointed ruler over nations *(V.43)*, and foreigners cringed before him and trembled as they came out of their stongholds. *(V.44-45)*

The final five verses put us back where we started, namely, that the LORD protects us like a rock! *(V.46)* David seems to be saying that he will praise God for all of his victories among the Gentile nations. But David is also apparently being prophetic. Verse 50 makes it clear that David is projecting future victories to all of David's descendents forever from God. For Christians this last verse refers to the Messiah, Jesus Christ. The Apostle Paul, writing under the influence of the Holy Spirit, saw this in Psalm 18 and uses verse 49 as a quote to reinforce the coming of Jesus from the Jews to the Gentiles to give them salvation. This can be found in Romans 14:8-13.

The dominate thesis in this psalm is that God is our "Rock"! God is a shelter under which we can be protected--a fortress into which we can go and be safe. God is a firm foundation upon which we can safely build. August Toplady (1740-1778) was traveling when a storm arose and forced him to take refuge in a cleft of a huge rock. While the storm raged, Toplady was inspired to write the words of a familiar hymn "Rock of Ages."

Maybe David did see into the future – we don't know. But we who stand on the Victory side of the cross know what Jesus did: He died for us, so that we might be saved from our sin, and so that we might be with God and Jesus for all eternity when we die!

# PSALM 19

## God's Revelation in the Heavens and the Torah

Some commentators theorize that David's Psalm 19 was originally two separate compositions: one, his thoughts on God's creation (verses 1-6); and two, the importance of God's Torah (verses 7-11). Some later editor joined them together.

### Segment One – God's Glory in Nature. Verses 1 - 6

Heaven and earth contain wonderful displays of God's craftsmanship. Day and night, they continually reveal God's creative power, His glory! *(V.1) ("Kabod")* is a Hebrew noun meaning "glory," "majesty," and "honor." When we observe the stars at night, we are made aware of the Creator's fantastic design. *(V.2)* It's also evident when we see the petals of a flower, or a snowflake, or a sunset – all testify to an all-powerful mind that lies behind them. The beauty represented by these aspects of the creation speak to who God is. *(V.3-5)* It's self-evident. One doesn't have to be a physicist or an astronomer to see it. This is what Paul writes in his first chapter of Romans. *(Romans 1:19-20)*

David is saying the heavens have been revealing God's glory ever since God placed the stars and moon in them (some 40 billion years ago, say the scientists). *(V.6)* One of the great and stately hymns of the church, *The Heavens are Telling* composed by Joseph Addison, is based on Psalm 19.

### Segment Two – Wisdom from God's Torah. Verses 7 - 11

In beautiful poetic language, David writes that the LORD's law is perfect and revives the soul. *(V.7)* The "law," (Hebrew *("Torah")* refers to the law of

Moses and the Hebrew word means "teachings," "a set of rules." David says the commandments of the LORD are clear and joyful. *(V.8)* The precepts (or proclamations) are not only fair, but they are true. *(V.10)* These decrees, including the Ten Commandments (see Exodus 20:1-17), give pleasure when obeyed – even the do not ones. When recited, they even give a warning to help erring servants back on track. *(V.11)*

David obviously had spent several days and nights contemplating the mysteries of nature, with its breath-taking beauty and grandeur. He had come to the conclusion that behind it all was the hand of God. Some days David was overwhelmed by the majesty of the sun and stars – yet still other times were the dark side of nature, the vicious storms, the earthquakes, and such that disrupt and destroy human life.

Paul had these same puzzlements as did David. Paul writes that against nature's will everything on earth was and is subject to God's curse. He looks to the future and says all creation groans for a future when it will join God's children from freedom of death and decay. *(Romans 8:21)* Paul then adds all creation has been in the pains of childbirth up the present time. The Holy Spirit is a foretaste of our future freedom from pain and suffering. *(Romans 8:22-23)*

In Segment Two (verses 7-11), David lauds the LORD for the laws given to Moses. He calls them perfect, true and fair. *(V.7)* The only problem is that no human beings have ever been able to live up to them!

Again, this is the conclusion Paul came to in chapter seven of Romans. He tells us the more we know God's law, the clearer it becomes that we aren't obeying it. In Romans chapter five, Paul writes that God gave us His Law to show all people how sinful we are. *(Romans 5:20)* He didn't say that the law was evil. No, the law showed Paul his sin. The good law, which was supposed to show Paul the way to the good life, instead gave him the death penalty. In chapter 7 Paul agonized saying that when he wants to do right, he inevitably does wrong. The law wins the fight and makes him a slave to sin. *(Romans 7:21-23)*

### Segment Three – David's Reflections. Verses 12 - 14

David, in Segment Three, questions God, asking why he (David) is aware of sins lurking in his heart. *(V.12)* Like Paul (and we Christians), David knows he is a sinner, and he realizes that his sin has erected a barricade that separates him from God. David asks the LORD to cleanse him from hidden faults. Deliberate sins *(V.13)* are sins like when David lusted after Bathsheba, and then after he committed adultery with her, he deliberately had her husband murdered! He pleads with God not to have sins control him. *(V.14)*

Again we go to Paul who triumphantly cries out that Jesus Christ our Lord is the answer. *(Romans 7:25)* Jesus fulfilled the requirement of the law in dealing with sin and His Spirit helps us not to subcumb to our sinful nature. *(Romans 8:3-4)*

# PSALM 20

## A Royal Psalm

Psalm 20 is designated A Royal Psalm. Psalm 20 and 21 were written to be sung by the Jewish people in the Tabernacle or Temple on behalf of their king and their nation. Both psalms are liturgies. The verses are not classified as a format prayer, inasmuch as the words are directed to the king himself, letting him know that his people are 100% with him and that they want God to protect him in battle.

### Segment One —May God Grant the King All His Desires. Verses 1 - 5

Psalm 20 begins by the Psalmist (the king) acting in his role as a priest to encourage the congregation that in times of trouble may the God of Israel response to their cries for help. *(V.1)* The word "trouble" *("Yowm")* in Hebrew refers to the sovereignty of God in a particular time sequence when the king needs protection. Yehweh God resides in His sanctuary (as the people of Israel believed) and when called upon He would send help. *(V.2)* In days past, He had rescued Israel on numerous times. For instance, when God confronted Moses at the Burning Bush, He told him that He saw the misery of the Hebrew slaves in Egypt and would deliver them by sending Moses to confront Pharaoh. Moses asks how he was supposed to do it? God said just tell the Hebrews "I Am" sent you. *(Exodus 3:14)* This was just one of the many times God had led His people against their enemies. So the people had faith that they could count on God's help, especially since they sacrificed many burnt offerings to Him. *(V.3)*

Note the *"INTERLUDE"* at the end of verse 3. Possibly this might be the occasion when a priest would offer a symbolic burnt offering on behalf of the king, and he would lead the congregation by praying that God would

57

grant them their hearts desires. *(V.4)* Also, that the LORD would answer their prayers. *(V.5)* Finally the congregation is instructed to shout for joy in anticipation of future victories. *(V.5)*

## Segment Two – Assurances for the King's Success. Verses 6 - 8

David writes in this psalm that God will give His "saving" help to David and to the future "anointed" kings in David's bloodline. *(V.6)* "Saves" in Hebrew is the word *("Yasha")* and it can mean "victory in battle." "Anointed" is the word *("Mashiyach")* and it implied that kings in David's line would be consecrated by God to become priest-kings (God's representatives on earth). These words reflect what Moses said in Deuteronomy. Moses wrote that the Hebrews should show no fear in battle because the LORD would join the fight with them against their enemies. *(Deuteronomy 20: V 1-4)*

Verse 7 of Psalm 20 says Isreal should not put its confidence in weapons of war but in its faith in the the LORD. These are wonderful sentiments. Unfortunately, even under David's son, Solomon, Israel had become very much like her neighboring nations acquiring a great standing force of military horses and chariots. David says the nations that put their trust soley in military force will be destroyed. *(V.8)*

## Segment Three – Concluding Prayer of the People. Verse 9

In the Tent of Meeting and in the magnificent Temple that King Solomon erected, the gathered congregation concluded worship by singing a prayer. David rightly requests victory for the king(s) of Israel. *(V.9)* In the same spirit – but in an entirely different perspective – the Apostle Paul counsels his spiritual son, Timothy, to pray for all the people and those in authority. *(1 Timothy 2:1-6)* Yes, we need to pray for all in authority over us, local, state, and national leaders, asking God to grant them supernatural wisdom.

We Christians can view Psalm 20 in two ways. One, we can see it as a piece of ancient Jewish political propaganda which says that God is on our side and He will give us victory. This kind of thinking says, "I'll plan it and then God will sanction what I've planned." Or, two, we can see the psalm as God being the primary actor, not the king. Naturally, we have to depend on our leaders, but the second approach teaches us to pray for those who hold power, asking the Lord to help them make the right moral decisions. At the same time, the second approach warns us not to let our dependence upon our leaders turn into the trust we owe to God. It also says we ought <u>not</u> to support policies based on pure military might. Taking our cues from this second approach, we need to prayerfully and carefully do our best to discern what God's will is for us, and then pursue it. We should never pretend that our will is God's will.

# PSALM 21

## A Prayer or National Thanksgiving

Psalm 20 and 21 are similar. Psalm 20 is a prayer asking for deliverance by God prior to going in to battle. Psalm 21 recounts a national thanksgiving for what God did for the Israelites—obviously the battle was won-- and enumerates what they hope He will continue to do for them (and for King David).

### Segment One –The King Thanks the LORD. Verses 1 - 7

In gratitude, the king thanks the LORD for (God's) victory. *(V.1)* The word in Hebrew for "victory" is *("Y shuw ah")*. It can also mean "salvation." David thanks God for giving him his heart's desire *(V.2)* and once again putting a gold crown on his head. *(V.3)* The king also thanks God for many blessings, which include preservation and long life *(V.4)*, honor *(V.5)* and eternal blessings *(V.6)*. David did live a long life, 70 or longer. He was King of Israel for over 40 years. A little exaggeration about the length of David's life is in verse 4, which says his life with stretch forever. The Hebrew word for "forever" is *("Olam")*. It can mean "most distant future" or "a short period." On the other hand, it could be referring to the Prophet Nathan's prophecy (in 2 Samuel 7) that David's dynasty would last forever.

From our Christian perspective, we see Jesus as a descendant of David who is God's Messiah and a continuation of David's dynasty. Verse 7 speaks of the king trusting in God's power and in the unfailing love of the most high God. This term "most high" to described God goes back to Abram's victory over Kedorlaomer's army in rescuing his nephew, Lot. Abram meets with the King of Salem, a priest of God. "Most High" was the name given to Melchizedek, who blessed Abram. In appreciation, Abram gives King

Melchizedek a tithe (a tenth) of all he had recovered in his victory. Many interpreters believe this could be a pre-incarnation appearance of Jesus. (See Genesis 14 and Hebrews Chapters 7 and 8.)

## Segment Two – Anticipation of Future Victories. Verses 8 - 12

In the Tent of Meeting (or the Temple), the congregation and the king would be assembled and a priestly spokesman would speak words about future victories. He would use the future tense and his words would express a confidence that Yahweh God (the LORD) would protect the king and his people in future times.

God's unfailing love could be counted on. God would be faithful to His covenant agreement (see Exodus 19:6). This would be the basis for the future confidence spoken by the priest. The language in this psalm is vicious at points (which was the norm for that era). Addressing God, the priest would acknowledge God's strong right hand would protect them. *(V.8)* That God's anger woud consume the enemy. *(V.9)* And, that the enemies' descendants would cease to exist. *(V.10)*

Of course, much depended on the king. In theory, each Davidic king was to become a faithful priest and spokesman for the widows and orphans. No sooner had Solomon died then Jeroboam, his son, paid no attention to the people's demands and the ten northern tribes of Israel refused to be ruled by a descendant of David (see 1 Kings 12).

## Segment Three – Concluding Prayer of the People. Verse 13

It is God who gives victories by his glorious power. *(V.13)* This was the congregational response—a song of praise celebrating God's mighty deeds. *(V.13)* It is important that we Christians learn from this psalm about what we should think concerning our own political leaders, especially our president: (1) If we have little or no respect for him, we fail to pray for him; (2) Or we think too highly of him and praise him to the skies and are, therefore, disillusioned or crushed when we discover in time that he is only a mere sinful human being as we all are.

In Psalm 21, the people value King David and want him to succeed. No leader can succeed without God's help and intervention. We always need to read the psalms from a Christian point of view. We know that David lived at a time in history when he (and everyone) felt that war was an inevitable fact of life. They, therefore, turned to God in prayer that He might give them victory over their enemies. They frequently prayed, like verse 10, and asked God to wipe out the descendants of their enemies. This kind of prayer is called imprecatory prayer, where you ask God to damn and destroy another group of people. In that day the extermination of enemies totally—men, women and children—was the accepted way of making certain your enemy would not come back and fight you in the future.

However, this teaching stands in stark contrast to the teachings of Jesus Christ! In Matthew 5, Jesus tells us to love our enemies and pray fo those who pesecute us. *(Matthew 5:43-45)*

# PSALM 22

## The Psalm of the Cross

Psalm 22 is the best prophetic description of the crucifixion of Jesus in the Old Testament of the Bible. In David's time, the Romans didn't practice death by crucifixion, but this psalm is a prophetic picture of the suffering endured by Jesus as He died on the cross to pay the penalty for our sins.

Parallels between this psalm and passages from the New Testament are as follows:

Psalm 22, verse 1 –God forsakes him.
Mark 15:34 and Matthew 27:46

Psalm 22, verse 7 – He is mocked on the cross.
Matthew 27:39 and Mark 15:29

Psalm 22, verse 8 -- Let God save him.
Matthew 27:43

Psalm 22, verse 18 – His clothes are divided.
Matthew 27:35, Mark 15:24 and Luke 23:34

Also, Psalm 22 has an affinity with Job 30:9-11 and Isaiah 40:55

David was a prophet and he meditated and spoke of the Messiah's suffering. Not only did David write Psalm 22, but Jesus quoted David's words in Psalm 22 when He was on the cross.

In the Apostle Peter's charismatic sermon at Pentecost, where thousands of folks were converted (see Acts 2:29-33), he reminded the people that David in Psalm 22 predicted how the Messiah would die.

Here is a quick review of the events leading up to the crucifixion. Jesus was arrested and kept under guard at the Chief Priest's house. The next morning, He was taken before the Counsel (the Sanhedrin), was tried and found to be guilty of blasphemy. He then was sent to Pontius Pilate, the Prefect of the Roman province of Judea. Pilate approved the death sentence sought by the Chief Priest. Then Jesus was led through the streets bearing a cross (a terrible humiliation). He ended up at Golgotha, where Roman soldiers drove nails through His hands and feet and attached Him to a wooden cross. While on the cross, Jesus prayed that His Father forgive the people for they were unaware of what they were actually doing. (*Luke 23:34*) While on the cross, darkness descends from noon to three o'clock, and during this period of agony, what do you suppose He was thinking about? He must have been thinking about Psalm 22 because Jesus quoted verse 1. All this can be found in Matthew 27 and Mark 15.

Psalm 22 begins with a description of Jesus's alienation with His heavenly Father as He was made to be sin for us (see 2 Corinthians 5:21). Psalm 22 continues with a vivid description of the crucifixion in verses 1-21, and concludes in triumph as Jesus ends up being fully and perfectly accepted by God the Father (in verses 22-31).

### Segment One – Prophetic Description of the Crucifixion. Verses 1- 21

I am deeply indebted to Rev. Dr. James Montgomery Boice* whose keen analysis saw an alternating pattern in the first 21 verses of this psalm. He divided the first 21 verses into six sections as follows: 1-2, 3-5, 6-8, 9-11, 12-18 and 19-21. The first, third and fifth sections speak about David's sufferings. The second, fourth and sixth sections are David's prayers to God. As Boice lays it out, the intensity and distress becomes less and less as the psalm goes along and David's confidence in God's help intensifies. We will follow the pattern that Boice described.

### No Help From God. Verses 1 - 2

On the cross Jesus cried out to God using the very words of verse 1 in this psalm, thinking He was abandoned by God. Jesus asks why has God forsaken

---

*Boice, James Montgomery, *Psalms, an Expositional Commentary*, Baker Books, Grand Rapids, MI, 1994, p. 198-205.

him? *(V.1)* There was no answer. In verse 2 Jesus in agony says day and night God does not hear his voice. As we see it, God had not abandoned His Son, but the very essence of the atonement is God letting Jesus bear the hell in order that we might share His heaven! In Jesus' suffering, He was undergoing the wrath of God in our place. In this sense, Jesus was forsaken during the interim of His horror. We Christians know that the crucifixion was followed by resurrection—so we know that God the Father did not abandon His Son. God loves us (the world) so much that He was willing to allow His son to suffer on our behalf so believers might have salvation (John 3:16).

## You Delivered Our Fathers. Verses 3 - 5

Yet Jesus acknowledges that God is holy and that Israel's praises surround His throne. *(V.3)* Obviously, Jesus knew this psalm well and knew that leaders in the past were delivered because they trusted in God. *(V.3)* He mulled this over in his mind when on the cross. He must have sensed the bitter irony—that His ancestors trusted in God and God rescued them. *(V.4-5)* He must have thought, I trust in You and yet I feel forsaken! David (in these verses) is simply stating his faith that a Holy God will be faithful and will deliver the Messiah, even though he feels forsaken.

## I Am Scorned and Despised. Verses 6 - 8

Jesus was scorned and hated as He hung on the cross. *(V.6-7) (Luke 23:35)* First God abandons Him and now He is being mocked. The people taunted Him by laughing and sarcastically saying they will only believe that the LORD (the covenant God of Israel) loves Jesus *(V.8)* when they see the LORD coming down and rescuing him. (See Matthew 27:39-43.)

## You Have Helped Me in the Past. Verses 9 - 11

This was David's memory of God's past faithfulness throughout his life. As a nursing infant he was taught to trust God. *(V.9)* From infant to now you have been my God. *(V.10)* The implication is that God helped him in the past and will continue to keep him safe. I am sure Jesus had similar thoughts, particularly given the last few words of verse 11 that point out that no one else could help him.

## My Strength Is Drained Away. Verses 12 - 18

David's words in verses 12-18 vividly portray the crucifixion. Can you just imagine how Jesus felt hanging on that cross of death? He must have felt just the way David describes it, as if he were surrounded by fierce bulls *(V.12)*, like a victim with hungry lions with open jaws attacking their prey *(V.13)*, with his bones out of joint by the weight of his body hanging there. *(V.14)*. His tongue sticking to the roof of his mouth. *(V. 15)* His hands and feet pierced with nails. *(V.16)* With his enemies staring at him and gloating. *(V.17)* And the soldiers dividing his clothes among themselves. *(V.18)* Almost all of this is repeated in Matthew 27:39-49.

## Hurry, God, and Rescue Me. Verses 19 - 21

In verses 19, 20 and 21, Jesus again pleads with the LORD to come quickly to his aid and rescue him from a violent death. Amidst all the agony of the horrible physical suffering, Jesus never ceased praying to His heavenly Father. He asked God to deliver Him from those dogs and from the mouths of the lions and the horns of the wild oxen. It is amazing how David's words parallel Jesus' experiences. The implication is that the darkness has passed and Jesus' time of alienation from His Father is over. In the midst of His agony and His torturous suffering, He is able to transcend everything and He and the Father are One—once more! He was surely rescued, because on the third day God raised Jesus from the dead, and today He is with God sitting at the Father's right hand in heaven interceding for us!

To accept His intercession for us, all we have to do is say to Jesus that we trust Him and thank Him for dying for us. We just need to tell Him we are willing to follow Him as Lord and Savior. *(Romans 3:22-26)*

In the first two chapters of the Book of Hebrews in the New Testament, we are told that Jesus died to cleanse and clear the record of all our sin. Having done this, He sat down in highest honor beside the God of heaven. Thus Jesus became far greater than the angels and the author of Hebrews goes on to say that God allowed Him to suffer in order to bring multitudes of people to heaven. Because of His suffering, God crowned Him with special glory and honor. Through all this, it was necessary for Jesus to share our humanity. So that by His death, He might destroy the devil who holds the power of death and, thereby, free everyone held in slavery by the fear of death. Then Jesus says He's not ashamed to call us His family. *(Psalm 22:22)*

Of course Psalm 22 was written by David's hand, but probably without his knowing that God was inspiring him to allow his words be that of Jesus. This is what Hebrews is telling us. The second half of Psalm 22 appears as if Jesus is talking to His brothers (and sisters) about His heavenly Father. It is in this spirit we will interpret the second half of Psalm 22.

Let's review the scene of the crucifixion: Jesus was forced to carry His cross through the streets of Jerusalem on His way to Golgotha. It was horrible, and when He got there the soldiers drove nails through His hands and feet, putting Him up on that wooden cross. Remember, He prayed for them. *(Luke 23:34)* When He hung there, He entrusted His mother, Mary, to John's safekeeping. He was always thinking of others, never of Himself.

All this changed at noon because a great darkness came over the land, and it lasted till about 3 o'clock. God sent this to shield Jesus. It was during this time that He was made sin for us. What was Jesus thinking about during these three hours? We don't know.

We do know that at about three o'clock, He cried out asking – using the words of Psalm 22-- why God had forsaken him. *(V.1) Matthew 27:46)* For that brief period, He felt alienated from His Father as He took upon Himself our sins. But later He cried out, dismissing His spirit, and died. But look! The curtain secluding the Holiest Place in the Temple was split apart from top to bottom, signifying the full atonement for sin had been made. Before this, Jesus already was assured that God had heard Him. Untold generations of people like us would be assured of salvation and they would become brothers and sisters in Christ.

## Segment Two – Proclamation of the Gospel. Verses 22 - 31

The Second Segment of Psalm 22 is a proclamation of the Gospel and of the growing and triumphant church. It can be divided into three phases: Part One: Brothers and Sisters, Verses 22 – 24; Part Two: Praise Before All the People, Verses 25 – 29; and Part Three: Generations Yet Unborn, Verses 30 - 31.

## Part One – Brothers and Sisters. Verses 22 - 25

If rescued, Jesus says, he will declare to his Jewish brothers and sisters the wonder of God's name. *(V.22)* He will give praise to the LORD to this and all generations of the descendants of Jacob *(V.23)* that the LORD has listened to my cries for help. *(V.24)* Also, Jesus would fulfill his vows to all who worship the LORD. *(V.25)* We are assuming in these verses that this is Jesus speaking, and it has to do with the Jewish people who are His brothers and sisters. But they also stand for all who have come to believe in Jesus as Savior; but, initially, it was for the Jews. The Apostle Paul, a Jew, said the salvation provided by Jesus was for the Jews first and also for the Gentiles. *(Romans 1:16-17)*

Jesus wanted His Jewish brothers and sisters to know, although He was despised and rejected by the majority of the Jews, that He wanted them to be a part of His heavenly family.

### Part Two – Praise Before All the People. Verses 26 - 29

One of Jesus' parables was called "The Parable of the Wedding Feast" found in Matthew 22:1-14. He likened the Kingdom of God to a wedding banquet that God put on for His Son. The Father sends out invitations to Jewish folks, but everyone had excuses why they couldn't come. When the Great Banquet was ready, God the Father sends out servants telling them to invite everyone they see, the good and bad alike, and the banquet Hall was filled with guests.

The parable was a prophesy of Jewish rejection and the subsequent salvation of the Gentiles. David in this section says that all who seek the LORD will have everlasting joy. The hearts of the poor will rejoice with everlasting joy. *(V.26)* The whole earth will return to the LORD. *(V.27)* The LORD will rule all nations. *(V.28)* All mortals will bow before the LORD. *(V.28)*

### Part Three – Generations Yet Unborn. Verses 30 - 31

David predicts that future generations will serve the Messiah (Jesus). *(V.30)* On the cross before He died, Jesus cried out that it is finished. *(John 19:30)* David says the same thing with different words. This righteous act by Jesus will be told to all those yet unborn. *(V.31)* What was concluded was the atonement. By dying on the cross, Jesus met the righteous demands of God. That is to say, because God is holy He cannot abide sin. Those mortals who sin must die; but due to Jesus' sacrifice of Himself on our behalf, God's righteous demands were fully satisfied. Now God can see those of us who are in Christ as righteous and not sinners. This is why Paul says there is no condemnation for those who accept Jesus Christ as Savior and Lord. *(Romans 8:1-2)*

Jesus is our Savior who shed His blood on the cross and that is what saves us from our sin. The author of the Book of Hebrews writes to Jews who had turned to Christ for salvation, but, because of intense persecution, they were contemplating the renunciation of their Christian faith. The author of Hebrews reminds them that the earthly high priests of Judaism cannot be their advocates to the Father in heaven. Only the Missiah, who was their blood sacrifice, can asccomplish that for them. *(Hebrews 9:24-28)*

Entrusting our life to the loving and living God, as David did and as Jesus did, changes everything. (A) Life can be understood not as a frantic search for satisfaction and self-security, but as a dependence upon God and a seeking of His Kingdom first (see Matthew 6:25-33). (B) Suffering can be understood not as something to be avoided at all costs, but as something to be accepted in the course of living—even embracing it on behalf of others. We can do this when we know that God shares out suffering,

# PSALM 23
## God Is My Loving Shepherd

The 23rd Psalm is one of the most beautiful, perhaps best-loved and best-known selections in the Bible. This psalm uses the metaphor of the relationship between a shepherd and his sheep to express the covenant relationship between God and His people. David, the author, was the shepherd of his father's flock of sheep when he was a young man. Later, when he became the king of Israel, he became known as the Shepherd King. (See 1 Samuel 16:11, 2 Samuel 5:2.)

Psalm 23 is relatively short, only six verses, and I will deal with it verse by verse.

### Verse 1 – LORD as Shepherd.

The personal name for the "LORD" in Hebrew is 'Yahweh." He is the all-powerful, all-present, all-knowing and all-wise God of the universe. A Shepherd is a person who cares for the sheep. His job is to protect, guide and nurture them. It is a 24-7, 12 months a year task. The amazing and perhaps the most awesome aspect of this psalm is that the mighty God has stooped to come down to earth as our Shepherd to take care of little people like you and me.

In Israel, as in other ancient cultures, a shepherd's work was considered to be at the bottom of the social scale. The lowest form of all work! If a family needed a shepherd, it was always the youngest son's job (like David who got his unpleasant assignment). Yet, God has chosen to be our Shepherd.

In the New Testament, Jesus refers to himself as the Good Shepherd for us Christians (see John 10:14). His parable in Luke 15 is about sheep and their shepherd. Jesus said that suppose you had 100 sheep and one of them strays. The shepherd would leave the 99 and search after his lost sheep. When he finds it, he will carry the sheep home on his shoulders and then tell all his friends the good news that he has found his lost sheep, and they would rejoice with him. *(Luke 15:7)* The Good News is that we are part of Jesus' flock and spiritually we have everything we need.

## Verses 2 and 3 —He Lets Me Rest and He Guides Me.

In Matthew 11:28-30, Jesus asks us Christians to let Him carry our heavy burdens. He asks us to rest in Him and that He will meet our needs.

The Hebrew word for "soul" is *("nephesh")*. It means "inner self," the vital principle that results in death when it leaves our bodies. Verse 3 is translated in the *King James Version* as *"He restoreth my soul."* This is an important part of our being that is strengthened.

## Verse 4 – Even in Death You Are There to Comfort Me.

For us Christians, it is Jesus who enables us to get right with God, and to know we will be with Him for all eternity. This is what takes the sting out of death and gives us a sense of safety and eternal security.

## Verse 5 – A Feast Is Prepared for Me in the Presence of Enemies.

If we allow God in Christ to lead us, we will find that He has prepared a table for us where we can break bread with our friends—yes even with our enemies. With God as our Host, our cups will be filled to overflowing with the wine of joy! Our blessings will indeed be a hundredfold.

## Verse 6 – I Will Experience Unfailing Love Throughout Life.

The Hebrew word for "unfailing love" is *("Checed")* and it is one of the most important words in the entire Bible. It is the love and mercy of God that will not let us go. It is the grace of God that sent Jesus to earth to be our Savior. He went to the cross and took our sins. He ensures us by means of His Resurrection that we will have everlasting life (John 3:16).

Psalm 23 sees life as a journey and the final destination is God's abode in heaven. When we arrive, God will be with us and there will be no more death or sorrow or pain. *(Revelation 21:4)*

Reading the Old Testament from a Christian perspective (as we must), we know that Jesus Himself, the Good Shepherd, will be in heaven to receive us. He says to us that the Father's home has many rooms for us. *(John 14: 2)* In the meantime, before you come to heaven, the Lord Jesus is saying to us if we love Him, keep his commandments, he will ask the Father to send His Holy Spirit to live in us and assist us throughout our lives. *(John 14:15-18)* It is so wonderful to have the Spirit of Jesus available to indwell us. God is good! All the time!

# PSALM 24
## The King of Glory!

When David brought the Ark of the Covenant to Jerusalem, it consolidated and made Jerusalem both the political and religious center of his regime. The Jews felt then, symbolically, that the God of Israel made His home in the Ark and so David composed this hymn for the occasion.

There is no mistaking things, David in this psalm is welcoming Jehovah God into the Holy city. In subsequent years, Psalm 24 would refer to King David or one of his descendants who were on the throne. For us Christians, we refer to the King of Glory as God's Son, Jesus, who entered Jerusalem on that first Palm Sunday. (See Luke 19:28 -38.)

Psalm 24 is a short psalm, only 10 verses. It is easy to organize into three sections. Verses 1-2 is a statement that all the earth belongs to God; the second section, Verses 3-6, describes the people who may stand before the LORD and the qualities of their lives they must have; the third and final section, Verses 7-10, welcomes the King of Glory coming into the city of Jerusalem!

### Segment One – Everything in All the World Is God's. Verses 1 - 2

This is a bold declaration telling us that God owns the world and everything in it. *(V.1)* It is also a veiled warning by the author so nobody should think of Jehovah in narrow or nationalistic terms. It would be easy for the Jews to think in terms of a Jewish God exclusively, that God loves Jews more than other people. Actually this idea became so dominant in the days of Jesus that His disciples seemed unable to think in terms of a worldwide Kingdom. Even after the resurrection when He appeared to them, they asked Him if He was to free Isreal from Roman rule. *(Acts 1:6)*

73

Actually Jesus had to teach His followers that the Kingdom was not a political entity, but a worldwide spiritual kingdom. *(Acts 1:8)* We are a part of that kingdom, and, as such, we owe Jesus our allegiance as our King. It is a great responsibility, but from our Lord flows wonderful blessings!

### Segment Two – Who May Enter Where God Lives? Verses 3 - 6

Who dares to come before God with dirty hands and besmirched hearts? *(V.3)* It's essential that our hands and hearts be pure. *(V.4)* Only those with pure intent may come before the presence of God. *(V.6)* Of course, being pure refers to having inward holiness. It is what Jesus taught in His Sermon on the Mount when He said the pure of heart will see God. *(Matthew 5:8)*

You should know that Psalm 24 is similar to Psalm 15. In Psalm 15:1, it asks who may enter into the LORD's sanctuary? Then it tells of some qualities of life that are pleasing to God. *(Psalm 15: 2-5)* Much of Psalm 24 sounds like justification by works, that is, people having certain outward requirements or actions in order to please God. It sounds like if we don't do certain things like telling lies, or do positive acts like being honest, we will automatically be unqualified to stand before God. *(V.5)* From a Christian perspective, these and other moral actions are good and praiseworthy. However, we consider them as fruit of our Christian commitment to Jesus Christ. These are the natural outcome or expression of our faith. The Apostle Paul puts it this way: you don't need to go to any particular sanctuary you just have to put your trust in Jesus. *(Romans 10:6-10)*

Once we have confirmed our saving relationship with Jesus and know in our hearts that we have been forgiven and accepted before God, then with thankful appreciation we will try to do our very best at living a moral life, such as is described in Psalms 15 and 24. We need to have standards, and that's fine; but not predefined measurements for our faith.

### Segment Three – Let the King of Glory Come In. Verses 7 - 10

The climax of the psalm comes in this last section. In verses 3-6, God's people (the inhabitants of the earth) have come and are prepared for the King of Glory. In verse 7, David, the Psalmist, asks that the doors of the Temple be opened to let the King of Glory in. The question is asked in verse 8 who is the King? And the answer comes forth, loud and clear: It is the

LORD. This is the accurate answer and the gates opened to let the pilgrims in. *(V.10)*

Many of the psalms are arranged for antiphonal singing or chanting. For instance, a priest or choir of voices will ask a question, such as we see in verses 3, 8 and 10, and these will be responded to by a second group or an individual.

For Christians, it was Jesus who entered the Holy City in triumph! He came and was crucified. But God raised Him from the dead after He had taken the punishment for our sins, and then made it possible for us to have eternal life.

# PSALM 25
## An Acrostic Psalm of David

One commentator called Psalm 25 an alphabetical lament. This is an acrostic psalm, one of nine such psalms in the Psalter that use the acrostic technique in which verses begin with a successive letter of the Hebrew alphabet. They are Psalms 9-10, 25, 34, 37, 111, 112, 119 and 145.

There are 22 verses in Psalm 25, each verse beginning with a successive letter of the Hebrew alphabet. In this psalm a few letters are left out and the final verse added outside the pattern. This is a rigid pattern that obviously limits the freedom of the writer's expression.

Many scholars feel this psalm was composed in post-exilic times. The superscription says it is of David, but his authorship is doubtful. The writer doesn't seem to be in serious trouble, but he is presenting a form of prayer in a time of distress for anybody seeking God's help.

The 22 verses can be divided into three segments: One – A Prayer for Guidance and Protection, Verses 1-7; Two – God's Dealing with His People, Verses 8-12; and Three – The Psalmist's Prayer for Protection and Intervention, Verses 13-22.

### Segment One – A Prayer for Guidance and Protection. Verses 1 - 7

The Palmist's prayer asks for several things. Because he trusts in God, he asks for his soul to be lifted up *(V.1)* and that his enemies not succeed. *(V.2)* He also asks not to be disgraced. *(V.3)* Then he requests God for guidance. *(V.4)* He then throws himself on God's grace. *(V.5)* Then he remembers how he was when he was a young man and requests God to overlook his youthful sins *(V.6-7)* and deal with him as God has dealt with His people in the past, that is with mercy. *(V.7)*

## Segment Two – God's Dealing with His People. Verses 8 - 15

The Psalmist reminds God that because God is good *(V.8)*, He teaches sinners through His Word but, he admits, we learn when we are humble. *(V.9)*. Also, God leads us when we keep His covenant. *(V.10)* Verses 12 to 15 are quite similar to the Book of Proverbs in content. The writer says if folks fear or are properly in awe of the LORD, the LORD will share the secrets of His covenant with them and they will be blessed with prosperity and their children will continue to possess the land. See Deuteronomy 4:40 where Moses says those who keep the laws and the commandments will have a long life in the land.

This segment closes with God sharing the secrets of His promises with those who are respectful of Him. *(V.14-15)* The *New Living Bible* indicates those who respect God will be God's friends. *(V.14)* It refers to a special intimate relationship with the LORD when worshipers reverence Him.

## Segment Three – The Psalmist's Prayer for Protection and Intervention. Verses 16 - 22

Having said all of this, the Psalmist now gets to the heart of his prayer to the LORD. His prayers have not yet been answered. In fact, he says things have gone from bad to worse. *(V.16-17)* He is distraught and interprets his helpless feelings to the result of his sins. He asks God to feel his pain and forgive all his sins. *(V.18)* Forgiveness in this context means having his pain and sorrow removed. He cries out to God to save him from his enemies. *(V.19-20)* He then says he puts his hope in God. *(V.21)*

Verse 22 is outside the acrostic pattern and scheme and was probably added later. It was an attempt to tie the psalm from an individual lament to worship in the Temple, which is tied to the nation of Israel. The added verse requests that God ransom Israel from its current and future troubles.

The Apostle Paul in his early pre-Christian life was a Pharisaical Jew who knew the Scriptures like the back of his hand! After his conversion on the road to Damascus, he became a flaming evangelist for the cause of Christ! In his letter to the church at Ephesus, Paul may have been quoting Psalm 25:5 when he writes that we need to be strong in the Lord's mighty power. *(Ephesians 6:10)* Then he tells us to put on God's armor – the belt of truth, God's breastplate, shoes that speed you on to preach the Gospel of peace, the shield of faith and the helmet of salvation (Word of God). *(Ephesians 6:11-18)*

# PSALM 26
## A Protestation of Innocence

The superscription on this psalm says it was written by David. This usually means it was written in honor of King David. We shall assume that David actually was the author.

At the dedication of the Temple, King Solomon reiterated a standing law that said that a person accused of a wrong doing was required to take an oath of innocence in front of the altar of the Temple. God Himself would then judge that person. *(1Kings 8:31-32)* In Psalm 26, we assume that David has been falsely accused and goes to the altar in this short psalm of 12 verses. For ease of interpretation, we separate discussion of this psalm into five segments.

### Segment One – A Plea of Vindication. Verses 1 - 3

David is asking for vindication from the LORD because he feels he has lived a blameless life. He is claiming that his motives are as pure as he can make them. *(V.1)* He asks the LORD to put him on trial and cross examine him. *(V.2)* He has taken God's *("Checed")* as his ideal (God's "unfailing love"). He also claims to have lived according to God's "truth" (God's*"Emeth"*, "faithfulness," "reliability," "covenant") *(V.3)* David feels strongly that he is innocent and is willing to have God test his motives.

### Segment Two – No Consorting with Evildoers. Verses 4 - 5

David tells God that in order to maintain his righteous character, he stays away from deceitful persons, those who are wicked and pious frauds. *(V.4-5)*

### Segment Three – I Love to Be in Your Dwelling Place, LORD. Verses 6 - 8

David dares to use the laver, the basin of holy water in the sanctuary that the priests used to purify themselves before sacrificing, to wash his hands to prove he is not guilty as charged. *(V.6)* This verse probably is indicative of David being the author of the Psalm. Only he, and perhaps Solomon, would have the courage to take on this priestly function. It's interesting to note that when Jesus was brought before Pontius Pilate, the Roman Prefect, Pilate, after hearing the accusations of the Jewish leaders, he asked for a bowl of water and washed his hands before the assembly, implying he was innocent of the blood of Jesus. *(Matthew 27:22-25)* Our Psalmist concludes singing praises to the LORD *(V.7)* and affirming how much he loves to be in the LORD's sanctuary. *(V.8)*

### Segment Four – Walk the Straight and Narrow Path. Verses 9 - 11

Having claimed his innocence, our writer comes before the Holy God and begs Him not to lump him in with gross sinners. *(V.9-10)* By implication he doesn't deny his own shortcomings, but his shortcomings do not include taking bribes. *(V.11)* So please, LORD, have "mercy" *("Chanan")* and save me. *(V.11)* The Hebrew word for "save " used here is *("Padah")*; it means "to set free," "deliver." It also can mean "redeemed," "being released from punishment."

### Segment Five – I Will Publicly Praise the LORD. Verse 12

David concludes this psalm by promising he will praise the LORD publicly. *(V.12)* Those of us who are followers of Jesus are called upon to know what we believe and to share our faith with others at opportune moments. There are several ways to witness. One obvious way is to know the right words to say so we can demonstrate to unbelievers that the way of following Christ is the most satisfying and successful way to live. We who profess inwardly to be believers in the Lord Jesus Christ have to ask ourselves if we are following outwardly in a manner consistent with our talk. James, the brother of Jesus, informed early Jewish Christians that their actions needed to speak for their faith and faithfulness. *(James 2:14-17)* Will it be clear to an unbeliever that our way of Christian living is attractive to him/her? This is our goal.

# PSALM 27
## Light and Lament

Psalm 27, attributed to David, is one of the better known and comforting psalms in all of the Psalter. Some critical scholars claim that Psalm 27 is really two separate psalms awkwardly put together. However, it is the thinking of this interpreter that what we have here is an unfolding of two closely related moods, put together like two movements of a well-honed symphony. Finite human beings have mood swings. This is what we find in this psalm. David is anxious and trustful, fearful and confident.

We will divide Psalm 27 into four segments: One, The LORD Is My Light, Verses 1-3; Two, The Security of Worship, Verses 4-6; Three, David's Lament, Verses 7-12; and Four, God Will Act, Verses 13-14.

### Segment One – The LORD is My Light. Verses 1 - 3

God is frequently associated with aspects of light in the Bible, but in Psalm 27 David calls Him specifically light and salvation. *(V.1)* Salvation here implies a deliverance from evil people who come to destroy David. *(V.2)* He says his heart knows no fear, though a mighty army surround him because of the security he has in his relationship with God. *(V.3)* As Light, God dispels the darkness of trouble and brings a quiet confidence that everything will be all right. These verses have brought inspiration and hope to countless millions.When we go to the New Testament, we find that light is our name for Jesus Christ. In fact, Jesus said He is the light of the world. *(John 8:12)*

## Segment Two – The Security of Worship. Verses 4 - 6

In many of the psalms written by David, he expresses his life-long joy and desire of worshiping in God's house (the Tabernacle). It is there, in concert with fellow believers, he is able to bask in the LORD's presence and be filled with supernatural power from the LORD. *(V.4)* (This sounds a lot like his words in Psalm 23.) The metaphor of being hidden and protected on a high rock *(V.5)* gives the spiritual security of a refuge from many of life's difficulties. One can sense the joy he expresses in wanting to sing his praises to the LORD. *(V.6)*

## Segment Three – David's Lament. Verses 7 - 12

David begins this lament pleading with the LORD to listen to him. *(V.7)* To talk to him. *(V.8)* Don't abandon him. *(V.9)* David responds to the hypothetical question of his parents abandoning him in verse 10 by saying God would take upon Himself the duties of a parent, that is, God would guide and protect and would hear him out. The one small ray of hope in this third segment is that God had protected and accepted him in his trials in the past. *(V.9)* David pleads with God to teach him how to live. *(V.11)* The question is will God continue to be there for him in the future? *(V.12)*

## Segment Four – God Will Act! Verses 13 - 14

The psalm ends up on a note of confidence once again. *(V.13)* What David is praying for does not always come at once. He says we must be patient with the LORD. *(V.14)* It is always about God's timing. When we pray for something and the answer is delayed, does this mean we lose our confidence in God? No. We need to be patient.

There are countless examples of inspirational Scriptures that tie into the 27th Psalm's wonderful ending of trusting God but being patient with God. Here are just a few: *(Psalm 23:4); (Psalm 40:1-3); (Isaiah 40:28-31); (John 1:14).*

Psalm 27 is a psalm of trust. Trust is nurtured and strengthened by the exercise of discipline. Here are four disciplines we recommend:

1. Trust grows by studying the Bible in a small group of other mature believers.
2. Trust is developed through regular worship and by hearing the proclamation of the Good News (the Gospel of Jesus Christ!).
3. Trust is nurtured by personal prayer and meditation.
4. And trust is maintained by having a prayer partner, a Confident who will hold us accountable.

# PSALM 28

## A Prayer for Mercy

When the remnant of the Hebrew people returned from 70 years of slavery in Babylon, they found their country in total disarray. It took them a year before they were able to rebuild and to track down all of the Hebrew Scriptures that had been destroyed – including the Psalms. Scholars think that what we have now in our Old Testament was reassembled in about the third century BC.

We also don't know why they placed certain psalms in the order they did, but we think it may have to do with certain themes. One hypothesis is that Psalm 28 was placed after Psalm 27 because Psalm 28 ends with the words that the LORD should lead Israel like a shepherd. *(V.9)* Psalm 27 begins with words that the LORD is the author of light and salvation. *(Psalm 27:1)* Both Psalm 27 and 28 suggest that Israel does not have to be afraid if the people put their trust in the LORD.

This psalm like Psalm 27 if about prayer. When we pray, answers don't always come to us at once. God's timing isn't necessarily ours. Sometimes God's answers are delayed. What then? We <u>need</u> <u>to</u> <u>wait</u>! What shall we do while we're waiting? The answer is to keep praying – be persistent. Maybe the editors placed Psalm 28 after the 27th Psalm because praying and waiting for God to answer prayers is the theme that connects the two.

Waiting for the Lord is <u>being</u> <u>persistent</u>. It reminds us of the story Jesus told. It was the "Persistent Widow." There was a certain judge who cared nothing about God or other people. Then there was a widow who had a case that needed to be heard, but the judge wasn't interested. The widow was persistent and kept coming to him again and again, trying to present her case. Eventually, she got on his nerves, and he satisfied her request because he just wanted to be rid of her. *(Luke 18:2-5)* The lesson Jesus said is that if even an evil judge will help us if we are persistent, how much more will our Father answner our prayers if we keep praying. *(Luke 18:6-8)*

## Segment One – A Prayer for Help. Verses 1 - 2

The psalm opens with a faith statement that God is a rock for safety, a metaphor that occurs more than 30 times in the Old Testament, and six times in the Psalter. God is like an impregnable fortress providing support and protection. It is not really clear, but the Psalmist seems to be mortally in danger from certain godless and deceitful persons. He prays for divine help. He says if he can't get help from God, he will die. *(V.1)* Throughout the Psalter, it is expressed that to live in the presence of God is life; but to turn one's back on the divine is the equivalent of death. *(V.2)* Then, as now, it is possible to live on earth and yet for all intent and purposes be dead.

## Segment Two – Punish the Wicked. Verses 3 - 5

Our Psalmist begs God not to let the wicked drag him away. *(V.3)* He tells us that these evil doers are deceitful persons even though they speak non-threatening words to their neighbors. So he asks God to punish them – and adds it ought to be in direct proportion of the evil they do. *(V.4)* They are like old buildings that should be torn down and not be rebuilt. *(V.5)* Back then the accepted code of fairness was based on the Mosaic law of an eye-for-an-eye and a tooth-for-a–tooth. (See Exodus 21:24.)

We Christians can understand why our Psalmist feels as he does. But from our perspective, we see God revealing His will more fully in the New Testament through the Messiah Jesus in His Sermon on the Mount. Much of asking God to damn (punish) enemies in the psalm goes counter to Jesus' teachings. Jesus asked His followers to pray for thos who pesecute us (see Matthew 5:1-47).

## Segment Three – Assured that God Will Act. Verses 6 - 7

Our author becomes certain that God has heard his cry for "mercy" *("Chanan"). (V.6)* He uses another metaphor "the shield"*("M Ginnah")*, which in this case represents God. He will ward off any arrows of danger, and with exhuberence the Psalmist shouts that he will trust the LORD with all his heart. *(V.7)* David (who is probably the author) is always the consummate musican and he ends the psalm by breaking out in a song of thanksgiving. *(V.7)*

## Segment Four – The Liturgical Appendix. Verses 8 - 9

Many or most of the psalms were sung or recited by the priests and congregations in the Temple worship. Obviously, these final two verses were appended by a later author asking the LORD to give victory to their king. *(V.8)* The Hebrew word for "victory" is *("S shuw ah")*. It also can mean "prosperity" or "good health." The Psalmist then cries out that God needs to save his people because they are a special possession of His. *(V.9)* God touches each person with His *("Yasha ")*, His "saving power," and gives them the necessary "compassion and love" *("Y shuw ah")* to take God's forgiving love to others. It is God who gives His people (His sheep) the spiritual power to love and care for others *(V.9)*, which is similar to what David wrote in Psalm 23.

We Christians look to Jesus as the Good Shepherd. Jesus specifically tells us He is our good Shepherd. *(John 10:11-14)* Jesus is also our light and there is no darkness in Him. *(1 John 1:5-7)* If we confess our own darkness, our own sins, Jesus will forgive us and cleanse us. *(1 John 1:5-10)*

# PSALM 29
## The Majesty of the LORD of Creation

Psalm 29 is one of the oldest songs in the Psalter. It is an Israelite adaptation of an ancient Canaanite hymn to Baal, the god of weather and fertility. In its present form, it is a hymn to the majestic God of Creation (from the period of Moses and Joshua).

The superscription lists it as a psalm of David, but it is doubtful he is the author. Because of the predominance of storms in the poem, it was probably written during the rainy season. It was probably written in the autumn of the year when strong thunderstorms sweep over the countryside – from north to south.

### Segment One – Summons to Heavenly Beings. Verses 1 - 2

**The Psalmist is calling to the angels of the LORD to recognize and praise God for His glory and strength because** He is the sovereign ruler of both heaven and earth. *(V.1)* In order to recognize His majesty, these heavenly messengers are called to be clothed in proper attire of holiness *(V. 2)* and to not only extol the LORD's magnificence, but to honor His great creative power. In these first two verses, the Psalmist pictures the angels worshiping God in a worship house similar to the earthly Tabernacle. We know this because in the Book of Hebrews it says the Temple was merely a copy of the heavenly Temple. In other words, the sanctuary (Tabernacle) on earth was only "a shadow" (a copy) of the one in heaven. *(Hebrews 9:24)*

## Segment Two – The Voice of Many Thunders. Verses 3 - 9

Our Psalmist visualizes the mighty God of the universe up in heaven with wonderful imaginative poetry. He pictures God's voice as it is identified with the ear-splitting thunder of a storm! *(V.3)* The darkened clouds move eastward over the Mediterranean Sea and then drop their moisture over the mountains of Lebanon and Sirion (Mt Hermon). So furious and powerful is the LORD's voice *(V.5)* in the wild thunderstorm that even the mighty cedars of Lebanon come crashing down! Even the mountains are shaken! *(V.6)* Once again the voice of God bellows forth in both reverberating thunder and crackling lightening and we're told that it even shakes the Kadesh desert. *(V.8)* While this tumultuous storm is raging, the faithful congregation of the Lord God of Israel is in the Temple joining the angels in heaven, crying, Glory! *(V.9)*

Having a violent storm come to their arid land would be a wonderful gift. It would mean the end of draught and a gift of new life. Israel's LORD is the all-powerful King who sends rain when it is needed. God is indeed glorious!

## Segment Three – The LORD Reigns as King Forever. Verses 10 - 11

The author goes back to the time of the flood to give glory to God as the LORD of all Creation! *(V.10)* He envisions the Genesis story when Adam and Eve rebelled against God. As consequence, sin became rampant in the land. God cannot abide sin so He brought a flood to cleanse the earth. There was one righteous man named Noah and God told him how to survive the Flood. *(Genesis 6:13-22)* The Psalmist closes this poem by saying the LORD strengthens the people and blesses them with peace. *(V.11)*

God's plans have been finalized in Jesus Christ! We Christians are the recipients of God's grace and love. The words of Psalm 29 can be applied to us. We are God's children, spiritual Jews and, as the Psalmist says, we can receive strength and peace from Him. However, it is inevitable that storms will come to us, for that is what it means to live on planet earth. So we need to be wise and build our lives on the rock-like foundations of Jesus' teachings. *(Matthew 7:24-25)*

# PSALM 30
## True Thanksgiving!

In Psalm 30, David is giving thanks for his recovery from an illness that could have been fatal. The superscription says that this psalm was used for the dedication of the Temple. This indicates that it was used at one of the rededications of the Temple – probably the Temple by Judas Maccabaeus in 164 B.C. This psalm probably was modified following the exile as an expression of the nation's experience.

### Segment One – The Reason for David's Thanksgiving. Verses 1 - 5

Not only is this a psalm of thanksgiving, but it is a partial autobiography of David. He is telling us that he was sick enough to die and he prayed to God for deliverance and the LORD kept him from death itself. (V.1-3) He gives God all of the credit for his healing. And he wants to praise Him! Furthermore, because of his deliverance, God saved him from having his enemies gloat over him. Also, because of his joy in his recovery, David calls upon all of his friends who are worshiping with him in the Tent of Meeting (the Tabernacle) to join him in singing praises to the LORD's name. (V.4) In verse 5, he mentions God's anger. Perhaps God was angry at David for some sin of his? But David says that the LORD's anger last for only a moment. But his favor (for David?) last a lifetime.

Because we stumble and fall into sin at times, we are recipients of God's anger. We are sinners, but thank God we Christians are sinners saved by grace! God's forgiveness and love far outweighs the negative. It is true that there are good and bad things in life and we don't always see a specific judgment or blessing of God in each one. What David is saying here is that God's favor always outweighs the disfavor for God's people. This helps us reevaluate the meaning of suffering because the ultimate end of human misery is not weeping but joy! Verse 5 anticipates verse 11, which says God changed his mourning in joy.

It needs to be said again that God is displeased with sin and judges it with anger, even in us Christians. What remains is His favor – and that lasts our lifetime, and <u>forever!</u> We Christians need to call upon God for healing when we get sick, like David did. We live in a scientific age that has the effect of removing many folks from a sense of God's presence and intervention during times of sickness. Many talk about the miracle of modern medicine rather than God's miraculous intervention. When we Christians go to a doctor for help and He gives us medicine and we get healed, it is really God who works through the physician's skill and knowledge and we need to be thankful!

### Segment Two – David Reviews His Former Condition. Verses 6 - 12

Here David is revealing a former sin of pride. *(V.6)* He confesses that he felt secure and really felt he had life by the tail. His sin was his feelings of self –sufficiency. He really didn't need God. Apparently he linked this sin as the reason for his illness. As a result, he felt that God turned His back on him, and he became panic-stricken. *(V.7)* In this recounting, David is so honest. He began to barter with God, appealing to His self-interest. He reminds God that dust can not praise Him. *(V.9)* What good will You derive if I am destroyed? I wouldn't be able to serve You or praise You if I am in the shadow-land of Sheol *("the pit").*

Psalm 30 has a happy ending. God hears David's petition. David repented and the LORD forgave him and turned his mourning into joy. *(V.11)* In beautiful poetic language, the psalm ends with God taking away the clothes of his deathbed. He then proclaims he will sing praises to the LORD and not be silent. *(V.12)*

David was a free spirit and a man described as being after God's own Heart. *(1 Samuel 13:14)* We Christians can learn much from studying these magnificent psalms he wrote. It is tremendously important to stay close to the Lord and not get so enamored with our own importance. The sins of self-righteousness and self-centeredness are such an easy trap to fall into, like David's feelings of self-sufficiency. James, the brother of Jesus, tells us if we draw close to God, God will draw close to us. *(James 4:8)* Having God close to us will give us sustaining power in spite of what we may have to face. The main thing we can learn from Psalm 30 is that with God's presence, joy is possible, even when things seem to go wrong. If we keep God near at all times we, will be able to praise Him for His gift of life.

Despite trouble or calamity, overwhelming victory is ours through Christ who loved us enough to die for us. For, as the Apostle Paul wrote in the Book of Romans, he was convinced nothing could separate us from the love of God. *(Romans 8:31-39)*

# PSALM 31

## David's Ups and Downs!

This psalm is a composite of two laments: the first seeks assurance of protection from impending difficulties (Verses 1-8); the second lament pleads to be delivered from an illness and enemies (Verses 9-24). This psalm is difficult to outline; no two interpreters agree. Some divide the psalm into three parts, some two.

We have chosen to follow the stanza divisions of the *New Living Translation*, describing them in the following manner: (1) Prayer for Rescue from Enemies, Verses 1-5; (2) Radiant with Joy Because of God's Mercy, Verses 6-8; (3) David's Distresses, Verses 9-13; (4) David's Future in God's Hands, Verses 14-18; (5) In God's Shelter, Verses 19-20; (6) God Heard David's Cry, Verses 20-22; and (7) God Is Just in His Judgments, Verses 23-24.

### Segment One – Prayer for Rescue from Enemies. Verses 1 - 5

The theme of the first five verses is that God is David's Rock and Fortress (metaphors used in many of his writings). *(V.3)* Throughout his life David had many enemies, beginning when he had to flee from King Saul and find shelter and safety in and among the rocks of the Judean wilderness. There was no wishy-washy about it, David trusted in the LORD. God had rescued him in the past and David calls upon Him again. *(V.1)* He needs God to rescue him quickly. *(V.2)* After beseeching God to get him out of this trap his enemies had set for him, *(V.4)* he gives himself totally over to God's care. *(V.5)* Amazingly, these are the words that Jesus used on the cross right before He died. Millions of Christians have heard these words preached at Easter time, but few know that they were quoted from Psalm 31.

## Segment Two – Radiant with Joy Because of Mercy. Verses 6 - 8

This segment begins with David proclaiming that he hates those who worship idols. (V.1) The prophetic part of David probably could instinctively sense the dissatisfaction that God feels when His creatures do not acknowledge Him as their creator. David, however, is full of joy because God has kept His promises. He listened to David's troubles. (V.7) He didn't hand him over to his enemies (V.4), and He gave him open ground in which to maneuver. (V.8) This last point meant that David didn't get caught in a dead end where he couldn't move. God's "mercy" is that wonderful word ("Checed"), one of the most important words in the Old Testament. It's a covenant word, and it is closely related to the forgiveness of sins and to God's unfailing love.

## Segment Three – Lament of David's Distresses. Verses 9 - 13

Segment three is the emotional heart of the psalm. David tells God all about his distresses and dangers. His enemies are threatening to surround him and take his life. (This sounds like the years he was running from King Saul.) Being constantly hunted was bound to take its toll on him physically as well as emotionally. He complains that his strength fails him, both body and soul are withering away. (V.9-10) Because of his precarious situation and his own vacillation, David is scorned by his enemies and neighbors. (V.11) Even his friends hate to be seen with him (V.12) and his enemies continue to plot against Him. (V.13) Some of his words may be poetically exaggerated, but there is no question that he was hurting!

## Segment Four – David's Future Is in God's Hands. Verses 14 - 18

This segment is a continuation of David's emotional roller-coaster experiences. In segment three, he was down in the valley and now in segment four he is in the upper slope again, saying three important affirmations: that God is his God; he trusts Him; and trusts his future to Him. (V.14-15) He calls himself God's servant. (V.16) He throws some theology in by saying God is so kind. Feeling a little better, he wants God to silence his enemies because of their atheistic beliefs. (V.17) If God will silence them their lying lips will be quieted. (V.18)

### Segment Five – In God's Shelter. Verses 19 - 20

Verse 19 is a beautiful expression of God's abundant goodness. When those of us who love Him are willing to place our faith and trust in His goodness, we know we will be safe in His everlasting arms for all eternity. Consequently, we'll not be hesitant to take our stand publicly and make our convictions known. As David says, great blessings will be in store not just for David but for all of us who put our trust in the LORD. *(V.19)* God shelters us in His presence. *(V.20)* This reminds us of David's words in Psalm 23.

### Segment Six – God Heard David's Cry. Verses 21 - 22

God showed David His unfailing love. *(V.21)* And he kept him safe when his was being attacked in his city. He heard his cry for mercy when he was fearful. *(V.22)* The good news is that God never deserted David.

### Segment Seven – God Is Just in His Judgments. Verses 23 - 24

David calls on all of God's people who love the LORD. He ends this up-and-down psalm by philosophically saying the LORD protects those loyal to Him and punishes the arrogant. *(V.23)* David loved the LORD and depended on Him for guidance and protection. He also encourages the people of Israel to look forward to the coming of the Messiah. *(V.24)*

We Christians also love the Lord! We are wonderfully blessed because the Messiah has already come in Jesus Christ! What this means to us who are sinners is that God sent Jesus to earth and He took the punishment for our sins; this is an act of sheer grace that ended God's wrath against us! Because of Christ's sacrifice on the cross, God declares all of us who choose Jesus as our personal Lord and Savior to be fully acceptable in His sight.

With the Good News of salvation - thanks to Jesus' death and resurrection – we are set free from the anxieties of death and dying. When we initially surrendered our life to Jesus Christ, we became one with the Father (Romans 5:11). Using the symbol of baptism, we became identified with Jesus. Through His death, the power of our sinful nature was shattered. Our old sin-loving nature was buried with Jesus by baptism. With Jesus' death, God's magnificent power brought Him back to life again and being identified with Him, we share in His new resurrected life! Putting this another way, our evil desires were nailed to Jesus' cross, part of us that loves sin was fatally weakened (or crushed!). Scripture says we are no longer under sin's control (or we are no longer slaves to sin). We still have to struggle daily against temptation, but we are free spiritually because God now sees us as having Jesus living in us (without sin).

What we have written (above) is what is going on inside a Christian. Outwardly we are no different from David. We have to face the same struggles he faced, and that is why we can learn from him. The exception is that we know we are going to heaven when we die!

# PSALM 32
## David's Confession and Pardon

Psalm 32 is one of seven Penitential Psalms found in the Palter (6, 32, 38, 51, 102, 130 and 143). This appears to be a companion psalm to Psalm 51, which was David's great psalm of repentance.

David had committed adultery with Bathsheba. If that was not enough, he manipulated the plan of battle that was going on so that her husband, Uriah, one of David's soldiers, would be killed. David tried to ignore or hide this sin for some time. Nathan, one of David's prophets, came to him and exposed his transgressions. David confessed his sin and God in His graciousness forgave David and allowed David to remain King of Israel. David then apparently sat down and wrote Psalm 51.

Psalm 32 was written some time later. In Psalm 51, David says that he will teach God's ways to sinners in hope that they will return to the LORD. (Psalm 5:13) Some experts tell us that Psalm 32 may have been written as the teaching that David said he would do in verse 13 of Psalm 51.

It is also interesting to note that the Apostle Paul quotes the first two verses of Psalm 32 in his letter to the church at Rome (Romans 4:7-8). Paul adds David's words to his own conviction that salvation is by God's grace in Jesus Christ through faith alone. Paul links David's words to the words recorded about Abram in Genesis 15, where it says that because Abram believed in God, God deemed him righteous on account of his faith. (V.6)

Psalm 32 can be divided into 4 segments: (1) Happiness of Forgiven Sin, Verses 1-2; (2) Confession and Pardon, Verses 3-6; (3) Advise to Other Sinners, Verses 7-9; and (4) Abiding Joy! Verses 10-11. I am using The Living Bible translation for this Psalm because I think it more accurately conveys David's intent in this psalm than how it appears in the New Living Translation.

## Segment One – Happiness of Forgiven Sin. Verses 1 - 2

David is enthusiastically happy about having the guilt from his sins covered over and taken away. *(V.1)*He obviously did not live up to God's laws and felt condemned, hence his guilt. Then he confessed those sins and God forgave him. *(V.2)* The words "covered over" were taken from the Day of Atonement in the Old Testament where the High Priest would take the blood of a slain animal and go into the Holy of Holies and sprinkle the blood on the mercy seat of the Ark of the Covenant. The blood was sprinkled on the mercy seat because, symbolically, it comes in between the presence of God and the sin (the broken law), thereby covering the sin or shielding the sinner from God's just judgment.

When sin is confessed and the sinner repents, God doesn't count the sin against the sinner. Sinners become justified, that is, they become just-as-if they had never sinned! God lifts away an insufferable burden.

## Segment Two – Confession and Pardon. Verses 3 - 6

David thought back to a time when he hadn't confessed and how horrible he felt! It even affected him physically. *(V.3)* Night and day he felt God's heavy hand on him. *(V.4)* When he turned his life around and came to God in repentance, he felt brand new with all his guilt removed – his slate was wiped clean! *(V.5)* Now he speaks a message of great urgency to all believers that the time for confession is this very moment before it is too late. *(V.6)*

One of Jesus's best-known parables is the Prodigal Son. The son had asked for his inheritance and headed to a distant country. He squandered his money in sinful living and finally made a decision to go back home and confess his sin. While far off, he was met by his father who was filled with loving pity and embraced him. The son said to his Father that because of his sin to his Father, he is no longer worthy to be call a son. *(Luke 15:11-32)* His father ordered the slaves to bring the finest robes and put them on his son, and a jeweled ring for his finger, shoes for his feet and that the slaves should kill the calf that was in the fattening pen. We must celebrate with a feast because my son was dead and has returned to life. He was lost and is found. So let the party begin! This is what it feels like when one's sins are forgiven! David would have been totally sympathetic to the message of this parable.

## Segment Three – Advice to Other Sinners. Verses 7 - 9

David is jubilant in verse 7 telling the Lord how great He is, and how He keeps David from trouble. From a poetic point of view, Psalm 32 could have ended after this. But no, everyone is urged to learn the lessons of David's mistakes. He tells others that God will guide them along the way. (V.8) Don't be stubborn like a mule! (V.9)

## Segment Four – Abiding Joy! Verses 10 - 11

These words are David's benediction. Yes, the wicked have many sorrows, but we need to listen to God and do our best to follow His instructions. V.10) If we will obey Him, we'll be able to rejoice and obey him. (V.11)

Psalm 32 recalls Psalm 1. Comparing the two helps us understand the concept of righteousness. To be righteous, one does not have to obey all the rules (we can't!). David tells us in this psalm that even the righteous are pervaded with sin. In verses 3-4, he admits what a sinner he was and how miserable it made him. To be truly righteous, one has to know God's forgiveness. Psalm 32 was the favorite scripture of St. Augustine, one of the great Christians of all time. He had its words inscribed above his bed so that its message would be the first thing he saw when awakening.

# PSALM 33
## Praise God for His Word and Works

This is a psalm of praise. It is one of the few that has no superscription, so we don't know who authored it. It has a logical relationship with Psalm 32 because of its description of how God's forgiveness restores a sinner. It would seem right, then, that such good news be followed by thankfulness, joyous singing and praising God, which Psalm 33 does.

Psalm 33 focuses on God's word and work. It has 22 verses, but it is not an acrostic psalm. It can be outlined as followed: (1) Sing Joyfully! Verses 1-3; (2) Praise the God's Word and Work, Verses 4-15; (3) God Watches Over Those Who Fear Him, Verses 16-20; and (4) God's Constant Love Surrounds Us, Verses 21-22. Again I am using *The Living Bible* translation instead of the *New Living Translation* because I think it more clearly reflects the intent of the psalm.

### Segment One – Sing Joyfully. Verses 1 - 3

The Psalmist says it is right to praise the Lord. *(V.1)* In the opening call to worship, he mentions three helpful aspects of praising God: (a) playing joyous melodies on musical instruments *(V.2)*; (b) composing new songs of praise *(V.3)*; (c) and singing lustily! *(V.3)* Musical instruments are mentioned here for the first time in the Psalter.

### Segment Two – Praise God's Word and Work. Verses 4 - 15

To fully understand the Hebrew mind as expressed in Scripture, it is necessary to know what is meant by two idioms – God's <u>word</u> and His <u>work.</u> They always go together.

God speaks (His word) and He creates (His work). That the words of God are right, means that God's character is always righteous. *(V.4)* All of God's initiatives in creating and in dealing directly with human history can be characterized by words like "righteousness," "justice," "faithfulness," and "tender love."*(V.5)* God's word spoke and the heavens and earth were created. *(V.6,7,9)* Let everyone, therefore, fear the Lord and be in awe of Him. *(V.8)* He accomplishes this with his word. *(V.9)* Much of this understading of God goes back to God's telling Moses who He is. That He is merciful, slow to anger and rich in love and truth. *(Exodus 34:6)*

God is also sovereign and omnipotent. His will over people and nations is supreme. *(V.10)* His own plan (His will) never changes. *(V.11)* Bless Israel, therefore, because the Lord chose its people as His own. *(V.12)* And He is omniscient, which means He watches over all we do. And since He made the people's heart, He understands their intentions. *(V.14-15)*

## Segment Three – God Watches Over Those Who Fear Him. Verses 16 - 20

The author is harking back to verses 4, 5 and 6, and is discussing God's character and His all-powerful abilities. First, he says, man's armies can't save anyone *(V.16-17)*; only God can save! Second, he says only those who rely on God's love and are in awe of Him will be delivered from all kinds of disasters (like famine). *(V.18-19)* The LORD alone will protect us. *(V.20)*

## Segment Four – God's Constant Love Surrounds Us. Verses 21 - 22

If we truly believe that God's constant love is holding us up and lifting us when we fall, why shouldn't we put our trust in the Lord. *(V.21)*We can't trust in man-made schemes, for they will falter. *(V.22)* As Christians, our only hope is in God, in Jesus Christ alone!

# PSALM 34
## Instructions for the Good Life

This is one of the teaching psalms, composed by the Wisdom School of Composers (see psalms 1, 37, 49, 78, 105, 106, 111, 112, and 127).

It is unsettling to ascertain how the Psalter was re-programmed after the exile in Babylon. Why they placed certain psalms in their present position remain a mystery. Another unsettling question is why, whoever masterminded the final arrangement, he (they) assigned the fourteen superscriptions relating to the life of David at the beginning of certain psalms. Many are not relevant to the understanding of the contents. The title to Psalm 34 says it was written at the time when David pretended he was insane before Abimelech. This incident, which is related in 1 Samuel 21:10-25, seems to have little connection to the content of the psalm. And the superscription is wrong! It was not Abimelech, before whom David acted insane, but King Achish of Gath.

Psalm 34 is an acrostic poem, each of the verses (including the last) begins with a successive letter of the Hebrew alphabet. For some unexplained reason the *"Waw"* letter was left out. Another interesting fact is that a portion of Psalm 34 is quoted by the Apostle Peter when he makes the point in his first letter how we Christians should act as one family. Verses 10-16 of Psalm 34 were inserted by Peter in his letter as an example of why God would bless them (see 1 Peter 3:10-12).

### Segment One – Praising the LORD at All Times. Verses 1 - 3

The writer of this psalm wants to continually praise the LORD. *(V.1)* He boasts of the LORD's greatness and he invites all who are feeling low and discouraged to be lifted up! *(V.2)* He wants everybody in the congregation to ascribe to the wonderful God they serve. *(V.3)*

## Segment Two – The LORD Answers Prayer. Verses 4 - 10

The leader of the congregation tells of his personal experiences as the basis for others to share his praise for God. He relates how he took his personal troubles to the LORD in prayer and God's Spirit came to him freeing him from fears. *(V.4,6)* When the Spirit comes we will be radiant with joy if we look for Him. *(V.5)* Putting God first (reverencing Him) opens the way for having the angel of the LORD nearby to be on guard. *(V.7)* After giving his testimony, our Psalmist tells his friends in the congregation that they can experience the very same benefits. Step out in faith, he tells them, experience that God is good. *(V.8)* But also show reverence to the LORD. *(V.9)* Then he invites his listeners to know that those who trust the LORD will never lack. *(V.10)*

## Segment Three – Instructions for the Good Life. Verses 11 - 14

In this section, our Psalmist wears another hat-- that of a wisdom teacher. He talks to his people as if they were his children. *(V.11)* He says he will teach them to show reverence and trust in God. Do you want to live long, he asks? *(V.12)* Then don't lie. *(V.13)* This section is very similar to many of the Proverbs, which teach godly conduct. He tells his sons and daughters not to gossip, tell the truth, be peaceful and stay way from evil and do good. *(V.14)* In other words, his message is for them to work hard at not sinning.

## Segment Four – God Judges His People. Verses 15 - 20

Our teacher continues by saying when folks strive to live godly lives, God watches and responds when they need Him. *(V.15)* However, it is like the wording of Psalm One that says the LORD watches over their path, but the path of the wicked ends in destruction. *(V.16)* When good people call on God, their troubles will be minimized. God hears and will rescue them. *(V.17)* LORD God takes care of the brokenhearted and those crushed in their spirit. *(V.18)* Although the righteous will face many troubles, they will be rescued from all of them. *(V.19)* Not a single one of their bones will be broken. *(V.20)*

## Segment Five – The Consequences of Righteousness. Verses 21 - 22

The Psalmist is teaching the young to keep right with the Covenant, which means keeping God's commands and following Mosaic laws. When this is followed, then God's "Covenant love" –His ("*Checed*") –will surround them and protect them from harm.

The author ends Psalm 34 with a contrasted theological statement: a bad end will take over the wicked (those who are in rebellion against God) *(V.21)*; but the LORD will redeem His own. *(V.22)*

The teaching of Psalm 34 is not too far from the teachings of Jesus, when he urged everyone to have reverence for the Father. Jesus also taught His followers not to worry about outward material things like clothes and food. *(Matthew 6:32-33)*

The Psalmist of Psalm 34 was used mightily of God. His words are so helpful. His contribution to the world is wonderful. He just did not know Jesus. We Christians have a big advantage of not only appreciating the message of the psalms, but of being able to worship the mighty God of the universe through His Son Jesus the Messiah!

The one big advantage we Christians have over those who lived in ancient times is the result of God's miracle of the resurrection. He raised Jesus from death and brought Him up to heaven to be King of Kings and Lord of lords. In doing so, God set Jesus' Spirit free from the limitations of time and space.

This means that Jesus' Spirit can come and indwell us Christians when we open our hearts and minds to Him in faith. With the Spirit of Jesus in us – in our inmost beings – we are empowered within to be Christ-like. God's Holy Spirit works to help us be what God wants us to be. The Apostle Paul knew about this miracle from God. He writes that God would not only work in the lives of those who serve Him but would provide a desire in them to obey Him. *(Philippians 2:12-13)*

Having Jesus in our hearts does exactly what Paul is saying – it is God's saving work within us, giving us the desire to want to be Christ-like and the divine power to actually resist evil and incorporate God's unfailing love in all we do.

# PSALM 35

## Blow Away My Enemies, LORD

Psalm 35 can be classified as an Imprecatory Psalm. This means that the author asks God to damn his enemies, to dishonor them, and blow them away like chaff in the wind! In the Psalter there are four imprecatory psalms listed as David being the author (Psalms 7, 35, 69, and 109). These four run the gamut from mild to devastating. We will want to analyze this psalm and then evaluate it from our Christian perspective.

Psalm 35 lends itself to be divided into three separate parts. Segment One (Verses 1-10) is a prayer to God asking Him to declare war on those who are attacking him. Segment Two (Verses 11-18) is where the people David has befriended in their illnesses have now turned against him, spreading scandalous lies that tend to defame his character. In Segment Three (Verses 19-28), David's adversaries claim to have witnessed him committing heinous sins, which he says are false. In the conclusion of each of these three parts, David is sure that God would comply with his requests.

### Segment One – Protect Me from My Ruthless Enemies. Verses 1 - 10

No gentle David is writing here. Right from the start David demands that the LORD declare war on his enemies. *(V.1)* Take up Your shield, lift up Your javelin, proclaim You will save me! *(V.2-3)* He is asking the LORD not only to fight his enemies but to humiliate and disgrace them. *(V.4)* Blow them away! *(V.5)* He even asks the angel of the LORD to pursue them once they are defeated. *(V.6)* Why? Because he did no wrong and they did everything to lay a trap for him. *(V.7)* The snare they set for me let them fall into it. *(V.8)* Once the LORD accomplishes all that for him, he promises to praise God from the bottom of his heart. *(V.9-10)*

## Segment Two – My Enemies Want to Slander Me. Verses 11 - 18

In this second part of Psalm 35, it sounds in some respects that David is in a court of law arguing his case before God, the Judge. He says malicious witnesses accuse him of things he doesn't even know about. *(V.11)* These are the same so-called friends he took care of when they were ill. *(V.13)* But he should have known who they were because when he prayed for them his prayers were returned unanswered. *(V.14)* They slander him continually now that he himself is in trouble. *(V.15-16)* Then in verse 17 he turns in prayer and chastizes the LORD for apparently doing nothing. He then pleads for deliverance and promises that, if protected, he will thank the LORD before the whole congregration. *(V.18)* Sounds a little like David is bargaining with the LORD.

## Segment Three – Vindicate Me, LORD. Verses 19 - 28

Again David itemizes to the LORD how his enemies hate him and gloat over his fallen state. *(V.19)* They plot against all innocent people. *(V.20)* He reminds God that He is God and knows all of this. *(V.22)* David approaches the LORD as if he were his defense attorney asking Him to take up his case. *(V.23)* You are all knowing, so vindicate me. He is seeking "justice" *("Tsedeq"). (V.24)* So exonerate me. Cover my enemies with shame. *(V.26)* He also asks the LORD to honor those who have stood up for David. *(V.27)* In verse 28, David once more implies that if God will do his bidding, in gratitude, he will praise the LORD before the congregation. *(V.28)*

How ought we Christians interpret Psalm 35? The question is the rightness of praying to God and asking Him to damn our enemies. One interpreter (Dr. Rev. James M. Boice) makes a point of justifying David's prayer by saying he did not write these words as a private citizen but rather as king and chief justice officer of Israel. Dr. Boice says that it is accepable to ask for justice on behalf of those who had been wronged. Justice is one thing, but to ask the Almighty to cover enemies with shame and dishonor is a little too much! *(V.26)*

While it is entirely legitimate for us to ask God for justice, we should never try and take matters in our own hands. Judgment is the prerogative of God. In Deuteronomy 32:35, God says He alone should take vengence. The Apostle Paul picked up this verse in Deuteronomy and uses it in Romans, saying that we should not avenge ourselves, that is the perogrative of God Almighty. *(Romans 12:19-21)* If we Christians believe that Jesus is our Savior and that He is our personal way to be made right with God, then we must do our level best to heed and obey His teachings. Jesus brought a whole new way of forgiveness and patient endurance into being. He told us that we must forgive our enemies. *(Matthew 5:43-45)* When the Apostle Peter asked Jesus how many times we should forgive someone, and then added the question: Seven times? Jesus replied: seventy times seven. *(Matthew 18:21-22)*

In both Old and New Testament times, godly persons were commanded by God to obey the commandments and follow the religious teachings. In Leviticus 19:2, God said we must be holy because God is holy. This is a universal principle. God wants holy men and women who will be set apart and be pure. Purity means not doing evil, which is rebellion against God.

The difference between those living in the Old Testament times and now is Jesus! He was sent by God to come into our world to show us the way – the way to God! When we Christians invite the Spirit of Jesus into our lives and let Jesus' Spirit merge with our spirit, then in time we begin to take on Jesus' characteristics of being loving and being able to say no to tempting sins. With Jesus in our hearts, we begin to develop supernatural spiritual strength. We don't become holy all at once, but having Jesus in our lives, He not only helps us to be holy and pure, but gives us the assurance that we will go to heaven and be with Him when we die.

# PSALM 36

## Contrasts of God and Man

Psalm 36 is a composition of David where he describes persons who are wickedly sinful, those who have no belief or concern for God, nor any overt fear of divine punishment (Verses 1-4) and then contrasts them with the character of God (Verses 5-12). Some interpreters theorize that these two conflicting modes of life were at one time independent compositions a later editor put together. From a literary standpoint, Psalm 36 can be classified as partly a lament and partly a hymn, with overtones of wisdom teaching.

For ease of analysis, we will divide the psalm into three segments: (1) Sin Dwells in the Wicked, Verses 1-4; (2) Blessings from the LORD's Character, Verses 5-9; and (3) A Final Prayer, Verses 10-12.

### Segment One – Sin Dwells in the Wicked. Verses 1 - 4

The Hebrew word for "sin" is *("Pesha")*, which can also be translated "transgression," "rebellion," or "one who breaks away from authority." The *New Living Bible* vivifies this in verse 1 by personifying sin as an evil spirit that has indwelt a person urging the person to do evil deeds.

David's great insight about wickedness begins with the individuals' rejection of God because they do not fear God. *(V.1)* They are not afraid of the consequences of God's judgment. Without being beholden to God or accountable to Him, there are no checks and balances on the wicked person. The worst part of rejecting God is that such sinners don't have any divine reference point to determine the difference between right and wrong! *(V.2)* Without knowing what sin is, their instinct is to be deceitful. *(V.3)* Instead of scheming how to stay on the righteous side, David says even at night they lay awake thinking up sinful plots. *(V.4)*

106

The fact that the Apostle Paul quotes verse 1 in his magnificent treatment of sin and evil in the opening chapters of Romans, tell us that the great interpreter of Christianity got many of his theological ideas from King David. In the Book of Romans, Paul analyzes the problem facing those who reject God. He wrotes in Chapter One of Romans that there are wicked people who neither know truth nor seek truth so that they will have no excuse when they stand before God on Judgment Day. *(Romans 1:18)* Rather than seeking God and worshipping God, they determine who they think God should be. *(Romans 1 V. 21-22)*

The tragic part of wickedness is in its downward slope. That is to say, if an evil person who has rejected God gets to the point where he cannot discern right from wrong, then in his thinking good becomes evil and evil good – his conscience gets hardened! *(Romans 1 V. 28-29)*

The Holy Spirit inspired David in this Psalm. His writing is a word from God about the nature of evil and evil persons. Psalm 36 has a lot in common with Psalm 1 in illustrating the contrast between good and evil, and what happens when a person chooses to go down the wrong path of life. The main difference between the two psalms is in the second half of Psalm 36, David zeros in not so much on the righteous person (as Psalm 1 does) as on the righteous character of God.

## Segment Two – Blessings from the LORD's Character. Verses 5 - 9

David lavishes his praise on God's greatness. In this section, he cites three characteristics of God's divine Being. The first, and perhaps the most important, is the Hebrew word *("Checed")*, which in English means "unfailing love." *(V.5)* This attribute of God is closely related to His covenant agreement with His people. It also involves God's forgiveness. Other words are "lovingkindness," "mercy," and "grace." These concepts epitomize God's nature and sum up His activity. The second characteristic is a word also cited in verse 5, God's "faithfulness." Faithfulness means that God always adheres to His promises, that is, we can count on Him. The third word characterizing God is the word "justice." The Hebrew word is *("Ts daqah")*, which can be rendered as "righteousness," or "rightness." This has to do with human affairs where God is perfectly just or impartial, or truthful. God is totally upright in all of His dealings with us mortals. *(V.6)* The Hebrew word *("Mishpat")* is a word meaning a verdict, having to do with judgment. (There are about 400 occurrences of this word in the Old Testament). All authority in judgment belongs to God. It is rooted in His character. All these three aspects of God's greatness shows us the distinctive quality of His Being. As someone put it, God never fails, falters, forfeits or forgets!

David now tells us readers how the merciful and loving God blesses His righteous people. *(V.6)* He tells us that all humanity finds protection in God, like under the wings of a bird. *(V.7)* Like birds the LORD feeds us and provides streams where we can refresh themselves. *(V.8)* This beautiful metaphor of David is used many times in the psalms (See 17:8; 57:1; and 63:7). Verse 9 uses the words "life" and "light." Jesus in the New Testment often refers to Himself in those terms. The Apostle John probably had been reading this section of Psalm 36 and was inspired to describe Jesus in the first chapter of his Gospel using "life" and "light." *(John 1-14)* God shone His light for us partially in nature, and faithfully in the pages of the Old Testament – which pointed to Jesus, the Light of the world.

### Segment Three – A Final Prayer. Verses 10 - 12

In the final three verses David prays for himself and for God's people, the upright ones. He prays that the LORD will bless those who love Him. *(V.10)* For himself, David petitions God not to let the wicked have influence over him. *(V.11)* Then in a spiritual flash of insight, he is able to see (through the eyes of faith) that God has acted: the wicked are vanquished! *(V.12)* Each time we read a psalm (like Psalm 36), we must read it through the eyes of our Christian faith. We must ask the Holy Spirit to take its words and apply them to our daily living.

# PSALM 37

## Wise Counsel from an Aging Psalmist

Psalm 37 is a psalm written by David in his old age where he reflects on what he considers important for readers to know. It is a long composition (40 verses) and it is also an acrostic psalm. Each two verses begin with a successive letter of the Hebrew alphabet. It is also a wisdom psalm along the lines of Proverbs, Job and Ecclesiates.

It is difficult to outline, mainly because of the acrostic restraints. I have organized it in terms of themes. (1) Don't Be Envious of Evil Men Who Prosper, (Verses 1-11); (2) Considerations About the Righteous and the Wicked, (Verses 12-22); (3) The LORD Never Forsakes the Godly, (Verses 23-33); and (4) God Will Honor the Righteous, (Verses 34-40).

### Segment One – Don't Be Envious of Evil Men Who Prosper. Verses 1 - 11.

The first two sentences give the gist of the whole psalm: we are not to worry about the wicked and not be envious of them. *(V.1-2)* We should not let the actions of the wicked upset us because if we are patient, God's justice will put them down! *(V.2)* Rather than being envious, David is telling his younger subjects to trust the LORD to do good in their lives. *(V.3-5)* Others will become aware of your innocence and how just you are. *(V.6)* God is in control and His justice will vindicate any disparity that seems to be taking place now. So be patient. *(V.7-8)* The wicked will be destroyed. *(V.9-10)* From David's own experience, he knows that humility before the LORD is the essential ingredient if his readers want to live secure and prosperous lives. *(V.11)*

109

## Segment Two – Considerations About the Righteous and the Wicked. Verses 12 - 22

This segement begins by stating that the wicked are defiant and plot against the Godly. *(V.12)* Psalm 37 echoes Psalm 2 when it says the LORD laughs at those who plot against Him. *(Psalm 2:2, 4) (V.13)* David sees God as the Sovereign LORD, and when the wicked plot against the godly a day of judgment will come. *(V.14-15)* If you don't have much its better still to be godly and not wicked with a lot. *(V.16)* What a wonderful way to look at life by viewing it through the eyes of faith in God who is pro-active on our behalf! Throughout this section, the LORD is rewarding the godly. *(V.17-18)* The pure of heart will survive even in times of famine. *(V.19)* Ultimately the wicked will go away like smoke. *(V.20)* In the short run, the wicked seem to prosper and the righteous suffer. However David says it is the long-run that counts. *(V.22)*

## Segment Three – The LORD Never Forsakes Godly Persons. Verses 23 - 33

The LORD actually directs the steps of the Godly. *(V.23)* Those who are right with the LORD may stumble, but the LORD will be with them and will keep them from falling. *(V.24)* David's testimony is that God never abandons anyone who loves Him. *(V.25)* However, he says to insure a place in God's heart one must not do evil and do good. *(V.27)* The land will be inherited by the Godly. *(29)* In the Beatitudes of Jesus, He says something very similar. *(Matthew 5:5)* The godly make good counselors because they can discern good and evil. *(V.30)* Evil people spy of the righteous hoping to do harm to them. *(V.32)* But the LORD will protect the righteous. *(V.33)*

## Segment Four – God Will Honor the Righteous. Verses 34 - 40

The last segment encourages the godly to be patient and not allow themselves to become discouraged. David encourages his people to walk along God's path. *(V.34)* The Hebrew word for "path" is *("Derek")*. It means a course of godly life following God's commands. David gives his own testimony. He says he has seen evil people fall like giant oaks. *(V.35-36)* Those who are honest will have a wonderful future *(V.37)*, but ultimately evil people have no future. *(V.38)* The psalm ends with David's usual reference to the LORD being his fortress. *(V.39-40)*

Our task as Christians – according to Psalm 37 – is to trust in God and commit our lives to walking along the paths of righteousness. Good words – but God sent us Jesus and He is the way to our knowing how to trust and live a useful life. *(John 14:6)*

Proverbs 3:5-6 is another wisdom saying that supports what David writes in Psalm 37. It instructs us not to depend on our own understanding but to trust God to give us enough light each day on our path through life.

# PSALM 38
## A Sick Man's Cry for Help

This is a psalm written by David. It is one of seven designated as a Penitential Psalm (see Psalm 6, 32, 38, 51, 102, 130, and 143). It is interesting that Verse 1 of Psalm 38 and verse 1 Psalm 6 are identical. Both verses cry out assuming that God is disciplining the writer because of some personal failing of the writer. Both were written by David and were composed within a short time of each other. The author is suffering from a serious disease (sickness) as well as from the plots of enemies and the indifference of friends. In accord with the thought of that time, David's sickness was felt to be a punishment for his sin. He does not name his sin, but he asks God for mercy. Psalm 38 is classified as a lament and prayer.

Psalm 38 anticipates Jesus' suffering and death, and His response to the treachery committed against Him. Our Lord was sinless, but the people around Him interpreted His sufferings as punishment for sins committed.

### Segment One – David's Sickness Described. Verses 1 - 8

David pleads with the LORD not to rebuke him in His rage. *(V.1)* David describes his physical pain metaphorically as like God's arrows shot at him and God's blows hitting him. *(V.2)* He tells us that his health is broken because his sins brought on God's anger toward him. *(V.3)* Whatever his transgression (and he doesn't say) he is overwhelmed by the feelings of guilt. *(V.3-4)* His wounds stink. *(V.5)* He is bent over in pain, has a running fever and completely exhausted. *(V.6-8)*

Today we realize that not all illness is a punishment. In fact, most sickness is not linked to sin. Physical suffering (whatever its cause) often depresses us emotionally. Often in a depressed state, we are inclined to ruminate on past sins. Job, for instance, was a righteous man, blameless and upright (see Job 1:8), and yet he suffered. The connection between sins and suffering might be that God can use suffering to develop a Christ-like character in us. All of us are sinners, including David, so we all have the possibility of suffering because of sin. Rightly or wrongly, David believed he was hurting because of his sins. (V.5)

### Segment Two – I Am Like an Untouchable. Verses 9 - 16

Speaking to the Lord (Adonai) and not directly to the LORD (Yahweh), David asks Him to listen to his prayer. (V.9) He cries out that his heart is beating wildly and he is going blind. (V.10) David tells of his feelings of isolation. No one wants to spend time with those who are hurting. His friends, loved ones and even his family stay away, fearing they may contract what ailes him. (V.11) He also is aware that his enemies consider his illness an opportunity to plot against him. (V.12) In agony of soul, David again turns to the LORD in prayer. (V.15) His prayer is that God won't let his enemies take joy in his downfall. (V.16)

### Segment Three – David's Confessions. Verses 17 - 20

In constant pain and facing possible collapse (V.17), he turns to God and confesses his sins. He humbly says he is sorry for his past sinful actions. (V.18) He reviews again the pain of having people oppose him. (V.19) As a king, there is bound to be opposition, even when David believes he has done nothing wrong. (V.20)

### Segment Four – Help Me, O God My Savior. Verses 21 - 22

Pitifully, David ask the LORD (Yahweh) not to abandon him. He ask his Savior to come quickly to his assistance. (V.21-22) The Hebrew word for "Savior" is ("T'shuw'ah); it means "deliverance," and "keeping me safe." The question is will God come? The answer: of course! Why? This is the very theme of the Bible. We Christians say, Salvation comes from Jesus Christ. He is the Savior of the world. No one else brings salvation. The Apostle Paul spells it out in Romans 6:22-23. Jesus sets us free from sin's power over us.

# PSALM 39
## The Brevity of Life

The superscription says this is a psalm of David. This is a prayer for help, and could have been authored by a person who was ill (see Verses 10-11). It is an unusual and strange psalm. The extended opening meditation (Verses 1-3) is for silence. The final petition asks God to lighten up (Verses 13). The middle part speaks of the brevity of life (Verses 4-6).

Psalm 39 speaks of despair and hope at the same time. Perhaps this is the way life really is – full of tension and complexity. There is an interweaving of four themes: silence; human transience; sin; and suffering.

Scholars tell us that Psalm 39 was composed sometime after the exile when Jews were reexamining their traditional faith in the light of the suffering and wretchedness they found when they returned from Babylon. Although the heading says David wrote the psalm, he obviously did not. Whoever composed this composition was troubled about the brevity and vanity of life. We can classify this psalm as a dirge and a lament.

Psalm 39 is beautifully written and it expresses many aspects of emotion – rebellion, despair, and resignation-- but sadly it leaves the reader with futility

### Segment One – Turmoil Within. Verses 1 - 3

The Psalmist is saying how difficult it is not to complain, especially with the ungodly listening in. He is trying to hold back while inside of him a fire is blazing! He is attempting to curb his tongue. *(V.1)* Finally, he says, his turmoil is so great that he is at a breaking point. *(V.2)* What is our author thinking about? What is troubling him? He obviously is pondering some serious matters. The Hebrew word for "pondering" is *("Hagiyg")*. It also means to "think about" or "muse."

Let's analyze the word "amusement;" its root word is "muse." If we put an "a" in front of muse (to think), the "a" makes it negative –a "no." Putting them together and you have amusement, and amusement means we are entertained "not to think." Many folks today are being entertained and drifting through life until they pass through the dark doors of death. This is not the case of our Psalmist. He looks out at the world and the turmoil becomes so great that he has to speak, to speak like a raging fire. *(V.3)*

## Segment Two – Vanity, All Is Vanity. Verses 4 - 6

What is bothering the author comes out at the beginning of verse 4. He has been thinking about the emptiness and meaninglessness of life. He asks the LORD to remind him that his days are numbered. *(V.4)* Life is only a short moment, then it is over! Life is but a breath. *(V.5)* The Hebrew word here for "breath" is *("Habel")*. It can also be translated "vanity," and "meaningless." *Ecclesiastes* begins with *("Habel")*. Solomon probably wrote *Ecclesiastes* later in life and had concluded by then that everything is meaningless, or "vanity" as *The King James Bible* translates *("Habel")*. *(Ecclesiastes 1:2)* It sounds a lot like verse 6 in our psalm.

## Segment Three – Turning to God. Verses 7 - 11

Our Psalmist desires some ray of hope and affirmation in his life, and so he turns to the Lord. *(V.7)* He asks the Lord to save him from his sins, from his rebellion towards God. *(V.8)* He doesn't shake his fist in God's face. He is willing to listen. *(V.9)* He begs God to cease his disciplining because he is exhausted. *(V.10)* He tells God that when He disciplines us we can be crushed like a bug. He goes on to say we human beings are but a breath. *(V.11)*

Job uses similar agonizing words. In Job's sorrow, he accuses God of testing us every moment. And he asks why God cannot just pardon him of his sins and take away his feelings of guilt. *(Job 7:17-21)*

Our Psalmist says to God that we are fragile creatures who walk the earth for a very brief time and cannot contribute anything to God who is eternal. Yet God continues to interact with what we do. God continues to (as Job says) scrutinize us.

## Segment Four – Spare Me, LORD. Verses 12 - 13

The final petition of the Psalmist is a prayer – an impassioned plea to the LORD to heed his tears of pity. He finally recognizes that now life has some meaning but only as God gives it meaning, he is merely a guest in what God has created. *(V.12)* He wants some happiness before he has to go down to the pit of oblivion. He feels some sort of hope in verse 12 but ends up with sad despair in verse 13.

It is true that life is brief on this earth, but for the Christian life does not end here. John 3:16 tells us clearly that God so loved the world (and us) that if we believe in Christ Jesus we will not perish but have everlasting life. God wants to save us and so He sent His dear Son, Jesus, to show us how to live while we are traveling through this world. Then, in an act of grace, Jesus made the supreme sacrifice on our behalf by dying on the cross and taking on Himself the penalty for our sins, thereby making us right with God. Because of this, the mighty Lord of the universe accepts and acquits us, declaring us not guilty because of our trust is in Jesus Christ. God sent His Spirit (not the world's spirit) to help us Christians understand our Father's wise plan to bring us into the glories of heaven when we die. The amazing Good News is that all can be saved by choosing Jesus as their Lord and Savior – no matter who they are or what they have been like in the past!

The Apostle John gives us wonderful words of Scripture to help us live by.

1.    We are the children of God and he cares for us. *(1 John 3:1)*
2.    We need to love one another for God is love. *(1 John 4:7)*

# PSALM 40
## He Lifted Me Out of the Pit of Despair

The first part of this psalm needs very little introduction because of its familiarity. It tells of a person who cried out to God and was rescued from being bogged down in a state of despair. That person was King David. The second part of the psalm (verses 13-17) is a plea for deliverance from enemies. The last section is repeated almost word-for-word in Psalm 70. Many scholars believe that verses 1-11 at one time were an independent composition, and verses 13-17 another. Sometime after the exile, when the Psalter was being reorganized, the two psalms were put together with Verse 12 added to serve as a connection between the two. Obviously Psalm 70 was placed further toward the back section to isolate it from the many psalms of David.

Psalm 40 can be organized helpfully into three segments: (1) David's Rescue from His Despair, Verses 1-3; (2) The LORD Has Done Glorious Things, Verses 4-10; and (3) A Prayer for Future Deliverance, Verses 11-17.

### Segment One — David's Rescue from His Despair. Verses 1 - 3

David begins by pointing out that he waited patiently for the LORD's help. *(V.1)* David developed patience as a boy taking care of his father's sheep. Being patient stood him in good stead later when he was hiding out from King Saul's soldiers who were trying to hunt him down and kill him. Now we don't know the circumstance around which David is describing when the LORD lifted him up out of pit of despair. *(V.2)* It must have been a time in his life when he felt trapped and hemmed in. It is assumed that pit, mud and mire are metaphors. And it is a good thing we don't know what they were,

117

literally, because now we will be able to think about our own experiences where we felt bogged down.

What could our pit of despair be? A physical illness? Some sort of ugly skin disease, like boils, or a wretched rash? Maybe a failed relationship? A friend who betrayed a trust? A death in the family? How about a bad habit when alcohol or a drug has gotten out of control? Or could the pit be an addiction to pornography?

In David's despair and hopelessness, he cries out to God and God hears him. God lifts David out of the pit and put his feet on solid ground. Because of David's gifted musical talents, he is given a new song to sing by the LORD. (V.3) He lifts his voice in sweet praises to his LORD. In gratitude for being blessed, he wants to bless those who are in awe before the LORD and who trust Him!

## Segment Two – The LORD Had Done Glorious Things. Verses 4 - 10

In this segment, after telling how God lifted him out of the awful his despair, David reflects on God's goodness. There is joy in trusting in God, he says. (V.4) Miracles were witnessed from God's hand, he says. (V.5) Best of all, he was in the LORD's thoughts.

David must have been thinking of the prophet Samuel's comments about the burnt offerings in I Samuel 15:22; he says almost the same thing--that sacrifices of burnt animals don't bring God any pleasure. (V.6) What God really desires is our taking joy in doing His will and in his heart the law of God is written. (V.7-8)

Several times in David's writings, he puts down words that have meaning for him but were later quoted by other writers in different contexts. That is what happened in Verse 7 and 8. David writes that God's law was written in his heart. What he probably meant was that he came prepared to obey God's laws. The prophet Jeremiah picked this up later when he spoke the words of God, saying the LORD will make a new covenant with Isreal and Judah in the future and write His laws in the peoples' heart. (Jeremiah 31:31-33) These words are familiar. The Book of Hebrews in the New Testament quotes them and applies them to Jesus. (Hebrews 8:8-12 and 10:15-17)

David continues to speak boldly to his fellow believers by telling them that God can forgive their sins and this is Good News! He hasn't been timid about telling them that this is the essence of God's power to save them. (V.10)

## Segment Three – A Prayer for Future Deliverance. Verses 11 - 17

In verse 11, David prays to God asking Him to continue His tender compassion toward him. He says he is desperate without God's mercy and faithfulness, because his sins threaten to overwhelm him. He doesn't know which way to turn. He is surrounded by his troubles. *(V.12)* I'm about to perish! He asks God to come quickly and help him. *(V.13)*

As we said in the opening paragraph, this section is loosely connected with the first part, verses 1-10. Throughout his long and illustrious career, David had many enemies to contend with, and it seems as if once more they are about to do him in. So he cries out for God to help him and to come quickly to his aid. *(V.14)* Zap them! *(V.15)* Dishonor them, LORD! He ends by asking God to bless those who search to find the LORD as their savior. *(V.16-17)*

In the end of the second part of Psalm 40, David comes before God and confesses his brokenness. Once again he is impatient for God's help. (Not too much patience manifested here that was evident in the first section.) Just another bit of evidence that says these two parts were once not connected.

In the first segment of Psalm 40 (Verses 1-10), we mention how frequently David's words in the psalms have been quoted by Old and New Testament writers. We cited Jeremiah's words coming from (or similar to) David's words in verse 7. We also said that the Book of Hebrews quoted Jeremiah 31:31-33 (in two places- Hebrews 8:8-12 and 10:15-17). In Hebrews 8: 10, David's words (Psalm 40, verses 6-8) are also quoted. Here is the context: The old system of Jewish laws entailed many sacrifices that had to be repeated over and over, year after year, but they were ineffectual for those who lived under their rule. If they could have one offering that would cleanse the worshipers once for all, then all their feelings of guilt would cease. But just the opposite happened. The yearly sacrifice where the Chief Priest made his sacrifice for the people merely reminded them of their disobedience and guilt, instead of giving them true peace. It was at this point that Jesus (according to the author of Hebrews) spoke David's words in Psalm 40. *(Hebrew 10:5-7)* After Christ said this, about God not being satisfied with the various sacrifices and offerings required under the old system, Christ then added, here I am, I have come to give my life. Jesus cancels the first system in favor of a far better one. Under this new plan, we have been forgiven and made clean by Christ's dying for us once for all. No more sacrifices are needed. *(Hebrew 10:18)*

A basic rule for Christians is to read the psalms through the eyes of the Christian faith. God inspired the Psalmists to write meaningful words to help all who read them to walk the earth with more courage and resolve. The psalms are basically God-centered and we Christians can learn many good lessons and insights. They were all written under the Old Covenant, which we believe has been superseded by the New Covenant. David's deliverance from his pit of despair is a wonderful example of how God works. Having read Psalm 40, it is helpful to supplement its lessons by turning to Paul.

In Romans Chapter 5 he writes that trials and temptations are good for us because we learn not only to endure but we learn to depend on God to help us through them. *(Romans 5:3-5)*

Paul goes on in chapter 5 saying that when we are feeling totally discouraged (as David expressed in verses 11 and 12 in Psalm 40), we can rejoice that Christ's sacrifice on the cross enables us to have a new covenant relationship with the Father. This not only gives us aid and succor in this life but eternal life. *(Romans 5:6-11)*

# PSALM 41

## A Plea to the God of Compassion

Psalm 41, like Psalm 38, describes a serious illness that David underwent. We are not sure, but it could be the same sickness. Psalm 38 focuses on the sickness itself, while Psalm 41 describes how his enemies and a false friend took advantage of him during his incapacitation. Psalm 41 marks the end of Book One of the 150 Psalter.

We can divide Psalm 41 into three discernable parts: One, The LORD Blesses Those Who Help the Weak, Verses 1-3; Two, David's Past Troubles, Verses 4-10; and Three, David's Prayers Are Answered, Verses 11-12.

### Segment One – The LORD Blesses Those Who Help the Weak. Verses 1 - 3

The Hebrew word ("*Checed*") is used to describe what God's covenant people should be doing. Because God has shown mercy and "loving kindness" ("*Checed*") on his people, He expects them, in turn, to share His saving love and mercy with one another and with their neighbors. We junior partners with God's covenant love and grace are called to share God's love and grace for us with others. This is a part of our mission to bring God's salvation to the world. This mission was not just commanded by Jesus (*Matthew 28: 18-20*) but it was first spoken of by Isaiah. (*Isaiah 49:6*)

There are many Christians today who feel that to be religious means to enjoy their personal salvation. They seek out other Christians and meet together week after week and feel happy in the Lord. They think that doing this will give them blessings. David wouldn't agree with them because he did not consider love a sentiment—he considered love an action! This whole new way of life when God puts us right with Himself has serious obligations for believers to pass spiritual gifts from God onto others, and do it in tangible

121

ways like being consider of the poor. *(V.1)* David was oriented to sharing with those less fortunate in society and when he fell ill he looked back and saw God's loving hand at work in his life. The LORD was there rescuing him. *(V.1)* The LORD kept him alive. *(V.2)* In retrospect, he realizes that God takes care of His own people who are faithfully trying to carry out their covenant obligations. *("Checed")* describes God's nature, His "loving kindness," what He is and how He acts, and so in David's serious illness, God stepped in and showed His *("Checed")* by easing his pain both physiclly and emotionally. *(V.3)*

## Segment Two – David's Past Troubles. Verses 4- 10

In this section, David looks back on his experiences with a debilitating illness, and his unfortunate encounters with his enemies and so-called friends. He begins by praying to receive mercy from God. *(V.4)* In His Beatitudes in the New Testament, Jesus spelled out God's wonderful spiritual law, by telling us we are blessed by God when we show others mercy. *(Matthew 5:7)* The Hebrew word for "mercy" or be kind is *("Chanan")*. David was able to humble himself and turn to God with a confession of any possible sins he may have inadvertently committed that might cause a disruption in his spiritual communication.

Throughout his kingship, David had many enemies from without, from the family of King Saul, and even his own son, Absalom. There were also many from his own administration jealous of his power and leadership. Whatever the sickness was, he was bed-ridden and those who opposed him would visit and say the obvious platitudes to his face, and then behind his back they would ask when David might die and be forgotten. *(V.5)* They would whisper to one another in mock tones of how better it would be for them when he was dead. *(V.7-8)* One of David's most difficult emotional hurts was when he discovered the friend he trusted most had turned against him. *(V.9)* Jesus sensed David's pain and used the last part of verse 9 to apply to Judas's betrayal of Jesus Himself. *(John 13:18)*

The last verse in this recollection by David entreats God not to desert him and make him well. *(V.10)* Here again David uses the same Hebrew word *("Chanan")* for "mercy." It would seem that David's motive for wanting God to heal him is so he could get back at those who hoped that he might die. This seems to be very vindictive. On the other hand, as the king he would have the responsibility to call these disloyal staff members to account.

We Christians have a totally different perspective given to us by the Lord Jesus Christ. The Law of Moses instructed the Hebrews to love their neighbor but hate their enemy. Jesus taught we are to love our enemies as well as our neighbors for they too are sons of God, disobedient sons (and daughters) of God, but sons of God nevertheless. *(Matthew 5:43-45)* Even in the midst of the crucifixion, Jesus prayed to God that the Father forgive those joyful of the suffering he was enduring. *(Luke 23: 34)* Jesus offers us a whole new way of life when we commit ourselves to Him. When this happens, He put us right with God, we are made righteous, and this gives us everlasting life! He gives us another wonderful gift through His abiding Spirit: the gift of compassionate, creative love. We are able (supernaturally) to show this love toward a neighbor. And with God's help, our love can bring this neighbor out of the clutches of sin into the joy and peace of God.

Jesus agreed with Moses that the two most important commandments are (1) love the Lord your God; (2) love your neighbor as yourself. *(Luke 10:27)*

### Segment Three – David's Prayers Are Answered. Verses 11 - 12

In these concluding verses, we are fast-forwarded to a time in the not-too-distant future when David's prayers were answered by God. He was healed and his enemies failed to harm him. *(V.11)* Furthermore, with humility borne out of his own commitment to God's covenant, David ends the psalm thanking God for protecting his life and then he adds that he was innocent. *(V.12)* The Hebrew word for "innocent" is *("Tom")*, which also can be translated "integrity" or "uprightness." David is saying he has been honest with God, not trying to conceal his faults, but doing the best he could with the light God has given him. Because of his dedication and sincerity, David feels he has been brought into God's presence forever! *(V.12)*

Verse 13 is a benediction, probably added by a later editor, making this verse the close of Book One of the Psalter. This verse is similar to the closing verses of the other four books of the Psalter. (See also 72:18-19, 89:52, and 106: 48.) The two amen responses are a liturgical added-on.

David's honesty and integrity in confronting his enemies are good examples for us Christians to emulate. We have some wonderful Christian ethics to help us. The Apostle Paul expresses the need for us to have the mind of Christ in Romans Chapter 12. As reborn Christians, Paul says our minds are transformed, making us aware of what God wants us to do. *(Romans 12:2)* Paul then adds that we must be authentic in our transformation, not just pretending to love others but to really love others. *(Romans 12:9-11)* Finally Paul exhorts us to learn to live in peace with others and never respond to the evil treatment of others toward us by being evil to them. *(Romans 12:17-19)*

# PSALMS 42/43
## Thirsting for the Living God

Book Two of the Psalter begins with Psalms 42 and 43. Some scholars theorize that originally these two poems were joined together as one. With the two compositions there are three pathetic cries to God for help from a very lonely person. They are arranged in three segments: first, Psalm 42, Verses 1-5; second, Psalm 42, Verses 6-10; and third, Psalm 43, Verses 1-5. An Identical chorus appears in Psalm 42, Verse 5 and Verse 11, and Psalm 43, Verse 5 with the Psalmist asking himself why he is so discouraged when God is his Savior.

From context we can surmise that the Psalmist is a committed Jewish believer who finds himself far away from home with the sadness that comes from not being able to worship with fellow Jews. Who is this depressed and lonely person? Where is he? How did he get to where he is? Many guesses have been made. Could this person have been captured and then sold into slavery by the slave-trade merchants from Gaza? (See Amos 1:6.) Was he in political exile? Some commentators suggest he might have been from the Northern Kingdom city of Samaria and was deported by the Assyrians when they destroyed that city in 722 B.C. Frankly, we don't know. All we do know is that our author is a very upset individual who was uprooted from home and the worship of God.

### Segment One – Thirsting for the Living God. Verses 1 - 5

The theme for these two Psalms is sounded in verse 1 comparing a deer's thirst for streams of waters to the Psalmist's search for God. (See Joel 1:20 and Psalms 63:1 and 143:6) The Psalmist's tears of isolation and loneliness are made even worse when others around him (his enemies) continually

125

taunt him, asking where is the God to save you. *(V.3)* With a broken heart, he remembers how it was back home when he could mingle with singing worshipers. *(V.4)* Discouraged and sad, he nevertheless, reaffirms his faith in God. *(V.5)*

## Segment Two – Exiled and Overwhelmed. Verses 6 - 11

Our Psalmist in verse 6 repeats his feelings of despair, but remembers (in a poetic way) Mount Hermon where the Jordan River begins (his home?). Verse 7 perhaps indicates the out-of-control forces that threaten to overwhelm him. It could mean that his heart is yearning to maintain a connection with his home community of faith – or the depth within him calling out to God's depth in order to keep him from drowning in his anguish. In verse 8 he addresses God as the LORD and acknowledges that the LORD shows him unfailing love. Then in verse 9, our author calls out to God, his Rock, and asks if God has forsaken him. In darkness again is the taunting question from his enemies, where is this God who is to help you? The chorus in verse 5, with him asking himself why he is so discouraged, is repeated in verse 11.

## Segment Three – A Prayer for Vindication. Psalm 43, Verses 1 - 5

The author prays asking God for help. Be my Advocate against those who want to harm me. *(V.1)* He is saying these people are not members of Your covenant. These are "Gentiles" (non Jews). The Hebrew word for them is *("Goy")*, heathen people. They don't know God's laws or His commandments. They don't know Your justice, God. They are a law unto themselves. In despair he has no answer and then asks why he is being pushed aside, oppressed by evil people. *(V.2)* He seeks spiritual peace asking God to take him to God's dwelling place. *(V.3)* His desire is to worship at the altar of God. Transport me home. *(V.4)* Then comes the chorus with him asking himself why he is so discouraged. *(V.5)*

Psalm 43 leaves things unresolved. The Psalmist (according to the belief of his day) implies that God is only to be found in His residence at His Holy Place in Jerusalem. The implication is that we cannot have joy unless we are in His vicinity. *(V.4)*

Reading the psalms from a Christian perspective, we have to admit that it is difficult to be alone in an alien culture like our Psalmist found himself. There is no question that without support from a loving worshiping faith community the conditions are ripe for depression. For us today when we bring Jesus into our hearts, He acts within us as a spiritual advisor encouraging us to walk-the-walk that God demands. Being God's partner, along with the Holy Spirit, Jesus gives us access to God's presence. When Jesus' Spirit comes into our lives, we give Him control, and the Bible says, with Jesus, our lives will produce wonderful fruits of the Spirit. With love, peace, patience, kindness, goodness, faithfulness, gentleness and self-control, we are able to have joy! You see, God doesn't just give joy at His altar on the Holy Mountain *(Psalm 43:3-4)*, He is joy! This is what is so great about our Christian faith! We'll let Paul tell us. In the 7th chapter of his letter to Rome, he says no matter how hard he tried, he couldn't do the right thing because he was a slave to sin. So, in despair, he cried out, and Jesus was there not only as his Savior but his Lord. *(Romans 7:24)*

Paul was supernaturally freed from the power of sin that leads to death through Jesus. He says the law of Moses couldn't save us because of our sinful nature. But God put into effect a different plan to save us – and we, too, are the recipients of God's plan. God sent His Son to die as a sacrifice for our sins. Paul goes on to say that if we have the Spirit of God living in us, we will be controlled by the Spirit and not by our sinful nature. *(Romans 8:11-17)*

# PSALM 44

## An Embarrassing Defeat

This poem was written by one of the descendants of Korah—Levites who ministered in the Temple-- at a time of national calamity. Apparently Israel had suffered an embarrassing defeat on the battlefield. He writes this lament on behalf of his people. Many experts in the field of biblical history are unsure of when and where this humiliation took place. We know it was after the exile, and before the Maccabean period. It has been suggested that the Jews suffered greatly in a general revolt against the Persian ruler, Artaxerxes the Third, in 351-349 B.C. While we don't know precisely, we do know that the Korahite poet wrote this selection for the Choirmaster of the Second Temple.

### Segment One – God's Mighty Deeds in the Past. Verses 1 - 3

The Psalmist reviews some of the miracles God performed for the nation of Israel – great stories passed down from generation to generation, like the Passover when God told Hebrews in Egypt to spread lamb's blood on the top of their doors so the LORD would pass over them but would strike down the Egyptian's first-born (see Exodus 12:21-29). *(V.1-2)* Another mighty deed was when the LORD brought the Hebrew people out of Egypt to give them the land He had promised their ancestors. *(Deuteronomy 6:22-23)* Joshua commanded a representative from each of the Twelve Tribes to carry stones and build a monument in the middle of the Jordan River to remind them when God stopped the River from flowing so the Ark of the Covenant could cross (Joshua 4:1-9). The Hebrew forefathers recorded that the Promised Land invasion was the result of God's miraculous leadership. The Psalmist says it was the power of God that they were able to conquer the land. *(V.3)*

## Segment Two – We Are Totally Dependent on You, God. Verses 4 - 8

Our author states the supernatural power of God accomplished Israel's success in the past. He reminds God that God still has the power to bring about victories for His people. *(V.4)* He then reminds God that it is only with God's power that God's people can defeat their enemies. *(V.5)* He says he does not trust his own sword or bow to save him only God. *(V.6-7)* Knowing this, the Psalmist praises God day and night. *(V.8)* David also knew this and, before he slew the giant Goliath, David reminded God that David's victory would be God's and not David's. *(I Samuel 17:47)*

## Segment Three – A Puzzling Present. Verses 9 - 22

All that talk in Segment Two about only You, God, can save us by pushing back our enemies and how much we thank You for watching over us gives way to Segment Three– but now we find ourselves having been invaded and dishonored! The Psalmist is remonsrating God for no longer fighting His people's battles. *(V.9)* We've been humiliated! *(V.10)* We've been treated like sheep and You sold us out as if we have no value. *(V.11-12)* We've been shamed and disgraced. We are a joke among our neighbors. *(V.13-16)* All these terrible things have taken place despite our loyalty to You. *(V.17)* We have not deserted You, God, nor strayed from you. *(V.18)* Darkness and death await us. *(V.19)* If we had not been loyal to You, then we could understand Your punishing us and causing us to undergo this tragic suffering and death. *(V.20)* Like sheep we are being led to slaughter. *(V.22)*

The writer of Psalm 44 feels as if the Covenant between the Jews and God has been broken by God. He feels totally disillusioned. The word, "Jew," the Psalmist feels is now a term of contempt. He feels despised and mocked! The anger, self-righteousness and pity that the writer is exuding come because of a literal understanding of the law. In Deuteronomy 28 it says if Israel keeps all the commanments, it would be exalted over all nations. *(Deuteronomy 28: 1)* Moses tells them they will be blessed, and one of the blessings in particular would be that they would conquer their enemies. *(Deuteronomy 28:7)* Moses further says for this blessing to keep occurring the Hebrews could not worship any other gods but God Almighty. *(Dueteronomy 28:14)*

The problem of the Psalmist is that he believes it is humanly possible to follow the letter of the law. The law of retribution told him that God would bless His people in exact proportion to how they (he and all his people) obeyed. Similarly, God would curse them according to their disobedience. Taking this literally is where the Psalmist went wrong!

The Prophet Isaiah in his 53ʳᵈ chapter speaks of the coming of the Messiah. He does not describe a coming king but a suffering servant, despised and full of sorrow who is wounded and killed for the sins of the people of Israel. Isaiah points out that all have strayed off the moral path like lost sheep. *(Isaiah 53:1-6)* Jesus didn't go to the cross and die because of His own sins. No, as Isaiah says, He died for our sins. He took the penalty that we—Jew and Gentile--deserve.

There is no one living who can follow the Law perfectly. *(Romans 3:10, 12)* In Romans 8:36, Paul quotes Psalm 44 to help us Christians see that we might have to face what the Jews in this psalm had to undergo. Paul points out the Christians in his day are being persecruted and threatened with death. But in death these Christian, Paul says, will have an overwhelming victory. *(Romans 8:35-37)*

### Segment Four – Urgent Plea for Help. Verses 23 - 26

Our writer is thoroughly upset at what has happened to his people and nation. He takes out his frustrations and anger on God. He beseeches the Lord to wake up. *(V.23)* Stop looking the other way! *(V.24)* Following the Deuteronomic code, he feels he has been betrayed, and perhaps God has cast him and his people out of His favor forever.

It all goes back to Deuteronomy where the Jews believed God told them if they followed all the commandments and ordinances given them, then they would be God's own special people. *(Deuteronomy 26:19)* The Psalmist states bitterly that the Jews have not violated their Covenant. They had not left God's paths, and yet by the defeat of Israel the implication is that God had violated His part of the agreement (Covenant). There seems to be no other explanation – at least not in Psalm 44. *(V.25)* He ends the psalm pleading with the Lord to rise up and help the nation. *(V.26)*

We need to understand that Israel is not the only nation God loves. John 3:16 says God loves the world! Yes, God chose the Jews to be a special people, and yes, He entered into a Covenant with them. We need to ask the question: Why did God choose the Jews? The answer: He called them to be a servant people and to take the Good News of God's love and salvation to the world.

They were to become a light in the dark world of the Gentiles and messagers to bring salvation to the world. *(Isaiah 49:6)* They were to learn to become a servant people and not just another political power.

Let's go again to the New Testament to the 8th chapter of Romans. Paul tells us that God entrusted the Jews with His laws, but there was not any way they could make themselves good enough to be acceptable in God's sight by trying to keep every jot and title of His laws. Trying to keep all the laws only allowed them (and us) to see that we are sinners! However, God in His grace and mercy showed us a better way to get right with God. He is willing to declare us righteous in His sight when we give ourselves to Jesus and to trust Him to take away our sins. All of us can attain salvation by bringing the Spirit of Christ Jesus into our minds and hearts no matter who we are or what we were like before. The Good News is that God sent His Son, Jesus, to come on earth to take the punishment for our sins. Paul, a converted Jew, tells us we are made right with God through faith in Jesus and not by observing a law that no one can fulfill except God Himself. *(Romans 3:25-27)*

Paul also spoke about Abraham, the patriarch and Father of the Jewish nation. The Scriptures tell us Abraham believed God and that is why God cancelled his sin and declared him not guilty. He says Abraham did not earn his way to heaven by all the good things he did. He was saved as a gift!

God declared sinners to be acceptable in His sight if they have faith in Jesus. *(Romans 8:1)* Through Jesus' death and resurrection, God has freed us from the cycle of sin and death! When Jesus went to His death on the cross, God raised Him from death and set His Spirit free from the limitations of time and space. Spiritually this means Jesus can come to us at any time or place as long as we are open and receptive to receive Him. Through Jesus' Spirit, God can be with us helping to direct our lives and working out His plan and purpose for reconciling the world to Himself (the original plan He had for choosing the Jews). Living in a broken and sinful world means we are vulnerable and subject to taking our share of the hurts and illnesses as we attempt to fit in with God's plan of bringing salvation to the world.

Continuing in chapter 8 of Romans, we are told that God's Holy Spirit speaks to us deep in our hearts to say we are His children. And since we are members of God's family, we will be able to share in His treasures – for all He gives to His Son will be ours in Christ Jesus, too. Paul says very plainly that if we are to share in Christ's glory, we must all be prepared to share in His sufferings! Yet, what we may have to suffer on earth will be nothing compared with the glory we will experience when we will be with God and Jesus in heaven for all eternity! (See Romans 8:16-18)

We Christians stand on the victory side of the cross and this is the major difference between the writer of Psalm 44 and us. We both live in a world of sin, death and decay. We both are vulnerable to the sufferings that are the result of wars and natural disasters. THE DIFFERENCE IS JESUS! God sent His Messiah, Jesus, and because we are able to put our faith in Him as our Savior, we have the optimism of walking by faith, which is a form of heaven on earth, and we know for certain that we will go to heaven when we die and will spend eternity with God and Jesus. *(Romans 8:38-39)*

# PSALM 45

## A Royal Wedding for the King

Psalm 45 was written for the occasion of a royal wedding. It also can be classified as a Messianic Psalm, written by one of the clan of Korah. We have no idea for which earthly king and bride it was originally composed. Some interpreters say it might have been written for the wedding of King Solomon and a princess of Egypt, but that is conjecture.

It is called a Messianic Psalm because the Holy Spirit of God was causing the author to look ahead to the coming of God's glorious King, the Messiah. We know this because the Book of Hebrews in the New Testament quotes (almost word for word) verses 6 and 7 of Psalm 45 in its first chapter. *(Hebrew 1:8-9)*

In order to better understand Psalm 45, it will be helpful to know something about ancient Jewish betrothal and wedding customs.

A. Betrothal – Similar to being engaged, but the parents do all the arrangements. After a legal procedure enacted before a magistrate, the couple can be called husband and wife – even if there is no physical union. We Christians can understand this when we think about the relatonship between Mary and Joseph prior to Jesus' birth. Part of the commitment of the husband's family is to provide a dowry. Many couples could be quite young which meant the actual wedding would be delayed for many years.

B. Day of the Wedding – Friends and attendants would gather at the home of the bride. She would wear her finest clothes and jewelry. At the same time, the groom's attendants would gather at his home. A grand procession would begin as the groom and his entourage would march through the streets to fetch his bride. When the groom arrives at the bride's house, a second procession would begin. The entire party (bride and groom) and those accompanying them would proceed from the home of the bride back to the groom's house. When they would arrive, a joyful wedding feast would take place that could last anywhere from a day to several weeks! (See Jesus' parable of the Ten Bridesmaids found in Matthew 25:1-12.)

### Segment One – Introduction: A Lovely Poem for the King. Verse 1

The poet's emotions have stirred wonderful thoughts. He begins by saying he will recite a lovely poem dedicated to the King. *(V.1)* The Holy Spirit was using his words as he describes a wedding of an earthly monarch and his bride and sends these words into the future to us in the twenty-first century to give us a glimpse of the divine Groom, Jesus the Savior, as He takes the Church as his bride. Indeed, God was truly inspiring the Psalmist!

### Segment Two – An Address to the Groom. Verses 2 - 9

In this section, the poet is praising King Jesus. Some of the language has to do with warfare, but we see it as metaphors. For us Christians, the Savior of the world is the best looking of all. *(V.2)* His words are God's directions for us. *(V.2)* Jesus won victory over sin, death and Satan. *(V.3)* He consistently stands for and defends truth and justice with humility thrown in. And His awe-inspiring deeds were miracles. *(V.4)* His sharp arrows of life-changing love are sent into His enemies hearts and they fall before him and become converts – His friends and followers. *(V.5)* His throne is everlasting. *(V.6)* It's true, You are God's Son and He has anointed you. *(V.7)*

### Segment Three – Advice to the New Queen. Verses 10 - 12

In these vereses, the Psalmist turns to the bride with loving affection (like a father). He assures this royal daughter that all is well and the future is secure! *(V.10)*

We will continue to apply the writer's words as metaphors of the Church.

The Psalmist instructs the bride to forget her people and her homeland. *(V.11)* He is echoing the words from Genesis 2:24 which say the married man and women leave their father and mother behind. Metaphorically, when we join the church – part of Christ's Bride – we become one with the Lord, and we are called to follow Jesus wholeheartedly. *(Matthew 16:24-25)*

It is difficult to leave worldly loyalties behind, but we Christians are called by God to make tough decisions. The other word of counsel in this segment is for the bride to honor her husband as her Lord. *(V.11)* When the marriage takes place between Jesus and the Church, it is a holy relationship that Jesus has for His Bride, and as members of the church we must hold this sacred relationship inviolate!

## Segment Four –The Bride and Her Attendants. Verses 13 - 16

The Church is the Bride wearing righteous robes as she is brought before the king. *(V.13-14)* Paul deals with marriage in his letter to the Ephesians, and he speaks of the church as being lovely. He tells us that husbands ought to show the same kind of love for their wives as Christ showed to the Church when He died for her. *(Ephesians 5:26-27)* Of course, Paul is speaking of a future church (which is the body of Christian believers) when Jesus returns to take us to heaven.

The Psalmist says another thing in this section that has meaning for us Christians. He says it is a joy procession when we enter the place of the king. *(V.15)* Here again is a future description of the marriage of the Lamb. What joy there will be in heaven when we Christians are with God and Jesus for all eternity. We will be living on the New Earth where there won't be any more death, or crying, or pain. All that will be left behind. *(Revelation 21:9-27)*

## Segment Five – A Look into the Future. Verses 17

Until that time when we will be in heaven, we Christians need to do our best with what God has given us while we are here on earth knowing of our great reward in the future. *(John 14:1-3)* In the meantime, we want to do everything possible to cause Jesus' name to be honored and to prepare ourselves for that wonderful Day! *(V.17)*

# PSALM 46
## God Is a Tested Help in Times of Trouble

The title says it is for the director of music and that the Sons of Korah wrote it. Many biblical experts think this composition was inspired by the failed takeover of Jerusalem either by the armies of King Sennacherib from Assyria (see 2 Kings Chapters 18-19) or the destruction of the armies of Ammon, Moab, and Mount Seir during the reign of King Jehoshaphat (see 2 Chronicles 20). We're not sure which one it was, but probably the former because of the prophet Isaiah's part in it. Whichever, it doesn't matter because the point of the psalm is that our eternal security does not rest in any earthly city, but culminates in the new earth, the Holy City, the New Jerusalem, coming down from God out of heaven! (Revelation 21:1-2)

In order for us to better examine its contents, Psalm 46 can be organized into three segments, as follows: 1) God Is Our Refuge and Strength, Verses 1-3; 2) When God Speaks, the Earth Melts, Verses 4-6; and A Future Look with the LORD, Verses 7-11.

### Segment One – God Is Our Refuge and Strength. Verses 1 - 3

The Psalmist begins by describing God as His peoples' refuge and strength. *(V.1)* A refuge is a place where we can be held safe from the tumultuous storms of life. The word "refuge" *("Mahseh")* is one of the definitive words in the book of psalms, especially in the first half. It occurs 24 times in the first 72 psalms. To take refuge in God is to trust Him, which is another key theme in the psalms. He is a safe-haven worthy of trust! We need not fear *(V. 2)* because God is the omnipotent ruler of the world!

The author has made one of the finest expressions of how God watches over and directs our destiny even when the oceans roar and mountains crumble. *(V.3)* He gives us strength not only for the present by His omnipotent control of history and His oversight in the affairs of this life, but also He has the last word over evil. He is able to work out things for our good when we love Him and are fitting into His plans. For our good, for those of us who put our trust in God's Son Jesus, will ultimately mean that we will be with Him in heaven for all eternity!

One of the great leaders of the Christian faith was a Roman Catholic priest of German origin named Martin Luther. An ardent student of the psalms, Psalm 46 was one of his favorites. One of the hymns for which we remember him is entitled, "A Mighty Fortress Is Our God," which is Luther's version of this psalm. Like us, Martin Luther read the psalms from a Christian perspective.

### Segment Two – When God Speaks, the Earth Melts. Verses 4 - 6

When King David captured Jerusalem and brought the ark of the covenant there, the city became both the political and religious capital of Israel. Then when King Solomon built the Temple, Jerusalem soon became known as the holy city. You have to know there wasn't an actual river in the city. The writer of Psalm 46 was being metaphorical when he speaks of a river in the city. *(V.4)* Perhaps he is borrowing from the likes of Isaiah when he writes tht the LORD is a wide river of protection. *(Isaiah 33:21)*

At perhaps the time this psalm was written, the Psalmist felt that God lived in Jerusalm and the city could not be destoryed. *(V.5)* Despite kingdoms crumbling and the world blowing up *(V.6)*, God is with us. We are secure! With a word from God the earth can melt in submission. *(V.6)* The mighty God makes His will known and those who oppose His plans and purpose for the world will be put down.

### Segment Three – A Future Look with the LORD. Verses 7 - 11

The final segment of Psalm 46 looks to the future with a sense of conviction and assurance so that the future appears to be present. Incorporating this kind of faith in our lives allows us to hold our head high and meet whatever comes our way with courage and optimism! After all, the omnipotent God who controls heaven and earth is with us and rescues us from all our enemies.

*(V.7)* This is the essence of the refrain found in verses 7 and 11 (and perhaps should have been placed after verse 3).

The Hebrew Prophets all looked forward to a Day in the future when all the nations of the world would look to Mount Zion and all its people would make pilgrimages to Jerusalem. In the last days, the Lord will rule the whole world from Jerusalem. They believed that He would issue His laws and announce His decrees from the holy city. He would arbitrate among the nations and because of Him they would beat their swords into plowshares and their spears into pruning hooks: nations shall no longer fight each other, for all wars will cease and there will be universal peace. Everyone will live quietly in his own home in peace and prosperity, for there will be nothing to fear. The prophets tell us that God Himself has promised this. (See Joel 4:1-4; Isaiah 2:2-4.)

Psalm 46 says that God will end wars of destruction *(V.8)* throughout the earth. *(V.9)* We Christians look forward to that time when nations will lay down their weapons and wars will become a thing of the past. God is saying to us through this psalm to be silent in His presence out of reverence for Him, and do our bit to make peace happen. *(V.10)* The Psalmist ends with a reminder that the LORD is here among us, our fortress. *(V.11)*

We Christians don't see Jerusalem as God's exclusive dwelling place. His Holy Spirit is everywhere present. It is our conviction that God has sent His Son, Jesus, to come into our world to save sinners. Jesus was a Jew and lived in Palestine as the Apostle John tells us in his Gospel. *(John 1:14)* Jesus calls us to make a decision to follow Him. When John the Baptist was arrested by King Herod, Jesus began preaching God's Good News. *(Mark 1:15)* Jesus is calling each of us to join Him and enter God's reign and find our ultimate security in God, rather than in self. The fundamental message of Psalm 46 is that God's truth abideth and his kingdom is forever.

# PSALM 47

## A Great King Over All the Earth

Once a year, the Hebrew king would make a dramatic reconfirmation of his kingship in the Temple in Jerusalem. It would be a colorful celebration. It was a reminder to the king that he was a human and the LORD's anointed. It also reminded the people that God was the real king of all nations and was ruler not only over all peoples but over the forces of nature as well. Thus took place a cultic drama – a re-enactment of the story of man's salvation, put on before the assembled congregation.

The priest would begin the liturgy by inviting those gathered to clap their hands and shout to God with a joyful praise song. Maybe another priest would tell the story of God's saving acts (escape from Egypt, Moses receiving the law, the manna in the wilderness, etc.).

The drama would follow Psalm 46, which speaks of turning foreign armies away from Jerusalem. Psalm 47 celebrates the same deliverance. Psalms 46, 47, and 48 all deal with God's protection of Jerusalem and they are called Psalms of Zion. Four other psalms are in this same category: 76, 84, 87, and 122.

Eventually, the king would lead the people to where he would ascend his throne amidst the sound of a ram's horn! This was an acted-out sermon that allowed the people to participate in the ascension of God!

### Segment One – God Is the Great King. Verses 1 - 6

Verse 1 begins with the priest's invitation that the people shout to God and clap their hands in joy that He is their King. We must acknowledge that not all of the people of the world see God as their ruler. But we believers are convicted of that. (V.2) In 1934 the English historian Arnold Toynbee began a monumental study of the history of the world. For the next 27 years (until 1961), he worked on his project, filling 12 massive volumes. In his study, he isolated 32 individual civilizations. Each of these took their place in history for a while and then passed away. Egypt, for instance, was once a world power, but not so today. Babylon was another power that was mighty, but her territory has been divided, and even the discovery of oil has not restored her to a dominant world power. Two other former world powers were Greece and Rome. In our lifetime, we have seen the Soviet Union fall apart. Even America, though still a world power, has begun to decline. Our country has not been able to escape the law of history. *(Proverbs 14:34)*

When nations are in the ascendancy, they think that they control their own destiny. But you know what? It is <u>God</u> <u>who</u> <u>controls!</u> *(V.2)* Our great God who is King requires righteousness, so when a nation goes its own way and acts arrogantly, God has a way of bringing them down. We don't have to have Arnold Toynbee tell us this because it is all written down in the Scriptures.

The Book of Daniel, for instance, made this very point. God humbled King Nebuchadrezzar who became insane and incapable of functioning. He had a son named Belshazzar. He gave a party and used the vessels that had been taken from the destroyed Jerusalem Temple. In the middle of the party, a finger of a heavenly hand appeared and Balshazzar and his guests were frightened. The finger produced writing that said, *"Mine, mine, tekel, parsin."* Nobody knew what it meant and so Daniel was called upon to interpret. "What does this mean?" the king asked. Daniel said that the Most High God says your days are "numbered," "weighted" and "found wanted." He said that your father's heart was hardened with pride. He was therefore driven from his throne and given the mind of an animal. But you, Balshazzar have not humbled yourself, though you knew all this. That very night the city was overthrown and Balshazzar was killed. Darius the Mede had taken over Babylon. *(Daniel 5:1-31)*

It is significant that Daniel used the words "Most High God." These are the same words that Psalm 47 uses in verse 2. The Kingdoms of this world rise and fall, but reigning over them and determining their course and their end stands the Most High God, the LORD of history! In verse 3, the Psalmist says that God subdues nations and crushes enemies. *(V.4)* Psalm 47 verse 4 also refers to the conquest of the land of Canaan under Joshua— God. In verse 5, most scholars see the shouts with sounding trumpets as the time when David brought the Ark of God back to Jerusalem. Verse 6 is the invitation to sing praises to God for his deliverance.

## Segment Two — God Reigns Over the Nations. Verses 7 - 9

Verses 7 and 8 repeat what the author said back in verse 2, that God reigns over all nations. Then in verse 9 he tells us that all of the non-Jewish rulers of the world joined the Jews in praising the God of Abraham. It is interesting that for a long time the Jewish leaders felt that God's kingdom was exclusively for them alone, but in reading this psalm we can see a gradual broadening of outlook. It has not yet happened, but it is just a matter of time before Jesus the Messiah will be praised throughout the world. *(V.9)*

Paul, the great Jewish interpreter, put some qualifiers in his magnificent Roman letter. He writes that Jesus' salvation is a free gift to all those who have the faith of Abraham. *(Romans 4:16)* God accepted and approved Abraham because of his faith. God the great King of the earth will accept us in the same way He accepted Abraham, when we believe the promises of God, who raised Jesus from the dead. The Good News is that Jesus died for our sins and rose again to make us right with God. Being blessed by God in this wonderful way should motivate us to share the Gospel with those we meet. With the help of the Holy Spirit, multitudes might give their lives to Jesus and become part of His Kingdom! All of us Christians need to pray that God's kingdom comes soon. *(Matthew 6:9-10)*

It is important for us to read the psalms through the eyes of the Christian faith. Through Christ Jesus we know there is just one way to heaven, it is a narrow gate. The roadways to hell are broad. Few will find it, especially on their own. *(Matthew 7:13-14)* With regard to the nations of the world, there are only two ways God deals with them: the way of God's grace in Christ Jesus; or the way of God's anger and wrath! We see this in the Book of Revelation. The author John of Patmos knew the psalms and they are reflected in his great vision of the future. The Jesus in the future is a judge with eyes bright like flames. The sharp sword of his mouth strikes down nations. *(Revelation 19:11-16)*

141

# PSALM 48
## Jerusalem, the Religious Center of Israel

Psalm 48 is a poem attributed to one of the descendants of Korah. It is a celebration of the City of Jerusalem as the center of Judaism and is, therefore, called A Song of Zion. This is one of several such psalms. The others are 76, 84, 87, and 122. Psalm 48 has some affinity with Psalm 46. The prevailing thought of the Jews of that day was that God's abiding place was connected somehow with the Ark of the Covenant. Since the Ark was located in the Holy of Holies in the Temple, this made Jerusalem the religious center of Israel. It meant that Jews from all over the world would want to make pilgrimages to attend various sacred festivals that were regularly held in the Holy City. Many of the Songs of Zion, besides being part of the Temple ritual, were often sung by the pilgrims as they made their way to Jerusalem from the hinterlands.

### Segment One – A Glorious Sight. Verses 1 - 2

It is quite appropriate to find the first word written about God is His greatness, and how much the people should praise Him! *(V.1)* Without God, the city of Jerusalem would be just another city. It is true that as the pilgrims approached the city from the north, west, and east it is uphill and breathtaking. Quite a beautiful sight! It is actually twenty-five hundred feet above sea-level. Our author exclaims it is fantastic. *(V.2)* He gets a little carried away and boasts everyone in the world rejoices when they see it. *(V.2)*

### Segment Two – God Defends Jerusalem. Verses 3 - 8

Verse 3 tells us that God is Jerusalem's protector and defender. This is one of the reasons why this psalm is linked to Psalm 46, with its recounting the deliverance from the invading armies of King Sennacherib when Hezekiah was the reigning monarch. (See Second Kings 18-19.) In the next three verses (4-6) there are some more generalized exaggerations, for example when the Psalmist says all the kings of the earth joined to attack the city (V.4), but once they actually saw it they became terrified and ran away. (V.6) The Psalmist compares God's mightiness to the awesome warships of Tarshish being shattered by powerful storms. (V.7) The Psalmist recalls how he had heard how magnificient the city was but now that he sees it he undestands why it is called the city of the LORD Almighty. (V.8) For a pilgrimming Jew seeing the city for the first time must have been a wonderfully exciting and uplifting spiritual experience.

## Segment Three – Jerusalem Is a Magnificent Place. Verses 9 - 14

The Pilgrims worshiped and praised God because of His covenant love for them, His ("Checed"). While in the Temple, they also heard the story of how God's name and His reputation will be praised throughout the world. (V.9-10) This is the story they will tell when they return home after their visit to Jerusalem. The Pslamist now becomes somewhat contemplative and says it is important to remember that God's judgments are just. (V.11) This implies that those who keep the LORD's covenant will be treated fairly. The pilgrims are then urged to tour the city in order to see all of its lovely sights so that they can tell their children who will be able to share it with generations. (V.12-13) The Psalmist begins his composition with a positive expression of praise for the LORD, and he ends in the same way. (V.14)

There are some pluses and minuses that we Christians have to deal with as we read this psalm. The minuses have to do with provincial beliefs that the everlasting God can be domesticated and tied to a specific locale, like Jerusalem. His Holy Spirit is there in the hearts of Jewish believers, yes, but He is too big a God to be there exclusively!

Actually, not all psalm writers picture Yahweh God (the LORD) as tied exclusively to Jerusalem and the Temple. In Psalm 139, for an example, the author sees God as all-knowing and everywhere present. It says God is not only in heaven but in the pit with the dead. (Psalm 139:8) Out among the furtherest oceans God is there to guide those who love Him. (Psalm 139:9-10) The Psalmist of Psalm 139 says those who believe in this kind of God can never be lost from His Spirit. (Psalm 139:7)

Another minus of Psalm 48, from our Christian perspective, is the implication found in verse 14 that says that God will only guide us up to the point of our death. At the very heart of Christianity is the conviction that God so loved us that He sent His Son, Jesus, to die for our sins – and this awesome sacrifice opened the way to ever-lasting life for us! It's very clear that if we bring Jesus into our lives, we won't perish but we'll have eternal life (see John 3:16).

God guided the hand of the great Prophet Isaiah as he looked into the future and envisioned a new Jerusalem where people can dwell with God and be guided by Him. Isaiah's prophetic words, as he speaks for God, says that in the future the LORD will create new heavens and a new earth. And it will be a source of joy for all His people. *(Isaiah 65:17-19)* Isaiah was right! We Christians have the assurance that when we die we will go to be with God and Jesus in the New Earth. The Apostle John tells us that a new Jerusalem will come down from heaven to be our new home, and God will live among us. *(Revelation 21:2-4)* This is a big plus! We can read Psalm 48 as a springboard and dive into the praising of God and see the earthly city of Jerusalem as a prototype of the New Jerusalem in heaven.

Because we are finite people, we cannot order the infinite God to be exclusively in a particular city of our residence (as Psalm 48 does for Jerusalem). We pray that God will guide our churches, but we cannot order Him to take up residency there. However, there is a big plus because we can say something more exciting. God can indwell us through the Spirit of Jesus. Before He went to the cross, He spoke to His disciples, telling them that He is the only way to the Father. *(John 14:6)* He said He would ask God to send us another Comforter, the Holy Spirit, who will never leave us. *(John 14:17-18)* One of His disciples asked Jesus why He would reveal Himself only to His disciples and not to the world at large. Jesus replied that all who love him will live with him and His Father. *(John 14:23-24)* The exciting part is that the Holy Spirit, the Spirit of Jesus, can indwell each of us believers giving us special capacities for doing ministries and seeing the challenges of the world through the eyes of the Lord! We can't order God to dwell in our churches, but we can bring God's Holy Spirit (the Spirit of Jesus living in us) into our churches! Halleluiah!

# PSALM 49

## The Foolishness of Trusting in Material Wealth

This is a wisdom psalm written by one of the Levites from the Temple related to Korah. Its thesis is that trusting in riches cannot save a person from death. Its purpose is not to denounce the rich, but to instruct and comfort the faithful.

Reading Psalm 49 provides a good background for studying Jesus' "Parable of The Rich Fool" found in the Gospel of Luke. Jesus told a story of a rich man who had a fertile farm that produced a bumper crop. In fact, one year his barns were full to overflowing, and he said he would build bigger barns so he'd have room enough to store extra crops. Then he would have enough stored away for years to come and he could sit back and take it easy and eat, drink, and be merry! But God said to him this night you will die. After telling this parable, Jesus said that in life it is best to build a rich relationship with God. *(Luke 12:20-21)*

### Segment One – The Psalmist's Introduction. Verses 1 - 4

Like the Roman Catholic Pope who speaks to the world from the balcony of St. Peter's Cathedral in Rome, our author begins Psalm 49 by calling on all those how live in the world. *(V.1)* All need to listen, whatever their station in life. *(V.2)* He has something really important to say, and his words are full of wisdom.

### Segment Two – Trusting in Wealth Is Foolishness. Verses 5 - 9

People who value their possessions and give them first place in their lives, as if they were gods, are like folks who act like they have divine power. They feel they can do whatever they want. *(V.6)* However, the Psalmist tells us that no matter how much money they have, they cannot keep themselves from dying. *(V.7)* God is eternal and cannot be manipulated, bribed, or controlled by human beings because God is the Creator and we human beings are His creatures! Verses 8 and 9 say that money will not keep them from the grave. Biblical language scholar, Eugene Peterson, says that in the original Hebrew language the psalms are not genteel. He says they are earthy and rough. English translations miss something vital. So back in 1994, he published a paraphrase of the psalms. I recommend that you read his translaton as well as *The New Living Translation.* The Hebrew word for "the grave" is *("Shachath")* and can be translated as "corruption," "destruction," "the pit," and /or Peterson's "Black Hole."

### Segment Three – The Inescapability of Death. Verses 10 - 13

The obvious statement is that we all must die. What wealth we might accumulate while alive will have to go to others when we die. *(V.10)* The Psalmist says that, in this sense, we human beings are no different from animals. *(V.12)* Human beings – despite their riches--will not long endure. This, of course, is a recurring theme in ancient literature. To live without understanding is to live like animals! To fail to comprehend the brevity of days allotted to us and not prepare for eternity is foolishness. An "INTERLUDE" is now injected in the text. *(V.13)* Generally the "INTERLUDE" was there to remind the reader (or listener) to think about what had just been said.

### Segment Four – Comparing Trust in God with Trust in Riches. Verses 14 - 15

In this segment, "death" becomes "the Shepherd" who leads the sheep – that is, those who think pleasure is the main objective in life – to their true home *("Sh'ol")* the pit. *(V.14)* After making this strong statement, our author goes personal and says that his own life will be redeemed by God. He will escape the pit. *(V.15)* He (or some editor) puts another "INTERLUDE" after verse 15 telling us readers to stop reading and meditate on this incredible faith statement!

The Old Testament doesn't generally speak about the afterlife; rather it concentrates on this life on earth. There are just a few exceptions in the psalms. David, in Psalm 16, says God will not leave his soul in the pit. That he will live in the presence of God forever. *(V.10-11)*

## Segment Five — An Appeal to Be Wise. Verses 16 - 20

Verse 16 says we are not to become over-awed when a person obtains a great deal of wealth. Why? Because the grave makes so all equal. *(V.17)* This section just reemphasizes what the Psalmist says in Segment Two *(V.5-9)*. In verse 18, the Psalmist acknowledges that many wealthy hedonists, due to their glamorous lifestyles, are loudly applauded by their contemporaries. But while this may sustain them emotionally, it is a poor substitute for having an abiding relationship with the Almighty.

Regardless of how much worldly goods we have accumulated, we Christians need to know that we are right with God. This is made possible by our trusting in Jesus as our Lord and Savior. When we have Jesus in our hearts, we know without a doubt that we will go to heaven when we die.

# PSALM 50

## Righteousness Demanded!

Psalm 50 is a judgment psalm in the tradition of the Old Testament prophets. The author, Asaph, is a priest in charge of the music in the Temple. One scholar characterized him as a stern moralist who taught as he sang. At the beginning of this psalm, Asaph takes us back to Exodus 19 where God descended on Mount Sinai and gave the law to Moses and his people. *(Exodus 19:17-19)* Asaph took these words in Exodus and transposed them with Jehovah God (the LORD) speaking judgment from Mount Zion in Jerusalem to the Jewish people in Asaph's day.

This psalm of 23 verses can be examined in four divisions in which the LORD is holding court and where He is both the plaintiff and the presiding judge. Part One – The Court Is Convened, Verses 1-6; Part Two – God's Testimony about Sacrifices," Verses 7-15; Part three – God's Charges Against the Wicked, Verses 16-21; and Part Four – Warnings and Promises, Verses 22-23.

### Segment One – The Court Is Convened. Verses 1 - 6

The Psalmist, speaking for the LORD, is calling for judgment not just against the Jews but all people worldwide. *(V.1)* The writer envisions God appearing amid smoke, fire and lightning (although he describes the LORD's appearance in less detail than the Exodus account does). *(V.2-3)* He announces that God will be fair in His judgments as He assesses the promises made by His people. *(V.4-5)*

The main focus of the Psalmist's ranting is upon God's covenant people and how they have used (or abused) the sacrificial system that God Himself gave Israel (see Leviticus 1:1-13). The essence of the problem back then had

148

to do with these less than faithful people. *(V.5)* Their problem was that they only outwardly kept their part of the covenant. When they had committed a sin, they were obligated to bring an animal (a bull or goat) to the Temple to have their sin forgiven. There a priest would slaughter the animal in place of the sinner. The sacrificed animal would take the punishment due to the sinner. Theologically, this procedure would make atonement for the sinner's guilt. God would then judge whether the guilty person who received forgiveness was totally sincere in seeking forgiveness. *(V.6)*

### Segment Two – God's Testimony about Sacrifices. Verses 7 - 15

In this segment, God lists His charges against His chosen people. *(V.7)* It is not the regularity of their sacrifices that is causing Him concern. *(V.8)* They are not doing Him any favors by having the blood of slain animals poured on the altars. *(V.9-10)* He doesn't need anything because every living creature on the face of the earth is His already. *(V.12)* What God wants is for His people to have a proper spiritual attitude. *(V.14)* The Prophet Amos, speaking as God's apponted prophet, voiced these same concerns—a sacrificing heart of the people is needed not just a priestly sacrifice of an animal. *(Amos 5:21-24)*

What the God of Psalm 50 wants is a true feeling of thankfulness that comes when people put their total faith in the LORD. An attitude of trust where worshipers know that Yahweh (the LORD) is walking close beside them and this gives them the security that allows them to give God true glory! *(V.15)*

### Segment Three – God's Charges Against the Wicked. Verses 16 - 21

In this section, Asaph is not talking to non-Jews (the heathen). No, he is talking to His people, those who have become evil. *(V.16)* They are the ones who come to the Temple and recite God's laws and claim God's covenant promises, but in their daily living they do whatever pleases them while ignoring the disciplines they supposedly espouse. Asaph says, they treat God's laws like trash. *(V.17)* These folk hob nob with other evil and immoral persons, they curse and use vile language. *(V.18-20)* These are the same people the Prophet Hosea railed against even adding that God's complaint is also with the priests. *(Hosea 4:1-4)*

Because God let these hypocrites get away with their wickedness for awhile, it seemed to them that God did not care. But the Psalmist is saying that God does care. God is a moral God. The Psalmist declares that God is using this psalm to make charges against the Jewish people. (V.21)

## Segment Four – Warnings and Promises. Verses 22 - 23

Speaking for God, the Psalmist calls on the people of Asaph's day to repent or God will tear them to pieces. (V.22) These ominous words sound very much like the Prophet Isaiah's prouncement in his first chapter where he accuses Israel's rulers and people of acting like the evil people of Sodom and Gomorrah. Like Asaph, Isaiah also informs the people that God is sick of sacrifices that are merely perfunctory. (Isaiah 1:10-17)

Asaph's second pronouncement is that God seeks the sacrifice of thanks. That indeed would honor God. (V.23) God is saying through Asaph that what He wants from His people are lives that have compassion for the widows and orphans, the victims of those who have been oppressed by the wicked in society. He wants his people to be grateful for all the blessings God has bestowed. God wants His people to honor Him by keeping the covenant He made with them (see Exodus 19:5-6). Keeping the covenant means obeying the Ten Commandments and the Law of Moses. The Psalm ends by God promising He will reveal to them His salvation. The Hebrew word for "salvation" is ("Yesha"). It also means "prosperity" and "deliverance." God is a God of second chances and He is promising that if His covenant people will repent and keep to His path, He will deliver them.

We Christians can read this ancient Psalm with appreciation. Its truth is applicable for all times. Asaph is right. The correct approach to God is embodied in thankfulness and honor. We Christians are especially thankful for what God has done for us in creating a wonderful world and giving us minds that can solve problems and hearts that can appreciate beauty. Most of all, we are exceedingly thankful for God's love and for sending His Son Jesus to be our Savior and Lord.

Psalm 50 is correct in saying God doesn't need us. But, oh how much we need Him! What God wants from us is our true thanks. He wants us to trust Him. We Christians have done that by bringing Jesus into our lives.

Then when God sees into the inner recesses of our souls, He doesn't see our finiteness and our sinfulness, He sees Jesus who is pure and righteous. We can rejoice with the Apostle Paul in his words to Timothy that, though Paul hunted down Christians and did them harm, God in His mercy not only forgave him but filled him with faith in Jesus Christ. *(Timothy 1:12-14)*

# PSALM 51
## A Cry for Mercy

David was extremely talented and competent, but also very complex with many contradictions. One writer classified him as a saint, lover and rogue. His successes were numerous, but his bad decisions caused him many a sleepless night! He was, however, totally committed to God. When he erred, he always turned to the LORD in repentance. Psalm 51 is a prime example. The title of this composition states that this is a psalm of David when the Prophet Nathan accused him of committing adultery with Bathsheba. (See 2 Samuel 11-12.) Not mentioned in the superscription is the fact that David also had Bathsheba's husband, Uriah, killed in an attempt to cover up his adultery.

Psalm 51 is one of the penitential psalms where David stood before the mirror of his soul and saw himself in dire need of forgiveness and cleansing. The problem back then was that the sacrificial system would allow every sin to be atoned for except two: 1) murder; and 2) rape. It was these sins that Nathan the prophet brought home to David in using the parable of the little ewe lamb (2 Samuel 12:2 – 15). David, man anointed by God and sweet Psalmist of Israel, found himself outside the realm God had chosen to grant forgiveness. David had literally divorced himself from God by refusing to abide by God's "covenant love" ("Checed") and thinking, because he was a king. he could run his own life better than God. He listened to Nathan's parable of how the rich man took the poor man's lamb and killed it to feed his guests. He was furious and said a man that does this should die. (2 Samuel 12:5) Nathan pointed his finger at David and said King David was that man. (2 Samuel 12:7) The Prophet Nathan was then very specific pointing out that David killed Uriah and stole his wife. (2 Samuel 12:9)) There was nothing left for David to do but throw himself upon the mercy of God!

### Segment One – David's Confession. Verses 1 - 2

There is no pretense here. David's sin is like a bright, blazing sun that blots out everything else from his consciousness. His words are honest and sincere. He ask God to have mercy on him because of God's "unfailing love." *(V.1)* "Love" *("Checed")* is a covenant word and God is love (I John 4:8). Then David goes deeper by asking God to have "compassion" on him and blot out his sins. *(V.1-2)* "Compassion" *("racham")* is a Hebrew word derived from "the womb." David is appealing to God's mother love.

### Segment Two – David's Offense Was Against God. Verses 3 - 6

David's offense against God was so all consuming in his mind that he ignores what his sin did to Bathsheba and her husband – and even to the people he governs, who eventually would suffer for his actions. He rightly says that his sin was against God alone. *(V.4)* Technically, he didn't commit a crime by his own hand, but he acknowledged that by his lust, his treachery and intrigues of having Uriah killed, he was personally guilty of breaking God's laws. In his heart David knows that he isn't fooling God because He is all-knowing, *(V.4)*, i. e., I have willfully broken the covenant. In Verse 5, David recognizes that everyone sins, so he looks back and, in effect, says all are sinners because sinful parents pass onto their children the potential for evil, brought about by self-centeredness. The act of sex is not sinful. When God is involved with a man and a woman, they together can do what God does – be creators. In Verse 6, David's suffering leads him to an insight – that more than anything God <u>wants us to be</u> <u>authentic</u>.

### Segment Three – Make Me Clean Again. Verses 7 - 11

In this segment, David is referring to the sacrificial system that was practiced in his day. He is asking God to do to him what the priests in the Tent of Meeting do to sinners who need cleansing. They put the blood from a sacrificed animal on the altar on behalf of the person seeking renewal. He is saying to God that he feels morally dirty, so wash away the filth of my guilty conscience. *(V.7,9)* There is no joy when unforgiven sin is sitting heavily on our shoulders. *(V.8)* I am a broken man and yes, I deserve it. I feel punished – then erase my sins and clean up my heart. *(V.10)*

David knows that there is always a cost involved in being cleansed. He begs God not to banish him from God's presence. *(V.11)* Forgiveness is actually <u>re</u>-creation by God, the giving of a new personality dedicated to righteousness. We Christians come to God with the coverage of Christ's indwelling Spirit, who is able to intercede for us. It was Jesus' once-for-all sacrifice on the cross that made it possible to get right with God. We can never take this gift lightly.

David begs God not to take God's Holy Spirit from him. *(V.11)* He would have to go to the altar and sacrifice an innocent animal (a bull maybe) to have it die in his place and have its blood cover his sin. David's confession of his sinful heart means he knows if he didn't have the power of God within (His Holy Spirit), he would undoubtedly sin again. We Christians know what David was talking about. Because of Jesus Christ's sacrifice on behalf of us sinners, God has shown us a different way of being right in His sight – not by obeying the Law but by the way promised in the Scriptures long ago. We are made right in God's sight when we trust Jesus Christ to take away our sins. We all can be saved (cleansed) in the same way, no matter who we are or what we have done. For God sent Jesus to take the punishment for our sins and to satisfy God's anger against us (for our rebellion). We are made right with God when we believe that Jesus shed His blood, sacrificing His life for us (Romans 3:21-25). So, in addition to seeking forgiveness, David needed God to give him a brand new personality. *(V.11)* This is what we Christians call "second birth." We are reborn with a new heart that can produce clean thoughts and right desires. It seems David was almost <u>bargaining</u> with God, saying if You, God, would restore me I will teach othe sinners about Your ability to save them, too.

## Segment Four – Restores the Joy of Salvation. Verses 12 - 15

Certainly in gratitude for being pardoned and being given the joy of God's salvation, David says he will worship the LORD with renewed zeal in prayer and singing. *(V.12)* In addition to being an evangelist for God in what he learned about sin and forgiveness *(V.13)*, David took up his pen and wrote another psalm on the subject Psalm 32. Like Psalm 51, it is beautifully written and just as pertinent today as when it was first written. The Apostle Paul expresses the same joy as David that sinners feel when God shows them mercy and forgives their disobedience. *(Romans 4:6-8)* In Verse 14, David is specific, he asks God to forgive him for shedding blood *('DAM').* This would permit David to have his lips unsealed in praising the LORD. *(V.15)*

## Segment Five – A Proper Sacrifice for David. Verses 16 - 17

David says God is not pleased with sacrifices unless they are accompanied with a repenant heart. *(V.16-17)* A repentant sinner must have a humble and contrite spirit. Actually, forgiveness of our sins is made possible for us Christians by Jesus <u>dying on the cross.</u> There is no forgiveness without having faith in Him. This is not new. When God promised Abraham that He would become the father of many nations, Abraham believed Him, even though this promise seemed impossible. Abraham's faith did not weaken even though he was too old to have children. Abraham never wavered in believing God's promise, in fact his faith grew stronger! This wonderful truth – God declared him to be righteous – and it wasn't just for Abraham's benefit. No, it was for us Christians too, giving us assurance that God will also declare us to be righteous if we believe in God, who brought Jesus our Lord back from the dead. The Apostle Paul explains and expounds of this Christian theology of forgivness through faith in his letter to the Romans. He specifically addresses this in Romans 5:1-2.

## Segment Six – An Added Thought. Verses 18 - 19

The original Psalm ended with Verse 17. The last two verses (18-19), which asks God to help the Jewish people rebuild the wall around Jerusalem and a new temple, obviously were added by a later editor after 520 BC when the Jews returned from exile in Babylon and were rebuilding the temple. They completed the second temple in 516 BC and rededicated the new worship center.

One final thought. Eugene H. Peterson was a pastor who felt God charged him with teaching people to pray with honesty and helping them to give voice to their experience of being human. Faced with the prospect of conversations with a Holy God who speaks words into being, it's not surprising that we have difficulties. We feel awkward and out of place. Give me a few months – or years – to practice prayers that are polished enough for such a sacred meeting. Peterson's response to those who felt unworthy in addressing a Perfect God with imperfect prayers, was to translate the 150 psalms in language that reflected the original Hebrew. (*Answering God: The Psalms as Tools for Prayer.*) A common response of those he gave his new translation was surprise at how folksy they appeared to be.

Particularly in the *King James* translation of the Bible, the psalms often sound smooth, polished and sonorous with Elizabethan rhythm and diction. As literature they are beyond compare. But as prayers, as the utterances of men and women passionate for God in moments of anger, praise and lament, these translations miss something. The psalms in Hebrew are earthy and rough. They are not genteel. They are not the prayers of nice people, couched in cultured language. In Peterson's work of teaching people to pray, he paraphrased the psalms to develop raw honesty. The type of prayer that that the very human Jesus Christ prayed more than two thousand years ago.

# PSALM 52
## Trusting in God's Unfailing Love

Not all of the psalms in the Psalter have specific historical settings. Some of them can be figured from context, and others from the headings. A number of the psalms concern incidents in the life of King David. Psalm 52 involves one of David's most upsetting experiences in his early life. This psalm by David concerns a time when Deog the Edomite informed King Saul, who wanted to kill David, that the High Priest Ahimelech had given refuge to David.

In this brief and fiery poem, David is expressing his anger with Doeg. But he then transcends his problem with Doeg to make a more general comment about those who neglect and compromise their religious obligations so they can pursue worldly power and success.

Here is the background (see I Samuel 11-23). David was a fugitive from the anger and jealousy of King Saul and, at the same time, a victim of a popular movement to make him king. After his compact of undying friendship with Jonathan, Saul's son, David has to flee to the city of Nob where he figured he'd be protected by Ahimelech, the chief priest. Ahimelech, an honest but frightened man, allowed David to eat some of the consecrated bread from the altar because he was hungry, and also gave David Goliath's sword, the giant David had killed. David then went to the city of Gath, still trying to escape from Saul's solders. However, before he left he was seen by Doeg, a man loyal to Saul. Later, Doeg returned to Saul and told him David's whereabouts.

Saul then summoned Ahimelech and put him on trial. Ahimelech protested his innocence and his loyalty to Saul claiming he did not know that David, who was the king's son in law, was allegedly conspiring against the king. King Saul's response was to order his bodyguards to kill Ahimelech and his entire family. But Saul's men refused to kill the Lord's priests. Then the king turned to Doeg and ordered him to do it. Doeg killed them, eighty-five priests in all, all still wearing their priestly tunics. Then Doeg went to Nob, the city of the priests, and killed the priests' families – men, women, children and babies, and all the cattle, donkeys, and sheep. Only Abiathar, one of the sons of Ahimelech, escaped and fled to David. Abiather told David the whole bloody tragedy. From then on David knew he was the confirmed leader of rebellion against a jealous and half-crazed king. Psalm 52 was composed by David in anger against Doeg.

### Segment One – Doeg's Evilness. Verses 1 - 4

In an angry but sarcastic manner, David begins his diatribe calling Doeg a hero who struts around convinced of his superiority and even boasts of his crime. (V.1) In verse 2, 3 and 4, David accuses Doeg of seeking to do evil more than good and liking lies more than truth. Ahimelech was a righteous man of God. By ruthlessly killing him, Doeg was currying up to Saul to gain his favor, and putting himself in the evil company of the king's deteriorating moral character.

### Segment Two – God Will Strike Him Down. Verses 5 - 7

The theme that runs throughout Scripture is that we live in a moral universe with a good God in control. Therefore, ultimately, David writes evil doers will be judged and brought down! (V.5) In verse 6 and 7, David prophecies that even the righteous will be amazed how God deals with evil people like Doeg.

### Segment Three – David's Commitment to Godliness. Verses 8 - 9

David uses an interesting figure of speech in verse 8. He compares himself to an olive tree living in God's house. The implication is he is sheltered by God, giving him adequate security. He puts his faith and trust in God's "unfailing love." (V.8) God's covenant love,– His ("Checed"), meant that David could be absolutely certain that God would uphold and guide those who were loyal to Him in worship and were doing their best to be faithful to their part of their covenant obligations. David ends Psalm 52 by saying he will be patient in awaiting God's mercies. (V.9)

We have to walk lightly here because when we see the downfall of some evil person like Doeg and we react with self-righteous delight at his demise, the implication is that we are not like him at all. We have to realize that we Christians are sinners and very vulnerable, and it is only by the grace of God that we are not in Doeg's shoes.

We must always read the psalms from the perspective of the New Testament. Of course there are many truths we can find in our reading. We agree with David that God is in control of our world and evil will be judged and righteousness will be rewarded. Believing this, David's words of trust in a merciful God is something we can agree with wholeheartedly. As we have pointed out in several of David's psalms, the word for God's "unfailing love" is ("Checed"), which alludes to God's commitment to His covenant. God will always be faithful and will deal with those of us who love Him with unfailing love and kindness. David is also correct in the ways we should respond to God's mercy. We always need to praise God (see verse 9), no matter what is happening around us, because we can't always get high enough above outward circumstances to see what God can see. We also need to trust God, as David says, forever.

This is where we Christians can go a step ahead of David because we live on the victory side of the cross, meaning we have the Good News that the Messiah has already come in Jesus Christ! By Jesus' sacrifice on the cross, our penalty for sin has been paid allowing us to know we will be with God and Jesus for all eternity! Because of this wonderful revelation, we have the courage to live victoriously in a fallen world. This gives us the faith to know that whatever happens – even like the senseless murder of the priests and their families – we can choose to live our lives committed to the path of righteousness. Yet all the while, we acknowledge we are finite mortals – meaning at times we will stumble and fall. But God's grace in Jesus will be with us and will lift us again and again.

A closing word is from Philippians in which the Apostle Paul reminds the new Christians of his day not to worry but to pray about everything and obtain the peace of knowing God will guard their hearts and minds so they can live in joy. *(Philippians 4:4-7)*

# PSALM 53
## Practical Atheism and Its Consequences

Psalm 53 can be classified as a Prophetic Liturgy. It was originally written by David as Psalm 14. Some later editor took it and, after making some minor modifications, placed it in its present position in the Psalter. It was probably a further commentary on the boastful individual who loved wickedness (Psalm 52) and the proud rich man (Psalm 49). The obvious dating of the composition is post-exilic.

### Segment One – The Results of Turning One's Back on God. Verses 1 - 5

This psalm, along with its identity twin, Psalm 14, begins by saying that the foolish say there is no God. *(V.1)* Actually, very few Old Testament individuals would make a remark that God doesn't exist. Most everyone back then acknowledged some kind of higher power created the world. What they didn't believe was that this God had anything to do with running the world. In essence, they believed He <u>was absent</u>. God not being a factor in their lives meant it gave them carte blanche to pull any kind of deal they wanted as long as it profited them. They could cheat and bend the law and do anything they could get away with – as long as it was to their own advantage (and they didn't get caught!). This is why David calls them fools! Not much has changed since he wrote Psalm 14.

The Apostle Paul read Psalm 14 and agreed with David's assessment. Writing in Romans, Paul says that everyone knows intellectually that God exists, but some choose to deny it, and they are fools. Paul writes that an awareness of God is hardwired into our DNA so there is no excuse not to be aware of Him. *(Romans 1:19-20)* Paul's magnificent exposition in Romans is something every Christian needs to read. Paul goes on in Romans to tell us God reveals Himself in nature. We can see evidence of His creation in the stars, snowflakes and flowers.

In verse 2 of Psalm 53, God looks down from heaven searching the entire human race to see if any of us are really committed to Him. The answer is not very pleasant. Verse 3 says all have foresaken God. The Apostle Paul quotes these words in Romans (Chapter 3:10). David goes on to say that people everywhere suppress the truth about God because they don't like God's moral demands! They don't like the fact that God is Sovereign – and they aren't; that God is holy, and they are not; that God is wise and they are foolish. They (we) don't want to acknowledge God because they (we) don't want to be accountable and responsible to God. Earlier in Romans, Paul explains that in not worshiping God, these foolish people begin to come up with their own ideas of what God is like. *(Romans 1:20-22)* Expanding on David's insight Paul writes that sinful people actualy push truth away from thenselves. *(Romans 1:18)* Paul goes back to Psalm 53:2 to make his point no one, without God's intervention, seeks Him. *(Romans 3:9-12)*

David in verse 4 asks whether those who do evil will ever learn. Could this mean the evildoers now are oppressing God's people? We don't know, but it may be referring to corrupt nobles, or even some foreign oppressors. Whoever they might be, verse 5 tells them to beware of God's judgment! The scattering of bones of God's enemies *(V.5)* is obviously an add-on in Psalm 53 to David's version. It was put in to emphasize the fact that God had rejected Israel (see 2 Chronicles 20).

## Segment Two – Looking to God for Restoration. Verse 6

Psalm 14, verse 7, is identical to Verse 6 in Psalm 53. Years later the Editor/Priest took David's psalm and was asking God for the same deliverances to a defeated people who had spent two generations in exile in Babylon. This tragic period of hardship and suffering, the prophets said, was because of their sin – a judgment of God. Psalm 53's main point is clearly put forth in the fool statement in verse 1 and reinforced by verse 3 in which David says all have turned away from God.

Psalm 53 is right on target to emphasize our sin (although we moderns don't like to hear this). We have repeatedly said we Christians need to read this (and all psalms) through the perspective and insights of the Christian faith. Therefore, we need to read Paul's understanding of David's words in

Psalm 14 and Psalm 53. The Holy Spirit, working through Paul, inspired him to write that given the fact that all have sinned, and no one can fulfill the law, God the Father made a provision that Jesus would be our annointment, our lasting sufficient sacrifice, and our right and righteous reconciliation with God. *(Romans 3:21-24) (Romans 3:25-26, 5:1-2)*

# PSALM 54
## Betrayal By a Friend

The inscription states that this is a psalm of David written when the men of Ziph tried to betray him to King Saul. This psalm was written in the same period of David's life described in Psalm 52. Jonathan, David's close friend, helped him escape from the clutches of Jonathan's father, King Saul, and David went to a city called Nob where he was given food and a sword by the chief priest there named Ahimelech. A wicked person named Doeg spied on David and went to Saul and told him where David was. Saul ordered Doeg to murder the chief priest and he killed eighty-five other priests, plus their wives and children!

The background of Psalm 54, according to I Samuel 23, has David and a few faithful followers getting word that the Philistines were attacking one of the small border towns named Keilah. David decided to help the inhabitants of Keilah and came to their rescue driving off the invaders. Saul got word that David was inside the walls of that town and so he marched his army there to capture him. However, David was able to slip out before Saul arrived and he went further south to the desert town of Ziph. Even in Ziph, David wasn't safe because the men of that town betrayed him and told Saul of David's whereabouts. Again he was able to escape and made his way into the wilderness. It was a day-to-day existence with very little security.

Psalm 54 is a lament. Anybody who has been betrayed by a friend will know how David must have felt. In these precarious times, David turned to God in prayer.

To help in analyzing this poem by David, we can break it up into four segments: One, Appeal for Safety, Verses 1-3; Two, God Is David's Friend,

Verse 4; Three, David Needs God's Help, Verse 5; and Four, God Will Triumph, Verses 6-7.

## Segment One – Appeal for Safety. Verses 1 - 3

David's prayer is for deliverance from strangers. He doesn't tell us specifically who these strangers are? Could they be Saul's soldiers? Doeg and his cohorts? Some of the inhabitants of Ziph called Ziphites? We don't know, but whoever they were we're told they were ruthless and had no relationship with God.

## Segment Two – God is David's Friend. Verse 4

In David's uncertainty and anxiety with enemies lurking around every corner, he turns to God to be sustained, for the LORD to be his helper. *(V.4)* David considers Yahweh to be a friend, which I believe is an appropriate description of the relationship between David and God. A friend is one who can be trusted and this is very important to someone who is running away from vicious enemies.

We Christians know God as we come to know Jesus. In Chapter 14 of John's Gospel, Jesus tells us that no one can come before the Father except through Him. *(John 14:6)* He told Apostle Thomas if he had known who He was Thomas would have known who God was. *(John 14:7)*

## Segment Three – David Needs God's Help. Verse 5

As Christians, David's prayer for God to destroy his enemies does not seem very godly. *(V.5)* It was different back then when violence and warfare seemed to be the norm. But Jesus tells us to love our enemies since they too are children of God. *(Matthew 5:44)* The Apostle Paul also knew the mind of Christ and so he tells us that we should not be vengeful toward those who do evil toward us. *(Romans 12:17)*

## Segment Four – The LORD Will Triumph. Verse 6 - 7

In gratitude, David wants to give the LORD a thank offering. *(V.6)* This is not a bribe. David was truly thankful for having the LORD as his helper and confidant. With God's presence, David had an entirely new outlook on what was happening in his life. His praise for God came as naturally as it was for him to pick up his harp and sing! Verse 7 is a good way to pray. It's like thanking God in advance for that which we are praying. God may have rescued David spiritually (in his mind), but his troubles and his enemies continued to plague him all his life.

# PSALM 55
## Wings Like a Dove to Fly Away and Rest!

This is a long prayer-poem for help by David. It contains a variety of features and can be classified as a lament, complaint and petition. It is titled a "Maskil," which means a "meditation." This is one of three psalms by David having to do with betrayal by a group or person (52, 54, and 55).

One commentator suggested a three-part outline for Psalm 55: Fear, Verses 1-8; Fury, Verses 9-15; and Faith, Verses 16-23. A more helpful way to examine it is this way: One, David's Upset, Verses 1-8; Two, Dishonesty in the City, Verses 10-11; Three, Betrayed by a Close Friend, Verses 12-14; Four, Cut Them Down, God, Verse 15; Five, God Will Rescue Me, Verses 16-19; Six, A Second Look at My Wicked Friend, Verses 20-21; and Seven, God Will Help, Verses 22-23.

### Segment One – David's Upset. Verses 1 - 8

David, in his usual direct manner in speaking to God of the universe, cries out to God to pay attention to his dire situation. *(V.1-2)* Enemies are theatening him. *(V.3)* David is beside himself! He is feeling devastated and is concerned for his very life. *(V.4-5)* With his back up against a wall, he thinks about an escape, wishing he had wings of a dove to fly off and escape his enemies. *(V.6)* Wouldn't it be wonderful, he muses, to fly away to some place of shelter – far away from my present anxieties? *(V.7-8)*

### Segment Two – Dishonesty in the City. Verses 9 - 11

David is enough of a realist to know he cannot just fly away. So he turns his thoughts to the city and visualizes the wicked prowling around creating havoc and upset. In verse 9, David ask the Lord to destroy his enemies. Back in verse 3, he speaks of his enemies and you'd think he was referring to the Philistines or one of the other hostile enemy nations that were constantly fighting with the Hebrews. But no! In verses 10 -11, he points out his enemies are from his own people and city. So he prays that God will cause them to have internal dissention so that they'll be destroyed in their own strife and confusion.

## Segment Three – Betrayed by a Close Friend. Verses 12 - 14

Now it comes out! His friend is part of the general evil that is upsetting him. A close friend has let him down! This is at the bases of his agony. It's not obvious who this friend is. David doesn't bother to tell us. He just says he was a close friend and companion. *(V.13-14))* This person (or persons) once worshiped with him in God's House. It is true that the greatest emotional pain can be inflicted by those most close to us.

It is fruitless to wonder who this might be. Ahithophel, David's time-trusted advisor, betrayed David when his son, Absalom, was in revolt. (See 2 Samuel 15:30-31) But this is mere speculation. We just don't know.

## Segment Four – Cut Them Down God. Verse 15

This is one of the most upsetting sentiments David expresses in this psalm. His words are hard to stomach! He is asking God to curse his betrayers and cause them to die before their time. He is essentially telling God to send them to "hell" *(Sheol)!* Morality in David's day, particularly toward one's enemies, was vicious and based on an eye-for-an-eye and a tooth-for-a-tooth kind of philosophy. By contrast, Jesus taught His followers to love their enemies. *(Matthew 5:44)*

## Segment Five – God Will Rescue Me. Verses 16 - 19

It is both wonderful and frightening how David can call on God to damn those who betray him and then, with seeming nonchalance, invite the LORD to come into his life *(V.16)* A long history of personal faith gives David confidence, and so he is confident his voice is heard by the LORD. *(V.17,19)* Although we Christians don't want to emulate David in certain aspects of his morality, particularly toward his enemies, we do admire his perseverance and his total reliance on God's grace.

## Segment Six – A Second Look at My Wicked Friend. Verses 20 - 21

David takes another look at the friend (s) who betrayed him. Earlier he is sorely pained by what happened, but now – having gone to God-- he is assured that the LORD is with him and his tensions are somewhat eased but still is aware of the deceitfulness of his friend (s). (V.20-21) It is important to remind ourselves that we live in a fallen world so it should not be too much of a shock to see sin in others. Little people fudge on their income tax, while Wall Street bankers manipulate the stock market and make millions.

## Segment Seven – God Will Help. Verses 22 - 23

In our determination to be godly followers of the Lord Jesus Christ, we need to stay close to God and bring the Spirit of Jesus in our lives. This will help us stay on the straight and narrow path. In verse 22 David tells us to put our burdens on the LORD. But then he ends the psalm reminding God to send his enemies to hell. (V.23)

The Apostle Peter picked up this wonderful verse 22 and quotes it in his first letter. Peter, the Big Fisherman, was a huge worrier in his early days. However, as he matured and got closer to the Lord, he counseled us Christians to go to Jesus and put our burdens on Him. (1 Peter 15:7) Giving our burdens to the Lord enables us not to run away from serious problems, but stand tall and do what God has assigned us to do.

The Apostle Paul in First Corinthians, the tenth chapter, reminds us that temptations come to everyone in life. But God is faithful. If we are faithful, He will not allow us to be tempted beyond what we can endure. (1 Corinthinians 10:13) This is the New Testament equivalent of verse 22 in Psalm 55, which says God will not permit the godly to slip and fall. The Lord will sustain us so that we might be able to live a righteous life. We Christians put our faith in Jesus and know absolutely that our salvation is secure!

# PSALM 56

## Running from Danger

This is a prayer-poem written by David. The title says the poem concerns the time when David was seized by the Philistines in Gath. David wrote this psalm shortly after his escape from the Philistines in their city of Gath. David was a young man, probably in his early 20's. Remember he had been anointed king by the Prophet Samuel, but couldn't take office because Saul was still king of Israel. Because of David's rising popularity after slaying the Philistine giant, Goliath, Saul became insanely jealous of David and set out to kill him. David spent the next twelve years of his life running away from Saul and his soldiers.

Psalm 52 picks up the story by telling us David goes to a town named Nob, where a group of priests lived. David was alone, hungry and unarmed. Ahimelech, the chief priest, befriends David, giving him Goliath's sword and some consecrated bread. One of Saul's spies, a man named Doeg, happens to be in Nob at the same time as David. Doeg went to Saul and told him what he saw and this led to the murdering of Ahimelech and eighty-five other priests and their families by Doeg.

Still running from Saul's soldiers, David goes to the fortified Philistine city of Gath, the home of the slain hero, Goliath. David thought he'd hide there but was recognized. His plight was from the frying pan into the fire! The Philistines wanted to kill him, but again he manages to escape and goes deeper into the wilderness and ends up in a cave at Adullam. It was there where he probably wrote Psalm 56. Much of the above was obtained from I Samuel 21 and 22.

### Segment One – An Appeal to God's Grace. Verses 1 - 4

David asks the mighty God of the universe to be merciful to him, that is, for God to stoop down in kindness and intervene on his behalf. *(V.1)* He feels hemmed in by overwhelming and superior military forces. *(V.2)* He confesses times of fear and some panic, but when he feels fearful he turns to God and experiences strengthening – giving him the courage and confidence he otherwise wouldn't have. *(V.3)* And in the shelter of God's presence, he proclaims he does not fear mere mortals because he trusts in God. *(V.4)* The last verse, together with verse 11, is the theme of Psalm 56. A similar refrain is quoted in Psalm 118:6 and in Hebrews 13:6.

### Segment Two – David's Enemies Want Him Dead. Verses 5 - 7

David feels like a bull's eye in a shooting gallery where his enemies are shooting at him. He feels as if everything is stacked against him. *(V.5)* His enemies are spying on him and eager to kill him. *(V.6)* David prays for God's anger (His wrath) to throw his enemies off him. *(V.7)* One thing about the psalms is the writers tell it like it is, and they don't try and soften their feelings or dress up their language.

### Segment Three – David's Trust in the LORD. Verses 8 - 11

David believes God is all-knowing (omniscient) and so he is confident that God will keep track of all his sorrows. He says God collects all of David's tears in a bottle, and writes them in His book. *(V.8)* God has been good to David in the past. There may be some exaggeration with his words when David says that when he calls on God the enemies of David leave. *(V.9)* David reminds the LORD that he trusts His word. *(V.10)* But certainly David's successes have to be attributed to the inspiration and power of the Almighty! He then lifts his eyes to the heavens and proclaims that God is on his side. *(V.11)*

We Christians owe a big debt of thanks to the Apostle Paul for his super-abundant energies in taking the Gospel over his known world. His inspired writings, particularly the Letter to the Romans, is a brilliant gift from the Lord. It is very evident that Paul leaned heavily on David's psalms for many of his insights. Specifically, verse 9 of Psalm 56, in which David proclaims that God is on his side, is probably where Paul got his idea and inspiration for Romans 8:31 in which he says if God is for us who can be against us. In verse 11 of psalm 56 David resolves not to fear because of his trust in the LORD.

## Segment Four – David Fulfill His Vow to God. Verses 12 - 13

As David does with many of his writings, he closes his psalms with full assurance as if his triumph over his enemies already happened. For instance, he closes Psalm 54 in a similar manner, vowing to bring a sacrifice to God when He acted. This is the case here in Psalm 56. *(V.12)* He optimistically says he has been rescued from death. He is thanking God in advance which is a marvelous way to pray. Out of gratitude for God's presence and power, David will surely do what he had promised. When and if the right opportunity presents itself, and he can meet with a worshiping community, he will give a thank offering celebrating his deliverance. David's faith and trust in God's goodness and mercy gave him the confidence to walk in God's presence. *(V.13)*

Confidence comes when a person places his faith and trust in God, as David did. We Christians put our reliance in Jesus, who told us, we need to walk in His presence. *(John 8:12)* Jesus brings His living light to those of us who put our trust in Him. When we invite His abiding Spirit to indwell us, He forgives our sin by giving us His own righteousness. He takes our sin with its killing judgment and covers it. Then when God judges us – as He must – all He will see will be Christ living in us, and so He declares us not guilty and accepts us. (See Romans 3:21-26.) In gratitude for being set free from sin's penalty, and the joyous anticipation of spending eternity with God and Jesus in heaven, we want to walk before the Lord in grace and mercy, to live in the light, to bear fruit, to do justice, to attempt to mend what is broken, and give mercy to our neighbors. It also means repenting from our self-absorption and self pre-occupation.

# PSALM 57
## Hiding Beneath the Shadow of God's Wings

Psalm 57 is a lament, coupled with a Hymn of Thanksgiving. The Committee of Jewish Priests-Editors who recovered and re-assembled the psalms (many years after the Babylonian captivity) put a number of psalms together that they thought were linked to that different time in David's life when he was continually running away from King Saul, who wanted David dead

Beginning with Psalm 52, we meet Doeg, the spy, who told Saul that Ahimelech, the Chief Priest, had helped David. As a result of this information, Saul ordered Ahimelech and 84 of his priests and their families to be killed. Psalm 54 continues another of David's hair-raising experiences where he narrowly escaped death because of a betrayal by his countrymen, the Ziphites. Worst of all, Psalm 56 tells of David's plight in the Philistine city of Gath. After another narrow escape, he runs into the wilderness and hides in a cave known as Adullam, which we know by the superscription of Psalm 57.

It was while hiding in the cave that his fortunes seemed to improve somewhat. His brothers and some of his father's household and others began to gather around David's leadership. Psalm 57 has a tone of being a bit more subdued.

### Segment One – David's Appeal to the God of Grace. Verses 1 - 3

David is asking for "mercy" *("Chanan")* even as he "trusted" ("Chacah") in God. Since David is hiding in the cave of Adullam, it became a refuge from the constant attacks of King Saul. The Hebrew word *("Chacah")* can be translated as "trusting," as well as "to make a refuge." Then he compares God's care for him like hiding him under the shadow of His wings until the storm passes. *(V.1)* This analogy of a little chick being protected by the mother bird is vivid and meaningful. Or maybe David was thinking of the wings of one of the golden cherubim's that adorned the Ark of the Covenant in the Holy of Holies in the Tabernacle. This is a very familiar figure of speech in the psalms. The shadow of God's wings is used in psalms 37:7; 61:4; 63:7; and 91:4.

David appeals to the "Most High God" *("Elyown")* for help. *(V.2)* This term for God means "elevated and exalted" and it was first used to describe Melchizedek, a priest and king of Salem, when he met Abram (see Genesis 14:17-24). After Abram won a battle in recapturing his nephew, Lot, Melchizedek brought bread and wine to Abram and worshiped with him and blessed him. In gratitude, Abram gave Melchizedek a tithe (a tenth) of all the goods he had recovered. Many biblical experts believe Melchizedek was Jesus in a pre-incarnational earthly appearance. They may be right.

In verse 3, David says God will send to him his His "unfailing love" (His *("Checed")* and "faithfulness"" (His *("Emeth")*. God does just not send abstract ideas or qualities. They have to be manifested in a person. We Christians see these dynamic aspects of love sent to us by God in His Son, Jesus. He came to earth and made those divine attributes live! And by faith, when we were able to bring Jesus' loving and living Spirit into our minds and hearts, then we too, will be able to experience an inner-directedness of God's love. In turn, we'll be motivated to direct this love outward – to others.

### Segment Two – Surrounded by Enemies. Verses 4 - 6

David probably felt like Daniel in the lion's den (see Daniel 6) and like Daniel, he was praying that God would shut the lion's mouths. *(V.4)* He obviously understands the seriousness of the situation. He describes his enemies as having set a trap for him. Exhausted, he sighs. But then he recalls that God is in charge, that His glory fills the earth. *(V.5)* He is encouraged and proclaims that Saul's troops who had dug a deep pit along a path will inadvertently fell into it. *(V.6)* "INTERLUDE" is interjected at this point in the psalm, which indicates that it is time for the hearer and reader to think about this!

Psalms are written for worship, and generally include liturgical instructions at the heading like to the Choir Director and the type of music to be sung or instruments to be played. In the midst of the dramatic action of Segment Two, of not knowing the outcome, the choir stands and to the tune of "Do Not Destroy," they sing the words of verse 5. It is a musical intermission of optimism and praise, and it gets the congregation (and us) in the mood for final outcome.

## Segment Three – Singing God's Praises. Verses 7 - 11

Now a very interesting thing is happening here in this segment. In the first half of the psalm, David is asking God to have pity on him and to send help down from heaven to rescue him from these angry lions. He is very fearful concerning his precarious position being holed up in a cave. Then in the second half of the psalm *(V.7-11)*, there is a completely different mood. David says his "heart"*("Leb")* is totally confident in God taking care of him. *(V.7)* So much so that our author can get up in the morning and praise God with song. *(V.8)* David picks up his harp and his anxieties are obviously gone and he rhapsodically gives out with a sing of praise to the Lord. *(V.9-10)* The two halves of the psalm are held together by a refrain in verses 5 and 11 in which David proclaims that God should be exalted. What is amazing is that despite his uncertain circumstances, David could put his total faith and trust in God's "unfailing love" *("Checed")*. David believed in God's steadfast love and His faithfulness. He believed that, come what may, God would see him through.

# PSALM 58

## We Have a God Who Judges Justly Here on Earth

This is a psalm of David that can be classified as a lament, where gods are called into judgment. It is also an imprecatory psalm where David calls on God to damn the ungodly. You have to realize that back then every nation had their own gods, who were created in man's own image. The problem was that those gods behaved like humans do – they fought and quarreled and did all the things their creators did. What makes Judaism (and of course Christianity) different from the gods of Babylon, Canaan, etc., is that the mighty God of the universe created people in His own image. God patterned them after Himself; male and female He created them. (Genesis 1:27)

The prevalent idea when David wrote this psalm was that God presides over a heavenly court (or a parliament) composed of the lesser gods of the nations. This assembly of gods was to legislate or make decisions about how human beings on earth should behave.

### Segment One – David Addresses the Gods. Verses 1 - 5

David begins by sarcastically asking these heavenly rulers if they really know what the word justice means? *(V.1)* It has to do with being fair, of honesty and having integrity. But that's not how they operate. David accuses them of being crooked and injust. *(V.2)* Then he tells us readers that these wicked gods were born sinners. *(V.3)* From their birth they lied and done what they thought was best for themselves. *(V.3)* The Psalmist goes after these man-made-gods and vituperatively criticizes them, saying are snakes that spit poison and ignore any kind of advice. *(V.4)*

David obviously was familiar with the account in Genesis 6 where God said about people in Noah's time that even their thoughts were consistently totally evil. *(Genesis 6:5)* These words and others had already convinced David that we are all sinners. We know this because he writes in Psalm 51 that everyone was conceived in sin. *(V.5)*

## Segment Two – Sevenfold Prayer Against the Wicked. Verses 6 - 9

David now calls on the LORD in an irreverent prayer to destroy them. *(V.6)* Will God do this? No, God won't sweep them away. Why? It can best be described in theological terms. He gives freedom to us human beings to make choices. Sometimes we make bad ones and become slaves to evil forces. He gives this same freedom for these god-rulers to exist.

We Christians face this same problem in the New Testament as God allows Satan (the Devil) to prowl around us like a roaring lion. *(1 Peter 5:8)* This is why God sent Jesus to earth to teach us and then raised Him from death when He went on the cross. When we accept Jesus as our Savior and bring His Holy Spirit into our lives, God gives us the power in Christ to make the right decisions to resist the evil in the world.

Getting back to David, he would like to oust these unjust judges, so he resorts to an ancient and popular belief of an omen – a seven-fold curse (seven is the perfect number). David's prayer has seven images that he is asking God to carry out. They are as follows:

1. Break off their fangs and smash their jaws. *(V.6)*
2. Let them disappear like water into thirsty ground. *(V.7)*
3. Make their weapons useless in their hands. *(V.7)*
4. Let them be snails and dissolve into slime. *(V.8)*
5. Let them die at birth and never see the sun. *(V.8)*
6. Sweep them away – both young and old. *(V.9)*
7. Destroy them faster than a pot heats on an open flame. *(V.9)*

## Segment Three – Righteousness to Be Rewarded. Verses 10 - 11

The last part of Psalm 58 is a prophecy – a confident statement of David that God will judge the wicked and the righteous will be rewarded. He looks imaginatively into the future in verse 10 and sees God's vengeance on the wicked judges and that the godly's feet will be washed in the blood of the wicked. We Christians cannot share in David's feelings of vengeance toward others, but we can share his real concern for a righteous God who will judge the wicked. It is important for us to take a stand for righteousness, knowing God is on the throne and will judge evil. It's important for us to keep the words of the Apostle John closely in mind that we should be bold in our confidence that God will receive our prayers because we obey him and do things to please him. *(1 John 3:21-24)*

The climax of Psalm 58 tells us that good is rewarded, and we have a righteous Father in heaven Who judges justly. *(V.11)* Can't you hear the earthly chorus singing the wonderful words of this last verse that those who live for God will be rewarded! *(V.11)* Again, let us turn to Paul, for his words in First Corinthians are helpful. He is talking about how we Christians will receive new bodies that are immortal when we get to heaven. *(I Corinthians 15:53-58)*

There is a resurrection! Victory is in Jesus! So we need to be strong and steady and abound in God's work. We all need to keep singing Maltbie Babcock's wonderful hymn, "This is My Father's World."

# PSALM 59
## Rescue Me from My Enemies, O God

This is another psalm of David where he was escaping from King Saul (along with psalms 52, 54, 56 and 60). Also the superscription on this composition says the psalm should be sung to the tune "Do Not Destroy." The last three of David's psalms (57-59) use this same tune. The story background for this poem is found in I Samuel 19-11-18. Psalm 59 can be classified as a lament with themes of deliverance, faith, imprecation, and gratitude.

Setting: David was still a young musician in the employ of King Saul. After David killed Goliath, the Philistine giant, his popularity grew. The women of Israel began chanting "Saul killed thousands, David killed ten thousands." *(I Sam. 18:7)* Saul became insanely jealous and twice tried to kill David by throwing a spear at him. After the second occurrence, David left Saul's court and went home to his own house. David had married Saul's daughter, Michal. She warned him that Saul's soldiers were coming to kill him and she helped him escape through a window. She then put an idol in his bed covered with a blanket and some goat's hair. When the soldiers came the next morning it looked like David was sleeping in his bed. He is ill, Michal told them. When they related this to Saul, he ordered them to bring the bed with David in it so he could kill David. When Saul found the idol in the bed, he was furious. But then David was long gone!

David may have expanded Psalm 59 some time later and added verses 5, 8, and 13b. This might explain why verse 9 is out of order. We will treat this as if that was the case and will move 9 to the last segment.

### Segment One – An Appeal for Help . Verses 1 - 5

David writes with desperate urgency that he needs to be rescued from his enemies who wish to murder him. *(V.1-2)* Nothing casual here! He is playing for keeps because these enemies want to destroy him. He can't go out for fear of an ambush. He reminds the LORD he has done nothing wrong. *(V.3)* Put yourself in his place. That's scary! Part of his prayer is protesting his innocence. *(V.4)* We ask, who are these wicked traitors? Verse 5 says they are hostile nations. Are they nearby neighbors? David doesn't say.

### Segment Two – More of David's Enemies. Verses 6 - 8

If we can believe the caption at the beginning of this psalm, King Saul sent soldiers to kill David. Verse 6 compares them to vicious dogs. You have to know that many of the ancient Eastern cities had hordes of wild, scavenger dogs roaming in packs at night, searching the city streets for food and anything else they could find. Can't you just hear them howling, prowling and snarling? David uses these vicious hungry mongrels to describe his enemies roaming around at dark seeking to catch and kill him. *(V.7)* Probably they were cursing and yelling that David had escaped. Then he prays that the LORD should laugh at them. *(V.8)* David may have said this to God because he remembered the same words of derision by the LORD in Psalm 2, when the combined nations of the world tried to rage against Him. The LORD merely laughed. *(Psalm 2:4)*

### Segment Three – Another Appeal to God. Verses 10 - 13

Instead of being seriously concerned about criminals and murderers who were doing everything they could to ambush him in verses 1-5, David in this segment of the psalm emphases a change in his attitude and is confident that God will help him. *(V.10)* David proceeds to implement his prayerful wishes, asking God not to kill them but merely stagger them with His power. *(V.11)* What David means here is that everyone can learn from God's Almighty-ness. They will know that the wickedness and evil within them are seeds of their own destruction. God is in control! He is still on the throne, and He will judge justly!

For us Christians, Romans 8:27-28 embodies what David is saying in Psalm 59. The Apostle Paul points out that all things work for good and God's purpose for those who love God. This does not mean we won't face trouble or that we won't suffer from evildoers, as David did. God gives His children freedom and this freedom gets abused by selfishness and thoughtlessness. But it is God's promise that wickedness ultimately will be judged and righteousness will be rewarded.

Another caveat – David's emotional prayer then asks God to not just stagger his enemies but destroy them completely. *(V.13)* This is (from a Christian perspective) the antithesis of what we Christians understand to be God's will. He is a God of love, not an angry killer.

## Segment Four – Another Look at David's Enemies. Verses 14 - 15

This is a re-play for verses 6-8. His enemies attack him at night like vicious dogs. *(V.14)* They haven't yet let up. Danger is ever present. Verse 15 is somewhat mystifying in its meaning. David is the food they are scavenging for, and they end up going to sleep at night unsatisfied, meaning they aren't able to find and capture David.

## Segment Five – The Refrain and Closing. Verses 9, 16 - 17

When Psalm 59 is presented in the place of worship, this last segment is the climax where the Choir Director leads the chorus. They sing in harmony that God is their place of safety. *(V.9)* Then an individual voice sings out he is joyful for God's "covenant love" (*"Checed"*) *(V.16a)*. Another voice perhaps stands and sings God is a refuge, a place of safety. *(V.16b)* Then the combined voices of the whole congregation sing praises to God. *(V.17)*

Nothing has changed as far as David's outward circumstances are concerned, but inwardly he is focused on God's strength and unfailing love. *(V.16-17)* That is what sustains him. That is what is so wonderful about reading the Scriptures, especially the Psalms. We can also read David's Psalm 23 and be lifted up! Or remember David's joy words in his 32nd Psalm in which he declares God forgives ours sins.

Then there are inspirational passages in the New Testament. We Christians have God's Son, Jesus, as our Savior. His Holy Spirit is our ever-present companion. In Philippians, the fourth chapter, the Apostle Paul writes that he can do everything with God's help.

Music was a big thing in David's life. He took his harp with him everywhere he went, and probably had it even when he was in the cave. Music in the Christian church means a lot, too.

# PSALM 60
## We Need God to Go with Us

The title (superscription) of Psalm 60 has the longest introduction in the entire psalter. It states that while David fought Aram Naharaim and Aram Zobah, he had to send Joab (the commander in charge of David's troops) back toward Jerusalem where Joab and his troops struck down 12,000 Edomites in the valley of the Salt. It tells the Director of Music of this psalm that he should sing it to the tune of "Lilly of the Testimony." Psalm 60 is a national prayer for God's help after Israel suffered a defeat by a foreign nation.

When David wrote this psalm, he had been king of Israel for a number of years. He and his army were off on a military campaign against the Arameans, somewhere in eastern Lebanon (Aram is the name for Mesopotamia). Apparently, while this campaign was going on, a group of hostile neighbors of Israel were able to rebel and score a devastating victory over the forces left to defend the homeland. David probably wrote this poem before returning to Jerusalem. There are two rather incongruous items here: as you can see the title is about Joab and his brilliant victory over the Edomites. However, Psalm 60 is also about the crushing defeat of the Hebrew people. The background information can be found in 2 Samuel 8:1-14.

Wars and battles are themes that occur endlessly in the psalms. Engaging in warfare has been mankind's chief occupation ever since people have been living in groups. Legends and epics revolving around battles and wars go back to ancient times. Unfortunately, we moderns have not been able to get much beyond them.

Psalm 60 is classified as a lament and verses 8-12 are quoted verbatim in Psalm 108: 6-13.

## Segment One – A Tragic Defeat. Verses 1 - 5

We don't have any of the specifics about the defeat, but David portrays it as a stunning disaster. He sees it as the result of God taking His hands off the nation of Israel. *(V.1)* We have been torn apart and our people have been shaken. The defeat is like You have hit us with an earthquake. *(V.2)* It's devastating! You have made us reeling like we were drunk with wine. *(V.3)* David is never a person to give up, so he says he expects God to rally Israel against a subsequent attack. *(V.4)* If this attack was a rebellion by the Edomites while David's army was away, David could only see it as God's anger against Israel, so he pleads with God to rescue his people. *(V.5)*

## Segment Two – God's Promise to Help. Verses 6 - 8

David asked God to come to the aid of those who have been attacked by the Edomites. Then in verse 6 through 8, God speaks from His sanctuary (by His holiness) a special revelation (an oacle). This explains why the prophecy in verses 5-12 also appears in Psalm 108:6-13—the prophecy was given to David by Nathan the Prophet. It is a promise from God here rephrased by David. This was the oracle: Shechem *(V.6)* was the place where Jacob lived after he returned from Paddam Aren (see Genesis 33:18). The valley fo Succoth *(V.6)* was the last place Jacob lived, and these two places represent the eastern and western side of the Jordan River. Gilead, Manasseh, Ephraim and Judah *(V.7)* are the Hebrew tribes. All these places are part of the territory God had promised to give to the Hebrews.

David is here representing a belief in God's word so that his people could act on it. God had promised him victory over the Edomites, Moab, and Philista. Later, David conquered Edom (see verse 8). This earlier oracle is rephrased and promises a reunited kingdom and victory over Israel's neighbors.

## Segment Three – Reflections upon God's Reply. Verses 9 - 12

David is attempting to understand lessons he needs to learn from the defeat of his people by Edom and the promises God gave him that will give him eventual victory! *(V.9-10)* He asks a rhetorical question: who will help him defeat Edom? *(V.11)* Only God can give supernatural energy and power to go against overwhelming odds, and in verse 12 he fairly shouts God will trample down Israel's foes. This psalm ends on a strong note of optimism, which comes from the promises of God that David grasped in faith!

Obviously, David remembered Nathan coming to him after he brought the Ark of the Covenant into Jerusalem, and telling him the Word of the LORD he had received that David's kingdom would be established forever. (2 Samuel 7:4-16)

While David doesn't tell us in Psalm 60, the inference from the superscription at the beginning of the psalm is that David must have dispatched Joab and part of his army back to the homeland. Joab met the Edomites in battle and was victorious over them thereby restoring peace and order that David spoke about in Segment One.

There are some personal lessons for us to learn as we read this poem. We are not kings and probabilities are that we have never meet a Moabite and we don't have any military battles to fight. Our battles generally are spiritual ones as members of the Church of Jesus Christ. We are commanded by our Lord Jesus to help promote God's Kingdom, and we are called upon to do this in a spiritually hostile world. Paul, writing to the Ephesians, says our fight is not against flesh and blood but mighty powers of darkness. (Ephesians 6:12)

To be victorious, we Christians need to be strong in the Lord's mighty truth and to use every piece of God armor to resist the enemy, so that after the battle we will still be standing firm. Paul further tells us in Ephesians to put on the full armour of God's righteousness to be victorious. (Ephesians 6:14-18)

# PSALM 61
## God Is a Towering Rock of Safety

In this psalm, David feels he is far away from Jerusalem, maybe on a military campaign. We don't know for sure. For a Jew, the Ark of the Covenant was where God resided, and the Ark was located in the Holy of Holies in the Tabernacle in Jerusalem. That is where David wanted to be.

### Segment One – Longing For Divine Shelter. Verses 1 - 4

Most of us have experienced times when we were far from home, and like David, felt overwhelmed. (V.1-2) Obviously, he feels alone and misses worshiping with his friends and family. Rock of safety, the metaphor in verse 2 and 3, gives an insight into David's rich and intimate relationship with God. Another meaningful figure of speech is in verse 4 where he desires to be between the shelter of God's wings, referring, of course, to the golden cherubim that adorned the lid of the Ark of the Covenant. Those wings opened to the Spirit of God. Philip Doddridge, the famous Scottish hymn writer of the 18th century, wrote a hymn entitled, "O God of Bethel," whose fourth verse uses David's metaphor of being protected by the wings of God.

We Christians know God as we come to know Jesus. He is our way to our heavenly Father (see John 14:6). As we read the psalms with a Christian perspective, we can identify with David's deep faith in God and make the wonderful metaphors our own. With David we can turn to God as our rock of safety. As God spreads His covering wings around us, we will know we are safe and secure, no matter where we might find ourselves.

David uses a slight bit of hyperbole in verse 4 when he rquests God to have him live in God's sanctuary forever. He probably doesn't mean actually

185

living in the Taberacle, rather he means being in God's presence. He wrote some very similar words in Psalm 27:4-6.

### Segment Two – David's Petition Granted. Verse 5

David began this psalm feeling homesick for Jerusalem and the familiarity of the ritual and music of the Tabernacle. He considered himself to be at edge of the earth. *(V.2)* and for a while felt some spiritual distance from God. But as he thought about God and went to Him in prayer *(V.5)*, words came to him from another poem he himself had written – words about how God's Spirit is always with him wherever he goes. *(Psalm 139:1-7)*

In *The Living Bible*, the translation indicates that David makes a vow to daily "reverence" *("Yare")* the Lord in grateful awareness of God's great Covenant love for him and for his people – to give daily praise for God's blessings. *(The Living Bible, Psalm 61:5)*

### Segment Three – A Prayer For The King. Verses 6 - 7

In this segment, David asks God to have his years as King span generations. *(V.6)* Then he prays (using the third person) that the King's reign be under the protection of God forever. *(V.7)* David knows only too well that an anointed king (which he is) has a sworn duty to reflect in all that he does the qualities of God, the heavenly King. He is painfully aware of his finiteness and sinfulness, so he must totally rely on God's power working in his life. His prayer, therefore, is to ask that God's "unfailing love" *("Checed")* and His "faithfulness"*("Emeth")* care for the king (David). *(V.7)* It's obvious that David is relating his kingship with the prophecy that Nathan gave him from the LORD of heaven (see 2 Samuel 7). Part of that oracle said that David's dynasty as king would be secure forever. *(2 Samuel 7:16)*

David was undoubtedly thinking of the coming Messiah when he wrote verses 6-7 in Psalm 61. As we Christians read David's words in Segment Three, we can identify Jesus, God's Son, not as the coming Messiah, but as God's Messiah who has already come!

## Segment Four – A Promise to Keep. Verse 8

David's words in verse 8 refer to a vow he made in gratitude for many blessings he received from God's merciful Hand. Throughout his long career as Israel's king, he took seriously his responsibilities on earth. Because the psalms are not dated, it's difficult to know when they were written, but whenever David took up his pen he almost always gave Jehovah God (the LORD) the glory and honor. His psalm 103:1-4 is an example.

David was no saint. He had his shortcomings, but his redeeming virtue was his total reliance on God for guidance and inspiration. God became for him a Father, forgiving him when he erred, and dealing justly with him when he needed disciplining.

Reading a poem like Psalm 61 from a Christian perspective means we can understand David's feelings and some of his vacillations. We can also admire his love of God. His God is our God! However, we can know the Lord even more intimately than David did because God sent us Jesus as our personal Savior. When God raised Jesus from the dead, He set His Spirit free so it was not bound from time and space. This allowed Jesus' Spirit to be everywhere present so that He could indwell those of us who opened our lives to Him – thereby giving us a part of His divine nature and guidance. Thus having Jesus' Spirit in our hearts and minds gives us the possibility and capacity to view things from Jesus' divine point-of-view! As long as we are "in Christ," (actually Jesus being in us), we are sharing His love and sensitivity, and are manifesting the fruit of the Spirit in our daily walk (see Galatians 5:22-23).

Jesus never forces Himself on any of us, but He is there for us when we need Him. Because we are fallible people (we are sinners), we can get preoccupied with our own affairs and inadvertently push the Lord out. However, because Jesus is so loving and forgiving, He always stands outside the door to our inner selves and knocks. *(Revelation 3:20-21)*

The psalms are good for us to read. They mirror life and keep us sensitive to staying close to the ways the Psalmists dealt with their problems. Some they solved; some they did not but all are valuable lessons. Remember we all share the same problems.

# PSALM 62

## Salvation Comes from God Alone

Psalm 62 is a beautiful affirmation of faith composed by King David. The superscription says for Jeduthun, director of music. In 1 Chronicles, it records David appointing Levites to serve in the Tabernacle, and one of the Levites was Jeduthun (Je-du-thun). He was a talented musician and many of his sons became Levites serving the Lord as Tabernacle musicians. (See 1 Chronicles 16:42)

### Segment One – David's Adversaries. Verses 1- 4

Verses 1-2 express David's total commitment to the Lord. In his closeness to God, he writes God is his salvation. *(V.1)* The Hebrew word for "salvation" here is *("Y'shuw_ah")*, the feminine form of the word, which also can be translated "deliverance." One interpreter suggests that instead of "salvation," it should be "sanctification," which means being holy--the Old Testament equivalent of becoming a true member of God's Covenant community (His redeemed person). David proclaims God alone is his salvation and his rock. *(V.2)* These first two verses express David's deep sense of inner peace, even in times of chaos.

Verse 3 is an example of the trouble David has to face—one man against so many enemies seeking to kill him. These are evil people who not only want to kill him but ruin his reputation. *(V.4)* He doesn't say specifically who they are, but, for instance, when David took over as king after Saul's death, most of the men from the tribe of Benjamin never gave their full allegiance to David, And, there were others who didn't want David as king. Some could be part of his staff in the palace. Then there was his son, Absalom, and his dream of replacing his father. We don't know who they are, and David doesn't tell us. What he does say is that they smile to his face but tell lies about him behind his back. *(V.4)*

## Segment Two – Protection Comes from God Alone. Verses 5 - 7

Notice that verse 5 repeats word-for-word what David says in verse 1, and the same thing is true for verses 2 and 6. He didn't mean for them to be refrains. No, he did this for emphasis. Then in verse 7 he tells the world, that his salvation and his reputation or honor come from God alone. The word "honor," in Hebrew is *("Kabod")*, which also can be translated "glory." Glory reminds us of what happened to Moses when he was up on Mount Sinai receiving the Covenant and the Ten Commandments from God. When he returned, Aaron and the people of Israel were afraid to come near Moses because being with God caused Moses' face to glow and be radiant with Glory!

David was experiencing something of God's glory, and so he uses two of his favorite metaphors – "refuge" ("Macheh") and "rock" ("Tsuwr") to describe his secure feelings. *(V.7)* This should be the logical ending for Psalm 62 – but no, there's more.

## Segment Three – David's Counsel to His People. Verses 8 - 12

These final five verses is where David turns his composition into a kind of "wisdom style" of writing. Psalm 62 becomes almost a hymn for use in public worship. In verse 8, David preaches to the congregation saying we need to trust God in all times. But when we come before Him we must be sincere. Next, David's writings sound like one of the great prophets, like Jeremiah or Ezekiel. He encourages us to hold onto our faith by telling us that many of the dealings of the rich and powerful (politicians, bankers and judges) are not always in touch with God's will. He says all—the lowest and the greatest—are mere puffs of air to the greatness of God. *(V.9)* So we waste our time if we put our faith and trust in mere man. *(V.10-11)* Proverbs says the godly spring forth like leaves in spring, but those who trust in money dry up like dead leaves. *(Proverbs 11:28)* In his final teaching, David tells the people (and us) the profound truth that God is infinitely kind and "loving" *("Checed")* and He rewards us according to our work for Him. *(V.12)*

We Christians have no quarrel with David. He just <u>didn't know Jesus as we do.</u>

# PSALM 63
## Longing for God

Another psalm written by King David, Psalm 63 is a combination of a lament and a strong affirmation of faith. The heading (the superscription) tells us David was in the wilderness of Judah. There is no evidence that he was escaping from King Saul before he became the head of Israel, so it must have been after he became king and had escaped from Jerusalem and was fleeing from his son, Absalom. (See 2 Samuel 15-19.)

Absalom's rebellion is a sad saga. Absalom became angry and jealous of his father due to what he felt was his father's overreaction to Absalom's murder of his brother Amnon. As a result, he set about winning the hearts of the people and finally declared himself king in the nearby city of Hebron. Having raised an army, Absalom marched to Jerusalem fully intending to overthrow his father. David got word at the last minute and hastily fled with a few loyal soldiers into the wilderness. Absalom failed to follow, allowing David to regroup. By the time Absalom's army marched to attack, David was ready and a brutal battle ensued with David's forces victorious. Twenty thousand men were killed that day, including Absalom. (See 2 Samuel 18:7.)

Knowing this background helps us appreciate the emotion David must have felt being separated from Jerusalem and the Sanctuary to which he was devoted. This psalm can be thought of as a love song for God. It is one of the most beautiful devotional writings in all literature.

### Segment One – Thirsting for God. Verse 1

David finds himself somewhere in the desert of Judah, which is one of the most barren spots in the world – hot and dry. He uses his need for water to satisfy his thirst as an analogy for his desire for God. He says his soul thirst for God. The Hebrew word for "soul" is *("Nephesh")* *("Neh'-fesh")*. It means "a whole person: body, mind, and spirit." David adds that his whole body longs for God. *(V.1)*

## Segment Two – Praises and Honor to God. Verses 2 - 5

David remembers with deep appreciation the inner joy he had when last he went into the Sanctuary of the Lord. It was like gazing upon the power and glory of God, a mystical envisioning of God. *(V.2)* Not too different, perhaps, from young Isaiah's experience when King Uzziah died and Isaiah went into the Temple and envisioned God sitting on His throne, and he beheld His glory! (Isaiah 6:1-8) The Hebrew word "to gaze or see" is *("Re ah")* and can also mean "to perceive," but not necessarily what one sees with the physical eye. Perhaps using his inner eye, David understands that God's love for him is greater than life itself. *(V.3)* This statement comes close to Jesus' words in His Sermon on the Mount in which He says we need to make God our primary concern and live for Him. *(Matthew 6:31-34)* Putting God's "Covenant love," His *("Checed")*, first was David's great contribution to the world.

David goes on to embellish his wonderful faith statement saying he will honor God as long as he lives. *(V.4)* In all of David's psalms, he always includes praying and singing, and Psalm 63 is no exception. He closes this section by telling God he will priase Him with songs of joy. *(V.5)*

## Segment Three – Wonderful Thoughts in the Night. Verses 6 - 8

When one is resting at night in bed, it is a time when many of us let our minds reflect on the day's activities and evaluate our situations. In this psalm, David shared his nighttime meditations with us. He says he lies awake meditating of God throughout the night. *(V.6)* He feels blessed and secure in God's protective wings. This beautiful metaphor he uses again and again in his writings. *(V.7)* The words in verse 8 where David is confident that God's strong right hand protects him depicts in a most profound way the actual meaning of God's Covenant with Israel. Remember God said to Moses – on behalf of the Hebrew people—that if they keep His Covenant they will be a special treasure of His among all the people in the world. *(Exodus 19:5-6)*

David had expressed his love and obedience to God. He has upheld his part of the Covenant. God, on the other hand, has promised to protect

191

David's people by His strong right hand. This is how God intended the Covenant to work. The Prophet Hosea interpreted God's love when He brought Israel out of captivity in Egypt, by saying, God is Israel's husband and David's people are God's bride. (Hosea 2:16-20)

## Segment Four – Consequence of Being Unfaithful to the Covenant. Verses 9 - 10

This magnificent devotional composition of David seemingly draws to a close at verse 8. Some later editor probably added the last three verses to turn David's soliloquy into a conclusion for Temple worship. If David did, in fact, compose these last three verses, we don't know if he wrote them before the battle his military forces had against Absalom's rebellious army or not. It really doesn't matter because he had many who opposed him and wanted to see him step down as king. David knew in his heart that he had been divinely anointed by God and that he kept his Covenant obligations, so that those attempting to destroy him will be destoryed. *(V.9)* If he wrote this after the battle, the demise of Absalom was a case in point! Verse 10 is somewhat grisly. The verse notes that those who plotted against David will be food for jackals. David was a military man who knew the realities of armed conflict and its consequences.

## Segment Five – The King Speaks for All Who Trust in God. Verse 11

David as the king – the head and spokesperson for Israel – rejoices in what has transpired (his victory over his rebellious son) and can and does speak for all his faithful followers who trust in God (those who are endeavoring to keep their part of God's Covenant of love!). They will know his joy in the Lord while tellers of lies will be silenced. *(V. 11)* – probably an add-on.

We Christians who read this inspired psalm can find some similar messages in the three other biblical passages:

1. While you can find Him, seek the LORD. *(Isaiah 55:6-7)*
2. Those who hunger and thirst for justice are blest by God. *(Matthew 5:6)*
3. The two most important commandments of God are: Love God with all your heart and soul; Love your neighbor as yourself. *(Matthew 22:36-40)*

# PSALM 64

## Evil Men Are Thwarted by God

The title of this psalm states that it is a psalm of David to be used by the choir director. This is a personal lament. David prays that God will preserve his life against clandestine plots of a group of sinister and cunning men. He doesn't reveal the nature of their hostility, but by context they appear to be dissidents and a powerful minority within his own court who want David ousted as king of Israel. Their strategy is not to come out in the open with any accusations, but to spread ugly rumors and false innuendos to undermine the king's credibility. This was no joking matter, and David reveals to us readers his fears and his serious anxiety as he confronts his political enemies.

### Segment One – David's Complaint to God. Verses 1 - 2

In just about every psalm attributable to David, the subject matter is twofold: (1) God, and (2) his enemies. Psalm 63 is mostly about David's relationship with the Lord (especially verses 1-8) with the last two verses about his enemies. Psalm 64 is a mirror opposite – mostly about evil men (his enemies). Because of the seriousness of the attack of his political enemies, David is wise enough to know he cannot take them on in the rough and tumble of political conflict. Why? Because they fight with skill and without scruples and David would be setting himself up for defeat. So what does he do? He doesn't have much human help so he turns to God and asks Him to listen to his complaint: You need to stop my enemies from overewhelming me. *(V.1)* In verse 2, he asks God to protect him from his enemies' plots. The Hebrew word for "plots" is *("Cowd")* which is a "conspiracy," a plot involving a secret agreement to do an unlawful act (in this case against the king). These evildoers are doing criminal things in as much as they are trying to

193

overthrow a legally authorized authority. They are making their attacks indirectly using slanderous and malicious gossip.

## Segment Two – A Description of the Enemy's Strategy. Verses 3 - 6

After making his appeal to God, David proceeds to describe in detail the strategy the enemy uses to discredit him. He uses metaphors for those who hunt wild animals because <u>he is the hunted!</u> (V.3) Their sharp tongues spread seditious propaganda that turns the average citizen against the king. Verse 4 says they shoot from ambush so nobody sees them. All this is done behind closed doors. What is worse, says David, they have no compunction about all their evil thoughts and plans. (V.5) They feel downright smug about what they are doing. They think they have the perfect plan to bring down King David and feel superior to the naïve king who thinks he's so righteous. (V.6)

David probably knew many of these ungodly individuals plotting against him. Oh, how hurtful it is when people we know turn against us and make accusations that are not true. They are like unseen rattlesnakes striking at us when we least expect it.

In a fallen world there are always people who are jealous of leaders and take great glee in wanting to embarrass them and see them toppled. The Apostle Paul, like David, was plagued throughout his many missionary journeys by dissident Jews (called "Judaizers") who followed him wherever he went. They would speak behind Paul's back, stirring up crowds against him.

## Segment Three – God Will Shoot Them Down. Verses 7 - 8

The wicked have been distributing their malicious schemes against David, doing it undercover, secretly. They think nobody will ever know about the traps they are setting. But God, who is omniscient and omnipotent, will see them and will act! God's own arrows will pierce them. (V.7) David speaks prophetically when he says their own words will destroy them. (V.8) This is a powerful prediction that the all-knowing and all-seeing God will act causing the evildoers to get so over confident that they will get caught in their own trap!

We Christians know this. In the New Testament, God is saying to us not to live to satisfy our own selfish desires. Live to please Jesus' Spirit and obtain everlasting lives. (Galatians 6:7-8)

## Segment Four — David's Confident Prediction. Verses 9 - 10

David is optimistic and confident that what he hopes for in Segment Three will become a reality. He proclaims that everyone will stand in awe when they see how God had protected the king. *(V.9)* Then those who are in a Covenant relationship with the LORD will rejoice and be protected by the LORD. *(V.10)*

Reading Psalm 64 gives us a healthy respect for morality and faith. It takes faith like David to trust the Lord. Christians put our faith in Christ Jesus and this is Good News! Like the Apostle Paul, we can say the Good News teaches us how God makes us righteous in His sight. *(Romans 1: 16-17)* It also motivates us to fight God's battles with His weapons, not those of the world. David makes clear to us, the Lord's weapons are His Word and prayer.

# PSALM 65
## Praise to the Lord of Creation and History

This is a psalm of David about the God of nature and can be classified as a Harvest Hymn to be sung during the Feast of Tabernacles (see Leviticus 23:33-34 and Numbers 27:12-29).

### Segment One – The Goodness of God. Verses 1 - 4

There is an intimate bonding between Jehovah God and his chosen people. *(V.1)* Since this psalm is focused on the Feast of Tabernacles, held each year at the end of September, one would naturally assume this poem only applies to Jews. It even speaks of Zion, which is another word for Jerusalem. But David, in verse 2, acknowledges that God is the true God of *all* peoples.

Jesus said this same thing many years later. He was in Samaria, in the village of Sychar at the well, having a conversation with a woman. She asked Him why Jews insist that Jerusalem is the center of worship. Jesus' reply was that a time was coming when the place of worship was not as important as worshiping the Father in spirit and truth. *(John 4:21-24)* It was Jesus Himself who manifested the spirit and truth here on earth. *(John 1:1-18)*

In Psalm 32, David tells us there was a time when he wouldn't admit that he was a sinner, but that his dishonesty made him miserable and filled his days with frustration. When he finally admits his sin to God and is forgiven, his guilt was gone. He then addressed his fellow countrymen to confess their rebellion against God while there was still time to be forgiven by God. *(Psalm 32:6)* In Psalm 65, David speaks of the joys of God's forgiveness. *(V.3)* The last verse in Segment One speaks of the privilege of being able to serve God. *(V.4)*

Back in David's day, the guilty sinner would bring an animal (bull, goat, lamb, etc.) to the Tabernacle, and it would be sacrificed with the idea that the death of the animal died in place of the sinner. The animal's blood would be placed on the altar to "cover" over a person's sin. This was necessary because God is a holy God and cannot abide sin. Sin's penalty is death for the sinner. The Hebrew word for "cover" is *("Kaphar")*, which also can be translated into English as "pardon," "expiate," "cancel," atonement," "forgiving," and to "hide sin with the blood of a sacrificed animal." The reason this matter of atonement is so important for a Christian is that when the right time came, God sent Jesus, His Son, to this earth to live among us. Then after a short three-year teaching and healing ministry, He died on a cross, sacrificing Himself and making atonement for our sins.

The writer of the Book of Hebrews is helpful in telling us about Jesus as the new High Priest not only became our sacrifice but now interjects Himself before God as our advocate. *(Hebrews 7:18-19, 24-25, 9:11-12)* Having our sins covered by Jesus' sacrifice on the cross, God can deal with us graciously once more. In the next two segments, David tells of the wonderful gifts God bestows on us.

## Segment Two – The Awesome Power of God. Verses 5 - 8

David is ecstatic in his praise of God's righteous power. He says not only is He our protector and Deliverer, but God is the hope of everyone of earth! *(V.5)* Then he envisions God's awesome power as the Creator and Sustainer of all the world. He created the mountains and calms the turbulent seas. *(V.6)* As an afterthought, David says, God even quiets the nations. *(V.7)* People everywhere will be awed by God's wonders. With charming poetic wit, our poet-ruler ends segment two with how God inspires joyful shouts. *(V.8)*

## Segment Three – The God of the Harvest. Verses 9 - 13

This section is about the harvest and God's blessings. The first thing we see is that God visits the earth and waters it making it fertile. *(V.9)* To those of us who live in places that get adequate rainfall, we have to know that Jerusalem and its environs are a rather barren and arid land. In that part of the world, the coming of abundant rains to water crops is a real blessing! David uses a metaphor saying God's rivers never run dry. *(V.9)* It's a wonderful symbol of God's action as He re-creates the world of harvest again and again. With water, crops come. Unless you have been a farmer, it is difficult to appreciate looking out at fertile fields and seeing crops grow and mature. Farmers work hard and long, but it is God who makes the crops grow! *(V.10-12)* Then there are lush "pastures" *("Na'ah")* filled with sheep and grain. *(V.13)* The climax of the psalm comes in the last sentence—all sing and shout with joy.

We Christians can read Psalm 65 with understanding and appreciation for David's sensitive insights about God's creativity and His awesome power. Most of all, we need to praise God for sending us Jesus as our Savior and Lord – for being our atonement for sin. David is right. We need to sing!

# PSALM 66

## A Wonderful Evangelical Psalm

The title at the beginning of Psalm 66 merely says it is for the choir director. We, therefore, don't know who wrote it or when it was written. If verses 10-12 allude to the Babylonian captivity, which we think it does, then it will have to be dated sometime after the exile which ended around 538 BC. Psalm 66 is made up of two parts: the first part is Israel's witness to all the earth (Verses 1-12); while the second part is by an individual witness within Israel concerning the greatness of God (Verses 13-20). The first part was probably sung in the Temple by an antiphonal choir, while the second part by a solo voice, either sung or recited. The similarity of Psalm 66's evangelical thrust to Isaiah, chapters 40 to 66, would be further evidence to date it following the exile.

### Segment One – The God for All the Earth. Verses 1 - 4

All the peoples of the earth are invited by our Psalmist to sing and give glory to God's name. *(V.1-2)* The Hebrew word for "sing" is *("Zamar")*, which can be translated as "give praise," as well as "to make music." God is wonderful and His deeds are awesome. *(V.3)* Because of God's tremendous power, His enemies cringe before him. *(V.3)* Everything on earth will worship God. *(V.4)* As you read these words, you can just feel the energy and enthusiasm of the choir singing these words and praising the Lord as they raise their hands!

### Segment Two – The God Who Works Miracles. Verses 5 - 7

All the nations of the world are invited to see the miracles God has done and especially the miracles He has done for His people. *(V.5)* He has worked incredibly for Israel in her history. *(V.6)* The Psalmist refers to the time when Moses and his people were fleeing from the Egyptian army and they came to the Red Sea. Moses stretched his rod over the water and the LORD opened up a path through the sea, with walls of water on each side. So the people of Israel walked on dry ground to the other side. When the Egyptians followed, the waters came back over them and they drowned (see Exodus 17). The writer of this splendid missionary psalm says we know God because of His power and then ends this segment with the affirmation that God rules forever. *(V.7)* We can say Amen! The one thing we know, that those back then didn't know, is God's Son, Jesus Christ – and that for us has made all the difference!

I like what the Apostle Paul says about being a Jew. You can read this in Philippians 3. Paul was a Pharisee. The Pharisees demanded the strictest obedience to every Jewish rule and regulation. Then came Paul's conversion on the Damascus Road. He says that he once thought all these rules and regulations were important but he now considers them worthless because of the saving grace he has obtained from Jesus' sacrifice for him. He no longer concentrates on his own goodness or attempt at goodness, but now he simply trusts in Lord Jesus. *(Philippians 3:7-9)*

## Segment Three – The God Who Purifies Us by Fire. Verses 8 - 12

Here again, like he did in Segment One, the Psalmist goes beyond narrow nationalism and invites everyone to bless and praise God. The Hebrew word for "bless" is *("Barak")*, and it also can mean "adore," "praise," or "salute."*(V.8)* He continues in verse 9 saying God keeps us from stumbling. These words were based on the belief that Israel is God's chosen people. In Deuteronomy it says that the Hebrew people were a holy people chosen by God as His speical treasure. *(Deuteronomy 7:6-8)* God chose Israel, yes. But He wanted her purified. So He put His chosen people through many trials. In verse 10, the Psalmist writes God tested His people and melted them in a crucible. (See Isaiah 48:10 and Jeremiah 9:7.) The dross had to be burned away! Consequently, Israel had to go through many humiliating experiences. But always they were in God's safety net. *(V.11)* The net is a metaphor meaning God had his hands on them. But God also, from the Psalmist's point of view, overburded His people. *(Psalm 66 V.11,12)* The plus factor in all of Israel's agonies is that God went through these burdens with the people. The

Prophet Isaiah pointed out that when the people went through great trouble, God was there with them as their Savior. *(Isaiah 43:2-3)*

Our writer ends this section with a positive word. God brought His people back to a place of abundance. *(V.12)* He brought them back from exile, and gave them new life!

## Segment Four – The God Who Receives Our Offerings. Verses 13 - 15

This segment is where the author provides his personal testimony. He is giving his burnt sacrifices to fulfill his vows to God. *(V.13)* In the past he had sinned. He obviously understood the spiritual implications that his sin was against God. When he was in deep trouble he made a vow to make this sacrifice. *(V.14)* He offers the best bulls and goats in sacrifice to God. *(V.15)* He needs to be forgiven from his past sin (whatever that was), because it is eating him up with guilt.

## Segment Five – The God Who Hears and Answers. Verses 16 - 20

In grateful awareness for what God had done for him, he cries out to all who would listen. *(V.16)* I confessed my sin and told God how sorry I was and He listened! *(V.17)* Especially God listened because I confessed my sin with a sincere heart. *(V.18-19)* Not only did He hear my prayer, but God gave His best gift of all His *("Checed")*, His "unfailing love!" *(V.20)*

What a wonderful message this psalm gives us. For Christians, this is the way for us to share our faith. Not by preaching, but by telling our friends and neighbors what Jesus has meant and done for us. We believe God chose the Jewish nation in order to work out His grand design for mankind. As we read the psalms, we are able to identify and claim the truths in them, because, in a real sense, we Christians are spiritual Jews! It was from this very matrix that God brought forth the Messiah, Jesus of Nazareth. He is our risen Lord and Savior!

In the first part of Psalm 66, we noted that the Psalmist invites us to come and see what God has done for His people. *(V.5)* Then in the second part, we are confronted with what God has done for the Psalmist. *(V.16)* When you read these words they are very similar to the way young Isaiah felt when he was in the Temple and experienced God's presence. He felt as a sinner his destruction was sealed. Then one of the Seraphim flew over to the altar and picked up a burning coal with a pair of tongs. He touched Isaiah's lips with it and said Isaiah's guilt was removed and his sins forgiven. Then Isaiah heard the LORD ask whom he should send as a messenger to His chosen people. Now cleansed, Isaiah could say, "Send me." *(Isaiah 6:5-8)*

Our call as followers of Jesus Christ is to take up our cross and be a witness for Christ wherever we find ourselves. *(Matthew 16.24-25)*

# PSALM 67

## God Blesses with an Abundant Harvest

Psalm 67 has a title affixed to it. It says this song for the choir diector should be accompanied by stringed instruments. This short psalm was most likely sung at the Feast of Tabernacles. Most biblical expositors think the date is post-exilic.

### Segment One – God's Grace Upon Israel and All the Nations. Verses 1 - 2

Verse 1 is a different wording of the Aaronic blessing found in Numbers 6:24-26. Having God's face shine upon us is, of course, a metaphor having to do with receiving His favor. Some editor placed an "Interlude" ("Selah") after verse 1 to make readers stop and meditate on God's grace. Verse 2 is a reflection of God's promise to Abram in Genesis 12:2 that he will be a father of a great nation and a great blessing to others. The Psalmist is praying a missionary prayer for the Jews to go to all the nations. He wants God's ways to be known and he wants God's saving power to be spread everywhere. (V.2)

### Segment Two – God Rules the Nations Justly. Verses 3 - 5

Perhaps the choir would be divided in two sections. Choir One may sing the first two verses; then Choir Two would sing verse 3 asking the nations to praise God. And, with typical Hebraic parallelism, Choir two would add yes they should praise you. Choir One could sing verse 4, telling how glad the nations will be because God is a just Ruler. Then there will be a few minutes of silence again for the congregation to reflect on these joyous but profound words. Then, maybe, both choirs will join together and sing verse 5 again suggesting that the nations should praise God and then repeat that refrain.

## Segment Three — God of the Harvest. Verses 6 - 7

Probably the entire congregation and choirs together will sing these final two verses because it is during the Harvest Festival and everyone is aware they need a rich harvest. The rich harvest is a blessing of God. *(V.6)* The psalm ends with a mighty crescendo with everybody (maybe including trumpets!) pouring forth seeking a blessing for all the people in the world. *(V.7)*

It's exciting to read evangelistic psalms like 66 and 67. Unfortunately, after the Hebrew people returned from their 70 years in exile, the nation turned inward and became quite narrow in its outlook. But God had a plan for Israel. Isaiah knew this and wrote that God would make Israel a light to the Gentiles, a light that would bring salvation to the entire earth. *(Isaiah 49:6)* God's eternal plan involves blessing Israel. Why? So she might <u>become a blessing for the world.</u>

God has blessed us Christians through Israel by giving us the Savior, Jesus. We can take this missionary Psalm 67 and read it as a splendid model. The Aaronic blessing is indeed God's favor on us *(V.1)*, and because of God's gracious favor in giving us salvation through the indwelling Spirit of Jesus, we need to be sent so that God's saving power includes all the peoples of the world. *(V.2)* The wonderful Hebrew word *("Yesha")* means "saving" or "salvation." We Christians too are commanded by our Lord Jesus to make disciples of all the nations. *(Matthew 28:19-20).*

Psalm 67 ends with the promise tht God will bless us. *(V.7)* We Christians have already been blessed by knowing our salvation is secure and we look forward to sharing the Good News of Jesus with those around us. And, when our life is through, we can enjoy heaven and reign forever with God and Jesus. Praise the Lord, it will be our joy to be able to see His face. *(Revelation 22:4)*

# PSALM 68

## God's Victorious March From Egypt to Jerusalem

The superscription (heading) for Psalm 68 simply states that this is a song of David to be used by the choir director. This composition appears to be a collection of episodes and material from early in Israel's history put together by some priest-poet for the use of congregational singing and drama for one of the many festivals in the Temple. David probably did not write this psalm but it was dedicated in his honor.

### Segment One – Arise, Mighty God. Verses 1 - 3

Verses 1 and 2 exhorts God to scatter God's enemies and drive them like blown smoke as they perish in the presence of God. The first episode that this poem describes occurred after Moses and the Israelites had received the law and commandments. The Tabernacle was erected in the encampment in and around Mount Sinai. Moses and a number of the tribes left Mt. Sinai on their way to the Promised Land, with the Ark of the Covenant carried forward. As they begin their march Moses cries out to the LORD that His enemies need to be scattered and flee (before the Ark). *(Numbers 10:35)* The warrior God of hosts was believed to reside in the Ark and thus it was carried by the Levites always in the front of the marching columns. The Shekinah Cloud would be seen going on before them leading them to victory! *(V.3)*

### Segment Two – The Compassionate LORD. Verses 4 - 14

It could be that the whole congregation would sing praises to God in verse 4 and then perhaps a single voice would remind everyone of the compassionate God, defender of the fatherless in verse 5. Verses 7-10 describes the march from Mount Sinai toward Canaan, comparing it to when God led them from Egypt. *(V.7)* The writer borrows ancient fragments from Exodus 19 such as powerful thunder and lightning storms. (Exodus 19:16) *(V.8)* Perhaps another voice would chime in about how God sent abundant rain. *(V.9)*

Verses 11-14 seem to be a thumbnail picture of the Hebrew conquest of Canaan. The Lord speaks to annouce victory *(V.11)* and their enemies flee letting Israel to divide the plunder. *(V.12)* It would appear that the Jewish women enhanced their personal appearance from the silver and gold taken off the bodies of their enemies. *(V.13)* The final verse could be a bloody recap of how Jewish forces destroyed a thousand men and women by burning them on Mount Salmon. (See Judges 9:49.)

### Segment Three – God's Home in Zion. Verses 15 - 23

If you travel to Israel and visit the Golan Heights you will find a range of mountains called Bashan. The poet says these peaks look enviously down at the small hill known as Zion. *(V.15)* Why? Because that is where God has chosen to reside. *(V.16)* He is there with His holy angels *(V.17)* having moved from Mount Sinai to His holy Temple. Of course, in this segment the writer has zoomed forward to the time of David who made Jerusalem his capitol, and to Solomon's time and the construction of the Temple.

It is also interesting to note that the Apostle Paul borrowed verse 18 and quotes it in Ephesians (4:4-8). Paul is talking about us Christians being a part of the body of Christ, which allows us to have the same eternal future as Jesus. Like in verse 18, Paul writes that when we ascend to the heights (heaven) we will be given gifts. The reason Paul took verse 18 is because God ascended to the heights and likewise Jesus was resurrected from death to join God in heaven. God also led a crowd of captives and Paul interprets captives as converts, who naturally would want to receive gifts from God. The author of the New Testament book of Hebrews picks this up and writes that Christians will ascend to a heavenly Jerusalem. *(Hebrews 12:22-24)*

Verse 19 is another wonderful chorus that could be sung by the choir praising the Lord our Savior who cares us each day. Verse 20 says the LORD rescues us from death. Then the author plunges into more of the bloody conflict in the conquest of Canaan, the smashing of heads and washing their feet in the blood of the enemy. *(V.21- 23)* Ugh!

### Segment Four — God Moves into the Sanctuary. Verses 24 - 27

These four verses describe the great festal procession into the sanctuary in Jerusalem. This segment could have been the occasion when David brought the Ark of the Covenant to the Tent of Meeting (1 Samuel 6). In poetic language, the King of kings leads the great solemn procession. *(V.25)* The tribe of Benjamin leads the way, then the rulers of Judah and Zebulun, Naphali to name a few. *(V.26)*

### Segment Five — The God of Peace. Verses 28 - 31

This small section of Psalm 68 is requesting God to again display His mighty power. *(V.28)* Tribute from the kings of the earth needs to be brought to the Temple in Jerusalem. *(V.29)* Nations that delight in war need to be scattered. *(V.30)* This future dream of all the nations of the world coming to worship the God of peace was the theme of the great Hebrew Prophets.

The Psalmist is recalling a prophery of Isaiah in which he writes that the mighty kings of the earth will come to Jerusalem and bring the best of their goods to pay homiage to the LORD and Savior of the world, the Mighty One of Israel. *(V.31)* *(Isaiah 60:1-3, 16)*

### Segment Six — Epilogue. Verses 32 - 35

God's Covenant people now join in singing praises to God who lives in ancient heavens. *(V.32)* In this Epilogue, the entire congregation sings praises to Yahweh God inviting the kingdoms of the earth to join in. In the prologue, God is called upon to scatter His enemies. Now His power is seen in the forces of nature. His voice is heard thundering from the sky. *(V.33)* While other nations are invited to participate in the worship, God shines down on Israel. *(V.34)* This tells us there is a fine line between exclusivity and universality. It's true that Jehovah is the supreme ruler over all the nations of the world, but He chose to work out His plans and purpose through the nation of Israel. Since the Israelites believed God dwelled in the Holy of Holies in the Tabernacle, and the Psalmist was no exception to this belief, he kneels down before Him in the sanctuary and is able to experience God's awesome power. *(V.34)* He thusly ends his long and cumbersome psalm with his own praise to God. *(V.35)*

A quick summary of what we Christians can get from reading Psalm 68: One, we can get an appreciation of what our Jewish ancestors went through during their wilderness days under Moses, Joshua, etc; Two, we can praise God for His compassion for the widows, orphans, and the fatherless; Three, we can appreciate the quote from the Apostle Paul in Ephesians 4:7-8, where he borrows verse 18 to reinforce Christ's triumphant return from heaven after His resurrection and gives His gifts of salvation (We better pass over the bloody conflict part where dogs feast on dead bodies and people walk in bloody fields); Four, we can appreciate the prominent place the Psalmist gives to women *(V.25)*; and Five, the future dream (called eschatology) where the nations of the world recognize and bow down to worship the God and the Father of our Lord Jesus.

# PSALM 69

## A Cry for Deliverance

The superscription states this is a psalm of David and should be sung to the tune "Lillies." This psalm is defintely a lament by a hurting individual bowed down with trouble and misery. This person is asking God's help to deliver him from a serious illness and some kind of false accusation from enemies of which he claims innocence.

There is no agreeement among biblical scholars as to the author or setting the date of of this psalm. Some claim it is one of David's poems, while others say it was written after the return from Babylonian exile, during the time of Ezra and Nehemiah. It would seem to this interpreter that the latter time is the more appropriate setting. The conditions described in Psalm 69 seem to be more in keeping with the return of those from Babylon, who rebuilt the walls of Jeusalem and tried to find some kind of order and stability in a land suffering from neglect and chaos. This would describe the sitaution throughout the land of Judah in the 5$^{th}$ century, B. C. The hurting individual in the psalm was probably one of the leaders of the community.

Psalm 69 is one of the most quoted psalms in the New Testament, directly or indirectly. Seven of its thirty-six verses were borrowed by New Testament writers to enhance the work of Jesus.

To help us examine this lengthy compositon, we will divide it up into seven segments: One, A Plea for Help, Verses 1-3; Two, The Psalmist's Predicament, Verses 4-12; Three, LORD Please Answer My Prayers, Verses 13-18; Four, Hear My Lament, Verses 19-21; Five, Imprecation, Verses 22-28; Six, Praises to You LORD, Verses 19-34; and Seven, God Will Save Jerusalem! Verses 35-36.

209

## Segment One – A Plea for Help. Verses 1 - 3

Our Psalmist is seriously depressed. *(V.1)* He cries out to God for help. He is fearful that he is about to die. He groans and and is overwhelmed. *(V.2)* This almost sounds like Jeremiah the Prophet. Jeremiah's enemies threw him down an empty cistern. It had no water in it, but in the bottom was a thick layer of muck and Jeremiah sank down deep into it. He probably felt he was going to die, just like the Psalmist. (Jeremiah 38:6-13)

The Psalamist is troubled and fearful. He tells us he is exhausted from weeping. *(V.3)* Help me God. Why are you so slow in answering me?

## Segment Two – The Psalmist's Predicament. Verses 4 - 12

In this segment, we're told that many influential enemies want the Psalmist dead, punished for something he didn't do. *(V.4)* He then reflects on his life and realizes God knows everything about him, and so he verbally acknowledges his humanity and admits he has sinned. *(V.5)* Then he appeals to God's self interest that He should protect those who trust in God. *(V.6)* Apparently many see the Psalmist as a role model. His reasoning is that if he is not vindicated, others will be confused and will stumble. He tells the Lord that he is being mocked for being faithful to God. *(V.7)* Even this own brothers are treating him like a stranger. *(V.8)* Those who insult him are really also insulting God. *(V.9)* In verses 10-12, the Psalmist is further excoriated because of his loyalty to Jehovah.

This reminds us of Jesus' teachings about suffering for righteousness' sake found in the Sermon on the Mount. (See Matthew 5:10-11.) Jesus endured many insults for God's sake and ours. If there was ever an example of One who was willing to bear abuse to please His heavenly Father, it is our Lord Jesus. His personal experiences in life certainly reflects the words in Segment Two.

## Segment Three – LORD Please Answer My Prayers. Verses 13 - 18

The Pslamist makes a second impassioned appeal to God for help, not too different from Verses 1-2. He is seeking deliverance from his predicament and plight. His appeal is on the basis of God's *("Checed,")*, His "unfailing love." *(V.13)* On this basis he begs the LORD not to let him sink deeper in dispair. *(V.14-17)* Free me now from my enemies! *(V.18)*

## Segment Four — Hear My Lament. Verses 19 - 21

This part of the psalm is more of the Psalmist's lament. The new element here is his claim that God knows everything. (V.19) He says that God knows how the comtempt for him by his accusers broke his heart. He is sitting on the pity pot asking God to comfort him. (V.20)

We Christians are sometimes called upon to take a suffering path in following our Lord. In verse 21 the Psalmist seems to predict what Jesus actually experienced in His crucification. The Palmist says his enemies offer him sour wine in an attempt to satisfy his thirst. (Matthew 27:34) Unlike the Psalmist, we have a wonderful High Priest who has gone to heaven to help us. The writer of Hebrews in the New Testament says we can come boldly to the throne of God and seek His grace. Grace may mean God might not end our suffering, which might have some purpose, but God will help us endure it. (Hebrews 4:15-16)

## Segment Five — Imprecation. Verses 22 - 28

Imprecation means to pray to God to damn someone. In this segment, the writer calls upon God to wreak vengeance on his enemies, to retaliate for what he feels has been done to him. (V.22-23) He wants God to consume them in His anger (V.24) and destroy their homes. (V.25) They mock God for the punishment he apparently has visited upon them. (V.26) Then he becomes more specific, he wants God to take their sins and pile them high! (V.27) In other words, if these accusers of the Psalmist repented and came to God and confessed their sins and said they are sorry, the Psalmsts is telling God not to forgive them. The Psalmist actually calls on God to erase their names from the Book of Life. (V.28)

This is where we Christians have to part company with this kind of false thinking. Jesus said we need to not just forgive our enemies but love them. (Matthew 5:43-46) The Apostle Paul spoke the mind of Christ when he said we must leave room for God's wrath by not taking vengence on our enemies ourselves. (Romans 12:19) In Psalm 69: 22-23, the Psalmist asks God to blind his enemies. It is also interesting to see that Paul quotes verses 22-23 of Psalm 69 in his letter to the Romans as a prophecy of a judicial blind on the majority of the people of Israel because of their rejection of Jesus as God's Messiah. Quoting the Psalmist in verse 22, Paul indicates that the chosen people who do not accept Jesus as their Savior have been blinded. *(Romans 11:10)* But then Paul provides hope for Israel by adding that those not accepting Jesus as the Messiah helped make Jesus's salvation available to the Gentiles. Further, when Israel does accept Jesus as its Messiah, it will be an even greater blessing for the world. *(Romans 11:9-12)*

## Segment Six – Praise to You, LORD. Verses 29 - 34

Still another plea for deliverance is brought forth in verse 29. The Psalmist pleads with God to rescue him, very similar with verses 13-15 and 18. The Hebrew word for "rescue" is *("Natsal")* which can also be translated as "deliverance." The author is now assuming God will answer his prayers and he will be rescued. In gratitude, he will present God with a thanksgiving gift of his singing. *(V.30)* He then makes a radical pronouncement for that time by saying his singing will please the LORD more than a sacrifice of an oxen. *(V.31)* One interpreter hypothesized that this point-of-view was what possibly incited some of his fellow Jews to oppose him. Incidentally, he was not the only voice expressing criticism of the sacrifical system. Many years before, Amos thundered his denunciation. Speaking for God, he says instead of religious festivals and burnt sacrifices God seeks justice and righteous living from His people. *(Amos 5:21-24)* The author of Psalm 69 ends this strophe by asking all those who seek God's help to be joyful. *(V.32)* For the LORD hears the cries of the oppressed. *(V.33)* He then calls on all creation to praise God. *(V.34)*

## Segment Seven – God Will Save Jersulsam! Verses 35 - 36

The end of Pslam 69 is in the form of a hymn—all the world, the heaven and the seas and everything under the seas are to praise Jehovah God, because with His help, the cities of Judah will be rebuilt and Jerusalem will be a safe haven! *(V.35)* And the land of of Israel will be inherited by all you obey God. (V.36)

# PSALM 70
## David Wants a Quick Deliverance

The subscription for Psalm 70 indicates that it was written by David. This short psalm is almost a word-for-word duplication with Psalm 40:13-17. We don't know why this sort of thing happened. Probably some kind of editorial mix-up when the Psalter was reassembled hundreds of years after the Jews returned from their captivity in Babylon.

David reigned as king of Israel for 40 years. He was installed after being blessed and approved by God. The Lord called David a man after God's own heart. *(Acts 13:22)* In this psalm, David seems to be in some kind of difficulty for most of his career. Someone is always threatening his life. Because it is a short psalm (only 5 verses), we will offer a commentary on it as a whole.

This is another prayer of David's. He prays for three things from the Lord:

One, he wants God to give him a quick rescue. *(V.1)*

Two, he prays that God will rid him of his enemies. *V.2-3)*

Three, David prays for those who are followers of God, asking that they may receive joy. *(V.4)*

We are not sure what is the emergency for which David wants an immediate response from God. He is not asking God to destroy his enemies, he just wants them to feel shame and be turned back. He wants God to frustrate them in their plans. Apparently they are ridiculing and mocking the king.

There is a close parallel between David and Jesus in some ways. When Jesus was here on earth, he had similar problems with the Pharisees, the Chief Priests, and the Teachers of the Law. They plotted His demise. When they crucified our Lord, the Gospel writer Matthew tells us the people watching the crucification of Jesus ridiculed and mock Him saying He trusted God let God demosrate that Jesus is His son by delivering now. *(Matthew 27:38-43)*

David was a powerful king, and yet he not only put his total trust and faith in God, he let it be known that only God could help and save him. His last words of this emotion-filled prayer were don't delay LORD. *(V.5)* These words are the theme of this psalm. It also was the cry on the tongue of the early church, for they prayed that Jesus would return soon. They had to undergo persecution and looked forward to a time when they would be in heaven with God and Jesus. At the end of the Book of Revelation, Jesus reassures His followers that He indeed is the heir of David's throne. That He is the bright morning star and the giver of life eternal. He then ends by saying He is indeed coming soon. *(Revelation 22:16-20)*

# PSALM 71
## A Psalm About Aging

There is no superscription for this psalm. The only other psalm in Book Two that has no title is Psalm 43, and that is linked to David's Psalm 42. Much of the first three verses of this psalm are taken from the opening verses of Psalm 31, which was written by David. The Greek translation of the Psalter called the Septuagint says David is the author. The evidence seems fairly conclusive that he wrote this psalm, so we shall assume he is the author.

There are many ways to look at this composition, but, for ease of interpretation, we will divide it into five segments: One, Rescue Me from My Enemies, Verses 1-4; Two, The LORD Is My Mighty Protector, Verses 5-8; Three, My Enemies Are Still At Work, Verses 9-13; Four, I Want to Share My Testimony, Verses 14-19; and Five, Looking to the Future, Verses 20-24.

### Segment One — Rescue Me from My Enemies. Verses 1 - 4

The psalm begins with David asking the LORD to save him from his enemies. In nearly every psalm he has written, there is invariably a mention of those who hate him and who were trying to do him harm. David had a strong personality and was endowed with wisdom and the ability to see the long view of things. Therefore, he was able to give orders and make unpopular decisions and had the strength of character to see that these orders were carried out. This combination of wisdom, strength and military acumen was what made Israel the powerful nation it became in David's day. However, his leadership stirred up jealousy and envy so that he always had his share of detractors, including the rebellion of his own son, Absalom.

As the years went by, David had to face what we all must deal with as we go on the downward side of the life cycle. We find ourselves slowing down physically as we age. Our hearing declines, our eyesight diminishes, and we aren't able to sleep as well as we used to when we were younger. The one good thing David had going for him in his maturing years was his wonderful commitment to Yahweh, his LORD. In writing this psalm, he is pleading with God that he not be disgraced and he be rescued. *(V.1-2)* David had this marvelous way of humbling himself before God, and yet being able to talk with the LORD man-to-man. He gets very personal with God pleading with Him to listen to him with His good ear. *(V.2)* He then reminds God that God is David's rock and fortress. *(V.3)* He ends this segment by again pleading with God to protect him. *(V.4)*

## Segment Two — The LORD My Mighty Protector. Verses 5 - 8

The aging monarch has spent most of his life in the shelter of God's protection dodging arrows and spears physically and figuratively from various and sundry enemies. Now in the twilight of his career, he steps back and reflects on God, his divine Partner, saying the LORD alone is his *("Yachal")* "hope." *(V.5)* I have placed my confidence in You ever since I was a child—even in my adolescent days when out tending my father's sheep, keeping them safe from predators. You were always watching over me that is why I praise You always. *(V.6)*

You, God, endowed me with Your special spiritual insights and gave me super-human abilities so that I could make the right decisions that brought me success, not only personally, but for our nation! LORD, you are my protection and strength. *(V.7)* That is why I always sing praises to you. *(V.8)*

## Segment Three — My Enemies Are Still at Work. Verses 9 - 13

In spite of David's indomitable faith, he still had to cope with members of his council who wanted to see him toppled. You'd think that as he got older these difficulties would go way. Not so. Actually, because of his diminishing eyesight and faltering strength, they got worse. So he begs God not to abandon him. *(V.9)* He knows these enemies would move in if they realize God had forsaken him. *(V.10-11)* In his younger days when he was active and virile, he had lots of supporters and helpers who would share his burdens. But now being old and more or less alone, he calls out to God to hurry and help him. *(V.12)*

Then feeling very vulnerable, he asks God to destroy those who want to bring him harm. *(V.13)* These are the words of an old man with his back up against the wall! As we Christians read these words, we are able to empathize with this wonderful king in his situation of suffering. However, as much as we understand his predicament, we cannot countenance his prayers of imprecation, that is, his asking God to damn his enemies.

Paul, the former Pharisee, had angry and hostile feeling against the early Christian believers. He did everything to destroy them. That is, until he met the Lord Jesus on his way to Damascus. God turned him around and he became the great advocate of the very group he originally despised! (See Acts 22:6.) Paul epitomizes in his writings the way we Christians should react toward our enemies. In his letter to the church at Rome, Paul says (reflecting the spirit of Jesus) not to curse those who persecute you but to pray to God that He bless them. We Christians are to conquer evil by doing good. *(Romans 12:14-21)*

## Segment Four – I Want to Share My Testimony. Verse 14 - 19

The aging David thinks back over his life and prays to God in his usual conversational style, for that is how he communicates with the Almighty. He again hopes that God will help him. *(V.14)* In return, he says he will proclaim God's saving power all day long. *(V. 15)* The Hebrew word "saving power" is *("T'shhuw ah")*, which also can mean "rescue" or "redeem." He goes on to remind the LORD that since his earliest childhood God has taught him and that David acknowledged this to all others. *(V.16-17)* David's lifetime discipline of sharing his faith with others is a marvelous example of why he is a special role model for us Christians. It is like playing the children's game of Red Rover. When we are caught, we have to spend the rest of the game catching others. In this segment, David is saying to God that He caught him when he was a child, and David has been catching others ever since!

David pleads with God that now that he is gray and old let him continue to proclaim God's power to a new generation. *(V.18)* David acknowledges that nothing can compare with the righteousness of God. *(V.19)*

In all of David's many writings his favorite word when talking about God is *("Checed")* which means His "steadfast love," His "grace," or "kindness." It is closely related to God's covenant relationships with His chosen people.

It also has to do with "forgiveness." David wanted everyone to know about God's *("Checed")*.

In the New Testament, God's salvation centers around Jesus Christ and what He did for us by His sacrifice on the cross. When we open our lives to the indwelling Spirit of Jesus, this is the first step in our being saved. But like David's experience, our redemptive activity is not complete, and we dare not claim we're saved if we do nothing more. It is essential that we put into action in our lives a whole new way of love and compassion that reflects the essential nature of Jesus, our savior. Remember after Jesus called Peter to be His disciple, He told Peter and the other disciples in no uncertain terms that they had to put away their selfish ambitions. *(Matthew 16:24-26)* The second step in our salvation means costly love, costly giving, and sharing our testimony with others.

## Segment Five – Looking to the Future. Verses 20 - 24

Life is not always tranquil. It has its time of struggle and hurts. David learned this early in his life and it was reflected in his writing of the 23$^{rd}$ Psalm. He had to go through some dark valleys, but his faith prevailed. *(Psalm 23:4)* Having God close beside him gave David the optimism to assert in Psalm 71 that God would give him eternal life. *(V.20)* In verse 22 of Psalm 71, David brings up his favorite way to give praise to God—through his music. The God who is holy has as His plan and purpose to make Israel Holy, which in turn would influence the whole world to be holy. The Hebrew word for "Holy One" is *("Oadowsh")*, which also can mean "pure" and "consecrated."

David tells the Lord he is joyful because God has redeemed him. *(V.23)* David closes this psalm of his old age by saying he will share with others all day long God's righteous deeds. *(V.24)* The word righteous has to do with the way God deals with His world. David is testifying that God is good and consistently fair and just in all His ways with us. He is a faithful God that we can count on. We can put our faith and trust in Him.

# PSALM 72
## The Reign of God's King

Psalm 72 is called a Royal Psalm. It was written for the coronation of a Hebrew king and was to be recited or sung at an enthronement festival. It was one of nine other psalms given this title in the Psalter (See Psalms 2, 18, 20, 21, 45, 89, 110 and 132.) The title at the beginning of this composition says its of Solomon, but we're not sure whether that means that the son of David wrote it, or some later editor placed Solomon's name on the front piece to give it a special prestige.

No matter who authored Psalm 72, its importance for us Christians is the contents and their significance for our personal journeys of faith. After all, that is why we read the psalms. What we find in this psalm is a description of a godly king who has been endowed with supernatural abilities on how to govern and deal with his people in a loving and righteous manner. If Solomon was, in fact, the author (and he could well have been) then we are assuming that he was under the inspirational power of the Holy Spirit as he did his writing. The words he wrote have meaning far beyond what he realized. Like the writers of the New Testament, who wrote with God's hand guiding their thoughts, Solomon is in this instance a visionary. He has a vision of what is to come (beyond history), and, naturally, beyond this immediate act of enthronement. Therefore, we are assuming that the exalted king in this psalm has to be more than a human ruler. He has to be Jesus Christ, the King of kings and Lord of lords.

One of the great prophetic passages in the Old Testament regarding the linking of Jesus Christ to the kingdom of David comes from the prophet Isaiah. Remember David received a word from the LORD that his kingdom would be perpetuated forever! However, when the Babylonians defeated Israel in 586 BC, the monarchy was smashed and that put an end to the succession of Israel's rulers. In Isaiah's eleventh chapter, he acknowledges that the royal line of David had been cut off but he writes that out of stump of the line of David will grow a new shoot, a new Branch. On this new Branch the Spirit of the Lord will rest. *(Isaiah 11:1-2)*

That shoot, which Isaiah is talking about, is the Messiah, Jesus. He is the new branch from the chopped down stump. Isaiah goes on the say that this Messianic King will delight in obeying the LORD and will destroy the wicked with the breath of His mouth. *(Isaiah 11: 3-5)* Isaiah's passage is almost a summary of Psalm 72. It describes the way a king should ideally treat the subjects of his kingdom. It is my opinion that what we are seeing in Psalm 72 is an overview of Christ's heavenly kingdom described in earthly terms.

### Segment One – Christ Will Judge Righteously. Verses 1 - 5

As Solomon writes under the inspiration of the Holy Spirit, he sees the ideal King – the Lord Jesus Christ – "judging" the people. He uses the Hebrew word *("Shapat")* which means to govern or rule justly with fairness. Solomon says, this king will judge fairly and take care of the poor, in particulary. *(V. 1-4)* We Christians understand from the Gospel of John that Jesus says that He and the Father are one. *(John 10:30)* Jesus certainly has the mind of God, and the LORD says in Leviticus 26 that if his people would live together in love and would obey the moral laws, there would be a close correlation between living in righteousness and enjoying prosperity! *(Leviticus 26:3-4)* This reinforces the words in Psalm 72 verse 3. With Jesus reigning in His eternal kingdom there will be prosperity for all. There's no doubt where Jesus' concern is with the poor and needy. Right at the outset of His ministry here on earth, He affirmed His ministry was to preach the Good News to the poor. *(Luke 4:18-19)* Verse 5 says this king (Jesus) will be king for eternity.

### Segment Two – Christ's Reign Will Be Gentle and Fruitful. Verses 6 -11

Solomon here uses spring time rains, a beautiful figure of speech, to describe how the Messianic King will reign. *(V.6)* Prosperity will also reign. *(V.7)* He will reign all over the earth, with nomads bowing before him, kings Tarshish, Sheba and Seba bringing him tribute. *(V.8-10)* When we Christians look to the future and anticipate living with God and Jesus in the eternal kingdom, we're overjoyed to know there will be wonderful harmony and all kings will bow before Jesus! *(V.11)* This is such a delight to look forward to being a part of God's everlasting fellowship, that I want everyone to have their names written in the Lamb's Book of Life.

## Segment Three – God's Concern for the Weak. Verses 12 - 14

We started out quoting Isaiah's chapter 11 and saying it mirrors Psalm 72. Verses 4 and 5 of Isaiah chapter 11 says the future king will protect the poor and destory the wicked. A good way to prepare for Segment Three is to read through the Gospel of Luke. In almost every chapter you will find Jesus having compassion on some unfortunate person. For example, in Luke 7 we read Jesus cured the sick of diseases and give sight to the blind. *(Luke 7:21)* Jesus is God's Son, whom God sent to earth to to show us the Way to the Father. Jesus is the Word of God become flesh, and while He was here on earth, He was God incarnate. This means He manifested God's compassionate love. He truly was merciful and gracious, slow to anger and filled with constant lovingkindness and truth. He naturally would feel concern for the weak and needy. Luke tells one of Jesus' parables about His eternal kingdom. A man prepared a great feast and sent out many invitations. When all was ready, he sent his servants to notify the guests that it was time to arrive. However, they all made excuses as to why they couldn't come. So the Master told his servants to got to the streets and alleys and invite the poor, crippled and blind. *(Luke 14:21)* In verses 12 through 14 of Psalm 72 it says the eternal king (Jesus) will save the poor because their lives are precious to Him.

## Segment Four – Heaven Will Be A Wonderful Place. Verses 15 - 17

Solomon (who we are assuming wrote this psalm) is still writing under the inspiration of the Holy Spirit. Current Jewish theology sees Jerusalem as the center where Yahweh God (the LORD) resides in Zion, and all the world will come to Israel and pay honor to the Lord. All this will happen when the Messiah comes. Of course, we Christians believe that Jesus is that Messiah who has already come. The kingdom which Solomon is talking about is the New Jerusalem described in Revelation.

In verse 15, gold from Sheba is presented to the king. This, I believe, is a metaphor for when we Christians will bring our gifts to the Lord. Obviously, it will be some time in the future. Heaven will be blessed with material abundance, including food and fruits *(V.16)* and there will be constant praise and His people will bless Him all day long. *(V.17)* When we get to heaven we will join hands with people from all the nations, honoring Jesus' name.

## Segment Five – Doxology. Verses 18 - 20

The psalm ends by the Psalmist givng a benediction blessing the LORD. Apparently we imperfect creatures are given the ability and perhaps the obligation to bless our perfect Creator.

This also concludes the 2nd Book of the Psalter.

# PSALM 73

## Asaph Does a Turnabout

This is the first psalm in Book Three of the psalms. Book Three consists of Psalms 73 to 89.

A paradigm shift is a radical change from one way of looking at a problem to another, such as a different way that a person sees things. Asaph, the writer of Psalm 73, does a radical turnabout when it comes to viewing his perception of evil persons and the way they seem to go free in terms of God's concept of goodness and justice. Asaph was a member of the tribe of Levi. King David put him in charge of the worship and music at the Tabernacle. (See 1 Chronicles 6:39.) A number of psalms are attributed to Asaph (50 and 73-83).

Initially, Asaph is bothered because so-called scoundrels apparently get rich but don't pay too much attention to the worship of God. By contrast, godly people appear to have such a hard time. From his youth, Asaph was taught that, in a moral universe, a righteous God would deal harshly with the wicked and the godly would prosper.

This is the same question David raises in Psalm 37; this question also is raised in the book of Job. David's solution to this thorny question was to wait and trust God, believing that in the end the wrongs in the world would be set right. In Psalm 37, David writes that we should not be impatient with the LORD. Ultimately the wicked would be destroyed. *(Psalm 37:34)* Job, as you will recall, was a righteous man who suffered the worst kinds of calamity. He lost his wife and children, his home and all of his worldly possessions. Three of his so-called friends, who came to visit him while he was scraping his boils off on an ash heap, tell him his sufferings was the result of his sin. He takes issue with them and finally takes his case up with the LORD. God's response to Job is not to really answer at all but to point out that He is the God of all creation. *(Job 38:12)* In other words, the LORD challenges Job in having any

223

understanding of the God of creation. Job's response is to acknowledge, as a creature of the Creator, who is he to question God. *(Job 40:4-5)* Job ends up contending that God is so far above us that we dare not question what is happening here on earth.

We need to organize Asaph's psalm into five segments: One, God Is Good—Or Is He? Verses, 1-3; Two, A Description of the Wicked, Verses 4-14; Three, The Turning Point, Verses 15-20; Four, A New Awareness, Verses 21-26; and Five, The LORD Is Our Refuge, Verses 27-28.

## Segment One – God Is Good—Or Is He? Verses 1 - 3

Asaph begins this psalm with a statement he learned from his youth—one with which he thought he agreed--that to those with pure hearts God is good. *(V.1)* The orthodox formula tells us that a good God will pay special attention to those who follow His laws and worship regularly. But as the Psalmist observes the world around him, he begins to have some doubt because God doesn't seem to pay any attention whatsoever to what the wicked are doing. Perhaps God has abdicated His role and is not in control of what goes on. This bothers Asaph to the point that he almost becomes suicidal and losing faith in a God caring about the pure of heart and being upset with the wicked. *(V.2)* One thing we can say about Asaph, he was an honest man. Maybe what others wanted to say but were afraid to say, he says. Most of us Christians have had similar occasions when we have gone through times of doubt. Asaph is also envious of those who are prosperous despite their wickedness. *(V.3)*

## Segment Two – A Description of the Wicked. Verses 4 - 14

In verses 4 to 13, Asaph documents how the wicked apparent seem to live painless lives *(V.4-5)*, have jewels, clothes and all their hearts desires. *(V.6-7)* They scoff at others and speak evil, are prideful and boast against heaven. *(V.8-9)* Seeing this what are the righteous to think. *(V.10)* Doesn't God understand what is going on? *(V.11)* Doesn't He understand how arrogant these wicked are? *(V.12)* In Asaph's reflection on the rich and famous, he wonders if he should join their ranks because—by comparison—his godly life has been filled with problems. Why should he keep his heart pure when it has only brought him pain and suffering. *(V.13-14)*

## Segment Three – The Turning Point. Verses 15 - 20

Asaph is aware that if he had spoken out like this he would be a traitor to God's people. *(V.15)* During the time these angry thoughts stuck in his craw, Asaph goes into the Tent of Meeting and somehow is able to see himself in the light of God's perspective. *(V.16-17)* It all came into focus—not all at once, surely, but as he meditates he realizes he was beginning to walk on the slippery path these wicked people are on. He is able to reflect how self-centered he has been, and that God is still in control of heaven and earth! God still hates sin and ultimately He will send these arrogant individuals to destruction. *(V.18-19)* The word "destruction" in Hebrew is *("Mashshu'ah")*. It also can mean "the end of the line," "desolation," and "meaninglessness." This is why Asaph can say the present life of those who are arrogant is dreamlike and will be gone when they awake. *(V.20)* They will awaken from a dream of things that never really were!

This psalm mirrors life in the 21st century. There are many today who attempt to milk the system for all its worth and will not hesitate to manipulate the stock market or other business enterprises in order to enhance their own coffers. When we Christians see them—like Asaph—at first glance it doesn't seem right or fair for them to have more than their share of material goods. But Psalm 73 teaches us that they have no more reality than a dream. God in Jesus Christ is true Reality. *(John 1:1-3) (John 1: 14)*

## Segment Four – A New Awareness. Verses 21 - 26

The Psalmist not only has a new awakening about the ultimate destiny of the arrogant ones, but he also gains a new perspective of himself. *(V.21)* He humbly utters that to God he was acting like a senseless animal. *(V.22)* Asaph had allowed his doubt to rule him. He almost became like those he envied. However, God reached out and gently restored his faith. *(V.23-25)* He doesn't impart any theological arguments that would enable him to intellectually understand divine Destiny or the problem of evil. No, God did something better. He gave him His love and His abiding presence! The wonderful thing about all of this is when life has run its course, Asaph feels he will be received into the glories of heaven. Asaph says he wants to keep God first in his life. *(V.26)*

Faith means placing one's life in God's hands and inviting Him to guide and be available to us throughout this life and into the unknown. Those of us who live our lives on the victory side of the cross, worship the same God as Asaph. We face many of the same problems. The only difference is the coming of Jesus, the Messiah, who became the atonement for our sins. In Christ Jesus, God will accept and acquit us, and declare us not guilty because of our sin. (See Romans 3:21f.) Putting our faith in Jesus assures us we will have eternal life. (See John 3:16.)

## Segment Five – The LORD Is Our Refuge. Verses 27 - 28

The final two verses contain Asaph's conclusions after his inner struggles. He sees God's "covenant love" (His *("Checed")* upholding those who love Him. But for those who serve other gods, like materialism, they will "perish." *(V.27)* The Hebrew word for "perish" is *("Abad")*. It also can mean "to wander away." This is what they had chosen for themselves. They have separated themselves from God's love and have wandered away from God's eternal care.

The Psalmist's final word in closing this psalm tells us that he wants to get as close to God as possible. Then in grateful awareness for his new found security and great joy, he announces he will be a witness for others of the blesses the LORD does for his people. *(V.28)* Asaph's conclusions and his need to share this testimony becomes a wonderful role model for us who profess Christ. The Apostle Paul also mirrors Psalm 73 in his letter to the Corinthians where he says that the light of Christ is such a precious treasure shining within him He has to share it. *(2 Corinthians 4:13)* Asaph concludes that he wants to be close to God. We, too, want to be close to God's Son.

# PSALM 74

## Our Homeland Has Been Ravished
## Do Something About It, God

This psalm is a lament concerning the fall of Jerusalem to the armies of King Nebuchadnezzar of Babylon in the year 586 B.C. The title says it is a psalm of Asaph, who was a musician and psalm writer serving under King David. Asaph obviously lived hundreds of years prior to the massacre and destruction of the capital city, so he couldn't possibly be the actual author. There was a person by that name who was a descendant of Asaph, serving as one of the court musicians in the reign of King Josiah (640-609 B.C.) who might possibly have written this psalm. (See the sons of Asaph in 2 Chronicles 35:15.)

Apparently for the 70 years the Jews were captives in Babylon they instituted a practice of fasting and mourning during the month of August and October. When they were allowed to return to Jerusalem, they continued to lament the awfulness of their experiences away from their homeland and about their sins, which the prophets said had caused the tragedy in the first place. However, in time this practice lost its significance. For the younger people who had not experienced the rigors of Babylon, it became just another time for fun, fellowship and food. We know about this, thanks to Zechariah, who was sent to Jerusalem to speak to the priests as to whether the people should continue this traditional practice. (See Zechariah, chapter 7.) This may have been the catalyst that gave the impetus for the writing of this psalm.

Psalm 74 can be broken down into five segments for ease of interpretation. One, We Feel Rejected and Our City Is in Ruin, Verses 1-3; Two, The Enemy Has Systematically Demolished Our Worship Places, Verses 4-10; Three,

God Protected Us in the Past, Verses 11-17; Four, Please Save Our People from the Arrogant Enemy, Verses 18-20; and Five, Arise, God, and Give Us a Reason to Praise You, Verses 21-23.

## Segment One —We Feel Rejected and Our City Is in Ruin. Verses 1 - 3

According to prophecy, the city of Jerusalem and God's Temple were to become the hub from which many lands would flow down the spokes to worship the Lord. For in the Last Days the world was supposed to be ruled from Jerusalem, the LORD's own chosen city. (See Isaiah 2:1-4.) So why, God, did You allow a foreign pagan army to completely demolish Your holy city? Especially when we were Your sheep living in Your pasture? *(V.1-2)* The author ends this section by inviting God to actually walk through the ruined city and observe the destroyed sanctuary. *(V.3)*

## Segment Two – The Enemy Has Systematically Destroyed Our Worship Place. Verses 4 -10

Whoever wrote this psalm must have witnessed the actual battle or saw the results shortly afterwards because his reports are like it just happened. The invading troops shouted cries of victory *(V.4)*, chopped down the entrance of the Temple *(V.5)*, smashed carved panelings *(V.6)* and set the sanctuary on fire and burned to the ground. *(V.7)* Disheartened, the Psalmist laments and says where are Your miraculous signs indicting You will save us? *(V.9)* These enemy soldiers want to wipe out every trace of God. *(V.10)* There is nothing left and we can't even witness or honor Your name. O God, this is the worst thing that has ever happened.

## Segment Three – You Protected Us in the Past. Verses 11 - 17

Lord, why are You procrastinating? You have the power and the ability to unleash it and deliver a death blow to our enemies. *(V.11)* You have helped Your people in the past; we need You to act! Then in a more subdued manner, the author expresses his faith, calling God his king and saying to Him that He has always helped His people when they needed Him. He recounts their escape from Egypt and the miracle of the crossing the Red Sea. *(V.13)* You are the Mighty God who controls the forces of nature and You subdued the Leviathan, the evil in the sea. The Hebrew word for "Leviathan" *(V.14)* is *("Tanniym")* and it means "sea monster," "dragon," or "crocodile." The Prophet Isaiah explained this metaphor. He says the LORD destroyed Egypt, the dragon of the Nile. *(Isaiah 51:9)* So the Psalmist's words in verses 13-14 probably mean that God took care of the military forces of the Egyptians during the Exodus days. The Psalm completes this segment by reminding God that He is the creator of day and night and winter and summer. In other words, He has the power to destroy His people's enemies as well. *(V.16-17)*

## Segment Four – Save Our People from Arrogant Enemies. Verses 18 - 20

Since You have always been with us and helped us in the past, LORD, this is a serious situation where we need You to intercede and protect your doves from wild beasts. *(V.19)* These men are cruel and have no pity. The writer appeals to God's covenant love and His promises. You chose us back at Sinai, remember? You said You would be our God and we were to be Your people. (See Exodus 19:3-8.)

God told Abraham that he would be blessed and he would be the father of a great nation; God also said to David that his dynasty and his throne would continue until the end of time. With Jerusalem in shambles and the king toppled, does this mean God's Word is false? No, we Christians see the new state of Israel that came into being in 1948, and the heir-apparent to David's throne being King Jesus, God's Son, keeping the promised dynasty in tact. These are two of the reasons why God is faithful to His side of the covenant. God is forever true to His Word, even though we limited and finite mortals cannot always fathom His ways. This is why God said, (speaking through Isaiah) that His thoughts are quite different than our thoughts. And His ways quite different than our ways. *(Isaiah 55:8-9)* God is all-knowing and all-powerful and is working out His plan and purpose for our world. He is faithful to His covenant promises, even though the nation of Israel was not. Perhaps that is why God allowed all this horrible tragedy in 586 B.C. to take place in the first place.

## Segment Five – Arise and Give Us a Reason to Praise You. Verses 21 - 23

Asaph is pulling out all the stops trying to get God to act. He tries everything he can think of to remind God that His people are constantly disgraced, poor and needy. *(V.21)* But, he also reminds God, that His people only want to have a reason to praise Him. Not only this, Lord, but You are the One who is taking the brunt of the insults. *(V.22)* Finally, one last time, the Psalmist informs God that His enemies' rebellion continues to grow. *(V.23)*

We believers in Jesus know that God is in charge of our world, no matter what happens – good or bad. However, we are left with the difficult question of trying to understand why God allows certain things that seem detrimental to us to take place? For instance, we know that the first disciples of Jesus could not comprehend why Jesus had to go to His death on the cross? Of course, later when God raised Him from the dead for the salvation of the world it all became clear that evil did not have the final say! God is ultimately in control and He is able to create good even out of evil (see Romans 8:28).

Paul, a Jew by birth, agonized about why the Jews, his countrymen, had turned their backs on Jesus as the Messiah. In chapters 9-11 in his letter to the church at Rome, he tries to make sense of it. But Paul then states that God's gifts to his Jewish people can never be withdrawn ultimately. *(Romans11:28-29)* Paul goes on to say that someday by the mercies of God, the majority of the Jewish people will turn to Christ Jesus as their Savior. When will this happen? Paul concludes that is impossible for mere mortals to understand God's decisions and methods. No mortal can know what the Lord is thinking. *(Romans 11:33-34)* Paul concludes this section of Romans chapter 11 by answering the writer of Psalm 74's attempt to make God take action, by asking who is God's counselor. What we do know, Paul writes, is that all is intended for God's glory. *(Romans 11:33-36)*

We Christians acknowledge that the world is in a sorry state, with regional conflicts adding to the woes of natural disasters. Our prayers to our heavenly Father are constantly asking for His help in creating peace and order to a war-torn globe. William W. Reid, Jr. expressed his hope that God might take the lead in redeeming the world in his hymn "O God of Every Nation."

# PSALM 75

## God Will Judge with Equity

This is a psalm written by Asaph, one of the musicians appointed by King David to be in charge of the worship in the Tent of the Meeting. The superscription says it is a thanksgiving song to be sung to the tune of "Do Not Destroy," probably a popular chorus of that day. Asaph also wrote Psalm 73, which deals with the same subject matter. The two psalms concern the just rule of God.

Psalm 73 speaks about the proud and wicked and how Asaph envied them. *(Psalm 73:4)* His complaint is that they prosper while the righteous have a much harder road to go down. In Psalm 73, Asaph agonizes and struggles before he meditates in the sanctuary and finally comes to the conclusion that God will deal with these wicked arrogant individuals ultimately with equity.

In Psalm 75, there is none of this agonizing and inner struggle. The author speaks with conviction that God is in charge of the universe, but he also implies that it is not always clear as to the specifics of God's judgments— particularly the matter of timing. However, he states unequivocally that the wicked will eventually be judged.

Psalm 75 can be outlined in four segments: One, God Cares for Us, Verse 1; Two, God's Words Are Reassuring, Verses 2-5; Three, Putting Down and Lifting Up, Verses 6-8; and Four, Praise for the God of Israel, Verses 9-10.

### Segment One — God Cares for Us. Verse 1

In the liturgy, the people of the congregation in the Tent of Meeting would lift up their voices singing and giving thanks to God. *(V.1)* Always when the Jews worshiped, they would remind themselves of how in the past God had delivered them from slavery in Egypt. They would remember His miracles of the parting of the waters at the Red Sea, or of God providing manna to feed the people, or of Moses striking the rock for water. (See Exodus 14-17.) These and other miracles would remind the people of God's love and care for them.

## Segment Two – God's Words Are Reassuring. Verses 2 - 5

In true liturgical order, a priest would stand up and speak for God. In verses 2 and 3, he would tell the congregation that in God's timing justice would be brought against the wicked. God will do things when He sees conditions are right. God sees the total picture while we see only our immediate situation. In verses 4 and 5, God warns the wicked and insolent to stop being arrogant. These are words of reassurance to the godly. They also inform the wicked that God is delaying His judgments to give the wicked time to reconsider what will happen to them if they don't change their ways, and, thereby, escape God's judgment. Paul, that great theologian for Christianity, writes about this saying God is tolerant of our sins because he is patient and merciful giving us time to repent. *(Romans 2:4)*

## Segment Three – Putting Down and Lifting Up. Verses 6 - 8

The priest now adds his positive reinforcement to the words that God speaks in Segment Two. The spokesman says the Almighty is the only One who lifts us up and who judges. *(V.6-7)* It is interesting that Hannah, the mother of the prophet Samuel, recites a prayer recorded in First Samuel that in many respects parallels Psalm 75. She said that the LORD alone makes one rich and one poor, one woman barren and another woman with seven children. God also protects the godly and casts the wicked into darkness. *(1 Samuel 2: 3-10)*

It also seems that the Psalmist has paraphrased the words written by Jeremiah. Jeremiah says that the LORD said to him to take God's cup of anger and make all the nations drink it. *(Jeremiah 25:15)* Asaph also tells us in Psalm 75 that the wicked of the earth one day will take from Jehovah's hand His cup of wrath—His judgment! *(V.8)*

We Christians face many of the same things in our day that Asaph had to face back in his day. We have the same arrogant and wicked folks who try to lord it over their weaker brothers and sisters. We share the belief with

Asaph that if these wicked people don't turn their lives around and repent, they too, one day, will have to take from Jehovah's hand His cup of fury. On the other hand, if we trust Jesus for our salvation, God, in His loving kindness, will place His hand on us so that we know our sins are forgiven and we will be renewed!

### Segment Four – Praise the God of Israel! Verses 9 - 10

A spokesperson for the congregation is the speaker in Segment Four. He speaks as one who is refreshed and who is in agreement with all that was said (and sung) heretofore. He speaks of Jacob, who God named Israel. Jacob, if you recall, was fleeing from his twin, Esau. Jacob had bilked Esau out of his legitimate inheritance. Jacob got the message that Esau was on his way to confront Jacob with an army of 400 men. Jacob was frantic with fear. He prayed that the LORD would rescue him from Esau who would kill him and his wives and children. He then reminded God that God had promised Jacob that his descendants would be too numerous to count. *(Genesis 32:11-12)* That night at the Jabbok Ford on the Jordan River, a Man wrestled with Jacob all night long. He struck Jacob's hip and knocked it out of joint at the socket. The Man asked Jacob to let him go. But Jacob said he would not let Him go unless He blesses him. The Man then blessed him saying he no longer was Jacob, which can mean "to supplant" "to circumvent," but his name now was Israel. Israel can be translated "a man seeing god," "a prince of God." *(Genesis 32: 26-28)* Asaph ends Psalm 95 by singing praises to Israel's God *(V.9)* and proclaiming that God will cut off the wicked and increase the power of the godly. *(V.10)*

If you are a follower of the Lord Jesus Christ, you will want to make a similar commitment. We Christians can say with the Apostle Paul that we can sing praises to the God and Father of Jesus Christ our Lord. *(2 Corinthians 1:3-4)*

# PSALM 76
## God Defends Jerusalem

After the Exile when the individual psalms of the Psalter were being re-found, the priest-editor(s) had three psalms that he thought were written by Asaph and had some linkage. Psalm 74 asks God to stop the violence and injustice in the world; Psalm 75 asks God when is He ready to intervene and judge the wicked and deliver the godly; Psalm 76 has God destroying an invading army and protecting His people in Jerusalem. All three have God acting in His capacity as Judge. Perhaps this is why they were placed in the order we now have them.

Most interpreters see Psalm 76 as a celebration of Jerusalem's deliverance from an Assyrian army when Assyria's King Sennacherib was on the throne in 701 B. C. It is interesting to note that when the Pilgrims first came to America, they named one of their first settlements in Massachusetts "Salem" from verse two in the *King James* translation of Psalm 76.

The background for Psalm 76 is found in two places: 2 Kings 18-19 and Isaiah 36-37. Hezekiah was a godly king of Israel who rebelled against Assyria and refused to pay any more tribute. During the fourth year of Hezekiah's reign, King Shalmaneser of Assyria attacked Israel and lay siege on the city of Samaria. Samaria fell and all of its citizens were transported to Assyria. Later, Sennacherib became Assyria's king and he captured all the fortified cities of Judah. Hezekiah sued for peace and sent a huge amount of tribute, most of it he stripped from the Temple. Nevertheless, a large Assyrian army marched on Jerusalem to destroy it. It was during this crisis that Isaiah the prophet sent Hezekiah a message from the LORD saying God Himself will defend this City of David to the point where no armies at all will enter Jeruslaem. *(2 Kings 19:32-34)* That very night an angel from the Lord killed 185,000 Assyrian troops, and King Sennacherib returned to Nineveh. Jerusalem was miraculously saved!

We have divided Psalm 76 into four segments: One, God's Home in Zion, Verses 1-3; Two, God Rebuked His Enemies, Verses 4-6; Three, God's Judgments from on High, Verses 7-10; and Four, Wonderful Praises for the LORD, Verses 11-12.

### Segment One – God's Home in Zion. Verses 1 - 3

Verses 1 and 2 state that God is well known in Israel *(V.1)* and that He resides in Jerusalam. *(V.2)* God also protects His people living in Jerusalem. (V.3) Back in the days when this psalm was written, the Jewish people believed that Yahweh God (the LORD) resided with them in Zion, which was a metaphor for Jerusalem. Because God is a Spirit existing outside of our realm of time and space, we human beings cannot connect with Him, that is, unless He chooses to make Himself known. But that is precisely what He did. In fact, the entire Old Testament (the Jewish Bible) is a record and an exciting account of times when God broke into human life and revealed Himself, first to Abraham, Isaac and Jacob, then to Moses, Joshua, then to David and on up to the present day. We Christians consider the Old Testament as our Scriptures, sharing them with our Jewish brothers and sisters. We believe that God revealed Himself to Israel, just like it says in verses 1 and 2. We cannot explain it rationally. We say, *How odd of God to choose the Jews.* But He did! And we believe God chose the Jewish nation to work out His plan for our world. The Book of Hebrews in the New Testament says that God long ago revealed Himself to the Jewish ancestors and in these final days he revealed Himself through His Son Jesus. *(Hebrews 1: 1-2)*

Although the Psalmist's language is rather primitive and presents the Lord as a warrior God in verse 3 of Psalm 76, God, in actuality, is portrayed as a divine, righteous Judge before whom all of us must stand. This is the underlying theme of Psalm 76.

### Segment Two – God Rebuked His Enemies. Verses 4 - 6

The author waxes eloquently saying nothing here on earth can compare with God. *(V.4)* For He has caused the defeat of the mightiest enemies of the Jewish people. *(V.5)* 2 Kings tells us that 185,000 Assyrian soldiers lay

235

dead (Do you suppose that is a bit of poetic exaggeration?) (*2 Kings 19:32-34*) Maybe not. (*V.6*)

## Segment Three – God's Judgment from on High. Verses 7 - 10

The Psalmist is reflecting on what happened with the Assyrians. He is saying that when people take God's judgment seriously, no wonder the Jewish people are greatly feared. (*V.7*) But it is God Himself who brandishes the sword of judgment. God's enemies only enhance the glory of God when he disposes of them. (*V.8-10*) Apostle Paul was an expert on the Hebrew law. Speaking to Jews (and to us Christians), he informs us that a day of judgment can be expected for all, past and present, by a just God. (*Romans 2: 5-12*) We need to take God's judgment seriously. We're not sure if verse 8 in Psalm 76, where the Psalmist says the earth stands still and trembles, means the final judgment, but everyone must stand accountable before God at Judgment Day.

No matter who we are or what we've done in the past, if we turn from our sins and put our trust in Christ Jesus, God will accept us and forgive us and treat us as if we have never sinned. What this means, as the Apostle Paul writes, Jesus was sent by God the Father to take the punishment for our sins. Jesus alone is our Savior and Lord. (*Romans 3:25*)

Yes there is a judgment side of God. But the other side of God's righteous anger is His "loving-kindness" (His *"Checed"*). When Jesus announced His ministry to the world, He spoke of God's mercy saying He was sent to the brokenhearted to free them from their oppressors. (*Luke 4:18-19*)

Verse 10 reflects a final insight that God's judgment on those who oppose Him actually enhances His glory. Just as light is enhanced by darkness, opposition enhances God's omnipotence. At first glance, this may be confusing. But look back to the story of Joseph and his jealous brothers. In their anger they wanted their father's favorite, Joseph, to be destroyed. This story may shed some light for us on verse 10. The brothers sold Joseph as a slave to Egyptian traders. Then, years later when a great famine hit, Jacob told his sons to go to Egypt and buy some food. By now, by God's grace, Joseph had become the number two person in all Egypt. Joseph had put food away for such emergencies and was able to help the very brothers who sold him into slavery. But when the brothers discovered who Jospeh was and the power of life or death he now had over them, they were rightly worried. But

Joseph eased their fears saying that what they meant as evil, God used for good. *(Genesis 50:15-20)*

## Segment Four – Wonderful Praise for the LORD. Verses 11- 12

In gratitude to God for His miraculous deliverance of Jerusalem from Sennacherib's hordes, the citizen's of the holy city owed Jehovah God (the LORD) their allegiance. They should make their vows and then live up to them! *(V.11)* When Moses led the children of Israel from slavery in Egypt, he went up to Mount Sinai and met Yahweh God. God reminded the Hebrew people through Mose that He carried them on eagles' wings out of the clutches of the Egyptians' claws. He then made a covenant with them. They were to be His own special teasure. Their obligation was to obey Him. *(Exodus 19:3-6)* The Psalmist ends this psalm reminding the people that they need to bring tribute to the God Who protected them. *(V.12)*

We Christians want to bring gifts to God, and the appropriate gift would be our lives. We too are Covenant people. Paul tells us the gift God seeks is that we become a living sacrifice, a sacrifice for doing God's will. Is this too much for a God Who promises us eternal life? *(Romans 12:1)* The answer is <u>no</u>! We are God's people, or as God said to Moses, we too shall be God's special treasure where Christ's creative love can take place. Verse 12 tells the world that it is all too silly for heads of state to feel their own importance and power. All leaders, including dictators and presidents, need to know that the Almighty God is in charge of what goes on in this world. He knows when heads of state get too big for their britches. They need to know that God is to be feared by the unrighteous. *(V.12)* Psalm 2 informs the rulers of the world that they need to come before God with fear and trembling and submit to God's royal son. *(Psalm 2:10-12)*

# PSALM 77
## Alone and Rejected

Psalm 77 is a mixture of a trouble-filled lament (first half) and a hymn-like recounting of God's mighty miracles in the past (second half). The superscription is not too informative. It says it is a psalm of Asaph written for Jeduthun, a choir director. It is a tragic prayer by a person who feels God has turned His back, not only on him, but on God's people as well. As a result, the author feels overwhelmed and dejected. While he doesn't tell us specifically, it would seem that the Psalmist is one of the group of exiles carried off to Babylon after the humiliating defeat of Israel by King Nebuchadrezzar in the year 587 B.C. This would appear to be the best case scenario because it explains the loss of the homeland, the monarchy, the worship center, even God Himself!

### Segment One – In Deep Distress. Verses 1 - 4

The first two verses of this section indicate the author is upset and has feelings of rejection. He sees himself in deep trouble and needs the help of the Lord. Nine times, in the first four verses, he uses either "I" or "me" and so we can see how self-centered this prayer is. When he thinks of God not responding, he just moans. (V.3) Finally, he gives up, telling God he is is too depressed to even pray. (V.4)

### Segment Two – The Good Old Days. Verses 5 - 6

In this section the author tells us how it was in the good old days. (V. 5) He is feeling sorry for himself, which is quite understandable, being far from home and in terrible circumstances. Back then he say his nights were filled with songs of joy. *(V. 6)* He says he has done a lot of soul-searching and meditating, thinking how it was then compared with now. The Hebrew word for "meditating" *("Hagah")*, tranlated here as "think" *(V. 6)* can also be translated as "to sigh," or "to moan," which reinforces the idea that the Psalmist is in exile in Babylon.

## Segment Three – Many Unanswered Questions. Verses 7 - 9

The one encouraging thing we can say about the author in this segment is that he is back to ruminating about God. Perhaps he doesn't sense God's presence with him now, but when he looks back he had an intimate relationship with God that made him feel happy. So he begins to ask a series of searching questions: will he be rejected by the Lord forever; when will He show me his favor again. *(V. 7)* Have You withdrawn Your *("Checeh")*, Your "unfailing love?" *(V. 8)* O God, have You turned Your back on Your own special people? And what about Your promises? And what about Your compassion? *(V. 9)*

These are profound questions that we Christians sometimes ask and are in need of answers. The Psalmist is saying that God has changed! Does God change? The answer is a resounding NO! The Jewish Christians back in Rome in the First Century were wavering in their faith, due to the persecutions by the Emperor Nero. The writer of Hebrews in the New Testament says to those Jewish Christians that Jesus Himself pleads to God on their behalf. *(Hebrews 7:24-25)* Then the writer proclaims that this same Jesus, like the Father Himself, is the same yesterday, today and forever. *(Hebrews 13:8)* In other words, Jesus pleads for us Christians today before the Father as well.

## Segment Four – A Difficult Verse. Verse 10

Because God seems to be absent and to have abandoned the author, he has jumped to the conclusion that God's love for His people has changed to hatred. *(V.10)* The Psalmist feels this way because from childhood he was imbued with the idea that God was a mighty warrior who drowned Pharaoh's chariots in the Red Sea and overthrew those who opposed His people (See Exodus 15). In other words, since God is not helping him or the Jewish people presently, God's love must have turned to hate. The Psalmist personalizes this as his fate. *(V.10)*

## Segment Five – Miracles Remembered. Verses 11 - 20

The Psalmist begins verse 11 by again recalling how the LORD did so many miraculous deeds in the past for His people. He can't stop thinking about them – about the stories of Joseph and how God had used him for God's glory. *(V.12)* Then a thought pops into his mind that God's ways are holy. *(V.13)* If the LORD's ways are holy, then He wouldn't manifest Himself in hatred. Then all of a sudden he understands that it isn't God who has changed, it's me! I'm the one who has allowed all this being captured and being taken into a foreign land to change my faith. God is still the God of miracles. *(V.14)* In veses two and seven, the Psalmist refers to God as the "Lord" as *"Adonai."* But in verse 11, he refers to God as the "LORD" as *"YHWH,"* a tetragrammaton that acknowledges the omnipotence of God.

He's the One who reveals Himself in specific acts, and He is still at work! We are the descendants of Joseph and Jacob. All religous Jews, when they think of God, think of the miracles of the exodus. *(V.15-16)* The Psalmist now adds to his day-dreaming by envisioning clouds, thunder and lightning which allowed the Hebrews to escape from the Egyptians. *(V.18-19)* This miracle allowed God's people to cross the Red Sea safely, led by Moses an Aaron like shepherds leading a flock of sheep. *(V.20)*

What is so helpful about reading the psalms is that we are privileged to look over the shoulders of these writers and see their struggles and see how they interact with God. There is no pretense here. No, they don't try to hide their feelings or their innermost doubts. We can learn from them.

In this case our Psalmist actually blames God for his sufferings. However, we are able to see how God's Holy Spirit is able to nudge him back to faith as He led him to remember that the LORD *("YHWH")* is still a mighty God of miracles. From that he realizes God's ways are holy. With this revelation, he is able to reorient his whole outlook! It didn't change his present situation in Babylon, but he realized he was a member of God's people who has already been redeemed! Spiritually, he was becoming a changed person! And because of his inner change, it obviously will affect his current situation with a more positive outlook. All this because he sees that the LORD cares! And he sees God leading His people like a flock of sheep. *(V.20)* He is once again part of that flock.

God is still at work through His Holy Spirit and through the living Spirit of Jesus. We praise You, God, that we Christians are able to relate to these Psalmists.

# PSALM 78
## A Long Historial Sermon

Psalm 78 is one of the great historical psalms. The superscription tells us it was written by Asaph. It is a composition recounting episodes from Israel's early beginnings, and God's interaction with His chosen people, especially when they were beng rebellious and blatantly disobedient! The purpose for including this long sermon (72 verses) in the Songbook (the Psalter), was to warn its readers not to make the same ethical and moral mistakes as their forefathers.

The Judeo/Christian religion is historical, that is, it is rooted in history. It has its beginnings and its continuation with individuals and groups who claim to have encounters and communications with the Living God here on earth. God is a Spirit who by definition exists outside of time and space. He is omnipotent. He is powerful. He is omnipresent—He is everywhere and at all times present. He is omniscient—having knowledge of all things.

The Judeo/Christian faith believes that this mighty God has a plan and a purpose for all who live on planet earth, which includes working toward a time when there will be total peace and brotherhood for everyone. In His divine wisdom, God decided to choose a people through whom He would work out His plan. For whatever reason known only by God, He chose the Hebrew people. He appeared to various individuals like Abraham, Isaac and Jacob. At a later time, he confronted a man named Moses and negotiated a contract (Covenant) with the Hebrew people saying He would be their God and would take care of them. Their part of the contract was to give total allegiance to God and to obey His commandments, which He gave to them. Prior to this, the Hebrew people were slaves in Egypt. He sent Moses to Egypt and through a series of miracles, engineered by God, He brought the people out of Egypt to be a free people. Psalm 78 tells us what took place after they left Egypt and how God worked His will through them.

We Christians are part of this history. It is our conviction that God's plan for all of us continued through the Jewish people. We believe the Hebrew Prophets foretold the coming of the Messiah, along the lines of the Davidic king, and we believe God sent His Son, Jesus, to be His messianic King.

It is important for us to know the historical and spiritual background of our faith. That's why reading the psalms is so important and helpful. So let's get on with Psalm 78.

We can better look at this psalm by dividing it up into seven segments, as follows: One, The Introduction, Verses 1-8; Two, Rebellion by Ephraim, Verses 9-16; Three, Putting God to the Test, Verses 17-31; Four, Sin In Spite of God's Goodness, Verses 32-39; Five, God's Mighty Miracles, Verses 40-55; Six, An Angry God! Verses 56-64; and Seven, The LORD Chooses Judah and David, Verses 65-72.

## Segment One – The Introduction. Verses 1 - 8

Asaph is the preacher—can't you just imagaine him talking to a big crowd at one of the many festivals? He starts off asking the people to open their ears to what he is about to teach. *(V.1)* The Hebrew word for "open your ears" is *("Azan")*, which is a command to "pay attention!" He continues to tell them they are to hear parables about their history passed down to them from long ago—stories that they (and we) will need to tell their (and our) children. *(V.2-3)* The word for "parables" is *("Mashal")*. It also means "stories," or "proverbs."

We Christians know about "parables" because that's the way Jesus taught. He would tell a story, for instance, of a woman who lost a coin. She'd searched for it and when she found it she rejoiced! The story was really a metaphor of a lost person who was found by God, and Jesus would add that similarly God's angels like the woman who found her lost coin rejoice when one sinner repents. *(Luke 15:10)* A "parable" is a teaching where the hearer can visualize the story in his/her mind's eye. The Psalmist says each generation needs to be reminded to obey His laws and not forget the LORD's miracles. *(V.4)* This is vitally important because we are commanded to teach our children these things. *(V.6)* Appreciating God's many benefits will go a long way in keeping them from being like their ancestors who were

unfaithful, subborn, rebellious and half-hearted followers of the LORD.
(V.7-8)

## Segment Two – Rebellion by Ephraim. Verses 9 - 16

This segment begins the historical interaction of God with His people. You
have to know that the tribe of Ephraim at the time of the conquest of the
promised land was the largest of the twelve tribes. According to verse 9,
the soldiers from Ephraim exhibited cowardice and fled in the face of their
enemies. The Psalmist attributes this to the fact that did not keep God's
covenant and laws (V.10) and even more important they forgot the miracles
He had shown them. (V.11) They were not mindful what God did to protect
them.

Going back to verse 2, Asaph says he will teach "hidden lessons" from
the past. In Hebrew "hidden lessons" is the word ("Chiydah"). It can be
translated into English as "puzzle," "riddle," "dark saying," or "a parable."
Verses 12 through 16, Asaph itimizes the various miracles of God in leading
the Hebrew people out of Egypt and protecting them as they wandered
in the Wilderness. It is clear that the Ephraim adults didn't get taught the
secrets of God's grace and loving power when they were children. Asaph
includes the above verses to show those of us who read Psalm 78 that the sin
of unbelief has serious consequences.

## Segment Three – Putting God to the Test. Verses 17 - 31

Despite the care God showed the Hebrews, they kept rebelling against God.
(V.17) They willfully tested God in their hearts. (V.18) They griped and
complained. (V.19) The preacher speaks of two sins in this section. The first
is the sin of ingratitude. It seems difficult for us to understand when God
supplied their every need yet they murmured and grumbled. This riled
God up. (V.21) The second sin was the sin of unbelief. They didn't believe in
God or trust Him to care for them (V.22) in spite of receiving manna from
heaven and birds to eat. (V.23) Their ingratitude was too much, and so the
God caused them to get deathly ill, killing many of Israel's finest young
men. (V.31)

Following Jesus' baptism, He was filled with the Holy Spirit of God, and
was tempted by the Devil. In one of the temptation episodes, Satan told Jesus

he'd give Him all the kingdoms of the world *IF* He would worship him. To this Jesus answers, quoting the scriptures, that He (and we) must worship the LORD and serve Him. *(Deuteronomy 6:13)* These Scriptural replies to Satan by Jesus *(Matthew 4:1-11)* are a necessary corrective to what the Israelites did to God prior to Jesus.

### Segment Four – In Spite of God's Goodness. Verses 32 - 39

The Pslamist begins at verse 32 pointing out that God's chosen people kept on sinning in spite of all that the Lord did for them. God's response was to end their lives. *(V.33)* But there were occasions when the people of Israel outwardly at least repented and return to worshiping God. *(V.34)* However, their repentance was not true repentance. And how they must have sickened God. Not only did they not keep His covenant, but their hearts were not loyal to Him. *(V.37)* Yet God was merciful and forgiving and only destroyed some of them. *(V.38)* He held back His anger. God was mindful that they were mere mortals. *(V.39)*

It is interesting to compare the words of the Prophet Hosea with the words of Asaph. Hosea saw Assyria rising in power and marching against the Northern Kingdom of Israel. Speaking the Word of the LORD, Hosea says that the LORD (not the Assyrians) will attack you for your rebellion and multipied sins. *(Hosea 10:10)* We can just imagine Hosea looking over the countryside and with a saddened voice, recalling that when Israel was a mere child, the LORD loved him as a son. Brought him out of Egypt. Lifted from his neck the yoke of slavery, and fed him. *(Hosea 11:1-4)* Hosea's predictions came true. The Northern Kingdom fell to the Assyrian armies in 722 B.C. and its inhabitants were all taken as slaves to Ninevah.

### Segment Five – God's Mighty Miracles. Verses 40 - 55

Asaph the preacher goes back to that period known as the Exodus once again. He covers how grieved God was when the people often rebelled against Him in the desert and in the wilderness. *(V.40)* How they forgot that God rescued them from their enemies. *(V.42)* In verses 43 to 51, he lists a half dozen miraculous plagues with which the Holy One of Israel assulted the Egyptian people. What God did were great displays of His power and love. God then led His own people safely to the border of His Holy land.

*(V.54)* He also drove out the nations and settled the Hebrew tribes into their homes. *(V.55)*

## Segment Six – An Angry God. Verses 56 - 64

In this segment, the rebellious people of God's covenant in the so-called Promised Land went beserk! Asaph says the people were as useless to God as a crooked bow. *(V.57)* God then rejected Israel completely. *(V.59)* He abandoned Shiloh as His dwelling place *(V.60)* and allowed His Ark to be captured by His and the Hebrew's enemies. *(V.61)* He even allowed His priests to be slaughtered. *(V.64)* The Northern Kingdom, led by the tribe of Ephraim, was totally crushed in 722 B.C. All this because of Israel's twin sins of rebellion and spiritual adultery.

The idea of God choosing the Hebrews and doing this so that He could work out His divine plan for our world seemed to be derailed! Was this the end of everything?

## Segment Seven – The LORD Chooses Judah and David. Verses 65 - 72

No! Not all was lost! Jehovah God (the LORD) rose up – fully awake after a sleep and He marched to victory! *(V.65)* Jehovah not only routed His enemies but cast them to eternal shame. *(V.66)* He then spurned Joseph's descendants, the Northern Kingdom of Israel. *(V.67)* But we will see in the New Testament that did not mean He stopped caring for them and loving them. *(Romans 11;1-12)* It just meant His plan for the salvation of the world had to do with the tribe of Judah and with David, the shepherd boy as His king, and Jesus the Messiah who came from the lineage of David, who was (and is) Lord of lords and King of kings. *(Psalm 78:68-72)*

245

# PSALM 79
## The Awful Slaughter of God's People

The gifted writer named Asaph was able to piece together snippets of other writer's accounts of the catastrophic and humiliating defeat of Jerusalem at the hands of Nebuchadrezzar and his army from Babylon in 587 B.C. This is the second lament on this subject authored by Asaph. His first lament was Psalm 74, and it centered around the loss of the Temple.

Psalm 79 is more concerned with the horrible loss of life and the shame it has brought to Yahweh God (the LORD). We do not know why there was such barbarous aggression by the Babylonian soldiers. It was as if they wanted to erase every vestige of Jewish life, so great and thorough was the destruction, including the profanation of the Temple. The heathen hordes not only detroyed much of Jerusalem but systematically went through the whole land of Judea and destroyed all the worship centers. The blasphemy was total! Thousands of God's people were indiscriminately slaughtered and dead bodies lay rotting all over the city and countryside with birds and wild animals feeding on their decaying bodies. So many Jews were killed, and there were so few survivors that they were not able to bury the dead.

Two hundred years before, the prophet Amos received a Word from the LORD concerning Judah. Amos was from the southern Kingdom of Judah put preached in the Northern Kingdom of Israel. Amos prodicted that the LORD would send down fire on Judah and all of the fortresses of Jerusalem would be destroyed. *(Amos 2:4-5)* He repeated this judgment again with his famous "ripe fruit" message. This time Amos says, speaking for the LORD, that the people of Israel are like a basket of fruit ripe for punishment and that the singing in the Temple would turn to wailing. *(Amos 8:1-3)*

Apparently, Amos' fruit wasn't ripe enough because two hundred years went by. Only by God's mercy did Judah survive. Ezekiel, the priest-prophet who was exiled in Babylon, looked through God's eyes and saw the end. Speaking to his fellow Jewish exiles, he writes that the day of judgment is about to occur. *(Ezekiel 7:1-10)*

Ezekiel's words came totally true! In the aftermath of the destruction, Israel as a nation had been <u>annihilated!</u> She ceased to exist: the king was gone, the army was no more, homes were destroyed, families were wiped out, the economy was wrecked, with the Temple demolished, the worship of God ceased, their final doom had come. There were very few survivors, and those who were alive were rounded up and marched off into captivity to Babylon. Stated in another way: the Holy people who had lived in the Holy land and who had resided in the holy city and who worshiped at the Holy Temple were gone – and so was their land, their city, and Temple.

### Segment One – Reason for Lament. Verses 1 - 4

The prayer of Asaph is heartbreaking. He reminds God that what was destroyed was His land, His special possession, and His Temple. *(V.1)* He points out that pagan nations did this to God's land. *(V.1)* The Hebrew word for "pagan" is *("Gowy")* which means, here in this context, "non Jewish." But it also has a negative connotation, "the uncircumcised, "wicked," and "idolatrous." The author bemoans saying God's special city is now a heap of ruins. *(V.1)* Asaph says that the pagans left bodies of God's servants as food for birds. *(V.2)*

In verse 3, Asaph says blood flowed around Jerusalem like water. Jeremiah the prophet was an eyewitness to this divine judgment of Jerusalem in 586 B.C. . In Lamentations, Jeremiah writes that during the seige of Jerusalem starving mothers considered (and possibly did) eat their little children. *(Lamentations 2:20-22)*

We can read about this in 2 Kings 24:10-25:21. On top of such destruction and terror, the surrounding nations self-righteously added insult to injury by scoffing and heaping contempt on those who survived. *(Psalm 79:4)*

The butchering of hundreds of innocent women and children seems so preposterous and outlandish to our naïve ears – yet some older folks can remember back to the days of World War II and the saturation bombing of cities of Dresden, and the atomic bombing of Nagasaki and Hiroshima where tens of thousands were incinerated. It would seem that we have not made much moral progress in the ensuing years. It's good to read psalms like 79 if only to remind ourselves to redouble our efforts to work for peace nationally and internationally. And, as the Apostle Paul writes, we need to do our part to live in peace with everyone. *(Romans 12:18)*

## Segment Two – Mercy and Vengeance. Verses 5 - 7

Asaph prays to the LORD asking if He will be angry with us forever? *(V.5)* This is an agonizing question. It is similar to the question the martyred Christians in heaven ask. Having died for their Christian faith, they ask the Sovereign Lord when will He judge the worldly people who martyred them. *(Revelation 6:10)* Asaph is praying for mercy. He knows that this wanton destruction was according to God's will, and not just the power of Nebuchadnezzar's troops. Any good Jew knowledgeable of the Torah knew Moses' words in Deuteronomy which said plainly if they make idols and worship anything other than the LORD they would be devoured in fire. *(Deuteronomy 4:20-25)* The Hebrew prophets were constantly reminding the people of Moses' words. Jeremiah and Ezekiel both thundered their messages of God's pending judgment to those in authority in Jerusalem. Jeremiah' explicitly quotes the Sovereign Lord saying the Jews lack of worship of the Sovereign Lord exclusively would result in the unquencable fire of God's anger. *(Jeremiah 7: 17-20)* He told them that the time will come when the land will lie in desolation. He even predicted that the bodies of God's people will be food for the birds and animals. Not only this, but Jeremiah specifically told them that the LORD Almighty would gather all the armies under Nebuchadnezzar to destroy them and make them an object of contempt forever. *(Jeremiah 25:7-9)*

Our Psalmist asks another question, perhaps acknowledging the truth of the prophets' words. In anger the Psalmist asks God to pour out His wrath on the pagan nations. *(V.6)* They're the ones who deserve Your punishment. They devoured Your people. *(V.7)* They are the heathens who don't acknowledge You. Since the unbelievers have punished us, God should retaliate, using Moses' law of an eye-for-an-eye. (Exodus 21:26)

## Segment Three – Deliverance and Judgment. Verses 8 - 13

Asaph asks God to forgive his people their former sins. He appeals to God's tenderhearted mercies. *(V.8)* God's "tenderhearted mercies" in Hebrew is

("Racham"). It also means "compassion" and "pity." The word comes from "the womb" and it is Asaph's appeal to God for His "Mother love."

The author again pleads with God asking Him for the sake of His name to forgive His people. (V.9) When he asks for forgiveness, the only way it could become meaningful for the Jews of that ancient day was when the High Priest made a sacrifice specifically on the Day of Atonement. But the Temple was destroyed! For the Hebrew people it would have to be some day in the future when the Temple was rebuilt, and sacrifices would be made once more. When the Babylonians took a small remnant of Jews as slaves to Babylon, this group tried to keep the flames of their religion burning, feeling God still had a plan for His people.

The Psalmist has two more requests of the LORD: one, was to save the prisoners, those condemned to die. (V.11) The second was to take vengeance on our enemies. He asks the LORD for a sevenfold venegence on these invaders of Jerusalem. (V.12) If You will do this, LORD, then we Your people for generation to generation will praise you. (V.13)

We Christians who see things from the Victory side of the cross, cannot help but see that the Psalmist was a child of his time and realize he misunderstood God's ways with Israel. The question Asaph raises about being guilty for former sins and how we can have our sins forgiven –the whole matter of atonement – is what God had in mind through His chosen people, the Jews. He sent Jesus to be born in Bethlehem and where he grew up to be a man. He walked the dusty roads in the shadow of Jerusalem, gathered His disciples, had three years of ministry in which He shared God's teachings, then suffered under Pontius Pilate, was crucified, dead and buried. The third day, He rose from the dead, and God took Him to heaven. He became the perfect and all-sufficient sacrifice for all who would come to Him in faith.

We limited and finite human beings cannot always fathom God's ways. We have the Bible, both Old and New Testaments, and it gives light on God's ways with us. We stand with our Jewish brothers and sisters. God's covenant is in force today. Jesus is our High Priest in heaven at the place of highest honor next to God Himself. Christ Jesus is a Minister in heaven. He has been rewarded with a far more important work than whose who served under the old Jewish law, because the new agreement God made contains far more wonderful promises. The old agreement didn't work. If it had, there would be no need for another to replace it. But God Himself found fault with the old one. He said (in Jeremiah 31:31-34), just like in Psalm 79, that His chosen people did not keep their end of the Old Covenant, so God had to cancel it. His new agreement with us is that God writes His laws in our hearts and minds. And, when we fulfill our end of the agreement, God will be merciful and will remember our sins no more. Fantastic promises! The author of the Book in Hebrews in the New Testaments thoroughly expains how this new agreement works. *(Hebrews 10:18-22)*

As we Christians read Asaph's heart-breaking words in Psalm 74 and 79 about the sinful ways of the Hebrew leaders and their people and God's judgment on them with the resultant slaughter by the Babylonians and the virtual end of the Jewish nation in 587 B.C., we are deeply moved and saddened! We cannot look down our noses at them because we are living in a time when many similar parallels are taking place in our nation. Greed, corruption, and selfishness characterize much of the tenor of our world. Because we are sinful individuals, we need to repent and ask God for His mercy! Each of us Christian believers dare not bask in personal salvation without doing what we can to counter the self-centered and worldly trends that are leading our nation and world to chaos and destruction! We need to pray that God will strengthen our churches and our leaders so that each Christian believer will be on fire for the Lord and His kingdom!

This is not a new problem. Over a hundred years ago, one of our great men of literature, John Greenleaf Whittier, penned "Dear Lord and Father of Mankind," a wonderful hymn that asks God to forgive our foolish ways and clothe us with purer lives.

# PSALM 80
## The Vine that Turned Sour

Psalm 80 is a pitiful lament about the demise of the northern kingdom in 721 B.C. The ascription at the beginning indicates that Asaph wrote this psalm and that it should be sung to the tune of "Lillies of the Covenant." Whoever wrote the psalm drew heavily upon other writings from the Scriptures, especially from the Prophets.

The two familiar names of prophets who were active just prior to the overthrow of the northern kingdom are Amos (760-750 B.C.) and Hosea (750-715 B.C.). Amos was a farmer/prophet sent to announce God's judgment on Israel; Hosea prophesied during or slightly after Amos. Their messages of doom are similar, except Amos didn't specify Israel's enemy, while Hosea identified it as Assyria. Amos was from the southern Kingdom of Israel but preached in the northern kingdom of Israel. Hosea conducted his prophetic ministries in the northern kingdom of which he was a native.

A little background will help to set the stage. Following Solomon's death in 930 B.C., the nation of Israel split in two. The leading tribes of Ephraim, Benjamin and Manasseh declared their independence in the north, from the tribe of Judah in the south. The headquarters of the tribes of Ephraim, Benjamin and Manasseh was Shiloh and Samaria. The headquarters of Judah remained Jerusalem.

Anyone who read the Torah knew that it was God who brought the Hebrews out of slavery in Egypt and led them into the Promised Land. He made it very clear that He would be their God, and they were to be His people. They, on their part, were to make no peace treaties with the people living in the land, and they were to destroy the heathens' altars, which they did not do. Because of this, it was implied that the Hebrews broke the covenant--God's promise to destroy their enemies was no longer in effect.

Therefore the people in the land became thorns in the sides of the Israelites – plus the worship of pagan gods was a constant temptation, to which they had succumbed.

Thanks to the discovery of how to smelt iron, the armies of Assyria were totally equipped with iron swords and helmets. This made Assyria a dominating power, with her eyes on Ephraim. While all this was taking place, Amos came on the scene. He denounced the tribes of Israel in the north for not having honest judges, not telling the turth, stealing from the poor, and taking bribes. Because of all these evils, Amos says God's judgment is that they will never again live in their beautiful stone houses nor drink wine from their own vineyards. *(Amos 5:10-13)*

His contemporary, Hosea, saw what was happening around him. Assyria was expanding westward. King Menahem of the northern kingdom accepted Assyria as the overlord and paid tribute as a vassal (see 2 Kings 15:19-20). Later in 735 B.C., Pekah killed Pekahiah, Menahem's son, who was the successor to the throne of Israel. Pekah then named himself King and challenged Assyria. This was the beginning of the end.

While all this was going on, Hosea came on the scene with his doomsday message. God ordered Hosea to marry an unfaithful wife named Gomer. His relationship with Gomer represented graphically the LORD's relation to the Israelites, who had been disloyal to Him by worshiping Canaanite gods. Disloyalty to God is spiritual adultery. Speaking for the LORD, Hosea denounced the people of Israel for putting up with gangs of priests murdering pilgrims going to worship at Shehem and the people themselves worshiping idols. *(Hosea 6:6-11)* The LORD's judgment, says Hosea, is that the LORD will smash the people's idols and break down their foreign altars and cart off the people as captives of Assyria. *(Hosea 10:6)*

When King Hoshea, successor to Pekah, was head of the Northern Kingdom, King Shalmanser of Assyria brought his army and laid siege to the city of Samaria (see 2 Kings 18:9-12). It can be hypothesized that it was during this period that Psalm 80 was written.

## Segment One – God Rescue Us. Verses 1 - 3

The prayer our Psalmist employs is a powerful image for God that David used in the 23$^{rd}$ Psalm. Asaph calls on the Shepherd of Israel to again take lead of His flock. *(V.1)* Perhaps the Prophet Isaiah read these psalms and borrowed this poignant image of the Lord when he wrote that once again God will feed his flock and carry His lambs in His arms. *(Isaiah 40:11)* Asaph then calls on God enthroned above the cherubim in the Holy of Holles in the Tent of Meeting. *(V.2)* On the lid of the Ark of the Covenant were two angel-like figures, cherubim, facing each other. It was generally thought that this was where God resided. The Pslamist asks this Covenant God to rescue His people. *(V.2)* When things were good and people were prosperous, they could care less about God. But now that the Assyrians are on their doorstep, it is a different story! The Psalmist now pens a refrain that entreats God to turn His people again to Himself and save them. *(V.3)* Asaph repeats this refrain in verses 7 and 19.

## Segment Two — We Are Fed with Sorrow and Tears. Verses 4 - 7

Asaph offers a second prayer, pleading with the Lord God Almighty to cease being angry and rejecting the peoples' prayers. *(V.4)* The Psalmist reminds God that His people are drinking tears by the bucketful. *(V.5)* His people are the scorn of nations. *(V.6)* Then the Psalmist repeats the refrain in verse 3. You need to smile on us like when You had Aaron and his sons bless our ancestors. *(See Numbers 6:24-27.)*

## Segment Three — We Are Your Tender Vine. Verses 8 - 11

The metaphor "the vine" is found throughout Scripture. Hosea called Israel a vine loaded with fruit. *(Hosea 10:1)* Both Isaiah and Jeremiah used the idea of "the vine" in their prophecies. Jeremiah said, speaking of Judah, that God chose a vine of the purist stock and it has grown into a corrupt wild vine. *(Jeremiah 2:19-21)* In Psalm 80, Asaph says God brought the Hebrew people out of Egypt as if they were a tender vine and carried them to His promised land. *(V.8)* He even cleared the land of pagen nations for the Hebrews and transplanted this vine in His land. *(V.9)* And He planted mighty cedars to provide shade for these choice vines. *(V.10)* And the vine branches spread from the Mediterranen Sea to the Euphrates River. *(V.11)*

God chose the Jews to be His instrument by which He was to bring peace and joy to the world. Instead they turned their backs on Him. From the Jews, of course, came the Messiah, Christ the Lord! Jesus also uses the metaphor of the vine. In John's Gospel, our Lord says He Himself is the true vine now and Jesus' believers are the vine branches. But the branches are expected to bear fruit. *(John 15:1-5)*

## Segment Four — We Have No Protection. Verses 12 - 13

We have in this section, described in two cryptic verses, the total and complete capitulation and destruction of the Northern Kingdom by the Assyrian warlords in 721 B.C. Asaph points out that the Assyrians have now broken down the walls of Israel. *(V.12)* This is Asaph's shorthand for the sad state of sin that caused God to remove His hands from Ephraim.

In similar fashion, the Apostle Paul describes the working of God among people who continuously and blatantly break God's commandments and sin willfully. To this Paul says those who push truth away from themselves and begin to think up foolish ideas of what God is like, obtain minds that are dark and confused. Ultimately they begin degrading their bodies with shameful desires. *(Romans 1:18-24)*

With the collapse of the capitol city of Samaria, those few who escaped death were taken as slaves to Nineveh where the wild beasts fed on them, probably figuratively and physically. *(V.13)*

## Segment Five — Come See Our Plight. Verses 14 - 19

In the desperate hours of pending doom, the Psalmist begs God Almighty to come back and look down and see how desperate His people are. *(V.14)* The Hebrew word for "come back" is *("shuwb")*. It can be translated in English to "turn," or "to change one's mind." You see God had already taken His hands off of them because of their rebellion and sin. Asaph then reminds God that his people are His vine. *(V.15)* But now His vine is being chopped up and burned by the heathen. *(V.16)*

The Prophet Amos went to Israel (the name of the Northern Kingdom) and warned them of impending doom. He was met by one of the priests, under orders from King Jeroboam. He told Amos to return to Judah and preach there. But Amos replied that he was under orders from God to give God's message to Israel. Then Amos prophesied that Israel's king would die in a foreign land and the people of Israel would be captives in exile. *(Amos 7:12-17)*

In Segment Five, what Amos had predicted, came painfully true. All of Asaph's cajoling of God was of no avail. It was too late. Assyria prevailed!

But then unexpectedly and somewhat confusingly, Asaph asks God to strengthen the son of your choice. *(V.17)* Some expositors think this refers to a Jewish king, someone like David. Others, including John Calvin, thinks this son refers to the whole people of Israel, which is probably correct. The third view thinks it refers to the Messiah. Some of the later Rabbis take this view. It is reasonable to look to the Messiah to bail out Israel when a crisis is in effect. It is true that Jesus was called the son of man. However, He is not one who is referred to here.

The essence of this last section is a prayer asking the LORD to turn Israel's people back to faith in God again. *(V.19)*

It is helpful to have psalms like 80 preserved in the Psalter.

# PSALM 81
## Oh, that My People Would Listen

Biblical experts have classified Psalm 81 as Prophetic Liturgy composed of two short selections: a hymn (verses 1- 5); and a prophetic oracle (verses 5b - 16). We shall call this psalm a sermon.

According to verse 3, Psalm 81 was delivered at the Feast of Tabernacles (Booths). Researching the *New International Version Study Bible*, with its notes on Chapter 23 of Leviticus, The Feast took place at the end of September. Tabernacles was a week of celebrating the harvest, and it included thanksgiving for the exodus from Egypt. The people were to construct booths or primitive houses to remind themselves of the hardships of the time spent in the wilderness after their flight from Egypt. Leviticus 23 says this should be a seven-day festival every year to remind each generation how God rescued His people from Eygpt. *(Leviticus 23:41-43)*

The *NIV Study Bible* lists John 7:2-38 as the New Testament reference. Jesus' brothers urged Him to go to Judea for the Tabernacle Ceremonies. Jesus told them to go ahead and He would come later. Midway through the Festival, Jesus went up to the Temple and preached openly. The Jewish leaders were surprised when they heard Him, wondering how Jesus could know so much when he had not studied with them. *(John 7:15)* On the last day of the Festival, the climax of the holiday, Jesus tells those who are thirsty in the crowd to come to Him, because the Scriptures declare that living water shall flow from within. *(John 7:37-38)* Jesus is saying that God will pour out His Holy Spirit on all who believe and put their trust in Him. All this happened at the Feast of Tabernacles.

To examine Psalm 81 in detail, we need to break it down into five segments: One, Times of Joy at the Festival, Verses 1- 5a; Two, God Has Done Wonderful Things, Verses 5.b -7; Three, Warnings About Idolatry,

Verses 8-10; Four, Sad Results, Verses 11-12; and Five, Listen to Me Today, Verses 13-16.

## Segment One – Times of Joy at the Festival. Verses 1 - 5a

This section is an invitation to all of God's people to sing praises to the Lord! *(V.1)* In God's infinite wisdom, He has given us these times of joy. He knows that corporate worship strengthens us in the Lord. The Hebrew word for "singing praises" is *("Ruwa")*, which means "to sound the trumpet" *("shofar")*, "to shout with joy," "praising God," or "to make a joyful noise." The Psalmist reminds the people that Festivals are times to remember what God has done on Israel's behalf. *(V.5a)*

## Segment Two – God Has Done Wonderful Things. Verses 5b - 7

The Psalmist in this section begins his sermon by telling the people gathered at the Festival what God did by delivering their ancestors from slavery in Egypt. He reminds them that God heard their pitiful cries and rescued them. *(V.5b)* He took the heavy burdens off their shoulders as they carried bricks for Pharaoh's building projects. *(V.6)* God saw their suffering and God cared! *(V.7)* The Psalmist is recalling the events described in Exodus 6: 2-6.

In verse 7 of Psalm 81, the Psalmist mentions that God tested the people at Meribah, when they complained that there was no water. According to Numbers 20, when the people protested God ordered Moses to command the rock to pour forth water. But Mose struck the rock with his staff, and water gushed out, enough to satisfy the people and their cattle. *(Numbers 20:2-11)* Meribah in Hebrew means "quarreling."

## Segment Three – Warnings about Idolatry. Verses 8 - 10

The sermon continues. The Psalmist tells the festival folks that they must listen to stern warnings. *(V.8)* Though our writer doesn't say it exactly, he paraphrases the commandments—particularly the first to worship the LORD exclusively. *(V.9) (Deuteronomy 6:4)* For it was the LORD who rescued you. *(V.10)* Jesus instructed the Jews of His day that this was the greatest of all commandments. *(Matthew 22:39-40)* The Psalmist of

Psalm 80 was obviously thinking of the *"shema,"* the prayer that serves as a centerpiece of the morning and evening Jewish prayer services.

The preacher's sermon in this segment was crucial to the people back then and it is the same with us today. The fundamental issue in all of our lives is not whether we are religious, but that we know the true God who revealed Himself in the Old Testament to the Jews through the Patriarchs, the Prophets, Psalms and in the New Testament through the Savior, Jesus Christ.

### Segment Four – Sad Results. Verses 11 - 12

What incongruity! God has been so good and gracious to His people, and yet how little awareness and concern for all His kindness. Instead of worshiping Jehovah God and Him only (as the introductory words to Exodus 20 demand), the Israelite people continued to worship the gods of Baal and go their own way. *(V.11)* It is interesting that the preacher uses the technique of direct speech of God Who complains in verse 11 that the people of Israel did not want Him around anymore. That being the case, the LORD goes on to say He decided to let the people follow their own stubborn and blind way. *(V.12)*

### Segment Five – Listen to Me, Today! Verses 13 - 16

In the festival, the preacher tells those gathering around him that their ancestors had a record of unresponsiveness *(V.11)* and how God dealt with them. *(V.12)* In this segment, God pleads for His people to listen to him and walk within His paths. *(V.13)* If only they would follow Me, then I would give them the blessings of covenant obedience, which means God would protect them from their enemies. *(V.14)* Those who hate the LORD would bow before Him. *(V.15)* Then too His people would have abundant crops. *(V.16)*

For added emphasis, our preacher might have quoted Jeremiah's earlier warnings to the people. Speaking for God, the great prophet says God repeatedly warned their ancestors to obey him. Instead they stubbornly submitted to evil desires. As a result God imposed on them all of the curses described in His covenant with them. *(Jeremiah 11:7-8)* God took His hands off and let Israel take the consequences of their willfulness. The punishment sounds very much like what the Apostle Paul describes at the beginning of Romans (see Romans 1:24-32).

As we 21st century Christians read these prophetic words, we find we are in many ways like the Jews who heard Paul's words in Romans. Paul suggests the Jews of his day wondered who were these terrible people he was describing in Romans Chapter one. *(Romans 2:1)* Paul replies that his fellow Jews in his day were no different than in the past. They were just as human and just as much in need of repentance. *(Romans 2:1-3)* In candor, we need to ask: Are we Christians just as bad? Paul goes on to say that God is being patient and tolerant with the Jews in his day in hopes that they will turn away from their sins. *(Romans 2:4)* Paul's message is one we Christians need to take to heart.

God is a gracious God who sent Jesus to earth to give us eternal life. He will also give us the good life, if we will listen and follow in His paths. The Psalmist in Psalm 81 provides us with a wonderful metaphor for the good life. He will feed us with the best of foods, with wild honey from the rock *(V.16)* We Christians know that the rock is Jesus.

# PSALM 82
## Human Judges Called "Gods"

In Psalm 82, Asaph, the author, is pondering the mystery of moral good and evil. Back in antiquity, Abraham, the father of Judaism, said he was looking forward to an eternal city, designed and built by God Himself. *(Hebrews 11:10)* By Moses' time, the faith had been carefully scripted to a divine mandate that demanded the Hebrew people worship God exclusively. *(Exodus 20:3)* Centuries went by and the pressure of pagan neighbors' gods took its toll, but the Jews could never forget the stern warning of the First Commandment. The immoralities of the religion of the Baals certainly corrupted many of the ideas and behaviors of Israel, much of which is reflected in the psalms.

During the time of the writing of Psalm 82, there were in the minds of most Jews the idea that God presided over a heavenly gathering of lesser gods and angels. This is reflected in the following Scriptures: Psalms 58:1; 103:19-21: 148:2; Job 1:6-12; and many others. Ultimately, the idea of lesser gods was set aside by the rabbis, and the heavenly host now is thought to consist of angels.

In this short psalm, the imaginary picture of the poet paints may seem a bit fanciful to us in the 21st century, but his contemporaries thought it totally familiar. A conference was being held with the gods who were Jehovah's judges on earth (His deputies) to see if they were living up to God's righteous standards, and, of course, they weren't! *(V.1)*

### Segment One – God Judges the Judges. Verse 1 - 5

Jehovah God points His finger at the judges and indicts them, asking how long these judges will be unjust and provide special favors for the wicked.

*(V.1-2)* Then God commands His deputies to treat the poor and the orphans fairly. *(V.3-4)* He is telling them to deliver the oppressed and helpless from the grasp of the powerful. Jesus told a magnificent parable (a *"Mashal"*) where He separates the people as a shepherd separates the sheep from the goats. On His right hand, He will place the sheep and say "inherit the Kingdom prepared by My Father." When the righteous sheep ask why, the Lord replied "when you took care of the least of My brothers and sisters you were doing it unto Me." Then He turns to his left, to the goats, and cursed them to eternal fire. And when they asked why, He replied "when you refused to care for the least of My brothers and sisters you were doing it unto Me." *(Matthew 25:34-40)*

The point of the psalm is that judges did not follow God's rules, so He calls them both ignorant and living in darkness. *(V.5)* Because of their disregard for common decency, the Psalmist says the world itself is shaken to its core. *(V.5)*

## Segment Two – "Gods" Are Mere Men. Verses 6 - 8

Question: What does it mean when the author calls these judges "gods?" *(V.6)* For one thing, the Hebrew word for "gods" is *("Elohiym")* and it can also be translated as "magistrates" or "judges." They have an important position of human authority and are representatives or spokesmen for God. Ideally, then, when they render a just or fair decision, it should be as if God Himself is acting through them. What the psalm is about, however, is that these "magistrates" are being unjust and taking unfair advantage of their privileged positions.

It was winter and Jesus was in Jerusalem at the time of the Dedication Celebration. He was at the Temple surrounded by the leaders of the Jews. They were asking Him if He was the Messiah? He said He was. He was quite specifice saying I and the Father are one. *(John 10:30)* The Jewish leaders picked up stones to kill Him, calling Him blasphemous. *(John 10:33)* Jesus replies that the Scriptures themselves say cerain leaders of the people are gods. *(John 10:34-35)* Actually Jesus was referring to the psalm that we are considering. Jesus was not trying to evade their charges, but wanted to point out to them that the judges of Israel were called "gods" and that wasn't too different from His title, "Son of God." Jesus' response is important because it reinforces the judges' position as God's spokes people.

Verse 7 tells us these so-called "gods" are mere men who will die like everyone else. Verse 8 asks God to judge the earth. Some interpreters claim this is a prayer for the LORD's intervention in history; when He will pour out His anger upon all doers of evil – judges included – in the last days. Actually many of the Hebrew prophets envisioned this. A good example would be Isaiah's words in Chapter 66. He envisions the LORD bringing punishment to evil doers like a whirlwind. *(Isaiah 66:15-16)*

We Christians read Psalm 82 and see parallel things going on in our day. Our world has its violence and greed with crooked financiers and politicians. There is economic unsettledness and widespread unemployment. Those of us who are not professional civil servants (judges) still have the same calling from God as the judges have. God wants us to be righteous and honest. Our task is to do what we can for God where we are. To treat everyone with fairness and, if we can, we should try and help those who are poor and in need. We should stand on the side of the good. Be patient in trouble and never pay back evil for evil. Don't take vengeance into our own hands. Leave that to God. The Apostle Paul offers a few more suggestions in Romans reminding us to pay our debts and to love our neighbor. *(Romans 13:8)*

# PSALM 83
## Enemies at the Boarders

Psalm 83 is a community lament. Right at the outset, God is cajoled by the Psalmist for not responding to the prayers of the people of Israel. He is indignant and orders Jehovah to answer us! *(V.1)* When God doesn't (implied), there follows a description of a consortium of nations banded together and marching their combined armies toward Israel with the aim of exterminating Israel totally! *(V.2-4)* The second half of this psalm is a petition where Asaph, the Psalmist, takes it upon himself to counsel God to destroy the oncoming horde. *(V.9-18)* He officiously reminds the Almighty that there is a good historical precedence for the imprecation (the damning to hell their enemies), and proceeds to enumerate the times back in the days of the Judges when God helped Israel with victory.

Experts have tried to determine when this historical situation actually took place on the basis of material cited by the writer in verses 2-8. Some interpreters think Psalm 83 might have taken place during the reign of King Johoshaphat of Judah, a half century or so following the death of King Solomon in 932 B. C. (see 2 Chronicles 20); others think maybe it was in the era of Ezra and Nehemiah, sometime between 458-432 B.C. when a remnant of Jews returned from exile and rebuilt the walls. In the book bearing Nehemiah's name, he reports that representatives from surrounding nations were furious and plotted to lead an army against Jerusalem (Nehemiah 4:7-9). Still others feel this attack should be dated at the time of Judas Maccabaeus, 165-160 B.C., and they cite I Maccabaeus 5:1-68. The problem is that none of the above citations have all of the people and nations Asaph mentions. It would seem as if we should not take the contents of this psalm literally. It may have been written during a time of national peril. Whenever an attack is, it conjures up a feeling on the part of the people that the whole world is massed against them.

## Segment One – Enemies Allied Against God. Verses 1 - 8

This psalm is about a time when Israel's enemies have come together with the intent of destroying her. *(V.2-4)* The Psalmist cries out don't just sit around God, do something. *(V.1)* We have no idea of when this was, but we can assume it was when Assyria was the dominant force and was attacking both Judah in the south and Israel in the north. God was allowing this to happen.

We humans, because we are finite, cannot fathom the mind of God, unless He reveals His intentions, like He did back in Moses' day. Back then He told us plainly that He chose the Jews to work out His plan for the world. He entered a covenant with them and said He would live among them if they would obey His commandments. He also told them that He would see to it that they would prosper and live safely in the land, and they would be His people and He would be their God. He stated to them plainly that if they didn't obey His laws He would set His face against them. *(Leviticus 26:25)*

God also communicated to them by means of individuals called Prophets.

Hosea was one of God's special messengers. Speaking for God, Hosea tells the people that their worship is mere pretense and they are playing the harlot, serving other gods, and deserting the one true God. He says that Israel is arrogant and will stumble from the load of guilt. That the flocks of sacrifices they are making are useless. God has withdrawn his protection from them. *(Hosea 5:5-6)* Isaiah, another Prophet, reiterated Hosea's message, saying the incense they are sacrificing to God is a stench in His nostrils. The evil deeds they are doing are stopping His ears from hearing their prayers. They need to do good, defend the orphans and protect the widows. *(Isaiah 1:12-17)*

It would seem that the people in this psalm were devastated by the possibility of an attack, for it would threaten their very life-style. So they turn to God for help in their anxiety. But God is silent. They cry out to God don't be silent and inactive. *(V.1)*

## Segment Two – Blow Them Away. Verses 9 - 17

This segment is a challenge put by His people to get rid of their enemies. It is a vindictive request for God to damn and destroy those opposing them. This really upsets us Christians because it goes totally counter to what Jesus taught and advocated. We are not to hate and damn our enemies, but love them and we are to pray for those who persecute us (see Matthew 5:43-44).

The nations in verses 6 through 11 can be identified as follows: The Ishmaelites were descended from Abraham; the Edomites and Hagarites came from Jacob's twin brother, Esau; Gebal came from south of the Dead Sea; Philestia and Tyre came from the west on the coast of Palestine. The last names were Assyria, who joined the Alliance. We don't know if Psalm 83 was written before or after the year 721 B.C., which was the date when Assyria, under King Shalmeneser, overthrew Samaria in the north and took all who were living into captivity to Ninevah.

The Psalmist then remembers in the past how God got rid of Israel's enemies, so he shouts for God to blow them away like chaff and dust. (V.13) Asaph gets carried away telling God to think back when Gideon demolished four Midianite kings and did it with only three hundred soldiers! (Judges 6-8) Then he reminds God how He defeated Sisera and Jabin at the KIshon River (V.9) when Barak won victory (see Judges 4-5).

There are many aspects of Psalm 83 that are mystifying. We don't know when or where this psalm took place. In the end, Asaph shouts to the LORD (V.16) that He needs to embarrass Israel's enemies forever. (V.17) This is not the most uplifting way to handle things. The only saving grace is in verse 18 where the Psalmist wants others to acknowledge that the LORD is supreme over all the earth.

# PSALM 84
## Meeting the LORD Of Zion

This psalm is a beautifully crafted song of peace and joy by the Sons of Korah, as they long for the experience of worshiping the Living God in His lovely Temple. The 23rd Psalm is probably the best loved and the most well known psalm, but Psalm 84 is certainly one of the loveliest in all the Psalter.

It can be outlined into three divisions, encompassing the following: One, The Joy of Those Who Live in God's House, Verse 1-4; Two, The Joy of Pilgrims to Zion, Verses 5-10; and Three, The Joy of Those Who Put Their Trust in Jehovah God, Verses 11-12.

### Segment One – The Joy of Those Who Live in God's House. Verses 1- 4

The Psalmist says (poetically) how lovely it is to dwell in the House of God *(V.1)*, that he almost faints from his longing to sense the inspiration of being in the presence of the courts of the LORD. *(V.2)* The Hebrew word for "the courts of the LORD" is *("Tsaba")*. It also can be translated as "the armies of heaven" or "hosts," "the Almighty," or "an army troupe of angels in heaven." What makes the Temple so special is not the building, but the living God. *(V.2)* The author sees how a sparrow and a swallow find a home for themselves in the Temple, and, in like manner, he feels that being in God's House is to be at home with God. *(V.3)*

It's interesting that in New Testament times sparrows were not worth much. But Jesus in Luke 12:6-7 says that God is mindful of them. Just imagine, Jesus adds, that if God cares for the sparrows how much more he cares for His children. The vary hairs on their head are numbered by God.

The Psalmist ends this segment extoling how happy are those you live in God's Temple. *(V.4)* Of course he is referring to the priests and Levites (the sons of Korah) who had the joy of living in the Temple as the sparrow and swallow do, and being able to sing praises to the living God. The author knew that God doesn't live bodily within the four walls, but His Spirit was manifested in the Holy of Holies, and the worshipers felt God's presence in a special way. David experienced this special presence. And in the 27th Psalm David asks the LORD if he could live in the LORD's house all the days of his lfe, delighting in the LORD's pefections. *(Psalm 27:4)*

## Segment Two – The Joy of Pilgrims Going to Zion. Verses 5 -10

Not only were the priests and musicians who worked in the Temple happy, but also most of the population of Judah who lived outside of Jerusalem and those who made pilgrimages to the Temple. These travelers often came a long way and their journey could be difficult and dangerous. That's why they had to be strong in the faith in the LORD. *(V.5)* Certain times of the year they had to go through arid territories, euphemistically termed The Valley of Weeping because of freezing and blowing rains. *(V.6)* However, the pilgrims' anticipation of the joy they would experience when they got to the Temple allowed them to get a new burst of strength as they envision appearing in the presence of God in Jerusalem. *(V.7)* The first thing they did when they arrived was to say a prayer for their king as their protector. *(V.9)* The Psalmist ends this segment by proclaiming that being a gatekeeper in the house of God is better than living well in the homes of the wicked. *(V.10)*

## Segment Three – The Joy of Those Who Put Their Trust in Jehovah God. Verses 11- 12

This final segment could be addressed to those who, for one reason or another, cannot get to the Temple but who put their trust in the LORD. True happiness is not reserved only for those who live and work in the Temple, or who make pilgrimages to Jerusalem. No, the truth for us Christians is that every man, woman and child who puts their faith and trust in God's Son, Jesus Christ, is blessed. However, we can garner in this psalm some needed lessons for us to enjoy the church.

Each visit we make to church for worship, in a profound sense, is a pilgrimage. We go to receive inspiration and instruction to help us with our daily walk with the Lord. Remember, we always have to read the psalms through the eyes of the New Testament. Psalm 84 has many insights and blessings for us. Verse 11 says our light and protector is the LORD. He watches over those of us who turn to Him in faith and God protects and blesses us. When we go to church and truly worship, in gratitude for what He has done for us through sending Jesus to be our Savior, we can go out from church refreshed and inspired to do what we can to love of neighbors. God is the same yesterday, today and forever *(Hebrews 13:8)* and as the Psalmist in Psalm 84 says that for those of us who do what is right, no good things will be withheld by the LORD. *(V.11)*

Language scholar Eugene Peterson in his rendition of the psalms* helps us to read the psalms again for the very first time. What does this mean? In most English translations, the Psalms sound smooth and polished. Elizabethan rhythms and style dominate. As literature they are beyond compare. But as prayer – God-directed expressions of anger, praise, and lament –most English translations miss something vital. In the original Hebrew, the psalms are not genteel – they're earthy and rough … they have an immense range of gut-level honesty and passion that provides them with terrific energy.

We Christians are not seeking an earthly Temple. We are seeking God in the company of His people in the church, and ultimately, we are looking toward heaven. It is the Living God we long for! In Hebrews 12:22-24, we are told that in the heavenly Jerusalem we will meet Jesus and He will mediate a new covenant between God and us.

---

*Psalms, Eugene H. Peterson. Navpress, Colorado Springs, Colorado 80935, 1994.

# PSALM 85

## Mercy and Truth Meet Together

It's awful to be discouraged particularly if the conditions that caused the discouragement persist over a long period of time. This was the situation with David when he was escaping from King Saul. He had to flee for his very life for at least four years from age 22 to 26. Much of the time David hid in caves in the wilderness. In Psalm 13, David tells us of his feelings of abandonment and discouragement. He began Psalm 13 with a prayer asking the LORD how long will He forget David. Reminding the LORD that He is the light of David's eyes. *(Pslam 13:1-3)* Can't you just feel the agony and pathos in David's words? He longed for the spiritual vitality and joy he had in former times.

Psalm 85 is this kind of a prayer by the sons of Korah. It's called a prophetic lament. We don't know for sure about the historical setting, as the writers are not explicit. However, we can surmise that this psalm was written shortly after the Jewish remnant returned from their captivity in Babylon.

Turning to the Book of Ezra in the beginning chapters, it tells us that Cyrus, king of Persia in 539 B.C., allowed a handful of Jewish people to go back to Jerusalem, which they found in ruins. They were enthusiastic at first but their ardor dimmed when they had to face the difficult task of building homes while fighting off attacks by surrouding neighbors who resented their arrival. In 458 B.C., Ezra the priest retured to Jerusalem with another small group of Babylonian exiles. In 444 B.C., another Jewish man named Nehemiah (from Persia) became governor of Jerusalem, and he led the people in repairing walls. By 516 B.C., another Temple was constructed, one much less impressive than Solomon's Temple earlier destroyed by the Babylonians (see Nehemiah 2:16-20; 4:6-23; 7:1-4).

## Segment One – Thinking Back on God's Grace. Verses 1 - 3

King Cyrus of Persia was God's instrument, allowing the Jews to leave Babylon. That in itself was one of God's amazing miracles! The Hebrew people had been figuratively dead for 70 years in their exile and now they were reborn. Their fortunes had been restored. The Psalm opens with the Psalmist thanking the LORD for restoring the fortunes of Israel. *(V.1)* And, of course, the most wonderful blessing from God was His covering or forgiving their sins. *(V.2)* The Hebrew word for "covered" is *("Kacah")* and it means "to conceal," "to hide from view." Their sins were gone from God's sight and also gone was God's anger. *(V.3)*

One of the reasons why we are quite sure that Psalm 85 is post-exilic is from the writings of the Prophet Zechariah. He was a contemporary of those exiled in Babylon and when he returned to Jerusalem he had a vision from God. He quotes the LORD as saying that He will again show mercy to Jerusalem. That His temple will be rebuilt and prosperity will overflow the people. *(Zechariah 1:16-17)* Zechariah spoke another oracle acknowledging a day in the future in which the dynasty of David would be restored and the peoples' sins cleansed. *(Zechariah 13:1)*

## Segment Two – Revive Us LORD. Verses 4 - 7

On behalf of the congregation, our writer petitions the LORD to be His peoples' salvation again. *(V.4)* The Psalmist asks God if He will be angry with His people always? *(V.5)* He acknowledges that the congregation needs to be faithful and obedient and then God can bless them. The Psalmist also acknowledges that it was the Jews' disobedience that stimulated God's anger and allowed the Babylonians to destroy Jerusalem and relocate the Jewish inhabitants in Babylon and beyond for 70 years. He says in verse 6 that they need the Holy Spirit to come to them so they can have a spiritual revival of putting God First in their lives. *(V.6)* The Hebrew word for "revive" is *("Chayah")* and it can be translated in English as "to be restored to life," "refresh us," or "refresh our spirits."

True life comes when we put God first in our daily living. The choice between life and death is up to us. Moses told the people of Israel that they had a choice between life and death. Life and prosperity would come with keeping God's commandments and putting God first in their lives. Death would come if their hearts turned away for the LORD. *(Deuteronomy 20:15-18)*

These are words for Jews and Christians alike. The big difference between us is that we Christians believe that no one can be made right with God by doing what the law demands. The more we try to follow God's laws, the clearer it becomes that we are not able to obey them. Actually, the law only serves to make us realize that we are sinners! The wonderful part of Christianity is that it says we don't have to be good enough to be right with God. What He requires is that we love Jesus and believe that He is our Lord and Savior. When we put our faith and trust in Jesus, and put Him first in our lives, then God will declare us not guilty and this will assure us that we will go to heaven when we die! In gratitude for this blessing, we will want to do what we can to follow the Great Commandment of Jesus, to love God with all our heart and soul and to love our neighbor as ourselves while we are able (see Matthew 22:37-40).

We Christians can read verse 7 with appreciation for the Psalmist seeks the LORD's unfailing love. "Unfailing love" is one of the most important Hebrew words in the Old Testament. It's the word *("Checed")* and it is a covenant word. It expresses the true nature of God, which is "mercy," "kindness," and "forgiveness." God made a covenant with Israel and to this agreement He remains true. But to which He demands loyalty. He chose the Jews to work out His plan for the salvation of the world. He chose David to be His king and made a divine promise that David's dynasty would last forever. He chose Jesus, from the lineage of David, to be the world's Savior. Jesus' sacrifice on the cross made it possible for those who believe in Him to be made right with God, to have their sins forgiven, and to become partners in the Lord in building peace, righteousness and justice here on earth.

### Segment Three – Listening Carefully to the LORD. Verses 8 - 9

In a quiet way, our Psalmist does something we all should do—he listens to what the LORD is saying. *(V.8)* And God speaks "peace" *("Shalom")*. This is a great Hebrew word that means much more than the absence of violence. It means being safe and prosperous and having well being. God's peace can only come when God's people practice His First Commandment –to worship the LORD only. *(Exodus 20:3)* Our job is to give God honor, and when we do that the Psalmist says the glory of the LORD will fill the land. (V.9)

## Segment Four – Longing for a Brighter Day. Verses 10 - 13

Our author looks to the future in verse 10 and says "unfailing love" *('Checed")* and "truth" *("Emeth")* will be joined together. God is faithful to His covenant promises. Bringing His people back from exile is an example of God keeping His covenant.

We can just visualize the little group of hardy pilgrims gathered around the writer as he shares with them the promises of God. He informs them that all who came courageously demonstrated their faith in God. Because they are the faithful ones who are loyal to the LORD's covenant, God consequently speaks "peace" *("Shalom")* to them. *(V.8)* He tells them that God's "unfailing love" *("Checed")* *(V. 7)* will result in the land being full of he glory of God. *(V.9)* Also, God's faithfulness to his covenant, will not only bring spiritual blessings but bountiful crops. *(V.12)*

This psalm is a marvelous read for Christians. The Psalmist is telling us that when God's Spirit is manifested in four aspects-- His righteousness, His peace, along with His love and truth--in a community of godly individuals surely His salvation is near. *(V.7)* In a beautiful poetic expression, the Psalmist says when the LORD is present peace and righteousness kiss. *(V.10)* As the Psalmist says in verse 12, real blessings will be poured into the hearts of those who honor God.

We can say without a doubt that these four spiritual attributes— unfailing love, righteousness, truth and peace--were present in the Savior, Jesus. It's difficult to express in words the experiences that are supernatural; but words are all we have. We turn to Scripture for guidance. In Colossians, it tells us that Jesus is the visible likeness of the invisible God. Jesus has in Him the full nature of God. *(Colossians 1.15-19)* Salvation happens when the Spirit of the Lord in all its fullness is at work through Jesus as we Christians bring Him into our hearts.

# PSALM 86

## Searching for Mercy

Psalm 86 is David's personal lament. It is a carefully crafted prayer asking for mercy from a compassionate God. This psalm is a composition of seventeen verses, and David waits until verse 14 before he informs us readers of the serious nature of his problem, which is that certain godless men want him killed.

The unusual aspect of this psalm has to do with the fact that many of the lines can be paralleled with other psalms or are quotes from various parts of the Old Testament. According to the *New Living Translation*, the use of "I" appears ten times; "my" five times; and "me" fifteen times. (Much self-centeredness on David's part.) Also, according to my count, our Psalmist makes sixteen petitions to God in the course of this composition.

### Segment One – Looking for the LORD. Verses 1 - 7

David begins this psalm asking the LORD to bend down from his high perch and listen to David's cry for help. *(V.1)* I'm hurting! Then he lays out for God's sake his spiritual pedigree. David reminds the LORD that he is devoted to Him and has served Him. *(V.2)* The Hebrew word for "devoted" is *("Chaciyd")*, which also can be translated as "pious," or "godly." Then in verse 5, he paraphrases his favorite passage in Exodus 34, which exemplifies God's very nature, i. e., that He is good, forgiving and helpful. It is this loving and forgiving God that David is counting on. In Verse 6 he repeats his prayer for help. He closes this segment by explaining to the Almighty that whenever I am in trouble I can call You and for this I am thankful that Your help is always near, and this is my comfort! *(V.7)*

273

## Segment Two – You Are a Great God. Verses 8 - 10

Here David goes into theology. He points out that among all the pagan gods, there is no God like the LORD. *(V.8)* None can do miracles like You. *(V.8)* You alone made all the nations. *(V.9)* David was probably thinking about the way God brought His people out of Egypt from slavery, and all the mighty miracles He performed. He ends up in verse 10 stating that the LORD alone is God.

## Segment Three – Show Me Your Ways. Verses 11 - 13

David now begins teeing up the LORD for David's request begining in verse 14. He asks the LORD to teach him His ways. *(V.11)* Grant him a pure heart. *(V.12)* David then reminds God that His love for David is great. *(V.13)*

These are magnificent sentiments expressed by David. In the New Testament Jesus tells a group of people that they are made unholy (defiled) by what they say or do, that is, by what comes out of an evil heart (or our unconscious). *(Matthew 15:19)*. This is why David is right. We need to give ourselves to God and ask Him to purify our hearts. This is why Jesus, in His Beatitudes, says that those of a pure heart will see God. *(Matthew 5:8)*

In verse 13, David says God has rescued him from death. This doesn't mean God has raised him from the dead. No. The word "death" in Hebrew is *("Sh'owl")*. It means (in this context) a subterranean retreat, a cavern below the natural creation. It also can mean the depth within human beings' unconscious or in their hearts.

## Segment Four – Grant Me Your Strength. Verses 14 - 17

As noted earlier, verse 14 is the principal purpose of David's prayer to the LORD: insolent people are trying to kill him. But the major theme of Psalm 86 is God's "unfailing love" and mercy, God's *("Checed")*. David is appealing to this aspect of God's character to save him. *(V.16)* In the final verse of the psalm, David asks for some kind of tangible sign that will let him know that God has heard him and will deliver him from his enemies.

Obviously David worked hard at his faith. He not only acknowledged the LORD through regular worship, but communicated with Him through a deeply disciplined prayer life. David had a high level of spiritual sensitivity – way above the average. In this psalm (and in others he wrote), we see him crying out for deliverance and help. He reminds God that violent people are trying to kill him. *(V.14)* What ways can God help? This is the question. What are God's ways? His ways are enunciated in Exodus 34:6-7. Chief among them is that He is slow to anger, rich in mercy and forgiving of every kind of sin. David spells this out in verses 15-16.

In addition, God's ways are the ways of justice, because He hates sin. We see this most dramatically in the crucifixion of Jesus on the cross. Jesus took our place and paid the penalty for our sins. This is the highest expression of God's love for us. The Apostle Paul explains the need for Christ to take our sins upon Himself to allow us through Christ to be brought holy and blameless into the very presence of God. *(Colossians 1:18-22)*

275

# PSALM 87
## Zion – Home for the World

Psalm 87 is a celebration of Jerusalem ("*Zion*"), which is referred to by the Jews as the City of God. This is another composition written by the Sons of Korah, who also wrote two other psalms about Zion (see Psalms 46 and 48). What is unique about Psalm 87 is that it foresees an ingathering of people from the other nations of the world into Jerusalem as equal citizens with Israel in God's coming Kingdom.

There are other prophetic visions into the future in the Bible, particularly by Isaiah. The Prophet Isaiah who lived in the eighth century before Christ, wrote that in the last days that people from all over the world will come to worship at the Temple of the LORD in Jersulem. (*Isaiah 2:2-3*) In some of his other passages, Isaiah speaks of Gentiles joining God's chosen people. He says God will bring them to His Holy City and they will love His name and serve Him. They will accept His covenant and worship Him. (*Isaiah 56:6-7*)

Similar predictions were made by other prophets (see Micah 4:1-3 and Zechariah 8:19-23, as examples). These men speak of people from around the world making pilgrimages to attend Jewish festivals, and being blessed by Jehovah God. Peace will come to the world through Zion. Micah's famous prophecy says Jehovah God will settled international disputes and in the end times swords and spears will be beat into plowshares and pruning hooks respectively. God Almighty promises this. (*Micah 4:3-4*).

Pslam 87 is a short one of only seven verses. It can be divided up for analysis into two sections: One, Zion, the LORD's City, Verses 1-3; and Two, Home for the World's People, Verses 4-7.

## Segment One – Zion, the LORD's City. Verses 1 - 3

When David became king (somewhere around 1010 B.C.), one of his first military operations was to capture the city of Jerusalem from the Jebusites. He then made Jerusalem his headquarters. His next move was to re-capture the Ark of the Covenant and bring it to Jerusalem, along with the Tent of Meeting. He placed the Ark in the Holy of Holies in the Tabernacle, and, in the people's minds, it became the new dwelling place for Jehovah God. With these strategic moves, Zion (Jerusalem) became the political and religious center of Judah!

David writes in this psalm that Jerusalem stands on the Holy mountain of the LORD. *(V.1)* And the God loves Jerusalem more than any other city in Isreal. *(V.2)*

## Segment Two – Home for the World's People. Verses 4 - 7

In His official register, God will list as a bonafide citizen one who was born outside of Jerusalem, but only one who has come into a covenant relationship with the Living God. Loving the LORD above all gods entitles that individual to all the privileges and benefits of a native (born) citizen. The various nations listed in verse 4 are just a few representatives of Gentile people who can become citizens of Jerusalem. You must remember this is a prophetic psalm, along the lines of the prophets who proclaimed that Israel was to become a Light to the nations of the world in order to bring them God's salvation (see Isaiah 49:6). In verse 5, David further emphasizes that everyone of every nation can become a citizen of Jerusalem. And as equal citizens, they can particpate in all the festivals. *(V.7)*

This psalm stands out by itself in the psalter in contrast to the many others that blatantly call forth the destruction of Israel's enemies. Psalm 87 is like a breath of fresh air, and its vision comes alive within the Christian church. The Apostle Paul perceived the church as coming out of the Israel of God in the Old Testament. He said the Jewish laws were our teachers and guides until God sent Jesus to give us right standing with God through our faith. But now that Jesus the Christ has come, we don't need those laws any longer to guard and guide us to Him. Now we all are children of God through faith in Christ Jesus. There no longer is Jew or Gentile, male or female, free or slave, we are all equal in and before Jesus Christ. *(Galatians 3:24-29)*

Like Psalm 87, the writer of Hebrews in the New Testament, joyfully proclaims the new covenant proclaimed and administered in and through Christ that all people of the earth now can come to the heavenly Jerusalem where thousands of angel joyfully assemble. *(Hebrews 12:18-24)* Jews, Gentiles, people everywhere are coming to discipleship in Christ, and that is why we can sing with joy and thankfulness the wonderful words of the hymn "In Christ There Is No East or West" by John Oxenham.

# PSALM 88
## Seeing in a Glass Darkly

This is a maskil written by Herman the Ezrahite, who was one of the sons of Korah. Scholars have suggested that maskil is possibly a technical term relating to the manner of a psalm's performance or a class of composition.

In the eighteenth century a writer named St. John of the Cross coined the phrase "Dark Night of the Soul" which refers to an inner state of intense anguish where a believer feels abandoned by God. Psalm 88 describes this state. Other psalms have misery in them, but they all reach a state of resolution or hope at the end. Not so with Psalm 88. It ends with the author telling God only darkness remains when you have taken away my loved ones and companions. *(Psalm 88:18)*

Reading this psalm reminds us that life is filled with difficulties, even for the mature believer. As Christians, we are optimistic because we believe in a good God who has a special purpose for each believer. But we also know that as Apostle Paul writes we see imperfectly as at a dark mirror. *(1 Corinthians 13:12)* Our overall understanding of life may not become clear in our lifetime.

Commentators have proposed several outlines for this psalm, which means no one outline is to be preferred. Therefore, we will organize it around five segments: One, I Am Cut Off from God's Care, Verses 1-5; Two, You Have Put Me in the Darkest Pit, Verses 5-9; Three, Is God's Love Declared in the Grave? Verses 19-12; Four, God Has Hidden His Face, Verses 3-14; and Five, My Life Is Darkness, Verses 15-18.

## Segment One – I Am Cut Off from God's Care. Verses 1 - 5

The first several verses in the psalm that are not in total despair are those in which Herman the Psalmist cries out to the LORD that he has sought Him day and night. Please listen. *(V.1-2)* Right away he says his life is filled with trouble and death itself is drawing near. *(V.3)* He tells us readers that in his depressed mental state he is good as dead because he is forgotten by God. *(V.5)*

## Segment Two – You Have Put Me in the Deepest Depth. Verses 6 - 9

What makes this darkness so depressing and awful is that the writer <u>blames God.</u> God, he says, has thrust him to the lowest pits. *(V.6)* He accuses God of taking his friends from him. *(V.8)* Each day the Psalmist begs the LORD for mercy. *(V.9)* There is a close similarity between Psalm 88 and the Book of Job. God caused Job's misery undoubtedly by allowing Satan to afflict him. Job, like this writer, did not know what was going on or why he was suffering so. In Job's case, God had a purpose in having him suffer. It ultimaely permitted him to better understand God and to be a witness for God. Both of these works were placed in the Scriptures to let us know that when we suffer we don't necessarily understand God's purpose. By faith, we Christians have to believe that everything ultimately works together for good for those who love God. *(Romans 8:28)*

## Segment Three – Is God's Love Declared in the Grave? Verses 10- 12

Verse 10 through 12 repeat what David writes in many of his psalms—if I am dead how can I praise you? *(Psalm 30:9)* When I am dead can I speak of Your miracles? *(V.12)* The implication is NO! It implies that the dead are not conscious enough to remember God. Death is the severing of ties, corruption and nothingness. However, it is not the whole truth. We Christians are on the glory side of the cross and as the Apostle Paul tells us that if we die knowing Jesus as our Lord and savior our bodies will be transformed and we will be raised never to die again. *(1 Corinthians 15:51-57)*

## Segment Four — God Has Hidden His Face. Verses 13 - 14

Like in verse 1, the Psalmist continues to cry out to the LORD to listen to him *(V.13)*, but he feels rejected. *(V.14)* One of the main reasons the Psalmist feels close to death is because <u>God apparently is silent.</u>

## Segment Five — My Life is Darkness. Verses 15 - 18

The Psalmist is totally desperate. Since his youth he has been sickly. *(V.15)* He feels totally cut off by God. *(V.16)* God's terrors encircle him. *(V.17)* His loved ones and companions are gone. *(V.17)* In many psalms (see Psalm 42 for instance), most of the negative psalms have an ending that is positive. Psalm 42 speaks of the Psalmist being downcast and in mourning, asking why God has forgotten him, but in the end he says he still has hope that God will be his savior. *(Psalm 42:11)* The writer of Psalm 88 sees nothing but misery, loneliness and death! Darkness is the last word. *(V.18)*

Darkness is not the last word for us Christians. It's true, though, if we don't repent and turn from our sin and come to God through faith in the Lord Jesus, we too, will have to face the possibility of darkness, death, hell and judgment. But if we believe the Good News of the Gospel and bring Jesus' Spirit into our hearts and minds, we know He will forgive our sins, and we will be able to look forward to being in heaven for all eternity with God and Jesus!

Psalm 88 is a reminder that even us Christians, although we are blessed with the Holy Spirit living in us, still can groan with pain and suffering. *(Romans 8:23)* In that same chapter eight of Romans, Paul says we Christians should not to be like cowering, fearful slaves, instead we should come as God's very own children and cry out to him in our grief calling him Father, dear Father. Everything the Father has given to his Son Jesus is ours also. *(Romans 8:16-17)*

# PSALM 89
## What about God's Faithfulness?

This psalm is a brilliantly crafted composition by one of the wise men of the east, whose name is Ethan the Ezrahite (see I Kings 4:29-31). In this poem, Ethan mourns the downfall of the Davidic dynasty and pleads for its restoration. After lauding the power and faithfulness of Jehovah, and his promise to King David, our writer is shocked and disheartened that God would abandon His anointed one.

The transcendent God had a plan and purpose for our world. He chose to use human beings in order to accomplish His plan. According to His divine wisdom, He chose the Jews as His instruments. This psalm is an example of how God's will can be subverted by the perverse will of men – for a time at least. But not forever! From the perspective of the Christian faith, God's plan ultimately will prevail!

In the light that he has, the writer sees the crushing defeat of Israel by the Babylonians in 597 B.C., and concludes that the Davidic dynasty is ended. (See 2 Kings 24:8-17.)

### Segment One – God's Solemn Agreement with David. Verses 1 - 4

Our Psalmist begins this psalm by singing of the LORD's tender mercies and that His unfailing love will last forever. *(V.1)* The Hebrew word for "unfailing love" is *("Checed")* and it is a covenant word. This reminds the Psalmist of 2 Samuel 7 where Nathan the prophet told King David *(2 Samuel 7:11-16)* that God will establish David's dynasty and kingdom forever. *(Psalm 89:2-3)*

## Segment Two – Jehovah Is the King of Kings! Verses 5 - 18

Ethan calls on heaven to praise the LORD's miracles, and many angels to join the praising for God's faithfulness. *(V.5)* God is beyond compare, and all the heavenly hosts revere Him. *(V.6-7)* He points out that the LORD's character is the epitome of faithfulnes. *(V.8)* In beautiful poetic language, the Psalmist calls Jehovah the ruler of the oceans and all nature. *(V.9)* He is able to scatter His enemies, and why not since He created all that exists in the world. *(V.11)*

Ethan is saying that human kings (i.e., David and his successors) are called to reign according to the divine pattern shown to them in heaven. This pattern is founded on two strong pillars – righteousness and justice. But both of these pillars are tempered by the LORD's unfailing love and truth. *(V. 14)* David and his dynasty will be blessed when they walk in God's steps and put Jehovah first. *V.15)* Verses 17 and 18 say when earthly kings follow the righteous pattern of justice set forth by the Holy One of Israel, they shall be strong and will be protected.

## Segment Three – Nathan's Oracle Re-told. Verses 19 - 37

Ethan now writes a lyrical poem re-creating 2 Samuel 7:4-17, where God chooses and anoints David, a warrior selected from among the common folk. *(V.19)* He rose to power and kept his power because of the Holy One of Israel. *(V.21-24)* In 2 Samuel 7:12-13 the Prophet Nathan prophecies that when King David lies down with his fathers, the LORD will raise up an offspring of David whose kingdom will last forever. Referring to this prophecy, the Psalmist says this King will be God's firstborn son. *(V.27)* Under this King, the Psalmist becomes very specific saying Israel's land in the future will extend from the Mediterranean Sea on the west to the Euprhates and Tigris on the east. *(V.25)*

The Psalm apparently is pointing to Solomon, David's son, as God's firstborn son not the Messiah. Because in verses 30 to 33 the Psalmist says if Solomon's sons forsake God's law and do not walk in His ways, God will punish them. But God's covenant with David and his dynasty will be forever. *(V.34)* Our Psalmist ends this segment by quoting the Prophet Nathan's words from God, saying David's dynasty will be as secure as the sun and the moon. *(V.36-37) (2 Samuel 7:16)*

## Segment Four – Promises Broken. Verses 38 - 45

Whoa! Ethan at once sees the wide gap between God's promises (in segment three) and the stark reality of things. Here is Jerusalem laid in ruins with its walls broken dawn, the Temple destroyed, and the Psalmist accusing God with throwing down the crown of David into the dust. *(V.39)* The seriousness of the situation is apparent when Ethan asks pointedly if God has renounced his covenant with David and the Jewish people? *(V.39)* He then rails against the LORD charging Him with strengthening Israel's enemies, refusing to help Israel in battle, allowing them to be publicly disgraced and mocked. Angrily he says that God allowed this pagan nation of Babylon to obliterate the Holy City and destroy the monarchy! *(V.40-45)*

There is no way anybody, who lived through the horror of the fall of Jerusalem and the systematic dismantling of David's and Solomon's empire, could understand what God was up to. It would be similar to how the disillusioned disciples felt after Christ was crucified. They thought the end of the world had come. Ethan probably felt that way, too. Certainly he could not have known what the prophet Isaiah wrote, for Isaiah was in Babylon in exile. Isaiah thought that Israel's troubles were a punishment from God for their sins. But God revealed to Isaiah those exiled in Babylon were His suffering servants. Then Isaiah prophesied that another suffering servant, one who would be wounded and crushed for the sins not only of the Jews but all people was to appear in the future. *(Isaiah 53:6)*

## Segment Five – Lament on Behalf of a Hebrew King. Verses 46 - 52

The writer wants God to act now, to demonstrate His faithfulness is still intact. How long, God? Will You be angry for our sins forever? Please, LORD, answer me as life is so short! *(V.47)* I cannot live forever. *(V.48)* He pleads with the LORD to fulfill his faithful convenant pledge to David and his people. *(V.49)* Lord (he now appeals to Lord and not LORD) your servants are disgraced. *(V.50)* LORD your king is mocked. *(V.51)* God's timing, unfortunately, is not man's. But Ethan has hope. The Psalmist ends blessing the LORD forever. *(V.52)*

Isaiah, the prophet of the exile, spoke some mighty words that again were not known to Ethan. Isaiah's words are answers for questions raised in this final segment for us who read Psalm 89. Quoting the Holy One of Israel,

284

Isaiah says that the LORD Almightly will abandon the people of Israel for only a brief moment and that His everlasting love for Israel and His covenant with His people will never be broken. *(Isaiah 54:5-10.)*

The exiles did come back, and from our Christian perspective, God's choice of Israel is still valid. God worked out His plan and purpose for the world through the Jewish people. God's promises to David are still true. Jesus, the Messiah, is a descendant of King David, and He is the Savior of the world! (See Matthew 1:1.)

God never changes. He is ever faithful. His plan and purpose for the world's salvation began with His choice of Israel. More specifically, He chose to work through His servant David, and promised that his dynasty would never end, saying there will always be an heir to David's throne. Faithfully, God sent Jesus, who was of the lineage of David, to the world as the promised Messiah. His sacrifice on the cross culminated in God's final plan where He was able to accept and acquit anyone who trusts Jesus to take away their sins. Because of this, God will declare us not guilty of offending Him because of our sin. He now can use Christ's blood and our faith as a means of saving us not because of our good deeds but because of what Christ has done for us and our faith in Him! This salvation is free, open to all – Jews, Muslims, anyone who wants to bring Jesus into their hearts. Those of us who have accepted the wonderful salavation of Christ need to sing in celebration William C. Dix's hymn "Alleluia, Sing to Jesus."

# PSALM 90

## Is the Only Dwelling Place that Counts

Psalm 90 begins Book Four (Psalms 90 – 106) of the Psalter. Book Three (Psalms 73- 89) contains a number of psalms of prayers and laments mourning the destruction of Jerusalem. Psalm 89 ends Book Three with the implication that God has rejected His covenant.

Editors credit Moses as being the composer of Psalm 90. During his lifetime there was no Temple or monarchy. Moses had to deal with the crises of the exile and all of its difficulties. Even without the promised land, Moses was able to respond to God and enter into relatedness with Him, as evidence in Psalm 90. Moses knew the LORD intimately. He was chosen by God to communicate face-to-face with God (see Numbers 12:8). It was through Moses that God offered Himself to the Hebrew people in a covenant relationship of love, mercy and forgiveness, which of course had reciprocal obligations.

In Psalm 90, Moses prays to God asking His compassion on His people who have known Him to insure the safety of their homes through all generations. *(V.1)* The second part of the prayer sees the other side of God as He displays His anger as the result of human sin, and this cuts life short. Moses asks God to teach us not to fritter our lives away, but teach His people to make the most of their lives and grow in wisdom. *(V.12)*

Probably the best interpretation of Psalm 90 was made by Isaac Watts (1674-1748) in his hymn "O God, Our Help in Ages Past." It portrays the brevity of life and the hope that God will guide as long as life shall last.

### Segment One – God, Without Beginning or End. Verses 1- 2

Moses led the Hebrew people out of Egypt, and, during those incredibly difficult years in the wilderness, he faced many heartaches, including the death of his brother Aaron and his sister Miriam. Then God commanded him to bring the people to the top of Mount Nebo, overlooking the Promised Land of Canaan, and at Nebo Moses gave his farewell address. Among other things, he reminds the Hebrew people that the eternal God is their refuge and that God's everlasting arms will protect the people. *(Deuteronomy 33.27)* The Hebrew word for "everlasting" is *("owlam")*, which can also be translated as "eternal," or "without beginning or end." The eternal God is the Creator, the one foundation for everything that exists. Moses says in the psalm that the Lord, the Creator God, has been the home to the Hebrew people through all generations. *(V.1)* This is so important because in this transitory world when we place our trust and faith in God's everylasting arms, we have our security. *(V.2)*

### Segment Two – Man's Frailty. Verses 3 - 6

In verse three, Moses points out that man's life time is short. In contrast God is eternal. Moses says a thousand years are as yesterday for the Creator God. *(V.4)* Compared with God's everylastingness, we human beings are weak, fragile, and very self-centered. Moses says we are like grass that springs up in the morning and withers at night. *(V.5-6)*

In the New Testament, the Apostle Peter pondered about this passage in Psalm 90 as to why God hasn't closed down the world yet. So paraphrasing Psalm 90:4, Peter says that a day is like a thousand years to God and a thousand years like a day. *(2 Peter 3:8)* Thoughtfully, Peter says that God is totally patient with us, not wanting anyone to perish so providing time for all to reprent. *(2 Peter 3:9)*

### Segment Three – Man's Sin and God's Wrath. Verses 7 - 12

In this segment, Moses sees the three characteristics of human beings: our weakness, our frailty, and our self-centeredness. The first two contribute to our short duration in this world; but God's greater concern is with our sin! It is our sin that causes God's wrath, and it is our sin that separates us from

God. *(V.7)* Moses tells us that the Lord knows even our secret sins. *(V.8)* It is our sins that cause havoc and cause us to be overwhelmed with God's wrath. *(V.9)* To prevent us from sinning too much *(Genesis 6:3)*, Mose says we are given a life of 70 years, some as many as 80 years. *(V.10)* Verse 11 fairly shouts to us that we cannot comprehend the power of God's anger. *(V.11)* Then Mose exhorts the people to make the most of their time on earth by seeking to grow in God's wisdom. *(V.12)*

For us Christians, the most important verse in Psalm 90 is verse 12. We read this in the light of God's revelation in Christ Jesus our Lord. We know that Jesus went to the cross and took our sins unto Himself, freeing us from God's wrath. Having Jesus' Spirit in our hearts gives us the security that we can face death confidently and triumphantly, knowing we will go to heaven to be with God and Jesus for all eternity. Yes, we know we are going to die, but being in Christ changes the character and quality of our life while we are living! Having the Spirit of Jesus in our hearts, we are able to use trouble as a discipline. The human predicament is real, and Psalm 90 doesn't allow any empty optimism. However, it does open our mind to the wonderful optimism of being in Christ.

## Segment Four — Our Need of the LORD's Grace. Verses 13 - 17

Back in verse 1, Moses tells us that the Lord is our refuge and now here in the final segment of the psalm, he pleads with the LORD to take pity on his people. *(V.13)* Moses asks God to help him and the Hebrew people to begin each morning with the joy in having faith in a God full on unfailing love. *(V.14)* And to replace evil years with good years. *(V.15)* Moses pleads with God that the Hebrew children could experience the miraculous glory of God. *(V.16)* Moses ends his psalm by asking the Creator God, the Lord, to make the efforts of His people successful. He repeats this request for emphasis. *(V.17)*

From a Christian perspective, God has shown us His approval by sending Jesus Christ to be our Savior! Jesus has taken away our sin and has allowed us great joy *(Psalm 90:14)*, every day of our lives, offering praises to God. As the Apostle Paul says in his Letter to the Ephesians, we should praise God the Father and Jesus Christ for the blessings that come to us from the heavenly realms. *(Ephesians 1:3)*

If we in the 21st century allow God to show us His approval in Christ, then we can become a blessing to others. When we become a servant of God, the Great Judge for our lives, we will be able to hear Jesus' voice interceding for us. He will say come eat and drink at my table in the heavenly Kingdom. *(Luke 22:29-30)*

# PSALM 91
## Sheltered by the Mighty God

Psalm 91 is a beautiful composition of confidence and trust. It was probably placed following Psalm 90 to act as a counterbalance to its more somber and melancholy tone. The author of Psalm 91 was apparently a Temple priest who wrote the psalm to lift up the spirits of worshipers. He does not take into account the seriousness of the problem of evil, but his faith is genuine and his words have encouraged and comforted countless numbers of readers who have been sick, lonely or troubled.

### Segment One – The Psalmist's Personal Faith. Verse 1

The message of Psalm 91 says the awesome LORD of the universe cares! He is willing to shelter us and allow us to live within His protecting shadow. *(V.1)* This is the Psalmist's personal faith and we would do well to make it our own.

### Segment Two – What This Faith Can Do for Us. Verses 2 - 8

In order to avail ourselves of God's power and protection, we must make the same decision the Psalmist does: we must put our trust in the LORD. *(V.2)* This is fundamental! The Hebrew word for "trust" is *("batach")*, which means "to attach ourselves to Him," "to rely on," "to have a "confident expectation." From every trap He will rescue us. *(V.3)* When we know who is in charge and we put our faith in God, then we can relax.

Look at verse 4. There are two meaningful metaphors we need to know. God, acting like a mother bird, will cover us with His wings. The other has to do with God's promises to put His arms around us like we're wearing armor. The mental picture of God treating us like a mother and holding us, and giving us a warm nurture, is very meaningful. Our world has many dangers, but with God's presence surrounding us, we do not need to fear the terrors of night nor dangers that might confront us during the day. (V.5-6)

Apparently the thousands who fall at the side of those protected by God in verses 7-8 are being punished for their wickedness (sins), but the writer says he is protected from those evils. (V.7)

Trusting completely in the Lord Jesus Christ, we too, will be spared from God's judgment because our sins have been forgiven and we have been made right with God, thanks to our Savior.

## Segment Three – The LORD Will Keep Us from Stumbling. Verses 9 - 13

In verses 9 and 10, the Psalmist repeats his theme that we are to make the LORD our refuge because no evil can conquer us then. The Psalmist tells us God's angels are assigned to protect us and keep us from stumbling. (V.11-12) The last verse in this section tells us we will be able to crush lions and trample serpents. (V.13) These feats of strength may be that our writer has taken some slight poetic exaggerations, but he is well-intentioned. Actually these are metaphors representing evils in the world. In the New Testament the Apostle Peter tells us that the Devil prowls like a roaring lion to devour us. (1 Peter 5:8) This is the kind of victim we can become. However, the Devil is no match for God's armor. Peter tells us strong faith can overcome evil. (1 Peter 5:9)

## Segment Four – God's Promises for Those Who Love Him. Verses 14 - 16

The Psalmist has used different pronouns in the writing this composition. In the beginning of the psalm, he used the pronoun "I" to express his personal faith. Then in verses 4-13 he changed to "you," as he wanted to communicate with us, his readers. In the final segment he changes back to "I," representing Jehovah God. God is speaking and telling us what promises He has for those who love Him.

The first thing God says to us readers is the importance of commitment. He says if we truly love Him, then we will be blessed and protected. (V.14) It's amazing, because He said the same thing to Abraham and Moses years earlier. Then in exile in Babylon, He revealed His will to Isaiah concerning

Israel saying when His people go through great difficulty, He will be with them. *(Isaiah 43:2)* God did not give up on His people and He is still faithful to His covenant promises. His plans for the world are still intact.

As we become more mature in the faith and more intimate with the LORD, our prayer life will become more productive. God says I will answer when you call on my name. *(V.15)* Then God tells us we will receive long life and salvation. *(V.16)* The Hebrew word for "long" is *("Orek"),* which means for the Jews they will have a long life in the land. To us Christians, Jesus said He came here on earth to give us life in all its fulness. *(John 10:10)* He is saying that we are to live fully each day being honored by God, and, when our life on earth ends, we will continue to be with God and Jesus in our home in heaven. Our goal in this life is to live for Jesus each and every day as Thomas O. Chisholm writes in his hymn "Living for Jesus."

# PSALM 92
## Celebration of God's Righteous Rule

Psalm 92 is designated as a Psalm for the Sabbath. It was written as a hymn by an unknown saint with the objective of praising God. We can observe by context (especially verse 3) that it was written for corporate worship. The Levites probably sang this psalm in the Temple on the Sabbath accompanied by musical instruments.

This psalm can be broken down into four segments: One, Saying Thanks to th LORD, Verses 1-4; Two, Evildoers Are Scattered, Verses 5-9; Three, Made Strong by the LORD, Verses 10-11; and Four, The Godly Shall Prosper, Verses 12-15.

### Segment One –Saying Thanks to the LORD. Verses 1- 4

Book Four of the Psalter resonates with joyfulness! Psalm 92 starts off reminding the congregation that it is good to sing praises to the Most High. *(V.1)* Psalm 95 begins by reminding the congrgation to begin the service with a joyous shout of thanksgiving. *(V.1-2)* Psalm 96 exhorts the whole earth to proclaim the good news that God saves. *(V.1-2)* Psalm 98 is a bit different, but similar. It calls for the congregation to sing a new song. A new song that the LORD has revealed His righteousness to every nation. *(V.1-4)* There is also calls for more singing in Psalm 99. But Psalm 100 is even more enthusiastic as it tells us to shout and sing for joy in our worship of the LORD. *(V.1)* Then in Psalm 100, the Psalmist parallels verse 2 of Psalm 92 saying the LORD's unfailing love should not only be praised in the morning and night, but that love continues for each generation. *(Psalm 100:5)* And the last psalm of Book 4, Psalm 106, contains the same wonderful joyous spirit, saying we can never praise Him enough. *(V.1-2)*

The instruction in verse 2 of Pslam 92 to sing morning and evening prayers come from Jehovah's instructions to Moses for daily offerings (see Exodus 29:38-42). Of course, "loving kindness" and "faithfulness" of God mentioned in verse 2 are two of the most meaningful Hebrew words: *("Checed")* the covenant word for "loving kindness" and "steadfast love," and *("Emuwnah")* for "faithfulness."

In verse 4 the Psalmist is really celebrating God's righteous rule! He is glad because he is so grateful! This is the motive for us Christians to worship the God and Father of the Lord Jesus – the attitude of gratitude!

## Segment Two – Evildoers Are Scattered. Verses 5 - 9

God is a Spirit and He exists outside the realm of nature. He has a supernatural way of entering into human life for the accomplishment of His purposes, like raising up inspired and charismatic leaders like Moses and David. He also at times uses non-believers to further His plans, such as using King Cyrus of Persia to free God's people in captivity (see Isaiah 43:1-8). He also occasionally does mighty works of interrupting the natural laws of nature, such as what He did in bringing the Hebrews out of bondage from Egypt (see Exodus 14).

The Psalmist probably remembered the many supernatural incidents of the Exodus, and exclaims that the LORD is a LORD of miracles. *(V.5)* Then he exclaims how great Jehovah is and recognizes the vast distance between God and man, especially God's thought and man's thoughts. *(V.5)* He was probably thinking of Isaiah's words from the LORD who says just as the heavens are higher than the earth, so are My ways higher than yours, and My thoughts higher than yours. ((Isaiah 55:9). The writer of Psalm 92 tells us only the ignorant don't know this *(V.6)* and fools can't comprehend it. He then remembers that the wicked seem to prosper, but, because God is in charge, those who oppose God ultimately will be scattered. *(V.9)*

## Segment Three – Made Strong By the LORD. Verses 10 - 11

Going back to verse 8, the Psalmist sees the LORD in the heavens powerful and mighty, able to be helpful for His people. Because of this, the author is reassured *(V.10)*, feeling strong and able to deal with the problems that life deals him. He is perhaps reminded of Solomon's proverb that a godly nation is exalted but sin disgaces a people *(Proverbs 14:34)* and realizes his enemies are doomed. *(V.11)*

## Segment Four – The Godly Will Flourish. Verses 12 - 15

The godly will become like a palm tree and be tall like the cedars of Lebanon. *(V.12)* These are magnificent metaphors because the palm tree has the flexibility to ride out even the fiercest storm; while the cedar trees have some of the choicest wood for building. David wanted to build a Temple for Yahweh; but Solomon built it using wood from the stately cedar trees of Lebanon (see 2 Samuel 7:7).

Another beautiful metaphor is having the godly transplanted into the LORD's garden where He can personally cares for each one of us so that we can be fruitful for Him. *(V.13)* Even in old age, we'll be able to witness for God, and stay vital and green. *(V.14)* The Apostle Paul spoke about giving our bodies to God as a living sacrifice, holy – the kind He can accept. Then Paul further challenges us not to imitate the world but be transformed into a new person wanting and willing to do the will of God. *(Romans 12:2)* This is a way we can honor the Lord.

Paul became more specific in Second Corinthians, saying that we need to be Christ's ambassadors speaking out to others that they too like us need to be reconciled to God through acceptance of Christ's sacrifice for us as our Lord and Savior. *(2 Corinthians 5:19-21)*

# PSALM 93
## God's Majesty and Strength

Psalm 93 is a hymn praising the everlasting reign of God as King! This psalm, and six others are termed Enthronement Psalms. (See Psalms 47,95-99.) All these proclaim that God reigns! The Hebrew word for "reigns" is ("Malak"); it also means "to be king." We Christians share with our Jewish brothers and sisters that the Father of our Lord Jesus is the Almighty King.

The term "monarchy" is used to tell us that a government is ruled by a human king. The term "oligarchy" tells us the government is ruled by an elite few. "Democracy" means the government is ruled by the people. An historian named Josephus coined a phrase to describe how Israel was theoretically governed. It is a "theocracy," he wrote. ("Theo") in Greek means "God," and Josephus believed that Israel was governed by God as King.

### Segment One – The Throne of the LORD Endures Forever. Verses 1 - 2

The theory behind the government of ancient Israel was that a human king was enthroned yearly. But he ruled under the watchful eye of the kingship of God. As Psalm 93 puts it the king is not the LORD, the LORD is the king. (V.1) Majesty implies being imbued with dignity, grandeur, and inner power. It's like when young Isaiah had his vision of the Lord. God was sitting on a lofty throne in the Temple of heaven, filled with glory. Around the LORD were mighty six-winged seraphs and they continually sang Holy, Holy Holy. (Isaiah 6:3)

Overwhelmed by God's majesty and power, Isaiah fell down before the King, saying that his destruction was now sealed since he a sinful man saw God. (Isaiah 6:5) Standing before God, we human beings are humbled as we recognize our frailty and sin.

Israel's kings were to govern their people as God rules everlastingly from heaven, with love and justice. As the Psalmist points out in verse 1, God established the world and his rule cannot be shaken. *(V.1)* And His rule is immemorial. *(V.2)* God is eternal! He is, always has been, and always will be. As Moses writes in Psalm 90 God has no beginning and no end. *(Psalm 90:2)*

## Segment Two – Turmoil in the World. Verses 3- 4

God is the creator! He established the oceans. The Hebrew word for "established" is *("Kuwn")* and it means "to bring something into an incontrovertible existence." Even nature obeys Him. *(V.3)* The waters pounding the shore symbolizes the disorder and the evil forces that threaten us, but mightier than this is the LORD. *(V.4)*

## Segment Three – The King in Decrees and Holiness. Verse 5

The Psalm ends by saying God's Word is inviolable, His Royal decrees cannolt be altered. *(V.5)* It is one of the few things that is. Our universe is not inviolable. It is constantly changing. Nature, like what happens to our bodies, is always in the process of change and decay. Even the sun is cooling and eventually it will not shine any more. All of our human resources one day will be depleted. The Apostle Paul knew this and reminded the new Christians that all creation is still subjected to God's curse when Adam and Eve sinned. The decay of their bodies is evidenced of that curse. *(Romans 8:20-23)*

Everything changes but God. He is our creator and sustainer, and He has given a gift that never changes – His Word! Aware of this truth, the Psalmist of the 119th Psalm proclaims LORD forever your laws remain true and serve your plans. *(119: 89-91)*

God's royal decrees cannot be changed. *(Psalm93:5)* His commandments, promises, and His covenant are our plumb lines, and our lives in this world are measured by them. (See Amos 7:7-8.) The Psalmist ends this hymn by pronouncing another great truth: holiness is the nature of the LORD's reign. *(V.5)*

The Apostle Peter picks up on this and says that because God is holy, then we believers need to be holy in everything we do. Jesus Christ, God's

Son, is also holy and He invites us to be His children. *(I Peter 1:15-16)* The Hebrew word for "Holiness" is *("Qudesh")* and for us humans it means being "set apart" for God, being "consecrated to the Lord." It is similar to the Greek word *("Hagios")* which Peter uses in the New Testament. God is King and He is holy!

# PSALM 94

## The LORD Will Repay Those Who Deserve It

This psalm is a lament in two sections. The first (verses 1-15) is a community lament; the second (verses 16-23) is a lament of an individual. There is no superscription on this psalm. The author was probably one of the Temple priests, and in this composition he represents the voice of the oppressed within Israel. Certain wicked men in the community tended to take advantage of people who are below them socially and have less economic power, and so they push them around and exploit them financially.

The theme of Psalm 94 is God's judgment of the wicked. Some biblical interpreters think this psalm is an interruption of the eight other psalms that deal with God's Kingship in Book Four. It is my opinion that one of the main functions of God the heavenly King is to make righteous judgments and be an overseer and role model for those involved in governing Israel, and, therefore, Psalm 94 has a rightful place and fits right in with the others.

### Segment One – Asking the LORD to Arise in Judgment. Verses 1 - 3

The Psalmist begins by acknowledging that the legitimate function of the LORD is to handle vengeances. (V.1) The Apostle Paul in his Letter to the Romans repeats this exhortation to leave vengenance to God. (Romans 12:19) The writer of Psalm 94, however, wants God's justice to be seen when He is punishing the evildoers exploiting the downtrodden and weak members of the community. His judgments are always carried on in an impartial manner that is fair and just. The writer apparently thinks those who are proud deserve to be punished by God. (V.2) According to verse 3, it has been a long time (too long?) since the wicked have been reprimanded for their unrighteous behavior.

## Segment Two – The Arrogance of Evil Men. Verses 4 - 7

The writer describes to the LORD the way arrogant men actually boast about the way they walk over less powerful persons. *(V.4)* They hurt the ones You love. *(V.5)* He says these evil people actually murder orphans, widows and foreigners (a bit of hyperbole?). *(V.6)* O God, You don't seem to be looking or making any effort to help these underdogs. Don't you care? *(V.7)*

## Segment Three – God Sees and Hears. Verses 8 - 11

The Psalmist calls the oppressors fools! *(V.8)* He then asks a series of rhetorical questions, but answers them for the benefit of those he is criticizing. Is God deaf? Is He blind? *(V.9)* Of course not! The God that punishes nations is very capable of punishing you, the Psalmist writes. *(V.10)* The thoughts of everyone are known by the LORD. *(V.11)*

## Segment Four – Discipline Is Helpful. Verses 12 - 15

This segment is a kind of detour, an aside, where the Psalmist gives the reader a teaching based on Solomon's Proverbs 3:11-12, in which Solomon reminds the people that God corrects those he loves like a father corrects His child. There is happiness resulting from God's discipline and teaching. *(V.12)* On the other hand, God permits the wicked to dig their own pit. *(V.13)* The Psalmist reaffirms that God won't abandon His people and, in fact, will reward them. *(V.14-15)*

## Segment Five – The LORD Quiets Me. Verses 16 - 19

In this section the Psalmist goes back to his original question of God judging the wicked and giving to them the kind of penalties they deserve. *(V.1-3)* He then looks around to see if others will protect and shield him from the wicked, but finds no one – he is alone. Only the LORD will protect him. *(V.16)* He confesses he would have died if the LORD had not interjected Himself into the Psalmist's life. *(V.17)* Thanks to God's love and mercy (My partner in the covenant), He supported me. All the while I assumed God's "judgment" *("Mispat")* was only on the ungodly. Not so! He disciplined me with His everlasting grace when my feet were slipping, otherwise, I would have gone down to the Pit *("Shachath")* and be lost forever. *(V.18-19)*

## Segment Six – Trust in the LORD. Verses 20 - 23

In this segment our writer gets back to the question of the wicked oppressing the underdogs of society. He asks what makes unjust leaders think that God sides with them and not punish them for their attacks on the righteous? *(V.20-21)* In back of this question is the Psalmist's understanding that God has revealed His plan and purpose for the world by giving His "eternal Word," His *("Choq")*. Psalm 119:89-91 reiterates this same belief that law (the eternal Word) was true, is true will be true forever.

Psalm 94 ends up saying that God does not approve of a government allowing wrong to defeat right. He says that God will destroy evil persons because of their sins. *(V.23)* In the midst of all this wickedness, the writer looks to God for protection. The writer is thus quieted and secure. But what about the wicked? His answer is to leave their fate in the hands of Almighty God. *(V.22-23)*

# PSALM 95
## True Worship Needs Total Commitment


Psalm 95 is one of the enthronement psalms (93, 96-99), but it has an added liturgy of divine judgment in the last verses. In the later years after the Exile, the first part of this psalm was adopted in the synagogues as a call to worship, explaining how and why one should properly and respectfully come before the LORD. The first part is also used in many Christian churches as a call to worship. The last part (Verses 7-11) warns the readers what can happen if one hardens his heart.

### Segment One —An Invitation to Worship. Verses 1 - 2

Psalm 95 is a gracious invitation to worship the LORD with gladness! When the worshipers would gather in the Temple, a priest (or a Levite) would call them to lift their voices and sing with enthusiasm and joy for the rock of their salvation. (V.1) All the gathered Jews would know that the rock was a metaphor for the Mighty God, popularized by King David when he was out in the wilderness among the rocks and mountains. In Psalm 18, which David wrote, he says that the LORD is both his rock and his fortress. (Psalm 18:2) In another psalm composed by David, he writes that God leads him to a towering rock to keep him safe, a fortress of refuge. (Psalm 61:2-3) In Psalm 95, the Psalmist says worshipers need to be thankful for all the many blessings God has given to them, and these wonderful psalms of praise are the best vehicles to express joy and thanks. (V.2)

## Segment Two – God Is Awesome. Verses 3 - 5

God is enthroned above the earth, watching over all of us and monitoring our activities. *(V.3)* He rules and judges all human rulers and kings. He is also the Creator who put all we have here on earth in the first place. *(V.4-5)* The Psalmist says everything in all creation is under His control – it is all His! To realize that God is our all-powerful King allows us to worship Him in humility and trust.

## Segment Three – He Is Our Shepherd. Verses 6 - 7

Kneeling is an act of recognizing our submission and dependence upon the LORD. The Psalmist begins this segment reminding us to bow down before the LORD. *(V.6)* Of course, there are other ways of expressing our feelings of reverence, like bowing our heads, or prostrating ourselves. It is not the position of the body, but the inner attitude that is most important. The Psalmist uses a common, but beautiful pastoral image of a shepherd. God is our Shepherd and we are part of His flock. *(V.7)* It is this personal relationship we have with the LORD that makes it so special. In David's most poignant writing, his 23$^{rd}$ Psalm, he expresses his secure belief that though he might walk through a valley of dread and destruction he is certain he will be protected and comforted. *(Psalm 23:4)*

For us Christians, Jesus is the Good Shepherd. In John's Gospel, in the New Testament, Jesus speaks about how He lays down His life for His sheep. He uses the metaphor of the Gate. He himself is the Gate through which the saved will find green pastures. *(John10:9)* Then Jesus says that His sheep even recognize His voice because it gives them eternal life. *(John 10: 27-28)* What wonderful words! The last part of Psalm 95 verse7 says we need to listen to his voice now! These words are so similar to Jesus' words in John's Gospel about how important it is to hear His calling, and for us to recognize His voice and come to Him.

Hymn writer Fanny Crosby took the words from Psalm 95 and wrote her beloved hymn, "Jesus is Calling."

## Segment Four – The Voice of Warning. Verses 8 - 11

In this section, the Priest/Psalmist speaks a word of warning on behalf of God to the people. He reminds the congregation what happened to the people of Israel. When they arrived at a place called Rephidim, during their forty years of wandering, there was nothing to drink. In their thirst, the people complained to Moses, "Give us water!" they wailed. Moses told them to be quiet! Are you trying to test God's patience? Then they cried out wanting to return to Egypt rather than die here in Rephidim. *(Exodus 17:3)* God told Moses to take his rod and strike a rock and it will cause water to gush out. This ceased the people's complaints. As a result, Moses named this place Massah, meaning "tempting Jehovah" and "Meribah," meaning "argument and strife." (See Exodus 17:1-7.) The LORD said His rebellious people had refused to obey His laws, and they did not put Him first in their lives.

Returng to Psalm 95, the Psalmist wants the people not to have hard hearts like the people of Israel had to Meribah. *(V.8)* The Psalmist points out that for 40 years God was angry with these ancestors. *(V.9-10)* The Psalmist ends the psalm reminding the people that the LORD determined that those at Meribah would never enter into the promised land of Israel. *(V.11)*

The priest is saying to the congregation, "How can you so-called Jews enter God's House unless you are 100% committed to following God, with all your heart, soul, and might (Deuteronomy 6:4-5) and are totally faithful to God's covenant obligations?" (See Exodus 19:5-6.) This is the essence of the warning in Psalm 95. This warning is just as relevant today as it was back then.

# PSALM 96

## Sing to the LORD a New Song

Psalm 96 has no title to identify its author, but when King David was in the early stages of his monarchy, he liberated the city of Jerusalem from the Jebusites and made it his capitol, the city of David. (See 2 Samuel 5:6-10.) His next major exploit was to defeat the Philistines and then bring the Ark of the Covenant from its temporary resting place at the residence of Obed-Edom to Jerusalem, accompanied by thousands of worshipers along the way.

This trip to the new capitol city was a gala affair, with orchestra, horns and cymbals! David placed the Ark in the Holy of Holies of a hastily constructed Tabernacle, making Jerusalem not only the political capitol, but also the religious center of all Judaism. (See 2 Samuel 6 and I Chronicles 15-16.) In honor of this occasion, David wrote a composition that appears in 1 Chronicles 16:8-36. There are a number of identical verses in both Psalm 96 and what David wrote in 1 Chronicles for the celebration of bringing the Ark to the new capitol. Also, other verses that are similar would lead us to believe that David authored Psalm 96.

Not all biblical authorities agree with this reasoning. They argue that other verses of David's composition in 1 Chronicles 16 are also quoted in Psalms 105: 1-15 and 106: 47-48. They say some later editor put these Psalms together with influences of the writings of Isaiah in his chapters 40-55. If David was not the author, Psalm 96 certainly expresses what David would have offered to God on the happy occasion of recapturing the Ark and bringing it back to the new capitol. It is a joyous expression of praise to the God of Israel as King, and an invitation to the nations of the world to join in praising Him! Also contained in this psalm is an oracle – a prediction that one day in the future, the great God Jehovah, the King of kings, will judge the world in justice and righteousness. We Christians can read and can catch a glimpse of the coming King Jesus.

## Segment One – Sing Out the LORD's Praises. Verses 1 - 2

There are a number of psalms in Book 4 that begin with "Calls to Worship," that are similar to Psalm 96. Psalm 96 begins with the need or opportunity to sing to the LORD a new song, one that the whole world should sing. *(V.1)* Psalm 100 is a bit more raucous, asking worshipers to shout joy to the LORD and that the whole earth should shout this joy. *(Psalm 100.1)* Psalm 101 is a bit subdued, but nevertheless very thoughtful. It begins with the Psalmist saying he will sing of the LORD's love and justice. All of these are happy expressions of joy. All of them have as their objective to praise and honor God, and to proclaim to the world that God reigns!

The phrase "sing a new song" declares what God has done for His people to give guidance and blessings. Specifically in Psalm 96 it is the celebration of David bringing the Ark to Jerusalem where symbolically it meant that God was making His home in Zion. Each day the Psalmist says in Psalm 96 verse 2 the congregation should proclaim the LORD's good news.

## Segment Two – The Creator God Is to Be Honored. Verses 3 - 6

Verse 3 tells the Hebrew people to inform all nations about the deeds God has done for his chosen people. His deeds are God's many miracles of choosing the Hebrews as His people, bringing them out of slavery from Egypt, and *now*, under David's generalship, they are becoming a force to be reckoned with. God is the creator. He is the living God, while other nation's gods are mere idols. *(V.4-5)* The Hebrew word for "idols" is *("El'yl")*. It has many meanings including "worthless," "useless" and "empty." Those idols back then were worthless and are just as worthless today when people make idols of sex, popularity and material things. The Psalmist ends this segment by citing two qualities of God that exemplify his exalted nature—majesty and honor. *(V.6)* The wonderful transformation then and today is that we tend to become what we worship.

## Segment Three – The Nations Join in the Praising. Verses 7 - 9

We can just imagine David, with a smile on his face, playing his harp and breaking into a joyful song singing that the nations of the world need to recognize the LORD as their creator and give Him the glory He deserves.

*(V.7-8)* The Hebrew word for "glory" in English has a multitude of meanings including "brilliance," "splendor" and "majesty." To give God glory is to give Him proper respect and honor by living our lives in such a way to manifest His divine qualities in dealing with others such as being righteous, loving and kind. Worship has a lot to do with how we approach God. Part of giving the Lord glory has to do with bringing the Lord something, an offering or a sacrifice.

Too many today come to worship expecting to get something. One of our great role models is young Isaiah. He came into the Temple and saw the mighty God. Hovering around God were Seraphim, each with six wings. In a great chorus they sang that the LORD is holy and that His glory fills the whole earth. *(Isaiah 6:3)* God's awe and majesty were too much for Isaiah so he bowed low and confessed his sin. Then one of the Seraphim flew to the altar and picked up a burning coal with a pair of tongs and put it on Isaiah's lips and pronounced that his guilt was removed and his sins forgiven. *(Isaiah 6:7)* Then Isaiah heard the LORD ask who should be His messenger to His chosen people. *(Isaiah 6:8)* In gratitude Isaiah calls out, Lord, fearing to address Him as LORD, that he, Isaiah, be sent. *(Isaiah 6:8)* Our Psalmist in Psalm 96 calls out to the world saying that its inhabitants should worship the LORD and to bring offerings. *(V.7-8)* He informs them that if they humble themselves and give Jehovah (the LORD) the glory, they will be rewarded with the beauty of holy lives. The Psalmist then encourages the whole world to worship God and tremble before Him. *(V.9)*

### Segment Four – The LORD Is King, Let Heaven and Earth Rejoice. Verses 10 - 13

Verse 10 is the climax of the Psalm, where the nations are told that their king is the LORD (Jehovah). There are two ways in which God reigns. One, He rules over nature. In picturesque language the writer says the sea, all in it, and the fields, and all in it, and the rest of the ground, trees and forest, should praise God. *(V.11-12)* The LORD of nature is always doing new things like creating new days, new seasons and recreating crops. Graciously God created nature for our sake—a place for us to dwell, a place for us to grow food so we can live, and a place where we can enjoy the beauty of his creation. The second way that God reigns is that He controls the future. Verse 13 says the judge of all things, the LORD, is coming to judge with righteousness and truth. *(V.13)* When we read that the LORD is coming, that is an eschatological message meaning God will make something wonderful in the future, when God thinks the timing is right.

This is difficult for people to understand today as it was in the past because there is so much violence and unrighteousness in the world. However, God is in control and by His mighty power He is able to hold evil in check in the world. The Hebrew word for "judge" in verse 13 is *("Saphat")* and it means God will do what is just and right. The word for "truth" in verse 13 can be translated as "faithfulness" and "trust."

We have to trust that God will do the right thing for us. It is surprising that the Psalmist could sing for joy that judgment is coming because usually judgment carries the overtones of hell and damnation. This is why it is good to be a follower of Jesus Christ. We Christians do not fear the final judgment day because we know that our Savior Jesus Christ took our sins when He died on the cross. When we stand before the Judge on that day, thanks to Jesus, we'll be able to pass on into heaven and spend eternity with God and Jesus. Psalm 96 is right—we want to give God the Glory. Fanny J. Cosby acknowledges this in her hymn "To God Be the Glory."

# PSALM 97

## The LORD is King!

This psalm is another of the enthronement psalms (see psalms 47, 93, 96-99). Its purpose is stated succinctly in the first verse that the King of all of us in the world is the LORD and we should rejoice in that. The author is not identified. He uses familiar vocabulary, much of it drawn from other psalms and postexilic Isaiah (chapters 40-42). He states that the righteous are called upon to praise God for His awe-inspiring power, justice and supremacy. There are also overtones that point to the end of this present age. As one looks at this short, twelve- verse composition, there is some repetition.

### Segment One – The LORD Reigns. Verse 1

The psalm begins by proclaiming that the LORD is king. The Hebrew word for "king" in verse 1 is *("Malak")* and can be translated "to reign," "to be Sovereign." Sovereignty implies that Jehovah God (the LORD) is all-knowing, all-powerful and everywhere present. Knowing that God is sovereign tells us He is in charge, is ultimately in control of everything that goes on in our planet, and that is a marvelous sense of comfort for God's people.

### Segment Two – Clouds and Darkness. Verses 2 - 5

The language in this segment seems to come from various manifestations of God in a number of Old Testament Scriptures. God appears at Mount Sinai amidst thunder, fire, lightning and smoke (see Exodus 19:16-19 and 35:5). *(V.2-3)* Moses and the Israelites were awe-struck and filled with fear at God's appearances. The author of Hebrews in the New Testament says God

309

was not only a consuming fire back then shaking up the earth but will be a consuming fire in the future shaking up the earth and the heavens as well. *(Hebrews 12:26-29)* What this says to us is that we can never be nonchalant with God or take Him with casualness. There is much hyperbole in these few verses of Psalm 97, like flashing lightning across the whole world *(V.4)* and melting mountains like wax. *(V. 5)* But it's just the author's way of saying how great God is.

## Segment Three – Jehovah Is Greater Than Other Gods. Verses 6 - 9

Look at the heavens, they declare the majesty and glory to all the nations. *(V.6)* The author is correct in saying it is disgraceful to worship idols. Because their very definition says they are worthless and not real. However, I think the Psalmist gets too carried away in verse 7. If idols are not real, and they're not, they obviously cannot bow down to God. When the New Testament writers speak about idols, they talk about meat sacrificed to idols and whether or not it is proper for Christians to eat the meat. The Apostle Paul boldly replies idols are not god. *(1 Corinthians 8:4-6)* Today's idols are anything that come between a person and God, such things like power, sex, fame and material things. Apparently, the author feels that the citizens of the cities of Judah are taking seriously the justice and righteousness of God and were not being enticed or tricked by the paganism of their day. *(V.8-9)* It was good they were obeying the Second Commandment.

## Segment Four – Putting the Reign of the LORD into Practice. Verses 10 -12

Evil is an abomination to the LORD, and we who love God cannot just stand around and allow the wicked to prosper at the expense of the weak. This is one of the reasons why we Christians need to work at our social action activities in the churches, because there is strength in numbers. The Psalmist in verse ten reminds the people that God is faithful and protects godly people. The Psalmist then says that God showers his people with light. *(V.11)* He probably considers this light to be the Word of God. The most familiar passage in the psalms comparing the word of God with light is found in Psalm 119. In this lengthy psalm, it says that the LORD's word is a lamp to the Psalmist's feet and the light that shows him which path to take. *(Psalm 119:101,105)* Pslam 97 ends by exhorting the people to be happy in the LORD. *(V.12)*

The Psalmist began Psalm 97 by calling God's people to rejoice in the reign of God, and he ends up calling them (and us) to take the initiative in putting the reign of God into practice in our own lives by opposing evil wherever it is found, and by turning our backs on the idols of self-indulgence, money, sex, fame, and self-glorification. An update on these wonderful words comes from the Westminster Shorter Catechism which points out that the chief purpose of God's people is to enjoy God and glorify God.

# PSALM 98
## A New Song of the LORD's Mighty Deeds

This poem is yet another enthronement psalm. It is an exuberant call to celebrate the righteous reign of God the King! It was probably composed by one of the Temple poets to be sung by the congregation at the newly restored Temple, sometime after 516 B.C. Psalm 98 is a lot like Psalm 96, both of them begin and end in similar fashion. Psalm 98 is all about praise, while Psalm 96 praises God and compares the worship of God with those who worship idols.

There are three stanzas in the psalm we are considering. Each progressively extends the call to celebrate: First to the worshiping congregation (Verses 1-3); Second to the peoples on earth who have witnessed God's mighty deeds (Verses 4-6); and finally Third where there is so much excitement about what God the King has done that even nature takes up the call to sing its praises! (Verses 7-9).

### Segment One – The LORD Fulfills His Promises to Israel. Verses 1 - 3

Like verse one of Psalm 96, Psalm 98 exhorts the congregation to sing a new song to the LORD. But Psalm 98 specifically challenges the congregation to sing about the wonderful deeds the LORD has done. *(V.1)* A new song is based on the mighty deeds God did for Israel during the later years of their being prisoners in Babylon. Isaiah, the amazing prophet of the exile, spoke prophetic words of the LORD that were the basis for the inspiration of this poem. Isaiah wrote that the LORD actually named Cyrus, the king of Persia, to end the rule of the Babylonians over their Hebrew exiles. *(Isaiah 45:1-5)* Isaiah also prophesied that Cyrus would restore the exiled Hebrew people to again reside in their beloved city of Jerusalem.

(*Isaiah 45:11-13*) This great victory, the Psalmist, says was accomplished by the LORD's holiness and power. (*V.1*)

Cyrus, king of Persia, invaded Babylon and won the victory and then allowed the exiled Hebrews to go home to Jerusalem. Truly a marvelous miracle – a victory! (*"Yshuw ah"*) is the Hebrew word for "victory." It can also mean "salvation,"or "deliverance." In chapter 40 of Isaiah, he writes that the exiled Hebrews' sins are pardoned. Their punishement fulfilled. (*Isaiah 40:1-2*) The Psalmist points out that the LORD announced this victory to reveal His omnipotence (*V.2*) and to demonstrate His faithfulness to Israel. (*V.3*)

All this took place in 539 B.C. In less than 25 years, the walls of Jerusalem were restored, homes built, and a new Temple constructed. In 516 B.C. the Temple was ready for worship – miracles of miracle! It was Psalm 98 that produced a new song for this marvelous occasion.

### Segment Two – The Earth's People Praise the LORD for What He Did for Israel. Verses 4- 6

The mighty God did not reneged on His covenant promises. No! He had just brought a struggling remnant of Jews home from slavery in Babylon and resurrected the nation of Israel! Talk about miracles! Verse 4 exhorts the congregation to shout out praise to the LORD because of this. The people of Israel were no longer cringing prisoners. They are back in their homeland as changed people –new people. Hallelujah! Verses 5 and 6 tell the congregation to break out the harps and trumpets. It's worth a fantastic celebration and all the people of the earth are excited for the Jews (some hyperbole?).

### Segment Three – All Nature Sings Praises to the LORD. Verses 7 - 9

What a victory! It is so wonderful that all nature is invited to shout. (*V.7*) Stand on the seashore and you can still hear the waves clapping their hands. And, oh yes, the hills themselves are joyful. (*V.8*) All this is happening because of the miracle of God's grace. The psalm ends with a eschatological prophecy that the LORD, the righteous King, will be coming with judgment (*"Shabat"*) to judge the world with His perfect judgment and love. (*V.9*) The Heavenly King will right all the wrongs and will continue to work out His mighty purpose – working through David's dynasty, like He promised, through King Jesus the Messiah, the Son of David (see Matthew 1:1).

# PSALM 99
## Give Praise to the Holy LORD

This is the last of the enthronement psalms and focuses on God's holiness. There are but nine verses in this poem and verses 3, 5, and 9 all express the holiness of God the King.

Throughout the Bible, we read about God's holiness. Here are two examples. In Isaiah 6, there are mighty six-winged seraphs hovering around the throne of God, singing a great antiphonal chorus praising the LORD for his holiness. *(Isaiah 6: 3)* In the New Testament in the book of Revelation, John of Patmos is taken up to heaven and sees God's throne with twenty-four elders around Him. Lightning and thunder issue from the throne. Four Living Beings, day and night, keep repeating holy, holy holy. *(Revelation 4:1-8)*

### Segment One – Reverence for the Holy LORD. Verses 1 - 3

The mighty LORD is on His throne in heaven between the cherubim and the majesty of His presence is so overwhelming that it causes the whole earth to quake! *(V.1)* We can see God amidst the smoke and fire hovering above the two Guarding Angels who are perched on each end of the lid of the Ark of the Covenant. These cherubim are God's angels who protect the heavenly King. In this segment we get a quick peek into heaven and immediately sense the awe and reverence. The main impact, of course, is God's holiness. The Psalmist envisions the LORD as the supreme ruler of all nations. *(V.2)* The nations are encouraged to praise God because He is holy! *(V.3)*

## Segment Two – Bow Before the Holy God. Verses 4 - 5

The second stanza begins by saying God is a lover of justice and rules with justice and righteousness throughout Israel. *(V. 4) ("Mishpat")* is the Hebrew word for "justice," and it is administered with "righteousness" *("Ts_dagah")*. This important Hebrew word means "fairness" and "without partiality." God does not create people as puppets on a string. No, He expects them to act with love and consideration for others. God chose the Hebrews and made a covenant with them. His justice was a part of the covenant. In Deuteronomy the Hebrew people are informed by the LORD that He did not choose them because they were a great and significant nation. He chose them because he loved them. He made a covenant with them and expected them to obey his commandmants, laws and regulations. *(Deuteronomy 7: 7-11)* God's plan for His people was that they should face up to all of the evil in the world without succumbing to it by means of the spiritual ammunition He gave them – His "unfailing love" *("Checed")*, His "peace" *("Shalom")*, and others.

The most important concept in this poem is God's holiness. It is very difficult to adequately describe it. Theologians have said its meaning comes close to moral perfection or human purity. This is true. The problem is that God dwells outside time and space and is transcendent. The Hebrew word for "holiness" is *("Qadosh")*, which means "sacred," "pure," or "consecrated." Because we humans are sinful, we can never be totally pure. God, on the other hand, is, by definition, fully good and totally pure and absolutely perfect! Another word close to holiness is "sacred," or "sanctified." It has to do with being "set apart" by God.

We Christians, who love God and have committed ourselves to following Jesus, are called saints in the New Testament. However, we are far from perfect morally. We are sanctified as God's servants, dedicated to helping and serving our brothers and sisters. God, who is holy, chooses to send His Holy Spirit to work through us as we do our best to be God's representatives in seeing to it that "fairness" and "justice" are actualized. There is one other aspect of God's holiness that we have not mentioned. If we turn our backs on God's plan for our world, like the Jews did prior to the Exile, then God's anger will be triggered. A holy God cannot abide sin! He cannot stand to have His people vacillate and put other values (gods) first in their lives. God's wrath is a scary thing and nothing to be fooled with. When Isaiah had his initial experience with God, it terrified him so much that he prostrated himself and intoned that his destruction was sealed because he was a sinful person. *(Isaiah 6:5)* This is the other side of God's love that keeps us mindful of our commitments to the LORD and why we need to be continually exalting the LORD our God and bow down before him. *(V.5)*

## Segment Three – God Punishes and Pardons. Verses 6 - 9

There are a number of Scriptural quotes that relate to the cries to the LORD for help by Moses, Aaron, and Samuel. *(V.6)* In Exodus 13, God led the children of Israel at the edge of the wilderness and guided them by a pillar of cloud by day a pillar of fire by night. *(Exodus 13:21-22) (V.7)*

Later Moses called the people together, and recited a song to them (see Deuteronomy 32:1-43). The Psalmist refers to the Song of Moses in verse 8 saying LORD you answered them, forgave them and punished them. They wanted to elect a new leader and return to slavery in Egypt. God's holiness meant that He forgave them, but He also judged them for their sin and rebelliousness. In Numbers 14:20-23 the LORD says He pardoned them because Moses pleaded with him to do so. But because of their rebellion, He also determined that those who rebelled would never step foot on the Promised Land.

The Psalmist ends Psalm 99 by asking its readers to exalt the LORD in Jerusalm because He is holy. *(V.9)* Always we Christians must read the psalms through our Christian perspective. We can agree wholeheartedly with the author and can join him in exalting the Lord God. However, the next part of the command we would have to disagree with him. We are under no obligation to worship at the mountain in Jerusalem. For us this is not a command.

The Apostle Peter wrote to us Christians and said Jesus's Holy Spirit has made us holy. We are born again into the holiness of God because of Jesus.

Peter then spoke about our having to go through trials to test our faith to make certain it is strong and pure. Ultimately our time on earth is to learn to obey God and be holy in all we do, with the help of the Holy Spirit. *(1 Peter 1:2-16)*

# PSALM 100
## Shout with Joy before the LORD

Psalm 100 is a joyous call to praise the LORD! It is the back half of the book end that closes the series that began with Psalm 90. It is similar in structure to Psalm 95 (verses 1-2, 6-7) and it may have been composed to accompany a thank offering in the Temple.

Reformer John Calvin in Geneva, back in the 16th century, promoted something unique in the church – congregational singing, but he limited the singing to the psalms. One of the most familiar renditions of the psalms is a tune composed by Louis Bougeois and the words by William Kethe in 1561. It is called "Old Hundredth."

### Segment One – How We Should Give Thanks. Verses 1 - 2

It is not possible to give the LORD of the Universe anything. Why? Because He has everything! The Psalmist tells us, however, that we can do two things to show our appreciation for all of His blessings. We can shout with joy *(V.1)* and we can worship with gladness. *(V.2)* This poem is a missionary psalm for everybody on earth.

### Segment Two – Explaining Why We Must Give Thanks. Verse 3

The Psalmist exhorts us to acknowledge that the LORD is God. This means two things: 1) He is the Creator, He made us *(V.3)*; and 2) He is our Redeemer, we are the sheep of His pasture. *(V.3)* David presented this same message beautifully in Psalm 23. In the Gospel of John in the New Testament, Jesus, our Savior, says specifically that He is the good shepherd, the shepherd who lays down His life for the sheep. *(John 10:11)* This is a magnificent way of saying that He is our Redeemer. He went to the cross on our behalf, taking our sins away and opening the gates of heaven for us. Oh, how wonderful it is to know that we are His people. *(V.3)*

## Segment Three – An Invitation to Give Thanks. Verse 4

Picture a group of pilgrims who have come from afar as they arrive at the outer gates of the Temple. They are met by a priest who will help them to enter with thankful hearts. *(V.4)* They are led from the outer courts into the main assembly hall of the Temple with singing. Inside, they worship and gather as God's people.

## Segment Four – Final Expression of Praise. Verse 5

The last verse of this magnificent psalm, like verse 3, explains <u>why</u> we should thank God. Segment Two tells us God is our Creator, and this section invites us to thank Him because of <u>who</u> He <u>is</u>. He is good and his unfailing love for us is forever. God is forever faithful. The Hebrew word for "good" is *("Towb")*. It is an adjective meaning "gracious" and "lovely." The English word "God" is a shortened form of good. His "unfailing love" in Hebrew is *("Checed")*, a noun meaning "merciful," and "full of grace." It is one of the most important words in the entire Old Testament, because it expresses the eternal nature of God's nature. God is loving and kind, and *("Checed")* is also closely related with the forgiveness of sins.

We Christians can identify with Psalm 100. For us, John 3:16 is at the heart of our faith. God gave His only Son to die for us so we would have eternal life. It is God's eternal and unchanging character that sent Jesus to us as part of David's dynasty, just as He promised. It was all part of God's plan to use the Jewish people to be an instrument for the salvation of the world. God is "unchanging." The Hebrew word is *("Emuwnah")*. In a world that is always changing, God's unchanging nature provided security and joy for Abraham, Isaac, and Joseph. It is a joy for us in this generation to know that God will keep His Word for generations. *(V.5)*

# PSALM 101
## A Moral Guide for Those in Authority

Psalm 101 is the first in a collection of ten psalms (101 – 110). The superscription says it was written by David, but whether he wrote this poem is debatable. Psalm 101 is a vow by a king to do the things in his reign that would mirror the righteous will of God. These ten psalms are termed the Little Psalter within the Psalter.

We do not know if this is one of David's compositions, but it certainly has all the reasons to attribute it to him. David knew he was anointed to be king by God, and so it would be appropriate for him to set down the standards to which he would commit himself. It was a good way to begin his rule. After all, he envisioned his reign as a theocracy, that is, he would rule as God's deputy. We will assume David wrote the psalm or at least the Psalmist knew how David might have written the psalm.

### Segment One – A King's Commitment before the LORD. Verses 1 - 2

The words in Psalm 101 were primarily written as proper standards for the running of a righteous government. But these words of David's apply equally to our personal life as well. David is here putting forth right conduct that would be pleasing to the LORD. He realized that he himself would have to practice them in his home as well as in the public domain. At the very first he says he will have to reflect (mirror) God's ("*Checed*") and ("*Mishpat*") – His "unfailing love" and "justice."(*V.1*) Both are extremely essential aspects of dealing wisely with his subjects. David was sharp enough to realize that if he only used "love" and "kindness," people would soon think he was soft and weak and would, therefore, take advantage of him. On the other hand, if he used "justice" exclusively without "love," he would soon turn into a tyrant.

So in order to reflect the wisdom of the All-Wise Creator God, he would have to temper "justice" with "love."

The use of these two aspects of God's wisdom applies to our personal life as well. We need to be loving and fair and just in our dealings with others, knowing full well we are all sinners and are apt to let one another down occasionally. Even God, whose standards are absolute and perfect, treats us with mercy and forgiveness at times. The LORD is like a father who has compassion on us because he knows we are weak. *(Psalm 103:13-14)*

David not only sets standards high for being the King of his people, but he also knows that he must set the standard high for himself in living a blameless life and having integrity in his own home. *(V.2)* He is a marvelous role model for us. He approaches God humbly and sincerely, realizing his limitations and weaknesses. Having committed himself to living a blameless life, he tries to maintain this stance throughout his career. Yes, he stumbles now and then, but it was never because his standards were unclear. When he sinned, he always acknowledged his errors and asked God to forgive him.

### Segment Two – David's Personal Ethics. Verses 3 - 5

David sang this song, and maybe the priests in the Tabernacle picked it up and asked that it be used for special occasions, like a coronation or some other special public ceremony. It could have been sung by the whole congregation. Here was their king promising some wonderful things on their behalf: David is promising as their leader that he will try to be a good husband and father to his family, and in order to fulfill this vow he must be a role model for all. He must be attuned to the LORD in a special way, and this implies a humble spirit. Perhaps the priest would interject the words of Micah, the Prophet, who says what God wants for all of us – king and people -- is to do what is right, be merciful and be humble before God. *(Micah 6:8)*

Next came David's words that he would have a covenant with his eyes, ears and mind not to be attracted to evil, vulgar or crooked dealings. *(V.3-4)* In order to do this, he would have to fill his mind and heart with godly thoughts and worship the LORD regularly. He would do this personally and would encourage his people to bring the Spirit of the LORD into their lives to overflow so there wouldn't be any room for evil! Old Testament scriptures are very clear on this matter. In Deuteronomy we are told to love the LORD only and with all our heart, soul and mind. *(Deutonomy. 6:4-6)* In Leviticus it explains that we need to love our neighbor as our self. *(Leviticus 19:18)*

The last thing David promises is that he will oppose anyone who criticizes or slanders his neighbor, particularly if he does it clandestinely. *(V.5)* Slander has to do with words, and they can have a deadly and harmful effect on the whole community. The ideal is to have a free discussion of ideas. These are the high standards for the government and for the people.

## Segment Three – David's Administrative Principles. Verses 6 - 8

David, the king, says he intends to gather those who are godly and make them the folks with whom he will associate. They are the ones he will invite into his home. His servants will have to be people of integrity, because they will be the ones who will influence his children. Inviting godly folks into his inner circle will be the ones he'll choose to help him run the country. *(V.6)* David was wise enough to know that if he is to have honest and clean government, he must have upright and responsible civil servants – not those who practice deceit or shade the truth. *(V.7)* David ends this psalm by pledging to free the city of the LORD of evil doers. *(V.8)*

This is a wonderful psalm because it spells out much-needed high ideals. Would that public servants today could live up to these standards.

# PSALM 102

## An Afflicted Man and His Lament

Psalm 102 is a lament by a person in distress, whose health is broken and is asking the LORD for deliverance. It is one of the church's seven penitential psalms, along with Psalms 6,32,38, 51,130 and 143. There are a lot of unknowns connected with this poem. We don't know the identity of the poet, the nature of his illness, or whether he was part of the exiles in Babylon in the sixth century. It seems as if he has incorporated a short hymn into his composition about God's eternity (see verses 12-22), and worked it into his overall purpose as a source of encouragement.

### Segment One – A Sick Man's Lament. Verses 1 - 11

The first two verses act like a kind of prologue where the suffering man asks Jehovah to hear his concerns. In the verses that follow there is a great deal of parallelism. What this means is that the author states an idea in one line, and it is followed by a second line where the idea is repeated in slightly different words. Sometimes it is synonymous, but other times it is antithetical. It can also add a thought to the second sentence to amplify its meaning. Notice in the first two verses there are five times when the poet makes a request to God: hear and listen; don't turn away; bend down and hear; answer when I call. As you can see, this is no half-hearted petition. Rather, it is a very impassioned concern from a desperate man.

The Psalmist is ill, his bones burn like hot coals *(V.3)*, but he is also concerned for God's wrath against him and bothered by his enemies. *(V.8)* However, his chief concern is about the brevity of life, due to his illness. He cries out that he is so sick that he has no appetite at all. *(V.4)* He is just skin and bones. *(V.5)* He says he feels isolated, like an owl alone on a far off tree.

*(V.6)* If his illness isn't enough of a problem, he is taunted by his enemies. *(V.8)* With a marvellous poetic touch, the Psalmist says he eats ashes and his drink is filled with his tears. *(V.9)* While he doesn't let us know the exact nature of his transgressions against God, he experiences feelings of being totally rejected by God's anger. *(V.10)* Again the poet's touch appears in verse 11. He compares his life to evening shadows and withering like grass. The fact that his enemies curse at him and he feels thrown out, would lend some circumstantial evidence that he is in Babylon with the exiles!

## Segment Two – Jehovah Looks Down from His Temple in Heaven. Verses 12 -22

Martin Luther made an in-depth study of Psalm 102 and came to the conclusion that everything that went before looks to verse 12. He's right! In Part One, the Psalmist tells of his mental and physical distress, but verse 12 is indeed the turning point where he minimizes his own troubles and places his trust in the Sovereign God! *(V.12)* In so doing, he projects his thoughts on other people and other situations. In fact, there are four things that occupy his mind: (1) He asks God to watch over Jerusalem. *(V.13)* He is concerned about his devastated city. He says the people love even the dust on Jerusalem's steets. *(V.14)* He has faith that God will rebuild the ruins. *(V.16)* Yes, and the LORD He will listen and not reject His peoples' pleas. *(V.17)* (2) The author looks forward to the day when a nation yet to be created will not only praise the LORD but attract the nations of the world (the Gentiles) and their rulers to come and worship Jehovah God. *(V.18, 21-22)* Perhaps our author was in Babylon, and perhaps he had heard the sayings of the great Prophet Isaiah, looking to the future where the LORD's temple in Jerusalem will be a house of prayer for all nations. *(Isaiah 56:6-7)* (3) Isn't it wonderful that our sick poet has almost forgotten his own ills as he prays for others? (4) And finally his prayers are for the release of the prisoners. *(V.20)* Our Psalmist is anticipating the release of God's people from their 70 years of exile! Looking into a future future, the great Prophet Isaiah envisioned a new Israel. *(V.21-22)* Isaiah writes that the LORD told him to say the time for the LORD's favor has come to all those who mourn for Israel. This vision would appear to transcend our current era. *(Isaiah 61:1-3)* Christians cannot help thinking of Jesus as He announced His mission of spiritual freedom for prisoners of sin. He used similar words of Isaiah. (See Luke 4:18-19.)

## Segment Three – Distress Repeated. Verses 23 - 28

The Psalmist reflects again on his own personal ills and on the brevity of life *(V.23-24)* and comments on the fact that everyone has to die. He then contrasts that to God who exists forever. *(V.25-26)* The words in verses 25-26 are quoted in the New Testament in the Book of Hebrews (Hebrews 1:10-12) pointing out that although the LORD laid the foundations of the earth it will perish one day too but the LORD will still exist.

In the first chapter of Hebrews, it says that in the past God spoke to our forefathers through the prophets. Then in God's own chosen time, He spoke through His Son, Jesus, who exactly represents God. *(Hebrews 1:3)* And after Jesus died to cleanse us from the stain of sin, He sat down at the right hand of God in heaven. *(Hebrews 1:3)*

We all grow old and die, we wear out like old clothing. *(V.26)* But the Psalmist forgets his own mortality and is pleased that the LORD will provide security for Isreal's children and her children's children. *(V.27-28)* It's a frightening thing to die unless we know with certainty that with Jesus in our hearts, we will go to be with Him when we die. The Apostle Paul tells us in Romans that we are all sinners, but God's abounding grace forgives and saves us, and provides life eternal. *(Romans 5:20-21)*

# PSALM 103
## Praising the LORD for His Glorious Blessings

Psalm 103 is an autobiographical poem where the writer reminds himself of God's wonderful blessings. He also tells the gathered congregation in the worship setting what God is like so they can praise Him. He ends this psalm proclaiming that everyone on earth and heaven should give the LORD glory! This is one of the many compositions attributable to David.

### Segment One – Gratitude for Special Blessings. Verses 1 - 5

David begins this poem by praising the LORD with his whole heart. *(V.1)* The Hebrew word for "heart" here is *("nephesh")*, and it means one's whole "personality." David is grateful and doesn't want to take for granted all the good God things does for him. *(V.2)* He then enumerates them. First and foremost, the God of the universe accepts him in spite of his sins. *(V.3)* God hates sin, and sinning automatically means one becomes separated from God. In Psalm 32, David affirms how joyful one is when their rebellion toward the LORD is forgiven. It permits them to live their lives in complete honesty, he says. *(Psalm 32:1-2)* Secondly, in Psalm 103, he praises God for His healings. *(V.3)* David was delivered many times from serious illnesses. For instance, in Psalm 6 he prays to the LORD to heal him from a body in agony. *(Psalm 6:2-3)* The LORD obviously heard him and healed him. In Psalm 103, the third thing he is grateful for is that God has ransomed him from death (probably many times since he was a warrior). *(V.4)* The Hebrew for "death" is *("shachath")*. It also can be translated as "the grave," or "the pit." Another wonderful benefit David realizes God has bestowed on him are two covenant blessings, love and tender mercies. *(V.4)* And finally, Jehovah God (the LORD) renews him to a physical and psychology youthful state. *(V.5)* No wonder David wants to bless the LORD with his whole heart!

## Segment Two – What God Does for His People. Verses 6 - 18

After David's soliloquy, (his personal testimony), he now addresses the gathered community in the Tent of Meeting and shares with them the blessings of God.

1. God gives "righteousness" *("ts daqah")* and "justice" *("mishpat")* to all who are treated unfairly. *(V.6)*
2. God is "merciful" *("checed")* and "gracious" *("channuwn")* toward those who don't deserve it. This is God's Mother love. *(V.8)*
3. He is slow to get angry and full of unfailing love. *(V.8)*
4. God doesn't bear a grudge, nor stay angry forever. *(V.9)*
5. He doesn't punish us as we deserve for all our sins. *(V.10)*
6. God takes away sins and doesn't remember them. *(V.12)*
7. He is like a father to those who fear Him. *(V.13)*
8. He understands how weak we are. He knows we are only dust. *(V.14)*
9. The love of the LORD remains forever. *(V.17)*
10. His salvation extends to the children's children. *(V.17)*
11. God is faithful to those who keep His covenant and obey His commandments. *(V.18)*

Most of the above come from God's graciousness and mercy. There are a number of citations where these are found. (See Exodus 36:5-7; Nehemiah 9:17; Psalm 86:15; and others.)

## Segment Three – Praise from Everywhere, Heaven and Earth. Verses 19 - 22

Because of the gratitude in their hearts, the redeemed are the ones who want to spend their lives serving and praising the LORD! David envisions the God of the universe ruling from His throne in heaven, ruling over everything! *(V.19)* So in joy he cries out that the angels should praise the LORD. *(V.20-21))* Then he ends his uplifting poem the very way he began it, singing that he too will praise the LORD. *(V.22)*

As Christians, the 103rd Psalm should make us more aware of our many blessings from our loving Lord. We need to ask ourselves three things:

1. Have we experienced our sins being forgiven?
2. Do we realize that salvation can be ours?
3. Are we aware of the good things that satisfy us?

# PSALM 104
## The Wonderful Creator

This magnificent hymn is one of four that centers in praises to God as the LORD of creation! (See Psalms 8,19:1-6; 29, 104) Although the author does not follow the Genesis account strictly, he is dependent upon it. Psalms 103 and 104 go together: 103 tells of the goodness of God in salvation; 104 tells of God's greatness in creation. 103 categorizes God's benefits; 104 categorizes His works; 103 has God as the Father with His children; 104 has God as Creator with His creatures.

### Segment One – The LORD Is Robed with Majesty and Light. Verses 1 - 4

Psalm 103 ends with praising the LORD who created everything. *(Pslam 103:22)* Psalm 104 begins the same way (Maybe the writer is the same for both psalms?). *(V.1)* It's difficult to picture God as Spirit. It is too vague. When we Christians think of God, we usually use the words found in John 14 where Jesus tells Phillip that anyone who has seen Him has seen the Father. *(John 14:9)* The Old Testament visualizing God as creator helped the people grasp who God was. The Psalmist of Psalm 104 uses verses 2 through 4 to beautifully describe the LORD through His creation. He is dressed in the stars of the night. *(V.2)* He rides on the winds' wings. *(V.3)* And His servants (Angels) are like flames of fire. *(V.4)*

### Segment Two – God Provides Land. Verses 5 - 9

The Psalmist continues describing the LORD through his creation in this segment. God created the necessary laws of gravity so that the world would never be moved. *(V.5)* He provided the waters for the oceans. *(V.6)* He rules the seas with a mere spoken word. *(V.7)* He arranges mountains and valleys. *(V.8)* He promises never to flood the entire earth again. *(V.9)*

### Segment Three – Water Is Essential. Verses 10 - 13

The Psalmist continues describing God's power as a creator. It appears that the Psalmist is relying on the fifth day of God's creation presented in Genesis in this segment. *(Genesis 1:20-22)* Springs gush through the earth's ravines. *(V.10)* They quence the thirst of the animals. *(V.11)* The birds nest by the waters. *(V.12)* There is vegetation because the abundance of the waters. *(V.13)*

### Segment Four – The Productive Earth. Verses 14 - 18

God gives us trees, vegetables and grain so people inhabiting the earth might have food, wine to make us glad, oil to soften our skin, and meaningful work to do. Our poet sees the creative ways the LORD interrelated everything for cycles of procreation with birds, goats and badgers. *(V.14-18)*

### Segment Five – God Creates Days and Nights. Verses 19 - 23

In verse 19, our writer seems to be following God's creation story in Genesis 1:16, where it says that God created two lights, the sun and the moon. But our poet takes his own liberties by saying God sends darkness and it becomes night. *(V.20)* Notice he then says the day is established at dawn. *(V.23)* Modern day Judism says that day begins at midnight.

### Segment Six – God's Ocean Is Teeming with Life that Depend On God's Spirit. Verses 24 - 30

The wisdom of the LORD has made a wonderful variety of things. *(V.24)* The ocean not only teams with life but permits ships to traverse its wide expanse. *(V.25-26)* Minnows and whales depend on the LORD to feed them. *(V.27-28)* Life is precious, and every one of God's creatures depends on divine provisioning. The Psalmist says, however, when God takes away their breath they die. *(V.29)* Verse 30 states the other side of the coin: it is the Spirit of God that brings new life and replenishes the earth. The Hebrew for "breath" and "Spirit" are the same word. It is *("Ruwach")*. It is the same word used in Genesis where it is written that the LORD God breathed into the dust of the ground and formed a man's body. *(Genesis 2:7)*

In the New Testament, Jesus said that no one can get into heaven unless he or she is born anew. In John's Gospel, a Jewish religious leader named Nicodemus, a Pharisee, came to Jesus, and was told he would never see the Kingdom of God unless he was born anew. *(John 3:3)* Jesus explained further saying humans reproduce human life but new life comes from the Holy Spirit. *(John 3:6)* We must depend upon God for our salvation. Jesus, God's Messiah, came to earth to be our Savior. He died for our sins, and said eternal life is given to those believe in Him as their Savior and Lord. *(John 3:15)*

## Segment Seven – Praise God for His Creation. Verses 31 - 35

Throughout the first chapter of Genesis as God spoke and created our world, the Scriptures tell us God remarked that what He created was good. *(Genesis 1:25)* This would tend to confirm the Psalmist's words in Psalm 104 that God must have rejoiced in His creation. *(V.31)* And His is still involved in His cration. *(V.32)* The poet cannot contain all of his enthusiasm and admiration for God's creative work. He will praise the LORD to his last breath. *(V.33-34)* The Psalmist ends the psalm somewhat viciously asking that all sinners and those who are wicked be removed from God's creation. *(V.35)*

In their understanding of God's self-revelation in His creation, the Jews made a lasting contribution to the world. By God's Word, He was able to bring into being all that we have in our universe – the mountains, the seas, the rivers, valleys, trees, everything. These are manifestations of God's power and glory. God is not identified with nature; in fact, the Jews understood Him to stand outside of His creation. In every other religion of the ancient world, gods were identified with nature (like the Baals of the Canaanites). Worship for the Canaanites was worshiping various nature gods, which meant they worshiped nature, like the sun or various animals.

King Solomon spoke of "wisdom" as a personal being who existed with God before the earth was created and who was the architect for creation. *(Proverbs 8:1-35)* God wants all who read this to have God's Voice of Wisdom. He has created a marvelous world and, those of us who are wise, need to do all we can to take care of it. We need to oppose those who want to exploit nature. God gave the earth to us as a gift. Like the Psalmist who wrote Psalm 104, we need to praise Him! We need to shout out Hallelujah!

# PSALM 105
## God Is Praised as the LORD of History

Psalm 105 is a poetic version of the history of the Jews, beginning back at the time of Abraham, leading to the famine and how God used Joseph to save his people by bringing them to Egypt. The Psalmist goes on to tell of their growth and enslavement, the choosing of Moses as God's agent in bringing the miraculous plagues to convince Pharaoh to set the children of Israel free, the wandering in the desert, and the entry into the land of Canaan. It is a masterful psalm with the exception that there is no mention of Israel's sins.

Psalm 105 is related to two other historical presentations – Psalm 78 and 106. The editor has paired Psalm 105 with 106. Both psalms make use of the material found in Genesis 12 through Exodus 17. Verses 1-15 of Psalm 105 are quoted by 1 Chronicles 16:8-36. It also quotes material from Psalm 96 and 106. The material in 1 Chronicles was in honor of bringing the Ark into Jerusalem, and was sung by a choir directed by Asaph.

### Segment One – Worshipers Rejoice. Verses 1-6

Our poet is giving us four springboards to which he wants us to jump on in order to get the most out of the psalm. He wants us (1) to be thankful to the LORD and proclaim His greatness. *(V.1)* (2) Tell the entire world what God has accomplished. *(V.2)* (3) Sing of God's praises to God. *(V.3)* And (4) Search for an understanding of the LORD, what He has accomplished and to develop a relationship with the LORD. *(V.4-5)*

## Segment Two – The LORD Never Forgets. Verses 7 - 11

This segment begins with the affirmation that the LORD is the God of Israel. *(V.7)* We are His people and He has our allegiance. This is the most important part of what it means to be a Jew! God has made a covenant with us. *(V.8)* He did it back in Genesis 15, with our ancestor Abraham. *(V.9-10)* God made a promise with Abraham that the land of Canaan would be Israel's special possession. *(V.11)* God never forgets His promise. This is the theme of Psalm 105.

## Segment Three – God Is in Charge. Verses 12 - 15

This section is a brief review of Israel's background, very similar to Psalm 78. But the emphasis here is upon God's leading and caring for His chosen people. In those early days, the Jews were not an impressive people. *(V.12)* They were a wandering people without land of their own. *(V.13)* This tiny group was driven among one kingdom to another, but even then God cared for them and their welfare. *(V.14-15)*

## Segment Four – Israel's Time in Egypt. Verses 16 - 36

This segment is a run-down of the Hebrews in Egypt. The famine was an act of God to ultimately force Jacob and his family to relocated to Egypt. *V.16)* (See Genesis 41-54.) Joseph, the second youngest of Jacob's twelve sons, was sent to Egypt as a slave by the providence of God. *(V.17)* The Book of Genesis emphasizes Joseph's helpfulness and service, but our Psalmist places emphasis on the cruel treatment he received in prison. *(V.18)* In this psalm the author says Joseph's character was tested by the LORD. *(V.19)* In God's good time, Pharaoh sent for him and set him free and put him to oversee all of Pharaoh's possessions. *(V.20-22)* Following this, Jacob's family come to live in Egypt and initally prospered because of their relationship with Joseph. *(V.23-24)*

It is interesting that throughout this section, the poet has God taking complete charge of all the action. He calls forth a famine. *(V.16)* He sends Joseph to Egypt. *(V.17)* God tests Joseph's character. *(V.19)* He turns the Egyptians against the Israelites. *(V.25)* He sends for Moses. *(V.26)*

The Hebrews are in Egypt in slavery and being oppressed, and so God sends Moses and Aaron to perform numerous miracles in the land of Ham. *(V.27)* These miracles are ten sets of plagues (as recorded in Exodus 7-11), but for reasons of his own, the Psalmist rearranges them, beginning the 9th plague (darkness) first *(V.28)*, and he only uses eight of them. *(V.29-36)*

In order to understand the plagues, we need to realize they were directed against the gods and goddesses of Egypt. There were 80 major deities in ancient Egypt all clustered about three great natural forces in Egyptian life: the Nile River, the land, and the sky. Several of the plagues were aimed at the gods of the Nile River (water turned to blood and the frogs), others were against the land gods (gnats, locusts, and flies), and the sky gods (thunder, lightening). Then God said He would kill the oldest child in each Egyptian home. *(V.36)* (See Exodus 11:1-12:30.)

## Segment Five – The Exodus. Verses 37 - 45

The last section follows Israel through the years wandering in the desert and finally to Canaan, which God had promised. Again God is looking after his chosen people. They are brought out of Egypt loaded with gold and silver and none of the Hebrew people were sick or feeble. *(V.37)*

The Psalmist's major concern is getting the chosen people to Canaan, their final destination, which God had promised to Abraham. During their desert years there were three additional miracles of God's grace: (a) the cloud that gave protection from the hot sun during the day, and the pillar of flame during the night to give them light *(V.39)*; (b) the quail and the manna from heaven when they asked for meat *(V.40)*; and (c) the rock when struck gushed forth rivers of water to quench the people's thirst in the hot desert. *(V.41)* These mighty miracles are part of the Judeo/Christian heritage. The Old Testament is the foundation for the Christian faith. We even sing about it in the second stanza of the hymn, "Guide Me O Thou Great Jehovah."

Verse 42 contains the psalm's key word—that God remembered his coventant promise to Abraham that the land of Canaan will be possessed by Israel. The psalm closes with the God sending the Hebrew people out of Egypt with joy *(V.43)* and giving them the lands of the Gentiles, complete with the crops that the Gentiles grew. *(V.44)* All this happened, the Psalmist concludes, so that the LORD's chosen people would obey His laws and follow the LORD's principles. *(V.45)*

Always we Christians must read the psalms from a New Testament perspective. The thing that makes reading the Psalter so meaningful for us is the knowledge that we find the hand of God always in evidence initiating and leading the chosen People. No matter how sinful and disobedient the Jews were over the centuries, they still were God's people and most recognized His sovereignty. This was in contradistinction to the pagan nations around them, that envisioned life as cyclical. They observed the seasons of the year go by and then begin again, always in the same cycle. Their gods were in nature, whereas Israel's God transcended nature and was Lord of it.

We Christians take our stand with our Jewish brothers and sisters in worshiping the God of the Old Testament. We affirm with them that God is the Creator and sustainer of the world. We agree that God chose the Jews and made them His special covenant people with the objective of using them as His instruments to work out His salvation for our planet. He began with His covenant with Abraham, saying Abraham would become a father of a great nation. *(Genesis 12:2)* Then He told Abraham He would give his offspring Canaan as their possession. *(Genesis 12:7)* As the Psalmist poetically describes it in Psalm 105, God guided the Jews into the Promised Land.

Where we Christians part company with our Jewish friends is two-fold: one, of course, is their rejection of Jesus as the Messiah. This is very basic. The Apostle Paul deals with this in chapters 9,10 and 11 of Romans. The second difference we have with them is with regard to the land.

The Old Testament is not future-oriented, that is to say, its ideas of eschatology are very limited. In the Psalms when a person dies he/she goes to the Pit *("Sheol")* and essentially is cut off from life and God. Therefore, the land plays an important part--this is where life for the Jews exists. For instance, there is a proviso attached to the Old Testament's commandment to honor father and mother. It adds then you will live long and have a full life in the land. *(Exodus 20:12)* Several times in their history, the Jewish nation was threatened with extinction. In 586 BC, they were shut down for two generations, and again in 70 AD when the Romans demolished Jerusalem. But miracle of miracles, in 1948, against all logic, the state of Israel was reborn!

Back at the time the 105th Psalm was written, the purpose that God had in mind in the giving of the Promised Land to the Jews was so that the world might observe a people living in obedience to God's laws and commandments.

We Christians see the promised Land of Canaan not as some place that we think is holy, but as the environment where Jesus grew up and was nurtured. Jesus was a descendant of David, and is the continuation of David's dynasty that God promised back in 2 Samuel 7. Jesus is the Messiah clearly predicted by the prophets. In the upper room, after Jesus had been raised from the dead, He appeared to His disciples and reminded them that everything written about him by Moses, the prophets and in the Pslams had to come true. That he had to suffer and die and be raised on the third day. *(Luke 24:44-49)*

God made a new covenant with us Christians and sealed it with the resurrection of His Son, Jesus Christ. The Apostle Paul speaks of this. He says as Christians we have become new persons, we are born again, and our task is to assist in the reconciliation of all peoples to God through Christ His son. *(2 Corinthians 5:17-20)* When God raised Jesus from death, it was like God saying, "This is My seal of approval on My plan to save the world. Jesus is back with Me in heaven, but I have released His Spirit so that it can come to anyone who commits himself to following Him. His Spirit of love can indwell you and can direct your life from within."

# PSALM 106
## The LORD's Grace in Light of Israel's Unfaithfulness

Psalm 106 ends Book 4 of the Psalter (Psalm 90-Psalm 106). In this Psalm, we are given a long litany of the sins of the Hebrew nation starting with the Exodus from Egypt to the settlement in Canaan. Israel's history is also a record of God's mercy and long-suffering as God chooses to remain with them. Much of the material in Psalm 106 is similar to that of Psalm 78, Nehemiah 9:5-37 and Psalm 105. The historical accounts were taken from the books of Exodus and Numbers. The rebellion and sin recorded in Psalm 106 are a rather somber way to end Book Four of the Psalter.

### Segment One – A Hymn of Praise of the LORD. Verses 1 - 5

We don't know who wrote Psalm 106, but it probably was written by someone in Exile, as indicated by the concluding verses that asks God to gather the Hebrew people back to Israel now dispersed among the nations. *(V.47)*
   The first five verses of Psalm 106 are written as a "hymn offering" asking God to bless and save His chosen ones. *(V.1-3)* In verse one, the Psalmist begins by saying the LORD is good. *("Towb")* is the Hebrew word for "good," and it also means "gracious." After pointing out how gracious God is to His chosen people, it's interesting that the Psalmist sneaks in his own request for personal deliverance. *(V.4)* Notice that he begins and ends this segment with praising the LORD. *(V.5)*

### Segment Two – Rebellion at the Red Sea. Verses 6 - 12

After speaking of God's love and goodness in segment one, the Psalmist begins this section in verse 6 by setting the tone for the rest of the psalm—that

336

both the ancestors and their current descendants have sinned and acted wickedly. *(V.6)* (And of course, we aren't any different from them.) The chief sin of the Hebrews back then was rebellion against God. *(V.7)* They took for granted the wonderful things God did to get them free from slavery. Coming up to the Red Sea and seeing the Egyptian army in close pursuit, they were terrified and complained to Moses that they were about to die in the wilderness. *(Exodus 14:11)* God acted and the sea opened up and they were saved! *(V.8-11)* God defended the honor of His name. Then at last His people finally believed and sang and praised God. *(V.12)*

## Segment Three – Demand for Better Food. Verses 13 - 15

Yet how quickly they forgot all of this. *(V.13)* Grumbling and complaining is a way of testing God's patience, and complain they did. *(V.14)* They demanded, "We want meat!" God gave them bread from heaven (Manna) and sent them quail to eat. (See Exodus 16 and Numbers 11.) Because of their bad attitudes, God sent a plague among them. *(V.15)*

## Segment Four – Jealousy Toward Moses and Aaron. Verses 16 - 18

Then Korah (a descendant of Levi) with 250 followers tried to overthrow Moses' authority, motivated by the sin of jealousy. *(V.16)* (See Numbers 16.) The Psalmist points out that the LORD is not to be trifled with. The earth opened up, Korah and many of his followers were swallowed up and flames consumed the rest. *(V.17-18)*

## Segment Five – A Statue of an Ox. Verses 19 - 23

In this segment, while Moses is up on Mount Sinai to receive the Ten Commandments from God, the Hebrew people down below in the valley ask Aaron for a "god" who would lead them. *(V.19)* Aaron should have put his foot down and said a thundering "NO! However, he was weak and succumbed to their pleas, so he collected all their jewelry and melted the gold down and made an idol. When it was finished the people fell down and worshiped it, forgetting what God had done for them.*(V.20-22)* When God saw what had taken place, He was furious! He said He would destroy the people, but Moses interceded on their behalf reminding the LORD that He is slow to anger and has unfailing love. *(V.23) (Numbers 14:17-18)* God reneged and pardoned them, but said none of them would enter the Promised Land – only Joshua and Caleb would be permitted to enter.

## Segment Six – Refusal to Enter the Promised Land. Verses 24 - 27

Moses was told by God to send men out to explore the unknown land of Canaan to see whether the people who lived there were strong. Were their defenses good? Were the cities fortified? The men went out and at the end of 40 days the explorers returned and gave their reports. The majority opinion was that it was too risky to attack the Canaanites. Joshua and Caleb gave the minority report: We should go and take possession immediately. The majority of the people refused to go in. They didn't believe the LORD would take care of them. *(V.24-25)* Caleb exorted the people to possess a land flowing with milk and honey. He warned them not to rebel against the LORD. But they did. *(Numbers 14:7-9)* Angered the LORD swore none of them would enter the promised land except Caleb and Joshua. All the rest died in the wilderness. *(V.26-27)*

## Segment Seven – Joining the Worshipers of Baal. Verses 28 - 33

As the Israelites began to gain entrance to the Promised Land, the men started mingling with the Moabite women at Peor and having sex with them. *(V.28)* The gods of Moab were considered fertility gods. Angered again, the LORD sent a plague among the Hebrews. Aaron's grandson, Phineus, killed two of the Hebrew adulterers, which ended the plague. *(V.30)* Phineus was rewarded with a permanent priesthood (see Numbers 25:13). *(V.31)*

At Kadesh there was a shortage of water. The people wailed and complained. *(V.32)* God told Moses to speak to a rock, but he became angry and hit the rock. Water gushed forth, but God then informed Moses he wouldn't be allowed to go with the people into Canaan, because he hit the rock with his staff rather than speak to it. *(V.33)* (See Numbers 20.) This place was called "the Rebel Waters" or Meribah.

## Segment Eight – Mingling with the Heathen. Verses 34 - 39

The terrible part of the invasion of Canaan was the fact that instead of opposing the evils of the Canaanite gods, the Jews joined in and actually accommodated themselves to worshiping the idols and demons. They also adopted the customs and culture. *(V.34-36)* The most dreadful of all of the sins was when the gods demanded infant sacrifice, and the Israelites actually sacrificed their infants, incredible as it seems! *(V.37-38)* The men fornicated with cultic prostitutes. *(V.39)* In Deuteronomy 12, Moses reiterated God's laws that must be obeyed and warned that the Canaanites even burned their daughters and sons in sacrifice to their gods. *(Deuteronomy 12:28-31)*

## Segment Nine – Israel Is Destroyed By Her Sins. Verses 40 - 46

Finally God had had enough, the Psalmist says. For a time, he handed them over to the pagan nations. *(V.40-41)* When the First Commandment gets broken repeatedly, God's anger is going to burn against His people to the point where something major will happen. This is why He allowed Nebuchadnezzar's armies to totally annihilate the nation of Israel in 586 BC and before that, He allowed the Assyrians to destroy the Northern Kingdom in 722 BC. There had been 600 years of adultery (apostasy) and the wages of sin is death! *(V.43-43)* But ultimately God came to listen to their cries of distress and remembered his covenant relatonship with them. *(V.44-45)* He even caused Cyrus of Persia to pity the Exiles and allow them to be freed from slavery in Babylon. *(V.46)* (See Isaiah 45:1-8.)

## Segment Ten – Prayer for Restoration. Verses 47 - 48

But as verse 47 indicates not all of the Israelites have been delivered from their enemies. The Psalmist pleads with the LORD to gather all of the Hebrew people from among the nations and bring them back to their promised abode. Our author ends with wanting to praise God and thank Him for His faithfulness. *(V.47)*

The Apostle Paul in his letter to the Romans in Chapter Three talks about the value of being a Jew. He tells us that God trusted the Jews with His laws so that they could know and do His will. And, although they were unfaithful, God will keep His promises to them. *(Romans 3:2-4)* But the power of sin knows no partiality, it can enslave Jew and Gentile. *(Romans 3:9)*

# PSALM 107
## Gratitude of the Redeemed

Psalm 107 is the first psalm of Book Five of the Psalter. (Psalms 107- 150). It is a praise song of the Jewish people after their return from70 years of Babylonian captivity. Psalms 105, 106 and Psalm 107 are related; the three form a trilogy. Psalm 105 recounts Israel's experiences from the time of God's covenant with Abraham up to their entrance to the Holy Land. Psalm 106 tracks the people's unfaithfulness during this period and reflects on their stay in Babylon. This current psalm thanks God for their deliverance from exile.

Psalm 107 can be organized into four parts: (1) The Redeemed Say "Thank You," Verses 1-3; (2) Four Groups of Redeemed Pilgrims, Verses 4-32; (3) God Sets Man Over Nature, Verses 33-38; and (4) The Wicked Are Stricken Silent, Verses 39-43.

### Segment One — The Redeemed Say 'Thank You." Verses 1 - 3

As Christians, we need to ask ourselves, are we among the redeemed? Are our sins forgiven? Are we assured that we will go to be with God and Jesus in heaven when we die? If so, we need to say, "Thank you, Lord, for being so good, for always being so loving and kind." Verse one in Psalm 107 begins like verse one of Psalm 106 exclaiming that the LORD is good. It also says that the LORD is loving. Verse two and three of Psalm 107 challenges the returned inhabitants of Israel to tell others that the LORD has redeemed them from lands in the east, west, north and south.

## Segment Two – There're Four Groups of Redeemed Pilgrims. Verses 4 - 32

Four groups of pilgrims were probably used as a congregational liturgy accompanying a thanksgiving sacrifice offered in the newly constructed Temple. These could be sung by a choir or spoken by a priest. What links these four groups together is the refrain in verses 8, 15, 21 and 31 where the Psalmist asks the congregation to praise the LORD for His great love and wonderful deeds. The Hebrew word for "love" is *(Checed")* and for "deeds" is *("Natsal").*

A.  Desert Travelers Who Have Lost Their Way. (Verses 4-9) – see especially verse 6.

The desert traveler typified the experiences Hebrews had in their exodus from Egypt and their 40 years of wandering in the wilderness, or the suffering they had to undergo in Babylon during their 70-year exile. *(V.4-5)* The key thought is captured in verse 6 in which the Psalmist calls out that these lost and homeless desert travelers needed help from the LORD. And the LORD responded by leading them to safety and satisfied all their needs. *(V.7-9)*

B.  Those Who Were In Prisons. (Verses 10-16) – see verse 13.

This group of verses reflects what happened to both the Northern Kingdom in 722 BC and Judah in 586 BC when they were taken into captivity. The Psalmist reminds the people that because they rebelled against the commandments of the LORD *(V.11),* they endured horrible years of being in hard labor in a foreign land. *(V.12)* However, due to God's faithfulness to His covenant, He heard their cries and He allowed them to return home. *(V.13)* Then the refrain is sounded in verse 15. Verse 16 personifies God in action for His people: He broke their prison gates and cut their bars of iron.

C.  Those Who Are Ill. (Verses 17-22) – see verse 19.

Back in those days, sickness was thought to have been caused by one's sin. *(V.17-18)* There is truth to this. Rebelling against God

341

brings on anxiety and guilt – which takes away one's sense of joy and opens one up to depression that can lead to death. In despair, they turn to God and He hears them and they are healed. *(V.20)* After the refrain in verse 21, they respond with sacrifices and songs of joy. *(V.22)*

D.  Those Sailors in Storms. (Verses 23-32) – see verse 28.

Some Jews took up the profession of seamen. *(V.23)* Anyone who has been at sea knows how quickly storms can blow in and winds and waves can wreck havoc with ships. The Psalmist describes the storms as God's power in action. *(V.24-26)* He controls nature and when He calls nature answers! When a hurricane comes, it is a fearsome thing to be at sea in a small craft, and when it hits even the experienced seamen stagger like drunkards. *(V.27)* The wonderful blessing is that when they call out for help from the LORD He saved them. *(V.28)* This was true back then and it's true today. With a whisper, God calms the sea. *(V.29)* Remember when the disciples went across the Sea of Galilee with Jesus asleep at the bottom of their small craft? Soon a terrible storm arose with high waves breaking into the boat and it was about to sink. The disciples were terrified and awoke Jesus. He then rebuked the wind and said to the sea be still. And there was a great calm! *(Mark 4:41)* He is the One who brings us safely into harbor! He is the One who is the truth, the way and the life. *(John 14:6)* He is the One we can put our faith in. With these redeemed sailors, we Christians can join them in praising the LORD for all His marvellous deeds. *(V.31)* And like them, out of gratitude, we need to extol the LORD before the congregation and leaders of nations. *(V.32)*

## Segment Three –God Sets Man Over Nature. Verses 33- 38

In Segment Two, we are reminded that the God who can turn rivers into deserts and fruitful lands into wastelands in response to the wickedness of the people *(V.33-34)*, also can turn deserts into streams of living water for His covenant people. *(V.35)* We must realize that we human beings are not just a part of nature, we also are placed to a degree over nature (see

Genesis 2:15), acting on God's commands. Our rule over nature must be a careful reflection of God's rule, which, of course, is characterized by His ("Checed"), His "faithful love." The Psalmist in Psalm 107 also points out that the blessings of the LORD permits people to settle in the land and build cities (V.36), plant fields that yield bumper crops. (V.37) His blessings permit the people to raise large families. (V.38)

## Segment Four – The Wicked Are Stricken Silent. Verses 39 - 42

The sinfulness of man is seen as he exploits nature without any consideration for what harmful effects it has for the planet. We see this in the mining of coal and oil (fossil fuels) and the resultant competition that leads to wars fought over these and other natural resources. Verse 39 tells us that people become poor because of oppression. God pours contempt on rulers who exploit the poor and causes them to wander in wastelands. (V.40) This was probably an allusion to rebellious leaders who flirted with power-politics that resulted in the destruction of their cities. What this is saying is that presidents, prime ministers and dictators cannot run roughshod over the poor and little people without incurring God's wrath on all unrighteousness. This Segment ends by emphasizing that God rescues the poor (V.41)and the wise are able to look at the history of the Hebrew people and see the "faithful love" ("Checed") of God. (V.41)

We Christians feel we are wise because we profess God's ("Checed") and we believe this "love" was in Jesus as He lived here on earth. It was this wonderful love of God that permeated His life and gave us His marvelous teachings. This love of God gave Him the steadfast courage to die on the cross to take away our sins, and, finally, it was this powerful, unfailing love that raised Him from the dead. This love made it possible for all of us who have committed ourselves to Him to know that with Jesus's Spirit in our hearts we will have eternal life. As Jesus' disciples, we will be reflecting this fantastic love that will enable us to hold our heads up high, even if we have to go through suffering or hard times in this life. The Apostle Paul writes that it is our awareness of this faithful love of the Triune God that permits us to come before God through Jesus Christ not like fearful slaves but as worshipful children. (Romans 8:14-39)

# PSALM 108
## Bringing Old Psalms Back

This psalm is the work of a poet-editor who lived in the period of the Second Temple. Faced with an uprising of some neighboring nations (particularly Edom), he is looking to God for some new deliverances. He wants his fellow worshipers to benefit from David's experiences, so he borrows two of David's songs and incorporates them into a contemporary song of praise. This is a rather short psalm of 13 verses.

We will examine the psalm by breaking it down into three segments: One, A Morning Song Hymn, Verses 1-4; Two, Come, LORD, with Your Mighty Power, Verses 5-6; and Three, Remember Your Sacred Promises, Verses 7-13.

### Segment One – A Morning Song-Hymn. Verses 1 - 4

With only minor variations, the first five verses of Psalm 108 are identical with David's Psalm 57:7-11 in which the editor/poet acknowledges his confidence in God and his thankfulness through song. Our editor/poet opens his Psalm asking the LORD to wake up his soul! *(V.1)* He takes this praise of thankfulness *(V.3)* to invite the worshiping congregation to sing God's praises because God's love is so huge it reaches the clouds above. *(V.4)*

### Segment Two – Come, LORD, with Your Mighty Power. Verses 5 - 6

Again the editor-poet borrows David's words (with some variations) in Psalm 57:11 and 60:5 asking the LORD to shine His glory over the whole world. *(V.5)* The editor-poet now gets down to the real purpose of the psalm, requesting that God again save His beloved people. *(V.6)*

## Segment Three – Remember Your Sacred Promises. Verses 7 - 13

Our editor-poet, borrowing words of David in Psalm 60:6-12, says in this segment of Psalm 108 that Jehovah God (the LORD) has made these sacred promises to the Israelites: to divide up Shechem (a Canaanite city) and secure Succoth for the Israelites *(V.7)*; to produce kings in Judah and warrors in Ephraim, Gilead and Manasseh *(V.8)*; assure that Israel will conquer Moab, Edom and the Philistines *(V.9)*; and specifically today to remind God and the Israelites that only God can conquer the Edomities protected in their fortified city. *(V.10)* The psalm ends asking God if He has rejected Israel *(V.11)* He then reminds God and Israel that only God can bring victory to Israel against Edom *(V.12-13)*.

Not much has changed in the ensuing years. Since 1948, when Israel became a state, it has been in continuous conflict with its neighbors right up until today.

Life is filled with conflicts for everyone who lives in our world. We Christians are no exceptions. Paul wrote in Ephesians similar words that we find in Psalm 108. He exhorts us to put on the Lord's spiritual armour to combat mightly dark powers that rule this world. *(Ephesians 6:10-12)*

# PSALM 109
## Calling Down Curses

Psalm 109 is one of the most upsetting passages of Scripture in the whole Bible for Christians. It is filled with imprecations, prayers to God asking Him to curse or damn one's enemies. The superscription on this poem claims it is of David, and it may have been written by him. It is a strange and difficult piece of writing to analyze. It is filled with vindictiveness. Cursing to the ancient Jews was not just a matter of words; it was action that caused bodily harm. Moses said God told him the penalty for injuring someone with malice was to injure back in the same way: fracture for fracture, eye for eye, and tooth for tooth. *(Leviticus 24:20)*

Here are some examples from David when he seeks God to curse his enemies. In Psalm 35, he asks God to dishonor those who were trying to kill him. Like chaff the LORD needs to blow them away! *(Psalm 35:4-8)* In Psalm 58, he prays that the LORD break their fangs off, smash them in their jaws and let them disappear totally like water in a thirsty ground. *(Psalm 58:6-8)* These are just a few samples. David had many enemies and in just about all of the many psalms he wrote, he mentions those who would like him destroyed.

### Segment One – Asking God's Help. Verses 1 - 5

David cries out to God don't be silent *(V.1)* while his enemies slander him *(V.2)* Their hateful words surround him. *(V.3)* And, though he has shown love to them *(V.4)* in return they are doing acts of evil toward him. *(V.5)*

## Segment Two – Imprecations on David's Enemies. Verses 6 - 19

It is difficult to understand why the post- Exilic editor would want to insert one more imprecatory psalm into the Psalter, as it literally reeks of the spirit of hatred! C.S. Lewis, in his book *Reflections_on_the_Psalms*, says Psalm 109 is ofensive to Christians, like heat from the mouth of a furance. David was a child of his time and probably felt justified in his cursing, thinking he was going along with God's laws. (See Leviticus 24.) As king, these attacks on David, because he was God's representative on earth, were in effect, an attack on God. From a Christian point-of-view, we can understand David's rationale, but we cannot condone it! In this case, his vehemence make his actions reprehensible; it is ironic because David tried so hard to pattern his life after God's "unfailing love" – His *("checed")*. Obviously this was one of his blind spots!

One thing we notice is an abrupt change here from segment one where his enemies were plural in verse 3, to David pointing in verse 7 at one man for God to prouncement a guilty judgment on him. When one reads verses 6-19, David is asking God to do the following horrible things:

1. Have an evil person turn on him. *(V.6)*
2. Have God count his prayers as sins. *(V.7)*
3. Reduce his lifespan. *(V.8)*
4. Have God make his children fatherless. *(V.9)*
5. Evict the family from their home. *(V.10)*
6. Have the creditors take over the estate. *(V.11)*
7. Allow strangers to get all his money. *(V.11)*
8. Don't allow anyone to be kind to the children. *(V.12)*
9. Have the enemy die – blot the family name. *(V.13)*
10. Have God punish the sins of the parents. *(V.14)*
11. Have God curse him; don't bless him. *(V.17)*
12. Get God to return curses to him. *(V.19)*

There are two things that make these imprecations so hurtful. The first is the curses David places on his adversary who was slandering him. David tells God he was praying for the person (or persons) in verse 4, but it seems as if David allowed his temper to flare up in the cursing. He curses not only the wicked man, but his wife, children, parent and home. It is true that no one lives

347

alone, and if one sins, it has a ripple effect. Even the Lord Jesus recognized the principle of solidarity of sin when He wept over the city of Jerusalem. In His divine wisdom, Jesus knew that in 70 AD the Romans would crush the Jews and completely destroy the city. Jesus wept because He knew that children would innocently suffer because of the sins of their fathers. The second thing about the man who is being cursed by David is that he is obviously a person who persecuted the needy and poor, hounding them to death. *(V.16)* He also is a man who who not only cursed others but loved doing it. *(V.17)* It wasn't a case of this man just being a sinner (we all are), but he needed to be judged and punished – but not by those awful prayers of David.

## Segment Three – Bless Me Publicly, LORD. Verses 20 - 29

For most of next nine verses, David methodically asks the LORD to curse and punish his accusers for the sake of God's own reputation. *(V.21)* He also seeks to be rescued from them because David's own heart is full of pain and he is weak from fasting. *(V.22-24)* Finally he ends this section by beseeching the LORD to make David's enemies' humiliation obvious to everyone. *(V.29)* It's also obvious one should not have gotten on the bad side of King David.

The Apostle Paul was an astute student of Judaism and he would probably agree that this person who has been attacking David was an incorrigible and wicked man, one who had no concern for repentance. However, Paul writes in his letter to the church at Rome, reflecting Jesus' words, not to curse those who persecute you but to pray that God blesses them. *(Romans 12: 14-17)* Then Paul gets down to the very basis of why we should not pray curses on anyone for whatever reason. He writes that God alone, because He is the creator of everyone, has the authority for vengence of those who deserve His vengence. *(Romans 12:19)*

## Segment Four – A Vow of Thanksgiving. Verses 30 - 31

The final two verses are a positive ending to a very disturbing and difficult composition. Verses 30-31 anticipate the deliverance that David requested from the LORD back in verse 21. As a result, David feels blessed. *(V.30)* In the final verse 31, David the king humbles himself in ackowledgement of God's unfailing love.

In the Beatitudes in Chapter 5 of Matthew, Jesus Himself methodically points out how God blesses those who are a blessing to God and others, but points out that if we curse someone we are in the danger of the fire of hell. *(Matthew 5:2-22)* In the same chapter of Matthew, Jesus also asks that we love our enemies and pray for those who persecute us. *(Matthew 5:43-45)*

# PSALM 110
## The Greatest Messianic Psalm

This Royal Psalm was composed in the early pre-Exilic days to celebrate the enthronement of a new Davidic king. The superscription says it is of David, but probably someone wrote it in honor of King David. The Psalmist is not only thinking about the king to be crowned, but a succession of kings from the family of David. The importance of this psalm, from a Christian perspective, is the fact that its words have been applied to the work and ministry of Jesus. Psalm 110 is the most quoted in the New Testament because it was given a messianic application. Back in those days when a new king was crowned, he was thought of as a representative of God here on earth. He also was supposed to take on the role of priest.

### Segment One – The First Prophetic Oracle. Verses 1 - 3

The Psalmist delivers his first prophetic oracle, which is the imparting of divine information about the future that is otherwise hidden. In this case, his revelation from Jehovah God (the LORD) is that this LORD requests the Psalmist's Lord, to sit on His right side. (*V.1*) Not only is the Psalmist saying this applies to David but whomever is the reigning king to be crowned, including the Messiah. The Lord's powerful dominion will be based in Jerusalem (*"Zion"*) and will extend over all the Lord's enemies. (*V.2*) The Lord will be arrayed in holy garments because He is righteous. (*V.3*) The word for "righteous" is (*"Ts̲daquah"*).

Jehovah (the LORD) established a lineage from King David that He promised would go on forever (see 2 Samuel 7:3-17). This was the plan of God from the beginning. He chose the Jewish people to be His instruments for saving the world, and made a covenant with them whereby He would be their God and they would be His chosen people, through whom the rest of the world's people could be brought to the Lord. God's plan was working and so He chose a dynamic young leader in David and promised that his dynasty would go on without end. Part of God's plan was to give His people the freedom to make choices and, unfortunately, they chose to run after false gods. This resulted in God taking His hands off of them, allowing the nation of Israel to be crushed, and the monarchy to be interrupted. But God was faithful to His Word and to His covenant obligations and so He brought back a remnant from Exile and reestablished the nation of Israel.

When the time was right, the LORD God sent His own Son, Jesus (the Lord), to be born a Jew, of the lineage of David. When plan A didn't work out, the gracious LORD turned to plan B, still using the Jewish people to work out His program for the world, and Jesus, His Son (the Lord), became the promised Messiah. When again, the Jews rejected God and had Jesus crucified, God stepped in and raised Jesus from death, thus allowing Jesus' sacrifice on the cross to take away the sins of mankind – providing a vehicle whereby we human beings can have a way of being reconciled with God and have our sins forgiven, and a pathway to eternal life.

The Psalmist held the traditional Jewish concept that God would help them fight their military battles so they could rule over all their enemies. (V.2) One of the major reasons they rejected Jesus as the Messiah was because of this idea that the Messiah was to become a military genius who would lead Israel against her foes. This is definitely not the way Christ Jesus ruled then or now! He quietly and humbly infiltrates the hostile powers of the world in a fearless but invisible manner. Even today, the Living Lord exerts His power indirectly through the people in His churches. In the kingdom of God, there is nothing that is parallel with secular government and power politics. We Christians cannot beat the hostile world powers by means of physical weapons. We fight them by being willing to suffer and knowing what we believe, and this takes faith. (See 2 Corinthians 10:3-4.) Our job as Christians is to live in the world in the midst of our enemies and try to persuade them of the truth of God in Christ. We don't use coercion, because we know it is by God's Holy Spirit who helps us win any of the battles we have to fight.

### Segment Two – The Second Prophetic Oracle. Verses 4 - 7

The second prphectic oracle is found in verse 4. Our Psalmist sees the Sovereign God (the LORD) taking an oath that cannot be rescinded, telling us that the newly installed king is to be a priest in the line of Melchizedek forever. *(V.4)* Melchizedek was a pre-Israelite (Genesis 14:17-29) priest and a king. Abram had just rescued his nephew, Lot, and after a successful battle met this priest/king of Salem, Melchizedek, who blessed Abram by the God Most High, the creator of heaven and earth (Genesis 14:19). They shared communion with each other (bread and wine), and Abram gave him a tithe (a tenth of the spoils of his recent victorious battle). Aside from this brief passage of Scripture, we don't know much about this priest/king. (Some biblical interpreters have wondered if he could be a kind of pre-incarnation of Christ?)

The writer of Hebrews in the New Testament quotes the Genesis encounter of Abram and says Melchizedek's name means king of justice. But Melchizedek is also king of peace, because Salem means "peace." The writer of the letter to Hebrews says there is no record of Melchizedek's father or mother and, therfore, he has no beginning or end to his life and he remains a priest forever, resembling Jesus Christ. (Hebrews 7:2-3) The author of Hebrews probably had Psalm 110 in front of him and he gives us a running commentary, substituting Jesus' name for the king in the poem. *(Hebrews 7:20-25)*

The Letter to the Hebrews was written to Christian Jews in Rome being severely persecuted by Emperor Nero, and they were considering reneging on their faith. The writer is arguing that Jesus Himself is a permanent priesthood and able to save completely. He says that there is no longer any need for the Christian Jews to have a High Priest in Jersualem to sacrafice for their sins because Jesus Himself, the Son of God, sacrificed Himself on the cross for their sins today, tomorrow and forever. *(Hebrews 7:26-27)*

The writer of Psalm 110 in verses 5-7 is dealing with the final judgments. He speaks of God striking down kings in the day of His judgment. *(V.5)* He will punish nations and shatter heads of state. *(V.6)* This brutal imagery tells us about the standard Near Eastern practice of warfare back in David's day. He will not only be victories but brooks along the way (living water) will refresh Him. *(V.7)*

We Christians want to make sure we are right with God when this matter of judgment comes up. Psalm 2 and Psalm 110 are both psalms that rival the last book of the Bible, the Book of Revelation. The three of them contain some strong language for those who are unprepared when the end comes. There is much talk about the armies of heaven and the wrath of the

Almighty and people being thrown into the lake of fire. The Apostle John is very comforting when it comes to knowing where we stand. John says that God is a God of love who sent His Son into the world that we might have eternal love. As we live in God, our own love becomes more perfect, and we should not have any fear on the day Day of Judgment. *(1John 4:9-21)*

# PSALM 111

## Praising the LORD's Works

Psalm 111 and its companion piece, Psalm 112, when combined are acrostic poems where the initial word of each descending line begins with the next letter of the Hebrew alphabet. Both psalms correspond in form and deal with similar topics. Psalm 111 praises the LORD's works by His godly people, while Psalm 112 commends the way of living by the pious. Both poems are carefully crafted presentations for use in public worship.

The Psalmist of Psalm 111 begins with praising the LORD! He thanks the LORD with all his heart as he joins with other like-minded believers in worship. Verse 2 expresses his thankful praise for the LORD's deeds. This is the main theme of the psalm and so he proclaims all godly people should ponder over God's deeds. *(V.2)* The word "ponder" in Hebrew is *("darns")* and it can also mean "seek," "search out," "study" and "inquire."

The Psalmist then ponders God's wonderful attributes. He says all God's works reveal the attibutes of God such as His glory, majesty and righteousness *(V.3)*; also he says how gracious and merciful is God. *(V.4)* The LORD also shows us His great power. He provides food for us. *(V.5)* The Psalmist is probably referring to when God fed the travelers in the desert with quail and manna. (See Deuteronomy 8:16.) God gave the Hebrew people the land previously occupied by other nations. *(V.6)* (See Psalm 7:8 and Deueronomy 4:21.) The LORD is just, good and His commandments are trustworthy. *(V.7)* He also ransomed His people remembering His covenant with them. *(V.9)* (See Exodus 19-24 and Psalm 25:10.) The Covenant and the Law are twin gifts given by God to Israel.

Our Psalmist ends Psalm 111 with almost an exact quote from Proverbs 1:7 that says to fear the LORD is the beginning of wisdom. *(V.11)* (See also

Proverbs 9:10 and Job 8:28.) The Psalmist adds that wisdom is the reward for all of us who obey the LORD. *(V.10)* What he is saying is that wisdom comes from learning and living out an understanding of the Torah. This is exactly what verse 1 of Psalm 112 says as well.

# PSALM 112
## Works of God Take Shape in the Life of the Godly

Psalm 112 takes its cues from the last verse of its companion Psalm 111, which says that wisdom is a reward for us who obey the LORD. Both Psalm 111 and Psalm 112 are acrostic poems and many words, phrases and actual sentences from Psalm 111 are repeated in Psalm 112. Both are expanded beatitudes; both commend a delight in the law; both describe the blessings of the righteous; and both contrast the wicked with the righteous.

Psalm 112 describes how the fear of the LORD works out in the life of the godly. The Psalmist says godly people are blessed because they delight in carrying out God's commands. *(V.1)* Also, their blessedness will pass onto their children. *(V.2-3)* And, when they and their children attempt to live within the commands of the LORD, they will begin to take on some of God's characteristics. Consequently, they tend to be compassionate, generous and righteous. *(V.4-5)* They tend to overcome misfortune because they trust the LORD to care for them. *(V.6-7)* Also, their trust in the LORD makes them fearless. *(V.8)* And their generousity gives them great influence in their communities. God honors the righteous, and, therefore, the godly will have influence to make others better as well. *(V.9)* It is their fear of the LORD (reverence and respect for God) that allows them to enter into the works of the LORD. In turn, this enables God to work in, on and through their lives. Psalm 112 tells how the person who truly respects the LORD is doing his best to obey His commandments. Thereby God honors him for striving to be obedient to his Covenant obligations.

Psalm 112 ends with verse 10 contrasting the wicked in society with those godly persons who are on fire for the LORD and are praising Him and adhering to His commands. The wicked obviously see God honoring the godly as a slap in the face (a rebuke) for their own selfishness and lack of discipline. It angers them because their own selfish hopes are thwarted. (V.10)

Reading these paired-poems from a Christian perspective makes us realize the richness of the Psalter. We can appreciate the thought and effort that went into the writing of both psalms.

Just a few final comments. Godly parents, who are doing all they can to praise and obey God, will certainly pass on their righteous heritage to their children. (V.2) Their sons and daughters will become overcomers, and will be able to transcend terrible circumstances. (V.6) The righteous are confident that the LORD will care for them. (V.7) This not only makes them confident but fearless. (V.8) We all can say Amen!

# PSALM 113

## The Mighty God Stoops!

Psalms 113 to 118 are known as the Egyptian Hallel and are sung at the various Annual Feasts, like Passover, Weeks, Tabernacles, and Hanukkah. At Passover, Psalms 113 and 114 are sung before the meal, and 115 and 118 are sung afterwards. When Jesus and His disciples celebrated Passover in the Upper Room, perhaps they sang this very hymn. In Mark's Gospel it says they sang a hymn and then left to stay over night on the Mount of Olives. *(Mark 14:26)* Psalm 113, in particular, is a hymn of praise to the name of the LORD. He is supreme over the universe, yet He stoops to meet the needs of His chosen people.

### Segment One – The Call to Praise. Verse 1

The Psalmist begins and ends this uplifting poem with wonderful words of praise. He calls on all of the LORD's servants to honor the LORD's name. It's important to understand that names meant a great deal more in Bible times than they do today. We use names mostly today to identify people and places. Back then, names were thought to disclose something of a person's character. In God's case, His name has to do with who He is. Jehovah God is the mighty LORD of the universe who revealed Himself to Moses (see Exodus 3:1-14). For us Christians, He has graciously made Himself known through His Son, Jesus Christ. (See John 1:14.)

### Segment Two – God's Glory Is Exalted. Verses 2 - 4

Our poet calls on God's servants to praise Him forever *(V.2)* and from east to west. *(V.3)* In other words, he wants God's people to make a total commitment that will result in singing God's praises at every possible moment! The idea that the LORD reigns above the nations and His glory transcends the heavens *(V.4)* means no other gods can compare with Jehovah (the LORD)!

## Segment Three – The Humble God Lifts! Verses 5 - 9

The Psalmist now asks who can be compared with the LORD? *(V.5)* This verse, of course, is a rhetorical question, and the answer is "<u>Nobody!</u>" God is transcendent and He is so high that He looks down far below Him through the heavens and sees the earth. In His observance, He notices human suffering and so He stoops to look more intently and then in His mercy He lifts us out of our garbage dump, setting us among princes and rulers. *(V.6-8)* Hannah, the mother of the Prophet Samuel, sings a magnificent prayer that is almost identical with verse 7 and 8. (See 1 Samuel 2:8.) Our God is concerned with the downtrodden and lonely. In ancient societies, one of the greatest humiliation for women was to be unable to bear children. Verse 9 is one more instance when the caring God is concerned with women who are hurting and made low because they are barren. When Mary learned she was to become a mother, she sang with joy and her Magnification reflects Psalm 113. *(Luke 1:46-52)*

The greatest moment in history was when God stooped to come down to earth and make Himself known in the person of Jesus Christ. The Apostle Paul exhorts the Philippians to imitate Christ's own humility. The Son of God took the humble position of a servant for us and actually died a criminal's death when he was crucified. *(Philippians 2:5-11)*.

# PSALM 114
## God's Holy Presence in the Midst of Israel

Psalm 114 is the second of six songs known as The Egyptian Hallel. This exciting small poem was read (sung) in the Synagogues at the time of Passover. It tells how God came to be the Holy Presence in the midst of Israel and how the Sovereign God chose Israel to be His people and His dominion. There are four-matched stanzas in Psalm 114. First verse augments or complements verse 2, verse 3 augments verse 4, verse 5 augments verse 6 and verse 7 augments verse 8.

### Segment One – The Exodus Experience. Verses 1 - 2

You have to know that Israel and Judah are not used here to denote two separate nations, as when they split into the northern and southern kingdoms. Israel and Judah are two names for one people who came out of Egypt—Judah became God's sanctuary and Israel the name of the kingdom. *(V.1-2)*

When God came down at Sinai, He took up symbolic residence in the wilderness tabernacle, and later in the Temple in Jerusalem. God came to rule His people, a nation ruled directly by God. This was the fulfillment of the promise God spoke at Sinai, recorded in Exodus 19:5-6. Yes, no other nation has ever been constituted a kingdom of priests and a holy nation, but we Christians are that people and the church is the people of God. The Apostle Peter referred to God's people in 1 Peter 2:9. Thinking of the above passage in Exodus and maybe Psalm 114, Peter says the church of Jesus Christ is a Chosen People, a Kingdom of Priests and a Holy Nation.

How do we become God's sanctuary and dominion? The answer is by opening our hearts and bringing the Spirit of Jesus to indwell us and rule over us as Lord and King! When this takes place, we become priests and we can intercede for others. Not, of course, as Jesus does because He is the only Savior. However, we can pray for others. We can also offer ourselves to God as living sacrifices, which is what Paul spoke about in Romans 12:1-2. Like our Jewish brothers and sisters, we Christians are a fellowship where Jesus reigns!

In Revelation 5, it says Jesus, the Lamb of God, stood before the throne in heaven, and the people of God sang a new song to Him. The song says that Jesus' blood ransomed people for God from all tribes, languages and nations to be a kingdom of priests. *(Revelation 5: 9-10)* How are we to reign? The answer is by serving others, for that is how Jesus rules and reigns in our midst. He doesn't lord it over us as a tyrant. No, He works for our good.

## Segment Two – Out of Egypt. Verses 3 - 4

This section of Psalm 114 is pure poetry! The Psalmist captures a whole lot of history in a small space. These two verses capture the totality of the desert experience after the Israelites had been called out of Egypt. Verse 3 speaks of the parting of the Red Sea at the beginning of the journey. The Egyptians were pursuing the people when Moses stretched out his shepherd's staff and a strong east wind blew and drove the sea back. The Israelites crossed over and the wind ceased and drove the sea back. The armies of Pharaoh were caught in the middle and drowned. Verse 4 refers to the trembling of the earth when God came down from Mount Sinai to give the people His law. (See Exodus 19:18-19.) Commenting on this, the author of the Book of Hebrews in the New Testament says that when Moses met God on Mount Sinai he was terrified and trembling. *(Hebrews 12: 21)*

## Segment Three – What Possible Cause? Verses 5 - 6

What would cause such a disturbance in the natural disruption of nature? The sea to part, river to reverse its flow, mountain to skip like lambs? *(V.5-6)* These are teasing questions to which the author knows the answer. He is asking only for effect. Notice that God is not mentioned by name. The Psalmist must have had fun as he wrote. He knew his audience knew the answer, but he was holding off. For six verses he allows our interest to peak for dramatic effect.

## Segment Four — The Answer: The Presence of the Lord! Verses 7 - 8

Finally the answer comes. The turmoil in nature is caused by the very presence of the Lord. Seas, mountains and rivers move at the command of the Mighty God! *(V.7)* And it was Jehovah God who brought the children of Israel out of Egypt, and it was the Lord who turned the rock into springs of water. *(V.8)*

If God is with His people, what can stand in their way to oppose them? The answer is! "Nothing!" The Apostle Paul asks this same question in his letter to the Romans in Chapter 8. If God is for us, Paul says, who can really be against us? Who can separate us from God. No one. Paul lists a number of forces pitted against us. Although they are serious obstacles, all will bow before God's presence. They are death, angels, demons, our fears, even the powers of hell. God's power is so great that no evil can stand against it. *(Romans 8: 31-39)* Verse 7 of Psalm 114 says even the earth trembles in the Lord's presence. Human beings – apart from Christ – face judgment and hell, and yet, many go their nonchalant way oblivious that they need a Savior. Paul, again writing to the people in the church at Rome in Chapter 8, says through the power of the Holy Spirit we can overcome our sinful natures. Like children we need to call upon our creator as loving Father, a dear Father and seek His care and guidance. *(Romans 8: 12-17)*

# PSALM 115
## Glory to God's Name

This Psalm of 18 verses is a liturgical hymn of praise – another of the Egyptian Hallel series. In this composition the author includes a polemic against idols *(V.2-8)*. The Psalm was probably written after the Jews returned from captivity in Babylon. The verses in Psalm 115 are highly sarcastic and mocking, much like Isaiah 44:6-20, 46:5-7; Deuteronomy 4:28, 28:36; and Jeremiah 2:8, 16:19.

### Segment One – Praise Through Lament. Verses 1 - 2

The psalm beings with the Psalmist shouting that to the LORD goes all the glory. *(V.1)* But then it quickly relates how the nations surrounding Israel scarcastically are asking the Hebrew people where is your God? *(V.2)* So the Covenant people pray that Yahweh God will raise them from their low estate – not for their own sake, but for the sake of God's glory and because such a blessing will demonstrate once again that God is true to His "Covenant love" (His *"Checed"*) and to His "faithfulness" (His *"Emunah"*). *(V.1)* (See Exodus 34:6 and Deuteronomy 7:7-8.)

### Segment Two – Praise Through Ridicule. Verses 3 - 8

The answer to the question where is the God of Israel *(V.2)* is that the LORD is in heaven and does what pleases Him. *(V.3)* Then our Psalmist, in contrast to the Omnipotent and Omnipresent God of the Hebrews, goes after the man-made gods of their assailants. Their idols are human made of silver and gold. *(V.4)* God's second commandment ordered the Hebrews not to worship any other gods because the LORD is a jealous God (Exodus

20:4-6). These idols are ridiculous, the Psalmist says: they can't talk or see *(V.5)*; they can't hear or smell *(V.6)*; and they can't feel, walk or talk *(V.7)*. The Psalmist concludes tht those who made these gods are just like their gods, and not to be trusted. *(V.8)*

## Segment Three – Praise Through Affirmation. Verses 9 - 13

Praise is now offered through a call to re-commitment! Isreal needs to trust the LORD, our helper and shield. *(V.9)* Our writer addresses himself to three groups within the congregation: (1) the priests of Aaron *(V.10)*; (2) the lay people *(V.11)*; and (3) everyone else who fears the LORD. *(V.11)* The Psalmist writing in Psalm 135:19-20 uses very similar words. The author of Psalm 115 concludes this segment by stating that Israel's God blesses His people without regard to status or rank. *(V.12-13)*

## Segment Four – Praise Through Priestly Blessing. Verses 14 - 15

This psalm was composed for worship in the Second Temple, and, at this point in the reading or singing of the psalm, one of the priests would probably stand and pronounce a benediction, saying may the LORD bless you and your children. *(V.14)* And then add that the LORD who blesses you created the heavens and the earth. *(V.15)*

## Segment Five – Praise Through Commitment. Verses 16 - 18

A little bit of theology is expressed to end this psalm. God is the creator of the heavens and the earth, but He chose to make us human beings to be the stewards of the earth. *(V.16)* Verse 17 tells us, according to Hebrew beliefs, that when a person dies he or she could no longer sing praises to God, because they now reside in the silence of the "grave" *("Sheol")*. *(V.17)* What then, as God's faithful stewards, is our response? The Psalmist tells us that our responsibility is to rise up and sing the LORD's praises now and forever. *(V.18)*

From a Christian perspective, we agree wholeheartedly that praising the Lord is our responsibility, along with our Jewish comrades. With Jesus in our hearts, we believe in eternal life (see John 3:16). Therefore, we Christians believe that when we die God will take us to heaven where we will spend all eternity praising and serving the Lord.

# PSALM 116

## God Saved Me from Death

This psalm is a song of thanksgiving written by a person whose prayer for help was answered. Some post-exilic editor placed Psalm 116 fourth in a series entitled Egyptian Hallal. So thankful is the Psalmist for God's mercy in responding positively to him in his troubles and sorrow that he says as long as he breathes He will pray to the LORD. *(V.2)* Deliverance is the theme of Psalm 116.

### Segment One – What the LORD Did for the Psalmist. Verses 1 - 9

The first two verses witness that the LORD has answered the Psalmist's prayers. Apparently the writer of this psalm was struggling with some serious form of illness to the point of death and the grave was about to be his final resting place. *(V.3)* The Hebrew word for "the grave" is *("Sheol")* and it is pictured as the realm of the dead, an abyss. It definitely had a negative and foreboding connotation. It was the land of no return. Psalm 88:3-7 says those in *("Sheol")* are cut off, forgotten. Verse 4 of Psalm 116 says the writer called on the name of the LORD to save him. The Hebrew word for "save" is *("Malat")* and can be translated as "rescue," or "deliver" or "escape from." God healed him! The LORD delivered him because the LORD is merciful, the Psalmist says. *(V.5) ("Racham")* is the Hebrew word for God's "mercy." Also, it can be translated into English as His "compassion." Looking back the Psalmist reflects on how the LORD answers the prayers of those who have child-like faith. *(V.6)* So he says my deliverance from death's door has taken away all my anxiety. *(V.7)* In verse 8, the Psalmist joyfully exclaims that the LORD saved him from tears, stumbling and death.

## Segment Two – What the Psalmist Will Do for the LORD. Verses 10 - 19

Even though our writer was troubled and anxious, he tells us that he kept his faith. *(V.10)* But perhaps when he was most anxious, he looked around at healthy unbelievers and in anger cried out to God that how can you let them be healthy when all of them are liars. *(V.11)* Not exactly a nice sentiment for a Godly man. But then he asks what can he do for God who has delivered him? *(V.12)* In gratitude to God for His deliverance from non-being (death), he makes a vow that he will lift up a cup, symbol of his salvation, and praise the LORD for keeping him alive. *(V.13)* And he wants to do this publicly before the whole congregation. *(V.14)*

He reflects again about death and dying saying the beloved of the LORD are precious to him. When they die the LORD grieves. *(V.15)* What he is telling us is that the life of each person who loves the LORD is valuable, and, therefore, death is costly to God. Our Psalmist happily calls himself God's servant. *(V.16)* He has been freed from the slavehood of death and he offers the LORD a sacrifice of thanksgiving. He is so happy that he repeats himself, saying he intends to keep his promises to praise the LORD in the house of the LORD. *(V.18-19)*

Let us make some concluding Christian comments on this provocative psalm. We can identify and say amen with much of what is said by our Psalmist. All of us experience sickness and the crises of being near death. It is only right and natural to pray for God's deliverance. God does hear and answer our prayers.

Let us go through the psalm and make comments from our Christian perspective. (1) The LORD is kind, good and merciful. *(V.5)* The Psalmist is thinking of God's righteousness in remembering His covenant and responding to His people with His "undying love" *("Checed").* We Christians praise God for His goodness. We reflect on God's goodness in sending Jesus to die on the cross to take away our sins. We believe the Old Testament is the foundation and first floor of our house; Jesus and the New Testament are the second floor and roof. We are glad to live in this Judeo-Christian home! (2) The Psalmist is at peace again after being saved from death. *(V.7)* Happily he realizes when he turned to God and was saved from death he was no longer in turmoil, but felt at peace and experienced an inner calmness. When we Christians open our hearts to the Holy Spirit and put our faith and trust in the Lord Jesus Christ, we too, can experience wonderful inner peace. In the letter to the Philippians, Paul encourages us to pray about everything and then thank Him for answering our pray so we can experience the peace of God. *(Philippians 4:6-7)* (3) Child-like faith is important. *(V.6)* *The Good News Bible* translates this as God protecting the helpless. The *New International Version* translates this as God protecting the simple-hearted. Isn't God good? He is loving, protective and gracious of folks like us – ordinary, everyday folks. This is one of the glories of God. When Jesus called His disciples, he called fisherman, tax collectors, and common folks. When the angels announced the birth of the Messiah Jesus, they appeared to shepherds! That's the meaning of God's glorious grace. The Psalmist of Psalm 116 is right. If we call on God in faith and love, He will come to us. *(V.1)* (4) He saved the Psalmist so he could walk in the presence of the LORD. *(V.8-9)* God delivers us so that we might live for Him! He blesses us so that we might be a blessing to others. We are right on with our Jewish brothers and sisters. (5) He is now a dedicated servant of the LORD. *(V.16)* In gratitude for his deliverance from the "abode of the dead" *("Sheol")*, our Psalmist says he wants to make his sacrifice of thanksgiving in the presence of the congregation. *(V.14)* We Christians and Jews can go to God in prayer in private at any time and any place. But we need to meet periodically to bolster our walk with the Lord in the company of a worshiping community. The author of Hebrews in the New Testament tells us not to neglect meeting together and encouraging one another. *(Hebrews 10:19-25)* (6) The Psalmist says as long as he has breath he will pray to the LORD. *(V.2)* Our Psalmist is on the right track. Jesus said the same thing. He said that the Father provides good gifts to those who ask Him. *(Matthew 7:7:11)* (7) In his fear of approaching death, the Psalmist only could think of trouble and sorrow. *(V.3)* One of the key New Testament verses is John 3:16. It tells us that it was God's love for everyone in the world that He gave His only Son to die for us so we could have eternal life. This is the main difference between Christians and Jews. When we Christians bring Jesus into our hearts and minds, we believe the same divine power that raised Jesus from death will take us to heaven when we die. This takes the fear out of death. In First John it says we Chrisitans need not be afraid of the day of judgment because the God of love casts out all fears. *(1 John 4:16-18)* (8) One more truth we learned from Psalm 116. GOD IS UNCHANGING. Everything about life, other than God, changes. Nothing stays the same. Because God is unchanging, we can count on Him to do for us today and tomorrow what He did in the past. This is why we read the Psalms. What makes this psalm so important is that the Psalmist called upon the LORD and God answered him and healed him. HE CAN AND WILL DO THIS FOR US – IF WE WILL CALL UPON HIM. GOD IS OMNIPOTENT – He is all powerful! He doesn't need anything from us, except our love and commitment. And we need to serve Him.

# PSALM 117
## A Wonderful Little Gem

Psalm 117 is comprised of two verses. It is one of the shortest psalms in the Psalter. It is the fifth of the so-called Egyptian Hallals. It is a call to the nations of the world to give praise to Israel's God because of what Yahweh God (the LORD) has been doing in and for His people Israel. The call to praise is actually a missionary invitation to everyone on earth. *(V.1)* The basis for this invitation is God's "unfailing love," His *("Checed")* and His "faithfulness," His *("Emuwnah"). (V.2)*

This missionary invitation comes with the conviction that the God of Israel is the LORD who rules the whole world! Notice the psalms that explicitly proclaim God's reign over the earth and its people are the ones who also invite a universal audience to praise Him. Psalm 47 says the LORD is the great king of the earth. *(Psalm 47:1-2)* Or check out Psalm 98: it says the LORD has revealed His righteousness to every nation. *(Psalm 98:1-2)* Psalm 95 is another: it says the LORD is King above all gods. *(Psalm 95:2-4)* Because God is the ruler of the universe, His people need to include everybody, along with all creatures. Psalm 148 gets carried away and invites every created thing, including angels, the moon and the twinkling stars in the heavens to praise Him. *(Psalm 148:2-5)*

The salvation of the Gentiles was predicted by the Old Testament Prophets. Isaiah has a number of messages from the LORD concerning this, the more famous one is that Israel will be a light to the Gentiles and a great salvation to ends fo the earth. *(Isaiah 49:6)*

The second wonderful aspect of Psalm 117 is the two terms the author uses in verse 2: "unfailing love" and "faithfulness" of the LORD. The two Hebrew words *("Checed")* and *("Emuwnah")* both come from one of the most important Old Testament text in Exodus 34:6-7. By recalling this text,

369

our writer is joining God to a sinful humanity, and announcing that He loves the world and its sinful people. He does this, not with the power of a military conqueror, but through the power of His love and faithfulness!

This little gem of a psalm communicates the Good News that God loves the world and its people. Israel was called to be God's mouthpiece and a community whereby the world could see what an obedient and faithful people were like. Unfortunately, Israel turned her back on God and when the LORD sent His Messiah, Jesus, the Jews not only rejected Him, but shouted for Him to be executed by means of a cross. However, the all-powerful LORD of the universe used Jesus' death as a means to save the world by raising Jesus from death. Jesus told us that all those who believe in Him will live again, have eternal life. *(John 11:25-26)*

Psalm 117 teaches us that life is meaningless apart from God and from God's love for the world. We Christians know this and we believe that God sent His Son into the world not to condemn the world but to save it. *(John 3:16-17)*

Psalm 117 speaks to us Christians. It says that we are called to be God's missionaries to those who don't know Christ Jesus. We are the recipients of God's unfailing love in Jesus and that means we now have a brand new perspective and a new relationship with the world's people. We are God's missionaries with the task of sharing His "unfailing love" (*"Checed"*) with everyone we meet. To live as God's people means we must accept one another as God in Christ has accepted us.

The Apostle Paul's words in Romans bring our discussion to a wonderful close. Paul says that Christ came to the Jews to demonstrate that God keeps His promises. He came to the Gentiles to demonstrate His love and His mercy for all peoples. *(Romans 15:7-12)* Paul quotes Psalm 117 in Romans 15:10 and he insists that the Christian church be open to all people – all genders, all races, all nationalities.

# PSALM 118

## God's People Bring in an Outsider

Psalm 118 is the last of The Egyptian Hallal series (psalms 113-118).

These six psalms were composed to be used in the Jewish liturgy at the great Festivals (Passover, Tabernacles, Weeks, Dedication and New Moon). (See Leviticus 23.)

When the Psalter was put together and reorganized after the Babylonian Exile, the Editor-Priest placed Psalm 118 after Psalm 117 because it commanded Israel to love the heathen. It would naturally follow that Psalm 118 would be a missionary liturgy designed to bring pagan converts into the worship and fellowship of God's people.

When the Jews returned from Exile, they found the land in and around Jerusalem inhabited by many heathen people. It took years of struggle and heartache to rebuild the walls and homes in Jerusalem that were destroyed back in 586 BC. Ezra, the priest during this time, reminded the returnees that a large part of the reason for their being taken into captivity in the first place was their turning their backs on God and ignoring their covenant obligations. So he spoke of the urgency of reconstructing the Temple. With prodigious and sacrificial effort, the second Temple was completed in 516 BC. Many of the first proselytes were neighbors in and around Jerusalem who were attracted to the faith of God's people when they witnessed their love and fellowship. What they saw and heard was in stark contrast to the many heathen gods and human immoralities. When a desire was expressed on their part, the candidate would be given some preliminary instruction and then invited to go to Jerusalem and be inducted at one of the many festivals. Psalm 118 was the liturgical vehicle.

## Segment One – A Call to Thanksgiving. Verses 1 - 4

The first verse of Psalm 118 begins with a familiar liturgical formula (see Psalm 106:1 and Psalm 107:1). It points out that the LORD is good and his "faithful love"("Checed") endures forever. (V.1) Ezra tells us that during the construction of the Second Temple when the foundations were completed, the worker-priests put on their priestly vestments and blew their trumpets and crashed the cymbals and everybody involved praised the LORD with the words in Psalm 118 verse 1, just as King David had prescribed. (Ezra 3:10-11)

The next two verses exhort the Hebrew descendants to praise the LORD. When the Temple was completed and persons surrounding Jerusalem wanted to be included into Judaism, a procession would form inside the gates of the walls and a priest or Levite would cue the participants so that each group would sing similar praises to the LORD in unison. (V.4) First the congregation, then the priests, and finally the God fearers (converts) would all say their part, and this would be the signal to begin heading toward the Temple.

## Segment Two – The Converts Would Speak Out. Verses 5 - 9

The person who wants to become a part of God's people and a part of the covenant has already been taught what he should say by a Levite in his village. The inquirer was, no doubt, asked to tell about his understanding of the unfailing love of Israel's God. He was taught how God's love can set a person free in times of distress (from Psalm 107). So when the procession stops again, the new convert is asked to speak. He tells the gathered about how God has rescued him, and how with God he is no longer afraid and how Jehovah God (the LORD) has rescued him from worthless idols. (V.5-9)

## Segment Three – The Congregation Responds. Verses 10 - 18

After the convert has shared his faith, members of the congregation, on cue, speak as if they were speaking the words of King David, the warrior king. With liturgical preciseness, voices would speak about destroying hostile enemies, which swarmed around them like vicious bees, doing their best to kill the convert. (V.10-13) Going back to the halcyon days of David and winning battles made the people feel a sense of pride. Then everyone

together might shout out that the victories are due to the LORD. *(V.14)*
Another two phrases are taken up: the LORD has done glorious deeds;
and the LORD has been triumphant. *(V.15-16)* Then in verses 17 and 18, a
member of the congregation celebrates how God has punished Israel for her
sins, but allowed her to come back from death (exile).

### Segment Four — Open the Gates of the Temple. Verses 19 - 22

They have come to the Temple gate and it is the convert's turn again. He
cries out that the gates should be opened for him so he can join the righteous
to thank the LORD. *(V.19)* A priest opens the gates and welcomes the
procession to the presence of the LORD. *(V.20)* As we read this psalm,
we realize that the Psalmist is giving us *acting out theology* of God's love
and mercy! The new convert speaks to God thanking Him for answering
his prayer. *(V.21)* That person is now accepted as a part of God's covenant
people. In entering the Temple, he has now become a spiritual Jew! And
a famous prophetic oracle is pronounced that Jesus used in reference to
Himself. Verse 22 states that the stone rejected by the builders is now the
cornerstone of the building. This has a two-fold meaning in this psalm: not
only was a non-Hebrew now included in the nation of Israel but Israel was
back after the nations of the world thought they had finished her off.

### Segment Five —The Wonderful Cornerstone. Verses 23 - 25

When the exiled Jews returned from Babylon they were nobodies. But now
they have rebuilt their city and the LORD's temple. Our author says the
LORD is doing this. *(V.23)* The stone rejected by the builders has now
become the cornerstone! It may have been the old keystone in Solomon's
Temple that had been lost in the rubble, but it was found and used in
Zerubbabel's day with great relish! (See Ezra 2:2; and Nehemiah 7:7.) No
longer was Israel the great power she was back in King David's day, but the
people who returned have been reborn! The congregation, thinking of their
new fellow member, tells him he needs to rejoice. *(V.24)* Our mighty God
has acted in giving Israel another convert. Another example of God's grace
in action. But, less they forget, the returned exiles are still surrounded by
hostile people. The Psalmist ends this segment pleading with the LORD to
save His people. *(V.25)*

373

## Segment Six – God Is Good – Final Thanks. Verses 26 - 29

In this segment, a Priest pronounces the final blessing on the new convert for coming into the house of the LORD. *(V.26)* Then the new member places his sacrifice on the altar *(V.27)* and acknowledges that the LORD is His God. *(V.28)* The psalm ends with everybody repeating verse 1 that the LORD is good and faithful. *(V.29)*

There are aspects of this wonderful psalm with which we Christians can identify. When Jesus entered Jerusalem on a donkey in what we call His Triumphal Entry, the crowds threw their garments along the road in front of Him and when He got near they all began shouting out verses from Psalm 118. *(Matthew 21:9)* Later, He met a group of Jewish religious leaders and He told them a parable about a vineyard where its owner rented it out to some farmers. At the end of the year, the owner sent a servant to collect the rent due to him, but the tenants drove the servant away. The owner then sent his only son and they killed him. When the owner of that vineyard returns, Jesus asked, what do you think he will do to these farmers? The religious leaders replied that the owner will but to death these wicked men. *(Matthew 21:41)* Then Jesus quoted the Psalm 118 verse 22 that the stone rejected by the builders is now the cornerstone of the building. *(Matthew 21:33-44)*

The Apostle Peter and the Apostle John healed a man, and the Jewish authorities summoned them before the Council to explain. Peter, filled with the Holy Spirit, tells them that the man was healed in the name and power of Jesus Christ. Peter then looked into the faces of the spiritual leaders of Israel and points out that the man from Nazareth that these leaders crucified is the cornerstone the builders rejected. Salvation for the Jews and all peoples, Peter says, comes from no One else. *(Acts 4:9-12)*

# PSALM 119
## The Longest Psalm in the Psalter

Psalm 119 is a devotional psalm centered on the Word of God. It also is a massive acrostic scheme, composed of 22 stanzas (or strophes) corresponding to the 22 letters of the Hebrew alphabet. Each stanza has 8 lines and each pair begins with the same letter. Most of the psalm's 176 verses are addressed to God, and the purpose of the composition is for godly instruction. It also can be classified as a wisdom psalm. Perhaps the most striking feature of this psalm is the inclusion of some important and striking aspects of the Word of God in each of the 22 stanzas. The author uses eight Hebrew terms and sprinkles them liberally throughout the verses. The eight terms are: <u>laws, decrees, statutes, precepts, commands or commandments, principles, Word or words and promises.</u>

We will identify the 22 stanzas with the Hebrew letter of the alphabet and comment on the various eight lines as they are translated in the *New Living Bible.*

### ALEPH Verses 1 - 8

The first three verses act as an introduction for the whole psalm. They tell us that those who obey God's <u>law</u> and seek His presence with their whole hearts *(V.1)* are those who are "happy" *(V.1)* or "blessed." The Hebrew word is *("Esher")*. Verse 2 says happy are those who obey God's <u>degrees</u>. Verse 3 is just another way of saying what verse 2 says. In order to do God's will, we cannot compromise with evil. *(V.3)* This sets the tone for all that is to come.

The author recognizes his humanity. Yes, we all are sinners, subject to lapses in our commitment to the LORD. The mark of a godly individual is consistency in keeping God's <u>commandments</u>. *(V.4)* Right at the outset, the Psalmist tells us that his actions need to adhere to God's <u>principles</u>. *(V.5)*

He also seems to acknowledge that when he considers God's commands and His laws he needed to be disciplined by God for some human failing. *(V.6-7)* Finally noting that he again needed to obey God's principles, he pleads with God not to give up on him. *(V.8)*

## BETH Verses 9 - 16

This group of verses asks how can a young person remain pure? The answer? Obey God's word, which is His law. *(V.9)* The Hebrew word *("Torah")* has a multitude of meanings. It means "law," "instructions" and it refers to the "Law of Moses." At the time of the Second Temple in 515 B.C., the phrase "Word of God" became popular. God's Word covers all the different expressions the Psalmist uses about edicts by God in this lengthy psalm. God's Word comes from the Almighty and conveys divine power to change the heart or mind of the reader (see Psalm 33:4-6, Isaiah 55:11-12 and John 1.1-4, 14). When we read (or hear) God's Word and try our best to find God *(V.10)*, we open ourselves to God's supernatural power and something gets changed inside of us. The Psalmist speaks of hiding God's Word in our hearts. *(V.11)* In verses 12 through 15, the Psalmist says he has been studying and reflecting on God's principles, decrees, commandments and word.

## GIMEL Verses 17 - 24

It is apparent there is very little reference to the idea of sacrifice in this psalm, although in the Temple in Jerusalem sacrifices were continually offered. When this psalm was written, sometime in the fourth century B.C., there were tens of thousands of religious Jews scattered all over the known world, and most of them had never seen, nor were they likely to see the Temple. The Word had taken the place of the Temple as the center of their faith, and the 119th Psalm interprets this shift of focus.

In this GIMEL stanza, we are told that to live one most obey God's word. *(V.17)* The word "live" in Hebrew is *("Chayah")*. Biologically "live" is a gift from God. When we are right with God, He gives us something of Himself: His love and care. At the conclusion of the "Torah" (the first five books of Moses), it says we have a choice between life and death, blessings and curses. We are to choose life. And life comes from loving the LORD and obeying Him. *(Deuteronomy 30:19-20)*

We are all travelers (pilgrims) in this life and to find our way, we need divine directions. The author says that he is a foreigner here on earth and, therefore, he needs God's guidance and His commands. He pleads with God not to hide from him because he has a deep desire for God's laws. (V.19-20) Apparently, our poet was a minor government official and those in authority (perhaps those persons were department heads) sneered at him for being so disciplined in obeying God's decrees. (V.21-23) However, he is adamant and unbending in his loyalty to God's word. He stands his ground but begs God to give him wise advice in dealing with those who scoff at him. (V. 23-24)

## DALETH Verses 25 - 32

All of us at times get feeling low, but our Psalmist says he is so low he is in the dust and completely discouraged. He needs reviving with God's Word. (V.25) One thing we can admire is the conversational way the poet presents his prayers to the Almighty. He says that he informed th LORD of his plans and the LORD answered. (V.26) But he still needs help in understanding how to implement his plans within God's principles and commandments. (V.26-27) He also needs to be encouraged by God's word. (V.28) He then says something totally startling. He asks God to prevent him from lying to himself! (V.29) We all know that in our meditations with God that sometimes we feel we might be deluding ourselves. I assume the Psalmist asks God to prevent him from lying to himself because he wishes to show God how humble and sincere he is in trying to understand God's laws, decrees, statutes, precepts, commands or commandments, principles, Word or words and promises. Desperate, he asks God not to put him to shame. (V.31) He ends this DALETH stanza by asking God to help him to follow God's commands.

That is precisely what Deuteronomy 30 commands. Throughout this lengthy psalm, our author seems to be pushing toward a goal. He admits he is unworthy and undeserving. The writer is properly humble and not buddy-buddy with God. When Moses received the Ten Commandments from the LORD, he then spoke with the people. They had seen smoke and lightning billowing from the mountains and hail and all of these frightened them. Moses tells them not to be fearful. God merely did this to demonstrate His awesome power and to let their fear keep them from sinning. (Exodus 20:20) Many Christians today lack the proper reverence for God. They have allowed their consciences to become tame, and think nothing about doing wrong—so long as they don't get caught!

The Apostle Paul in the New Testament writes similar words. He asks the Philippians to obey God with fear and deep reverence. *(Philippians 2:12)* Then he makes a profound spiritual statement that we must never forget. He writes that God Himself (through Jesus Christ's Spirit) is working within us to put a desire in us to obey God and please God. *(Philippians 2:13)*

## HE Verses 33 - 40

The HE stanza concerns the right paths. It begins with the Psalmist asking the LORD to teach him to follow His principles *(V.33)* and to understand His law. *(V.34)* He then asks the LORD to help him walk on the right path. *(V.35)* The Hebrew word for "path" is *("Orach")*, which can also be translated as "the well-worn road" or "the way." The poet then makes a series of requests: that he not be inflicted with the love of money *(V.36)*; that he turn his eyes from worthless things *(V.37)*; for God to reassure him of God's promise (presumably to take care of him) *(V.38)*; that God help him abandon shameful ways *(V.39)*; and finally that his life be renewed with the LORD's goodness. *(V.40)*

Walking along God's paths is tantamount to obeying His commands and having His presence in your life. Jesus, God's Messiah, proclaims that he is the way (the path) and that no one can come to the Father except through Him. *(John 14:6)*

## WAW Verses 41 - 48

When God chose the Jews (see Exodus 19:4-6; 34:10-11), He made an everlasting covenant with them and bestowed His "covenant love" *("Checed")* on His people. In verse 41, the writer asks for renewal of this covenant love and salvation that God promised him. The Hebrew word for "salvation" is *("Ts shuw ah")*, which is the feminine noun asking God for "assistance" or "deliverance" so the Psalmist can give help and assistance to his neighbors (reflecting God's own kindness and love). This divine love the Psalmist says frees him from those who mock him. *(V.42)* By concentrating on God's Word and filling his life with spiritual things, he will be able to walk the path of righteousness with freedom. *(V.44-45)* Feeling free, he will be able to speak to those in authority about God's <u>decrees</u>. *(V.46)* The Psalmist ends the WAW stanza by delighting in the LORD's <u>commands</u> and <u>principles</u>. *(V.47-48)*

It was the Apostle Peter, filled with the freedom of the Holy Spirit, who spoke boldly in front of the Council (Jewish Sanhedrin) about the saving and healing grace of Jesus Christ. *(Acts 4:8-12)*

## ZAYIN Verses 49 - 56

Over and over the Psalmist exclaims that the <u>promises</u> of God's <u>Word</u> is his only hope. *(V.49)*. The Hebrew word for "hope"" is *("Yatchal")* and it has a sense of expectation that God's <u>promises</u> will revive him. *(V.50)* He tells God that he is being belittled because he uphold's God's <u>law</u>. *(V. 51-52)* Then we get a special insight into the Psalmist. He says he is furious with those who do not respect the <u>law</u> of God. *(V.53)* Perhaps his fury was somewhat responsible for those in authority over him taunting him. He ends the ZAYIN stanza by extoling the LORD's <u>principles</u> *(V.54)*, His <u>law</u> *(V.55)* and His <u>commandments</u>. *(V.56)*

## HETH Verses 57 - 64

All that we have examined and spoken about in Psalm 119 is now culminated in verse 57—he promises to obey the LORD's <u>words</u>. The poet is saying he has finally placed Jehovah God first in his life and expects the LORD's blessings and that He will be merciful to him. *(V.58)* This seems to indicate he has gone all the way in his commitment. The word for "merciful" in Hebrew is *("Chanan")*. It can be translated as wanting God to be "favorable" or "gracious" to him. Being human, the author thinks back to a time when he was only lukewarm in following God's way, but he caught himself and turned himself around. *(V.59)* Now he is all in in obeying God's <u>commands</u>. *(V. 60)* He realizes God's <u>Word</u> is the greatest treasure. But then he cannot help himself, he blames evil people for trying to drag him into sin. It's their fault! *(V.61)* He also realizes that he is not alone in his pilgrimage on God's way. Many of his covenant brothers and sisters are walking that road along with him. *(V.63)* Thinking about how blessed he is, the Psalmist smiles inwardly and, with joy in his heart again, asks the LORD to teach him His <u>principles</u>. *(V.64)*

## TETH Verses 65 - 72

The Psalmist is feeling blessed because, as promised he says, the LORD has done many good things for him. *(V.65)* God's promises are binding. He will do what He says He will do, and these promises are found in the Torah. The Psalmist apparently has graduated in his understanding of God and now seeks knowledge and good judgment. *(V.66)* Good judgment is a gift of being able to differentiate between good and what isn't. Knowledge comes gradually as we walk along God's paths (with Him). The poet says he used to wander off until he was disciplined by God. *(V.67)* Don't we all! But the Psalmist is not beyond criticizing others perhaps for his wardering off. In verse 69 he notes that arrogant people have made up lies about him. He then says that these people are dull and stupid. *(V.70)* He doesn't go into detail, but, by inference, it would apear that the Psalmist strayed away from the Covenant fellowship. Like the Prodigal Son in Jesus' parable, the punishment was his alone when he was in a far country. However, the Psalmist admits his resulting suffering was good because it taught him to pay attend to the LORD's princples *(V.71)* and also God's laws. *(V.72)*

## VODH Verses 73 - 80

This stanza confesses that God is not only the Creator, but He is the giver of the moral law as well. The Psalmist, like the Prodigal Son in Jesus' parable, has returned home and asks God, His loving Father, to give him the sense he needs to follow the LORD's commands. *(V.73)* He also seems to have spiritually grown to understand that he needs to be a joy for others who trust God's word. *(V.74)* At this point in the Psalm much of his concern has been about himself. Perhaps the discipline he received from God made him more aware of the needs of others. *(V.75)* Now that he is back in the Covenant fold, he asks for the comfort of God's unfailing love, just as God promised him, *(V.76)* and asks God to surround him with God's tender mercies. *(V.77)* But then his mood changes and again he says he is still upset by his unbelieving co-workers who lied about him and requests that God bring disgrace upon them. *(V.78)* Instead of brooding and feeling further upset, he says he will concentrate on God's commandments. *(V.78)* He makes another wise statement as he ends the VODH segment seeking to be blameless in keeping God's principles so he will never be ashamed. *(V.80)*

## KAPH Verses 81 - 88

Psalm 119, because of its length, is something akin to an epic poem, like the Arab *"Diwan."* Up to this point, our Psalmist has been on an emotional high. When God surrounded him with His tender mercies, it permitted him to really live (see verse 77). "Tender mercies" is the Hebrew word *("Racham")*, which is God's "mother love" that accepts us in spite of our unacceptability. However, no one can remain on a high forever, so the inevitable reaction comes in. Our poet now says he faints in his longing for God's salvation *(V.81)*, his eyes strain to see God's promises to come true *(V.82)*, and he is striveled up and exhausted *(V.83)* as he tries to obey God's principles. In verses 84-87, he cries out asking when is God going to punish the arogrant people who persecute him! It would appear that God is helping our Psalmist to learn a difficult lesson. To become a mature believer, one has to go through times of suffering and disappointment. He concludes this section by asking the LORD to spare his life and he will in return obey God's decrees. *(V.88)*

## LAMEDH Verses 89 - 96

The writer extols God's Word as something that exists beyond his own life. *(V.89)* Also, that God's faithfulness is from generation to generation. *(V.90)* And His laws remain true today as when they were first created. *(V.91)* He says God's law gave him the joy that kept him alive. *(V.92)* And God's commandments restored his health. *(V.93)* But he is still concerned about his life *(V.94)* because the wicked want to kill him. *(V.95)* But he says he is sustained by God'd decrees and commands. *(V.95-96)* It is true, God's law is forever! When Jesus came to earth as God's Messiah, He told the world that he didn't' come to abolish the law, but to fulfill it. (See Matthew 5:17-19.)

## MEM Verses 97 - 104

This stanza stands out as one of the more uplifting and encouraging in Psalm 119. It begins with our Psalmist proclaiming how he loves God's law. *(V.97)* Every spare hour he meditates on it. He feels that Jehovah God's plans for our world are working and God needs to share them. Because God's Word is his constant guide, it makes him wiser than his enemies *(V.98)*, gives him more insight than his teachers *(V.99)*, and makes him even wiser than his elders. *(V.100)* He proudly exclaims he refuses to walk the path of evil, remaining obedient to the LORD's word. *(V.101)* God's Torah teaches that God's Covenant people are to care especially for widows and orphans. The spirit of the law is to put love into practice so that each believer should love his neighbor. This is why the Psalmist can say with conviction, that God's Word has taught him well *(V.102)* and gives him an understanding that is sweeter than honey. *(V.103-104)*

## NUN Verses 105 - 112

The will of God is to be God-like as we walk our path in life. Our task (like that of the Psalmist) is to be faithful to the Word (be obedient). The Psalmist begins the NUN stanza by saying that God's word is a lamp for his feet and gives light to his path. *(V.105)* This is a helpful illustration because a light only brightens one or two steps ahead in the darkness. We Christian pilgrims are on our journey. Jesus says He came into the world as a light to shine in this dark world. *(John 12:44-46)* Life for us is precarious; it is a day-to-day adventure. We are like the Psalmist who says that he has suffered much. And like the Psalmist we expect our lives to be restored as the LORD promises. *(V.107)* Although his life hangs in the balance, the Psalmist will not stop obeying God's law. *(V.109)* The wicked are still setting traps for him. *(V.110)* But God's decrees *(V.111)* and His principles *(V.112)* are his heart's desire. God is faithful. He has placed His people in His Covenant fellowship and even though there are traps along the way, we believers need to be determined to the very end. *(V.112)*

As we read the Bible, and Psalm 119 in particular, we see what kind of character a Christian should have. God walks with us in our journey and He gives us His truth (His *("Emeth")*. These help us deal with the vicissitudes that meet us along the way. God's grace gives us our priorities and when things seem to be dark, God's light shines a step or two ahead of us so we can keep going.

## SAMEKH Verses 113 - 120

In segment (NUN), we are introduced to walking according to God's Word. There are many circuitous pathways for us to travel and we need God's Word to light up the way. In this SAMEKH stanza, even though there are those who are undecided about obeying Gods' Word, the writer is our role model for he says his choice is clear, he loves God's law. *(V.113)* He follows up by using words often found in David's psalms, that God is his shield and his refuge. *(V.114)* He asks evil-minded people to get out of his life, because he intends to obey God's commands. *(V.115)* There is much to admire in the Psalmist's decisiveness. He doesn't fool around! He is asking God to keep him safe because his enemies are vicious. He knows God cannot include them in His eternal Kingdom, and so he says they are only fooling themselves. *(V.118)* Being a bit more mean spirited he calls them scum that God will skim off and throw away. *(V.119)* There is judgment! God is omniscient and knows when we do things contrary to His will. The last verse is one we Christians need to heed and take seriously. Our author says he trembles in fear of God's judgments. *(V.120)*

All of us need to have a reverent awe of the Lord. Many today do not take God seriously. If truth be known, they don't think much about God, and, consequently, He has very little influence on them and how they live their lives. The Apostle Paul is talking to his friends in Corinth about what they (we) can expect when they (we) die. He says that each of them (and us) will one day stand before Christ and be judged for the good and evil they/we have done. *(2 Corinthians 5:6-10)*

## AYIN Verses 121 - 128

We are not sure what is the situation of our Psalmist. We think he was a minor official in the government. Because of his zealous adherence of the laws of God, in both his life-style and speech, he has gotten into serious trouble with his superiors who are probably secular Jews, and may have been placed in custody. He pleads with God, asking Him for protection from enemies since he has done what is right and just. *(V.121)* The Hebrew word for "right" is *("Tsedeq")*, which means "righteous." He cries out for God to bless him. *(V.122)* He seeks delivance as God promised *(V.123)* because he is God's servant. *(V.124)* He is aware that he needs discernment to understand the LORD's decrees. *(V125)* Then he informs the LORD that it is time to act on his behalf. *(V.126)* He is saying that he is God's servant, one who does God's bidding and, therefore, God should protect him now! As this stanza closes, and with the Psalmist upset, he can still affirm two trulys: truly he loves God's commands; and truly each of God's commandments is right. *(V.127-128)*

## PE Verses 129 - 136

In this segment, things have not changed for our Psalmist, although he may have been released from protective custody. He still is oppressed but is able to cheerfully remark that God's <u>decrees</u> are wonderful. *(V.129)* He sees God's plan unfolding, as more folks become a part of God's Covenant fellowship. They come together and share God's <u>Word</u> and then the Holy Spirit opens the Scriptures and when this happens even simple folk can understand God's <u>words</u>. *(V.130)* Humbly the Psalmist asks God in verse 132 to show him mercy. The word "mercy" in Hebrew is *("Checed")* and it can be translated as "unfailing love." God's mighty truth in sending us His love makes it possible for ordinary folks to be made right spiritually with Him. Then they, in turn, can help others get right with God by doing what God does for them—that is, by accepting sinners, forgiving them, and by loving them. God's <u>Word</u> is wonderful, of course, because it comes from the mighty Creator. Here are a few reasons why God's <u>principles</u> are wonderful: (1) They are so clear that even the simple can understand them *(V.130)*; (2) they make us aware of the mercy God shows on all who love Him *(V.132)*; (3) they give guidance so evil won't overcome us *(V.133)*; and (4) they help rescue us from oppression *(V.134)* The author ends this HE stanza tearfully (and without anger) because others disobey God's <u>law</u>. *(V.136)*

When Jesus rode in triumph on the first Palm Sunday and came in view of Jerusalem, the procession paused and Jesus began to shed tears and prophesied that Israel's enemies would again destroy Jerusalem, not a stone left in place, because the Jew's would reject Him as their Lord and Savior. *(Luke 19:44-46)* Does verse 136 look forward to this rejection of the LORD's plan to save them through Jesus Christ?

## TSADHE Verses 137 - 144

Because God is "just" *("Tsod oq")*, which also means "righteous," the Psalmist knows the LORD's judgments and demands are fair and right. *(V.137)* Also His <u>decrees</u> are perfect and are to be trusted. *(V.138)* But now the tears the Psalmist shed because others disobey God's <u>law</u> *(V.136)* are replaced with his rage since they have disregard for God's <u>words</u>. *(V.139)* He is not referring to foreigners or heathens. The people he is speaking about are those he is working with—folks who supposedly are people of the Covenant, those who grew up being exposed to God's Word but now have willfully turned their backs on God. In contrast to these so-called secular Jews, our poet further tells God how all his struggles and tribulations have given him opportunities to put his faith in God's promises to the test and that he found them to be true and that is why he loves them. *(V.140)* In his prayer, he tells God that even though he is just an ordinary person who is despised *(V.141)* because of his zeal for the LORD's Word, he won't ever forget God's commandments. *(V.141)* Why? Because Your goodness, LORD, is eternal. *(V. 142)* He then goes on to say God's unfailing love for him will never cease. Yes, he does experience stress and pressure in this life, but as he walks God's path on earth he finds joy in God's commands. *(V.143)* He closes this stanza by once again affirming God's decrees are forever fair and asks God to help him to understand them and bring them into his life. *(V.144)*

## QOPH Verses 145 - 152

Throughout the QOPH stanza our Psalmist lifts up his prayers to the LORD, beginning with Our Psalmist praying with all his heart. *(V.145)* He asks to be saved. *(V.146)* He gets up early in the morning to lift up his prayers *(V.147)* and late at night. *(V.148)* He seeks the LORD's justice *(V.149)* because lawless people are coming near to attack him. *(V.150)* He now knows that when he has all the fullness of God within him, he will have the divine motivation and ability to carry out God's will through the obeying of God's Word. He also now believes that the LORD's love in action will give him victory as he struggles to obey God's decrees.

In many of the segments of this psalm, we hear of our writer being persecuted. But when God is near him, he has the strength to withstand any crisis. *(V.151)* And he has known this from his earliest days. *(V.152)* It is the same for us Christians. When the disciples of Jesus met with Him after His resurrection, Jesus gave them His Great Commission. He told them and us to go and make disciples in all nations. *(Matthew 28:19)* Then Jesus gives wonderfully inspiring words, similary to Psalm 119. He said that His disciples need to teach these new disciples to obey all of the commands that He has given them. *(Matthew 28:20)*

## RESH Verses 153 - 160

In this segment the Psalmist continues his prayer. Our author is saying to us readers that life is difficult and all of us have to undergo times of physical suffering, sickness and crises. He himself is having problems. He begins by pleading with God that he needs to be rescued from his sorrows because he has not forgotten God's laws. *(V.153)* He asks God to protect him as God promised. *(V.154)* He looks around and sees the wicked being far from salvation and not living up to the LORD's principles. *(V.155)* He then asks God to give him back his life *(V.156)*, because he is being persecuted *(V.157)*, that he hates these traitors who care nothing for the LORD's word *(V.158)*, while he loves the LORD's commandments. *(V.159)* He ends his pray by stating God's words and laws are eternal. *(V.160)*

Our Psalmist knows that obeying God is not optional. To be a believer one must follow in obedience because without obeying one cannot make a claim on God for His intervention on our behalf. The great prophet of the Exile, Isaiah, speaking for the LORD, says that He alone is God, there is no other savior, and, from eternity to eternity, no one can oppose what He intends to do except Himself. *(Isaiah 43:10-13)*

As Christians, we know that salvation can only take place when we personally dedicate ourselves to God and follow His will. Of course, with us it is through His Son, Jesus Christ. However, the principle is the same as the Psalmist puts forth. The wicked in verses 155 and 158 are very far from salvation because they think they can go through life without God's guidance. When the Day of Judgment comes, they will want to call upon His mercy, and what will happen when they're not in God's will?

## SIN AND SHIN Verses 161 - 168

Our Psalmist is a humble man probably made humbler by being persecuted and looked down on by self-important powerful people. But he adds that his heart trembles only at the words of the LORD. *(V.161)* The Hebrew word for "trembles" is *("Yare")*, which also means "reverence" or having "holy respect" for God's Word. Our writer also rejoices in being able to walk in the way of God's word. He says it is like finding a great treasure. *(V.162)* He sees the whole Torah as a treasure that he loves. *(V.163)* He says he will praise God seven times a day. *(V.164)* (7= a perfect spiritual number!) The good thing about doing God's will, even if we get harassed for doing it, is the peace that comes to us, and knowing that it helps us not to stumble. *(V.165)*

Our poet ends this stanza by announcing that God is Omnipotent—all-powerful, and Omniscient—all-knowing. This means he cannot ever pull the wool over God's eyes, because God knows everything the Psalmist does. *(V.168)* This is very similar to another wonderful psalm, the 139th, in which that Psalmist indicates that the LORD has examined his heart and knows everything about him. He knows when he stands up and sits down. He can never, never escape from God's Spirit. *(Psalm 139:1-7)*

## TAW Verses 169 - 176

We have come to the end of this lengthy psalm. Throughout the many claims by the author that he has obeyed God's teachings in the Old Testament (the Torah), he has not become self-righteous. If he had known Jesus's teachings about the proud and self-important Pharisee and humble tax collector, he would have stood with the sinful tax collector and return home forgiven. *(Luke 18:10-14)*

In the TAW stanza, the Psalmist is again praying to God in a very humble manner. King David wrote the 23rd Psalm and, in his masterful composition, tells us because the LORD is his Shepherd he has everything he needs. *(Psalm 23:1)* God, the Chief Shepherd, has given him rest, renewal of strength and guides him along right paths. *(Psalm 23:2-3)* And the LORD lets him live in the LORD's house forever. *(Psalm 23:6)* In contrast, our poet in Psalm 119 is asking God to supply him with the things he doesn't have. He is asking for a discerning mind. *(V.169)* He also wants God to keep His promise and rescue him. *(V.170)* "Rescue" is another word for "salvation" in Hebrew. Many interpreters think the poet is asking God to rescue him from his enemies. That may be on his mind, but it sounds more like he is thinking of spiritual matters. Like all good Jews, he probably thought about the coming of the Messiah. He knew about God's mercy with Israel in entering a Covenant with them. He repeatedly asks Gods' mercy in delivering him from death. (See Psalm 119 verses 149-150.) In verses 171-172 the Psalmist encourages himself to let his lips burst with praise for God and let his tongue sing about His word. Then he again pleads with the LORD to help him *(V.173)* because he delights in God's law *(V.174)* and let him live so he can praise the LORD. *(V.175)* In verse 176, the poet finally prays (and problably finally fully realizes) for God to come and find him for he has wandered away like a lost sheep. But he quickly adds tht he has not forgotten the LORD's commands. *(V.176)* It is sad in a way that he waits until the very last verse in this epic poem to categorize himself with the same sin he accuses his enemies of having—that of wandering way from God's Word.

We are all fallible human beings who have to live in a broken and complex world. We all fall short of the ideals that God has established for us as exemplified in the Torah. Because of this, we all have to live under both the judgment and mercy of God.

We Christians have the informative testimony of the Apostle Paul to help us understand the law of God. In his letter to the church at Rome, Paul confesses he wanted desperately to do what was right, but it was the commandments that showed him his sin. He had all sorts of forbidden desires hidden in his heart, and he says yes the law is good but the trouble is not with the law but with Paul himself. He was conceived in original sin and that made sin his master. The Law of sin made him the miserable person who he is. *(Romans 7:14-24)* The Psalmist in Psalm 119 is in the same fix. However, because of God sending the Savior, Jesus, to us, we Christians have an advantage on the Psalmist.

Paul finishes his comments on this by asking who will free him from a life dominated by sin? The answer: the Lord Jesus Christ. *(Romans 7:25)* Then in chapter 8 of Romans, Paul continues his thought by writing that the life-giving Spirit of Jesus Christ frees us from the power of sin that leads all of us to death. Jesus' sacrfice on the cross satisfied the requirements of God's law for all of us once and for all. God Himself destroyed the power of sin that leads to death. And God's power in us through the Holy Spirit will help keep us from succumbing to our own sinful original nature. *(Romans 8:1-4; 9-11)*

# PSALM 120

## The Upward Journey to Zion and Peace

Psalm 120 is the first of fifteen psalms (120-134) that bear the title, "Songs of Ascents." These were songs sung by Jewish pilgrims making an annual journey to the Temple in Jerusalem to attend one of the three special festivals: Passover, Pentecost and Atonement. The Hebrew word for "Ascent" is ("Alah"). It was used because Jerusalem is some 2,300 feet above sea level. All fifteen of these psalms take their spirit from Psalm 84, which describes how a pilgrim feels making his/her way up to the Holy City. Psalm 84 is well known for comparing a single day in the LORD's dwelling place to a thousand days anywhere else. *(Psalm 84:1-2, 10)*

### Segment One – A Prayer of an Unhappy Pilgrim. Verses 1 - 4

Initially in this psalm the Pilgrim is upset and feels as if he must take his troubles to the LORD in prayer. *(V.1)* The Psalmist cries out to be rescued from deceitful people. *(V.2)* He obviously loves the LORD and is very sensitive when others around him do not have the same respect for things of God. The song is like a soliloquy where he talks to himself asking the question of those with deceitful tongues how will God punish you. *(V.3)* He answers his own query by saying deceitful ones will be burned with hot coals and pierced with arrows. *(V.4)* It's interesting to speculate why this particular strong composition was placed first of the fifteen "Songs of Ascents." We'll never know for sure, except that it tells us that living in that post-exilic day was not too different from our own time.

## Segment Two – Living with Violent People. Verses 5 - 7

The Psalmist now becomes more specific. He tells God how he has suffered among the scondrels of Meshech. *(V.5)* Meshech is east of Jerusalem somewhere beyond the Black Sea in northern Turkey. So this Pilgrim has come a long way in his journey. It also pains him to live among people of Kedar, he says, again being quite specific. *(V.5)* Kedar was a son of Ishmael, and, at the time when this was written, Kedar was a wild Arab tribe who spent their time robbing and plundering. They came from the Muslim faith, but obviously they did not practice it. The author also says he no longer wants to live among those who hate peace. *(V.6)* So by inference, the Pilgrim leaves these violent and greedy people and begins his arduous journey to the Holy City. It was a long way, and it was filled with dangers. It was an upward journey, but the writer is not daunted because he yearns for "peace" *("Shalom"). (V.7)* Seven is considered a perfect or complete number by God Almighty (the LORD).

From a Christian perspective, we can identify with this Pilgrim. But we followers of Christ have a special gift from God that the Psalmist does not have, which is, of course, God's Son, Jesus Christ! Jesus gives us His gift of *("Shalom").* The Apostle Paul in his letter to the Ephesians explains that the crucifixtion of Jesus resulted in the end of the whole system of Jewish law which exluded all Gentiles. This enabled the development of peace between Jew and Gentile by Christ creating in Himself one new person (a born again person) from the two racial groups. *(Ephesians 2:15-18)* Jesus Himself told us that he was providing all races with a special gift—peace of mind and heart. The peace He gives us is nothing like the peace that the world gives. *(John 14:27)*

# PSALM 121
## The LORD Watches Over Us Coming and Going

This psalm is the second in the "Songs of Ascents" series sung by Pilgrims in a caravan heading up to Jerusalem to attend special religious festivals. Everyone knew its words, but certain leaders would sing the verses and others would respond antiphonally. These songs were a Book of Devotions. Some small groups traveled together for mutual protection and fellowship. Some came from afar and had as many as five days of travel, carrying provisions.

### Segment One – The LORD Is Our Helper. Verses 1 - 2

This is a beautiful psalm where God's protection is the dominant theme. Along the way, someone in the group would call out "look at the mountains," and then would sing the question "does our help come from them?" *(V.1)* The whole group would sing a response—"no our help comes from the LORD!" And perhaps another individual would chime in, singing, "the heavens and earth were made by the LORD!" *(V.2)*

### Segment Two – The LORD Watches Over Us. Verses 3 - 7

When the caravan stopped to rest, maybe a leader in the group would give a devotional using the beloved 23$^{rd}$ Psalm, telling them that God is their divine Shepherd watching over them. The familiar poem of David was centuries old and most of the travelers knew its words by heart. Then perhaps the leader would tell the story of how the prophet Elijah defeated the priests of Baal (see 1 Kings 18:20-39). In telling this story, he would relate how in the heat of summer the god Baal would go underground and sleep (1 Kings 18:27). He then would recite the wonderful words of Psalm 121 that the One who watches over you does not sleep *(V.3)* and never tires. *(V.4)* He also is our protective shade *(V.5)* and stands beside us at night. *(V.6)* Because it was a long and often dangerous journey, the Pilgrims would be comforted when the devotion leader sang out that "the LORD protects us from all evil, preserving our lives." *(V.7)*

## Segment Three – The LORD Is with You Now and Forever. Verse 8

The Jews were aware they had a Covenant relationship with God Almighty. The last verse of Psalm 121 reassures that to them and was one of the reasons they made the often treacherous pilgrimage to worship in Jerusalem. But unlike we Christians, they did not have the assurance that they would be watched over forever. *(V.8)* How much more then should we be willing to undertake arduous journeys and tasks for our Lord Jesus Christ in gratitude for our assurance of a life with him throughout eternity.

# PSALM 122

## Praying for the Peace of Jerusalem

This psalm is the third of fifteen in the series entitled "Songs of Ascents." It carries a superscription of David. It seems obvious that Jerusalem would not be the focus of pilgrimages prior to the dedication and the placing of the Ark of the Covenant in the Most Holy Place in King Solomon's Temple (see 1 Kings 8:1-11). This throws serious doubt on David being the author. Actually most of these Ascents psalms were written post-exilic.

### Segment One – Reflections on Arrival. Verses 1 - 5

The Psalmist begins by being thankful that he was encouraged to go on this pilgrimage. *(V.1)* He now is standing inside the gates of Jerusalem *(V.2)*, and, as he has a chance to look around, he realizes what a marvelous city is Jerusalem. *(V.3)* It seems to him that all of the Jews living in the hinterlands are with him in the Holy city giving thanks in the name of the LORD as the law requires. Another thought enters the Psalmist's mind. Israel is composed of twelve tribes, but they all come here to this wonderful capitol city to worship and sacrifice as one. *(V.4)*

We can just picture the author standing inside the city gate viewing the crowded city of many buildings, homes, offices and palaces. To his right, beside the city gates, he can see judges deciding disagreements among the people. *(V.5)*

It is interesting that today the church of Jesus Christ is composed of the extended twelve tribes, symbolized by Jesus' twelve apostles, and yet they are one in Christ. In John's Gospel, Jesus prays for His disciples and for all of us that we will be one in the belief that the Father sent Jesus to be our Lord and Savior. *(John 17:20-23)*

393

## Segment Two — Praying for Peace. Verses 6 - 9

Our Psalmist was probably full of excitement as he experiences Jerusalem for the first time and considers what a memory he will have to take home with him. Then he thinks about the concept of *("Shalom")* and immediately he turns to his companions and says pray for the peace of Jerusalem and that those who love the city may prosper. *(V.6)* He expands his prayer to include everyone within the city's walls. *(V.7)* He thinks about home and prays out loud for his family and friends, many of whom probably encouraged him to come, that peace be with them, too. *(V.8)*

The writer of Psalm 122 fervently wants "peace" *("Shalom")* within the walls of the city of Jerusalem. He ends this short psalm, saying he will always seek what is best for Jerusalem. *(V.9)*

We Christians can appreciate the wonderful spirit of *("Shalom")* in this psalm. We worship the same God, and it was out of this same environment that God's Son, Jesus, lived and taught and died on a cross. But God raised Jesus from death and took Him up to heaven, freeing His Spirit from the limitations of time and space, so that Jesus can come to everyone who has faith in Him. The Apostle Paul, filled with the Holy Spirit, says while we were dead in our sins, God gave us life when he raised Jesus from the dead. *(Ephesians 2:4-5)* He further tells us not to worry about anything, but to pray about everything since Jesus' peace will guard our hearts and minds as we live in Jesus. *(Philippians 4:6-7)*

# PSALM 123
## Keeping Our Eyes on the LORD

Another of the "Songs of Ascents." This is the fourth in a series of 15 psalms composed for pilgrims traveling to the Holy City of Jerusalem.

The pilgrims make their way up to Jerusalem, which is the goal of their pilgrimage. However, the writer of the 123$^{rd}$ psalm knows that their real objective is not Jerusalem, as important as the city is, or even the newly constructed Temple. No, the real reason for their journey is to worship and be in the presence of Jehovah God (the LORD) enthroned in heaven. To the LORD they lift their eyes in adoration. *(V.1)* Perhaps they experience a similar feeling of awe as Isaiah did when he went into the Temple. Isaiah said that when he saw (experienced) the LORD Almighty, he was overwhelmed with how unworthy and sinful he was. *(Isaiah 6:5)*

The writer of Psalm 123 sings that the eyes of all the pilgrims (that is all of us) should be on God. He is the Creator. It is His laws and commandments that guide us and direct our paths in our journeys here on earth. The Psalmist is overwhelmed with how much mercy he and the rest of us need from such an exalted LORD. *(V.2)* The author makes an analogy of an obedient servant keeping his eye on his master and a female servant watching her mistress so she can serve her. These are the Psalmist's examples of how we need to depend on God and be obedient and submissive to His will. *(V.2)*

Every loyal Covenant Jew knew the Torah. How Moses went up on the mountain and received the Ten Commandments from Jehovah and how Jehovah came to him in the form of a pillar of cloud and said He is merciful, slow to anger and rich in "unfailing love" *("Checed")*. *(Exodus 34:6-7)* Then this gracious and loving God tells Moses He has chosen the Hebrews to be His people. I am making a contract - a Covenant – with your people and I will be Your faithful Provider and will watch over you. For your part of the agreement, you and your people must obey my commandments, and you must not worship other gods. *(Exodus 34:10-27)*

All of these 15 Songs of Ascents were probably written some time after the Jews had returned from exile in Babylon and were able to reconstruct Jerusalem and rebuild the Temple (516 B.C.). The last two verses of Psalm 123 reflect the bitterness and hurt the pilgrims felt from being treated as inferiors by those who were proud and arrogant. *(V.4)* There was a great deal of anti-Semitic feeling aimed at the Jews following their defeat (even after they returned from exile). In the case of these pilgrims, they are expressing relief from the cruel effects of the contempt they experienced from living in an environment where they were maligned and treated as second class citizens. The writer cries out that because of the comtempt the exiles have endured, their hearts need to be filled with the LORD's mercy. *(V.3)*

Mercy is one of three words in the Bible, along with love and goodness, that best describes God's character. When we pray for God's mercy, like the Psalmist does in this psalm, we are asking God to do what He is able to do for us in Jesus Christ – to bestow on us His favor and grace even when we don't deserve it. He forgives our sins when we repent. His mercy is not a reward for our goodness. When He bestows His love and mercy on us, we want in gratitude to return that love by being obedient and doing what we can to help others. The Apostle Paul in his letter to the Hebrews, probably those living in Rome at the time, says that by keeping our eyes on Jesus we too can emulate the mercy God has for us on others. *(Hebrews 12:2)*

# PSALM 124
## Praising God for His Protections

This is the fifth in the continuing series of 15 "Songs of Ascents." It bears also the title of David, which means it could be in honor of Israel's greatest king, or he could have actually written it. Because we don't get any background information in these "Songs of Ascents," we don't know where these pilgrims came from or the circumstances that led them to come to Jerusalem. These songs were sung by Jewish pilgrims coming to Jerusalem, after the second Temple was constructed, for one of the three annual festivals (Pentecost, Passover and the Day of Atonement).

The psalm begins abruptly with the pilgrims singing: let all Israel rejoice that, without the LORD on our side *(V.1)* when people rose up against us *(V.2)*, we would have been swallowed up by their anger. *(V.3)* Their fury would have taken our lives *(V.4)*, and like raging waters they would have overwhelmed us. *(V.5)*

Making their way through the gate still singing, they are met by an official who welcomes them and might have asked the question, "What was that song you folks were singing?" The leader of the caravan replies, "It goes back days of Saul. He was fighting a battle against the Philistines at Mount Gilboa and was overwhelmed. King Saul's three sons were killed, and Saul himself was badly wounded. He ended up taking his own life. (See I Samuel 31:1-7.) Then the Philistines set out to capture the new king David. The two armies met at the valley of Repaim with David being victorious. (2 Samuel 5:17-20) It was a precarious time. The Philistines threatened to swallow up the young Jewish state, and our song is about praising God for His protection! We serve a wonderful God!"

In verses 6 and 7, the Psalmist exhorts the pilgrms to bless the LORD because their enemies would have torn the Jews apart with their teeth *(V.6)* and trapped them like small birds. *(V.7)* The writer concludes his small psalm by reminding all the pilgrims (and us) that our help comes from the LORD who created heaven and earth. *(V.8)*

We Christians share the Old Testament stories with our Jewish brothers and sisters. Like Psalm 124, we too agree that God is the Creator of the heavens and earth. We also claim Abraham as our spiritual ancestor. The Apostle Paul in his letter to the Romans puts forth a marvelous insight about how we are spiritually connected to Abraham. God promised Abraham that he would become the father of many nations saying his descendants would be like the stars in the heavens. *(Genesis 15:5)* Because of Abraham's faith, God declared him to be righteous. In similar fashion, we Christians believe that Jesus, a descendant of King David, was sent by God to die for our sins and to be our Savior. Paul says that God did not just declare Abraham righteous for Abraham's benefit but for us Christians as well. The same faith that saved Abraham now saves us through out belief in Jesus Christ. *(Romans 4:23-24)*

# PSALM 125
## God Surrounds and Protects His People

This is the sixth in a current series 15 psalms entitled "Songs of Ascents." Psalm 125 is a short celebration of Israel's security.

When the pilgrims arrived at Jerusalem for a Festival, Psalms 125 and 126 (companion pieces) were part of the Temple liturgy. When they heard this sung, they were reminded that those who put their trust in Jehovah would have a solid faith that is as secure as Mount Zion. *(V.1)* Their faith could be compared with the mountain upon which Jerusalem is built. It is bedrock and surrounded by other mountains. *(V.2)* God can be likened to these other mountains as He envelops His people in His loving arms. They would be reminded that the great King David used these metaphors frequently in the psalms he wrote. For instance, in Psalm 18, David says that the LORD is not only his savior but his rock and fortress. *(Psalm 18:2)*

It seems that throughout much of Israel's history, following their return from exile in Babylon, they witnessed oppressive foreign rulers. However, Psalm 125 says that God would not allow the wicked to influence the righteous. *(V.3)* After a priest gives voice to verses 1-3, the worshiping community would lift their voices in prayer for God's blessing on themselves asking the LORD to do good to those whose hearts are good. *(V.4)* Then a warning would be issued. For those who oppose God and pursue evil they need to be banished so Israel can have peace. *(V.5)*

The Apostle Paul knew the psalms, as he was trained as a Rabbi in the Jewish faith. Then he met Jesus and became a flaming Apostle to the Gentiles. He wrote many letters that were incorporated into the New Testament. The Galatian letter is one of his best. In it he writes that we should not get tired doing good because we reap what we sow. We need to live to please the Spirit that lives within us and then we will reap God's blessings at His approprate time. *(Galatians 6:7-10)* The Psalmist concludes with a benediction very similar to Psalm 125 asking that God give us His mercy and His peace. *(Galatians 6:16)*

# PSALM 126
## The LORD Has Done Amazing Things

This is the seventh in a series of 15 poems that are known as "Songs of Ascents" concerning pilgrims traveling to Jerusalem. Obviously, Psalm 126 was written in response to the return of the Jewish exiles from Babylon, which began in the year 638 BC. God had led His people, because of their many sins, to repent by putting them through a period of painful slavery of two generations in exile. King Cyrus of Persia conquered Babylon and allowed a remnant of the Jews to return home. It took many years for the defeated people to rebuild their city's walls, homes and Temple. Now after many years, Israel's spiritual leaders were determined not to allow their nation to make the same mistakes twice, so they re-initiated the annual festivals and urged all the towns and cities outside of Jerusalem to send their people to attend these worship opportunities. They wanted to keep the faith of their nation strong!

### Segment One – Back from the Nightmare of Exile. Verses 1 - 3

Psalm 126 is like a primer to remind the young and old pilgrims how great it is not to be in exile. It is like they are living a dream now. *(V.1)* They can imagine neighboring nations saying what a amazing thing was done for His people by the LORD. *(V.2)* And all the pilgrims would respond with a shout "What joy!" *(V.3)*

### Segment Two – Tears Changed to Singing and Joy. Verses 4 - 6

It still wasn't easy. There were neighbors who weren't in sympathy, and they did what they could to disrupt the rebuilding process. When the returnees tried to farm, the weather didn't always cooperate. No, there were droughts (see Ezra and Nehemiah). But they persevered. They weren't out of the woods yet. They prayed to the LORD to renew the desert with streams and restore their fortunes. *(V.4)* We still have tears, but our faith is in You, God. The Hebrew word for "restore" is *("Shuwb")* and it can mean "refreshed" or a "spiritual return to the LORD."

Perhaps when the caravan traveled to Jerusalem, they had to cross the barren desert called Negev and saw gullies that at one time were streams. They knew when it rained, which in the desert was infrequent, water would fill those dry wadis with pure life- giving and refreshing water. With this analogy, the Psalmist is telling the world what God can do. He brought His Covenant people out of slavery in Egypt; brought them back from exile in Babylon; and would refresh them again! Yes, the author says, we cried over those dry times and we've had our setbacks when we didn't know whether our crops could be harvested – but they matured! We had to work hard, but we trusted Yahweh God (the LORD) because He is the God of hope and we harvest in joy. *(V.5-6)*

As we Christians read this psalm (and others), we can identify with many of the characters and their dramas. We can learn from them because we all have in common the fact that we are fallible human beings who must live and work in a fallen world. Like the men and women we meet in the psalms, we have our own times of disappointments. We stumble. Sometimes we even fall. God knows this and that is why He sent us the Savior, Jesus our greatest blessing.

Two closing quotes from the Apostle Paul, both from Corinthians. He is telling us about his friend, Apollos, and how both he and Apollos have special abilities. He says that the Corintihians are God's fields. Paul's role is to plant seeds and Apollos' role is to water the seeds. But it is God who makes the seeds to grow. *(1 Corinthians 3:6-9)* Paul then goes on saying that brothers and sisters in the Lord need to be enthusiastic about doing the Lord's work, for nothing done in the name of the Lord is ever useless. *(1 Corinthians 15:58)*

# PSALM 127
## Depending on the LORD!

Psalm 127 is another of the "Songs of Ascents" (the eighth of 15 psalms). The heading says of Solomon. Whoever put this superscription probably did so in the spirit of Solomon. David's son, Solomon, lived around 950 BC and this psalm was written after the returnees from exile rebuilt the city and the second Temple (516 BC), so obviously someone other than Solomon wrote it. Another probable reason for linking this psalm and Solomon is because of the wisdom style of Psalm 127.

### Segment One – We Must Put God First in Our life. Verses 1 - 2

The author originally tried to give the pilgrims who read this psalm some wise advice. Segment One begins by saying it doesn't do a builder any credit to build a house unless he has the LORD's purpose in mind. *(V.1)* A builder wants to do the best job he can, and his laboring should reflect a worthwhile contribution to the common good. His work should honor the LORD. This same idea can be applied to every other kind of worker. The writer uses the illustration of watchmen (sentries) on the wall. *(V.1)* If the Covenant population of the city, where the sentry is working, turn their backs on God like they did prior to the Babylonian captivity, then the sentry's job will become meaningless because God will have withdrawn His protective support from His people. In verse 1, the writer says unless the LORD protects Jerusalem the watchmen's protection will do no good. Hebrew for "will do no good" is *("Chav")* and it also can mean "useless" or "in vain." Workers (be they builders or sentries) will be working in vain unless they put God in the equation. They need to trust in God's *("Checed")*, His "unfailing Covenant love" and mercy. And they need to take each day as it comes, putting their faith in God, knowing that God will take care of them. Sure, builders and other workers need to work hard during the day, doing their best. When the day is over, they should not worry and go to their rest for God gives a good night's sleep for those He loves. *(V.2)* Sleep is God's gift.

## Segment Two – The Joy of Family and Having Children. Verses 3 - 5

In this section, the Psalmist is saying that a fruitful family is also a gift from the LORD, a reward. *(V.3)* The Hebrew word for "reward" is *("Nachalah")* and it also can be translated as "an inheritance," or "heritage." Children are our portion from the LORD, His gift. They are like arrows for a warrior. *(V.4)* Happy or blessed is the man (and woman) whose quiver is full of sons and daughters. *(V.5)* Many children in an agricultural society provided needful help on the farm and, in time of war, supplied soldiers for needful defense against enemies.

The creation of a happy home is God's will, where peace *("Shalom")* is present. A man of peace who could live and work in harmony with God's Covenant was rewarded with a large and happy family. The author mentions the justices of the peace whose offices were at the city gate hearing disputes on a daily basis. Our God-fearing family man will never be brought before a justice of the peace *(V.5)* for he knows the true meaning of love and peace.

# PSALM 128
## The LORD Blesses the Family

This psalm is the ninth in a series of 15 compositions known as "Song of Ascents." These are songs written for pilgrims to sing as they traveled to Jerusalem to attend the annual festivals. Many of them were also sung as part of the worship in the Temple. Psalm 127 and 128 are similar; both are so-called "wisdom psalms." Psalm 127 says all blessings come from God alone; whereas, in Psalm 128 it says we human beings have to take responsibility for the things <u>under God</u>. We will be blessed if we reverence God and obey Him! Back then, obedience meant being loyal to the Covenant.

Right at the outset the Psalmist says how happy or blessed are those who follow the ways of the LORD and are fearful of Him. *(V.1)* This language is similar to other "wisdom literature," such as Psalm 119, Proverbs, Ecclesiastes, and the Beatitudes of Jesus. The essence of this psalm is found in the words "those who walk in God's ways." The Hebrew word to "walk in God's ways"" is *("Derek")* and it means "a way of life." As a family man, the father must be responsible for others in the family, including his wife and children. He must also find satisfaction in his vocation. (Notice how the author changes "those" in verse one to "you" in verse two – making it more personal.) You, he says, will enjoy the results of your labor. *(V.2)* Part of the happiness promised by God are contented children. They are as healthy as young olive trees. *(V.3)* Certainly a happy family is a reward, a family where God is at the center. *(V.4)*

This is a beautiful idealistic picture of domestic joy. From a Christian perspective, however, we have to say that families are made up of people, and because all of us are sinners, sin can and does disrupt even the best of family relationships. Psalm 128 gives us excellent general guidelines. Its words are similar to Proverbs 22:6 which exhorts people to teach children when they are young to do what is right and when they are older they will also do what is right. Righteous parent training will produce righteous children.

The last two verses of this song are probably spoken (or sung) as a benediction by a priest for a family that goes to Temple. The priest asks that the LORD not only bless them that day in Jerusalem (V.5), but that the LORD bless them that they may enjoy their grandchildren in a future peaceful day in Jersusalem . (V.6) This sounds like the Aaronic blessing found in Numbers 7:24-25. It was given to all of the people of Israel. It means that a man's primary responsibility is to his family – but the family is not an end in and of itself. All of God's covenant people have responsibilities toward those around them, in neighborhoods and in the wider environment of the city. The last verses are a reminder that it is wonderful to be personally blessed by God, but those blessings would be incomplete if it didn't include the neighbors and those outside the city.

# PSALM 129

## Persecuted but not Destroyed

Another "Song of Ascents," the tenth in a series of 15. It can be classified as an imprecatory lament. This psalm is similar in content to Psalm 124 but also closely matches with Psalm 130 in length and the number of syllables. This is a prayer-song for the defeat of Israel's enemies. Written in first-person, it is the personification of the nation Israel. The people on the pilgrimage to Jerusalem are called to remember the suffering their nation has undergone. Someone may have read from the first chapter of the prophet Isaiah. It says Israel was sick from head to foot and if the LORD Almighty had not spared some of its people, Israel would have been totally wiped out. *(Isaiah 1:6-9)*

### Segment One – Remember the Perils of Our Nation. Verses 1 - 4

The author speaks now for all the people on the pilgrimage, lamenting the fact that he had been persecuted from his earliest youth. *(V.1)* It's so important what he's saying that he repeats himself. Speaking for the nation, he tells the travelers because of the LORD his enemies did not finish him off. *(V.2)* Look at my back. Like our nation, it is as if a farmer had plowed deep furrows into it. *(V.3)* We've been persecuted by the Egyptians, the Canaanites, the Babylonians and others, but the important truth is that our enemies have never been able to destroy us! The LORD has cut the cords that binded us. *(V.4)* In the New Testament, the Apostle Paul suffered a similar fate in his missionary journeys for the Lord. Writing to the Corinthians, he says he endured troubles on every side and was hunted down. God alone saved him. *(2 Corinthians 4:8-9)*

## Segment Two – Asking God to Keep Our Land Peaceful. Verses 5 - 8

The second part of this "Song of Ascents" fast-forwards to the time of the Second Temple when the Jewish community was struggling to maintain its identity and existence. The writer was obviously a leader in one of the pilgrim groups ascending up to Jerusalem to attend one of the annual festivals. He and his group of pilgrims are thankful to be free to make this arduous journey, but praying that God will defeat their enemies. *(V.5)*

As the author says in the first half of the psalm hatred of the Jews has been around for a long time. He uses an analogy from agriculture. He asks God to make the enemies of the Jews like the grass that grows in the shallow soil on the rooftops that soon sprouts, but, because of the lack of soil and water, it becomes dry and withers. *(V.6)* No reaper wants that kind of withered up grass, nor are the binders interested. *(V.7)* This is similar to Jesus' parable in Matthew 13:4-9 concerning seeds of truth when planted in shallow soil soon die off.

Because so many of the surrounding nations hated the Jews, especially now in her new-born status, there were no friendly greetings to the Jews as they passed by. But now as they walk up together to the city of Jerusalem, they can look forward to being greeted by the friendly welcoming committee as they enter the gates, hearing the LORD's blessings on them. *(V.8)*

# PSALM 130
## Counting on the LORD

This psalm is the eleventh in a series of 15 psalms called "Songs for the Ascents" to Jerusalem. It is a testimony of the writer's trust in the LORD. It is also what is called "A Penitential Psalm," which comes from the word "Penitent." This means one is sorry for one's sins, and is attempting to change or turn from wrongdoing. It is from this word that we get the term "penitentiary," where offenders of the law are imprisoned. When Martin Luther was asked which psalms were his favorites, he answered, "The Pauline ones." When asked to be more specific, he replied, "the four penitential ones – Psalms 30, 32, 51 and 143.

### Segment One – In Despair, I Ask for Forgiveness. Verses 1 - 4

The Psalmist calls for the LORD's help because he is in great despair. *(V.1)* It is interesting to note that the geographical climb up to Jerusalem that the author and his fellow pilgrims must make will surely help him in his spiritual approach to God. We don't know what his transgression was, but whatever it was has caused him to have a guilty conscience, and his guilt has alienated him with God. Impatiently he cries out that the LORD should pay attention to his prayer. *(V.2)* He rightly says that if the Lord kept a record of eveyone's sins no one would survive. *(V.3)* This is no superficial cry to God. His only hope for rescue can only come from God's forgiveness. *(V.4)*

### Segment Two – My Hope Is in the LORD. Verses 5 - 6

Still desperate, our author says his only hope is in the LORD's word. *(V.5)* It is apparent that the Psalmist has a heart-felt longing to be reconciled to his LORD. *(V.6)* As we Christians read this, we all would say, oh yes, we can identify with the writer. We've all been in the pit of despair at times. But we have the divine resources that the Psalmist didn't have – the Lord Jesus! God sent His only Son who comes to us by His living Spirit and He can go into the pit of despair of our own making and by God's grace and mercy, He can bring us up to a newness of life!

## Segment Three – Israel's Hope Is in the LORD's Unfailing Love. Verses 7 - 8

In placing his hope in God's Word, the Psalmist searches the Old Testament and turns to the profound words in Psalm 103. He reads that the LORD forgives all of or sins and ransoms us from death. *(Psalm 103:1-4)* Bolstered by these wonderful words of Scripture, he joins his fellow pilgrims as they go into the Temple for worship and he is able to experience renewal, a release from his guilt. He feels like a new person. In gratitude for becoming a whole new person, because of his feelings of being forgiven, he shouts out to anyone who will listen that the LORD alone is the hope of Israel. *(V.7)* People of the Covenant, he calls out, hear my testimony God alone will free Israel from each and every sin. *(V.8)*

Psalm 130 tells a marvelous truth. God's power and His presence can be with us in every human experience, yes, even when we are in great despair. We who call ourselves Christians know what Jesus went through when He hung on the cross to die for the redeeming of our sins and to provide an entrance into eternal life. Reading this psalm helps us realize that there is no place or circumstance that is beyond the reach of the Savior's love and redeeming power and presence. Whether or when God chooses to bring Israel to Christ is problematical. (See Paul's chapters 9 and 11 in Romans.) He will do it in His own good time.

# PSALM 131

## Quiet before the LORD

In this little gem of a psalm, the writer offers his personal testimony telling us how he has quieted himself. The inplication is that he is now ready to listen to the LORD. This composition has been classified as a "Song of Ascents" (the 12ᵗʰ of 15) and, because there is an honest humility about it, some later editor thought it sounded like what King David would write so he added the title that it was written by David.

In every society since time began there is a system of competition for sports. Those who excel and become leaders can't help but feel a little superior over those beneath them. The person who wrote this prayerful song confesses to God that he is not proud or haughty. *(V.1)* He is revealing to the LORD the "true feelings" of his inner self. The Hebrew word here is *("Leb")* and it can be translated as "coming from his deepest and innermost feelings."

Remember toward the beginning of Jesus' ministry how his disciples misunderstood the Master, thinking He was soon going to set up His earthly Kingdom they wondered if they would have an important position in it. So they asked Him who would be greatest in the Kingdom? Jesus called a small child over to Him and put the child among them, saying unless they turn from their sins and approach the Kingdom of Heaven like a little child they would never enter there. *(Matthew 18:3)*

Clearly the writer has had his share of struggles and disappointments, but he says that like a little child with his mother he has quieted himself. *(V.2)* I have put my trust completely in God's unfailing love and mercy, and as a result, like a child at my mother's breasts, I have found peace and security.

Finally, our Psalmist feels so content that he adds another verse aimed at God's Covenant people, to be sung in the Temple, that Israel's hope is in the LORD alone. *(V.3)* "Hope" is the Hebrew word *("Yachal"),* which means being "patient" and "having expectations that God will take care of things."

This is an inspirational psalm and we Christians can identify with it. We too put our hope in God's Son, Jesus. And when we bring Christ's Spirit into our hearts, His mighty power not only helps us to live triumphantly in our day-to-day struggles, but knowing we are in Christ gives us the absolute assurance (He is our Living hope) that we will share in His glory! Paul's words in Colossians tell us that because Christ lives in us we will share in His riches and glory. *(Colossians 1:27)*

# PSALM 132

## A Home for the Ark of God

Psalm 132 is the 13th in a series of 15 entitled "Songs of Ascents." It is also known as a "Royal Psalm." The emphasis upon the Davidic Covenant and the Ark of the Covenant dates it in the pre-exilic period. The first half of the psalm (verses 1-9) is about David's oath to bring the Ark to Jerusalem; the second half (verses 11-18) is about God's corresponding oath regarding David's dynasty. Verse 10 tells us that David did not author the psalm – it is an appeal to God in David's name – by another king who looks back to David and claims David's promise.

### Segment One – Prayer for the Davidic King. Verses 1 - 5

The author, speaking for King David, asks the pilgrim travelers to remember when he took his oath as king before the LORD. *(V.1-2)* He said he wouldn't go home or let himself rest until he built a sanctuary for Israel's Mighty One, the LORD. *(V.3-5)* Maybe at one of the stopping places in the pilgrims' journey to the Holy City, someone would read to the travelers the background information found in First Chronicles 16 and Second Samuel 6. This would refresh their memories about how David brought the Ark of the Covenant to Jerusalem and how he danced before the LORD and celebrated this wonderful event! So great was David's desire to construct a fitting home for God's Ark that he made a solemn promise vowing that he personally would see to it that a Temple would be constructed.

413

## Segment Two – Transfer of the Ark, Re-enacted. Verses 6 - 10

It has been suggested that when the procession of worshipers were just outside the city, a choir representing David and the priests and musicians would sing the hymn. David gets word of the Ark when he is in Ephrathah, and later found it out in the fields of Jaar. *(V.6)* (See 2 Samuel 6.) The choir beckons to the travelers to go up to the Temple. *(V.7)* As the pilgrams are about to enter the Temple, the Psalmist now recalls back when the Arc first came into the Temple. *(V.8)* The pilgrims meet the priests who sing for joy in their praise of the LORD and in acknowledgement of the prilgrms. *(V.9)* This is reminiscent of when the Israelites left Mt. Sinai with the Ark in the front of the column to choose a place for them to stop. *(Exodus 40:36-38)* When the procession of happy travlelers enter the inner court of the Temple, a person representing King David, prays for divine favor saying for David's sake do not reject the king chosen for your people. *(V.10)*

## Segment Three – God's Vow to David and His Choice of Zion. Verses 11 - 18

The third part of this psalm tells how God made an oath to David. Again speaking for God, the author says one of David's descendants will be on the throne forever. *(V.11)* But then God is quick to qualify that this royal line would never end if the descandants obeyed the terms of God's covenant. *(V.12)*

God's oath to David was that his descendants would always occupy the throne provided they would be faithful to His covenant and His commandments. As we all know, the earthly throne did not go on forever. It obviously ended with the Babylonian exile. (2 Samuel 7:4-17)

We Christians look to Jesus, who was of the lineage of David, as the successor to the throne. Zacharias, husband of Elizabeth, filled with the Holy Spirit, gave the prophecy that a mighty Savior from the line of David was about to be born and that Zacharias's son, John the Baptist, would prepare the way for the Lord. *(Luke 1:68-79)* We Christians believe that Jesus is the fulfillment of Zacharias' prophecy. *(John 1:14)* And the Book of Revelation in the New Testament declares the the entire world has become Jesus's kingdom forever. *(Revelation 11:15)*

The Old Testament gives the account of how God chose His special Covenant people and told them He would be their God and would watch over them. The Ark was, of course, the symbol of God's dwelling place, and that is why David wanted to bring the Ark to Jerusalem. When he did so, Jerusalem became not only the political center of the Jews, but became the religious center for all Judaism. This is why the 15 psalms—Psalms 120-134–are called "The Songs of Ascents. These psalms were grouped together and given to those travelers to sing and study on their way up to Jerusalem. The Jews believed God was omnipotent, omnipresent, and omniscient, and realized this when they read psalms like 139, which says that none of us can escape from the Spirit of God. *(Psalm 139:7-10)*

But, for the Jews, God was also personal, and they believed, because of the Covenant relationship He had chosen Jerusalem for His special home. *(V.13)* They also believed that Jerusalem would be the home of his chosen people forever, keep its inhabitants prosperous, its priests agents for salvation and increase the power of its kings. *(V.14-18)*

# PSALM 133
## True Unity Is a Foretaste of Heaven

This is the fourteenth of a series of fifteen psalms known as "Songs of Ascents." It is titled of David. He well could have written this beautiful poem about unity. It has been suggested that after the divisive reign of Saul, David's crowning by all twelve tribes of Israel in Hebron would have been the inspiration for the writing of this little gem.

The Pilgrims who journeyed to Jerusalem to attend the annual festivals came from all over, some from great distances. They came from all walks of life and with all sorts of differing backgrounds. We can just picture them as they walked along and then someone in their midst would recite or sing this psalm as an inspirational reminder of what it is that brings them together. Perhaps they would sing this in combination with Psalms 127 and 128, which deal with the harmony of the family. It is the pilgrims' mutual awareness that they have been chosen by God; He has put them together and bound them in one family by His covenant love. *(V.1)*

Living in harmony occurs when members of the Covenant fellowship exhibit a positive intent, care, and concern for each other. This oneness can be symbolized by the annointing oil flowing down Aaron's head. *(V.2)* This reference goes back to the time of Moses when God set aside Aaron and his sons as priests to minister to the Covenant people. (See Exodus 30.) The annointing oil poured over them sanctified them so that they could minister to others. The symbolism of the pouring and the running of the oil over Aaron's head, down his beard and unto the border of his robe has to do with God's blessings coming down onto His people! Of course, the underlying message of this small gem of a psalm is that unity and harmony are precious gifts from God.

This beautiful poem speaks to us Christians. We acknowledge we are sinners, and we know that it is sin that separates us from God and others. Our sinful, selfish behavior causes disharmony and pits us against our neighbors. Only God through Jesus Christ can remedy this problem by forgiving sins and giving us a whole new orientation. The Apostle Paul in writing to the Corinthians says that when we become a Christian, we are a brand new person inside, we are born again. God does this for us, we do not it. God does this through His son Jesus Christ who restores us to Himself and the Father through His sacrifice on the cross. *(2 Corinthians 5:17-20)*.

In this marvelous little poem, we are asked to visualize the divine blessings on the Covenant fellowship and, in our case as Christians, the present-day Church. Several things can be derived from Psalm 133: A) The spirit of unity is not cheap. It comes at a high price of commitment and dedication; B) Like the oil being poured down on Aaron's beard and the dew coming down on Mount Hermon, we can receive God's refreshing grace giving us new life; C) It is God's *("Checed")*, His mercy and "loving kindness," that motivates us to put the needs of others first and humbly love and care for the brothers and sisters in the fellowship; and D) The resultant harmony that is God-created, is a foretaste of heaven. The Psalmist closes the psalm by having God pronounce His blessings on the Covenant fellowship in Jerusalem and forever. *(V.3)*

# PSALM 134
## Praise the LORD through the Night

This small psalm concludes the 15 "Songs of Ascents." It was composed by an unknown psalmist for the Second Temple liturgy, as the concluding benediction for the festivities in the pilgrims' departure for their journey homeward.

The essence of this short psalm is a hymn in verses 1 and 2 where pilgrim congregations speak these words to the priests who are charged with responsibility of ministering throughout the night. These priests are compared with watchmen and they are greeted as servants of the LORD. As the pilgrims leave the LORD's House and return to their villages, they charge th priests to lift up their hands in holiness *(V.2)* and continue to pray and praise the LORD. Then the Levites (the priests) respond, assuring the worshipers that everything humanly possible will be attended to in the Temple, day and night. They send them off with a benediction that the LORD, creator of heaven and earth, continue to bless them even while they are away from Jerusalem. *(V.3)*

The pilgrims who have made their way to Jerusalem to worship at the festival are now returning to the villages from which they came, singing this psalm. This may be the only time in their life they will ever worship in the God's House. As they leave the city, they are gratified to know that the Temple priests will be on the job day and night representing them. It is encouraging to them to know there is a continuous offering to God of prayers and praise.

# PSALM 135

## The Worship of the Covenant God

The author begins Psalm 135 with multiple praises to the Mighty God of Israel, an apt way to initiate the liturgy he was writing for worship in the Second Temple. Psalms 135 through 150 are generally consider "Praise Psalms."

### Segment One – The LORD Is Great and Good. Verses 1 - 4

This is a celebration hymn. Its purpose is to give thanks and glory to the LORD and to have His faithful people glory and rejoice in His wisdom, His judgment, and God's love for them. (V.1-2) The Psalmist then says the LORD is good. (V.3) After all, the word "God," is a shortened form of the word "good."

In verse 4, it refers to Old Testament scripture that says the LORD chose Jacob and the nation Israel as God's special treasure. This is first mentioned in Genesis 32 where God meets Jacob when he is being pursued by his twin brother Esau. Jacob wrestles with God and God changes him physically and spiritually and gives Jacob the new name Israel. Jacob, being chosen, becomes one of the Patriarchs, one of God's special treasures.

Later at the base of Mount Sinai, Moses goes up to meet with God. In Exodus 19, the LORD says to Moses if the Hebrew people keep their covenant with Him, He will consider them His special treasure, a kingdom of priests and a holy nation. (Exodus 19:4-6)

God, in His vast wisdom and goodness, has chosen Israel. It is like the story of an ancient king who owned everything. He looked out over his vast land and saw all the buildings, the street, and the land. But they didn't give him real satisfaction. What did turn him on was up in his room in the palace. There was a jewel box and in it were his most prized possessions – his jewels. He would go there and open the box and run his fingers through those precious jewels. The Hebrew word for "special treasure" in verse 4 is *("C'gullah")*. Going back to Exodus 19, God used the same Hebrew word *(C'gullah)*. *(Exodus 19:5)* God's precious jewels are His covenant people.

## Segment Two – The LORD of History. Verses 5 - 12

In this segment, the Psalmist describes who the LORD is and what He has done for Israel. He is greater than any other god. *(V.5)* (See Exodus 28:11.) He created and controls all of nature. *(V.6)* The author says that the Mighty Ruler works out His loving purpose for our world because that is what pleases Him. *(V.6)* In verse 7, the Psalmist quotes almost verbatim from Jeremiah 10:13. The Psalmist now turns from nature to history. *(V.8)*

In verse 8-11 he tells how God brought the Hebrew people out of bondage in Egypt and led them into Canaan, mentioning two victories over the Amorites and Bashans. (See Numbers 21:21-35 and Deuteronomy 2:24-3:11.) The writer celebrates these victories and implies others by saying God gave Israel the land of the Canaans as an inheritance, Israel's special possession. *(V.12)*

God's purpose in choosing the Jews was to save mankind. The Apostle Paul in his letter to the Romans says that God knew His people in advance and chose them to become like His son Jesus. *(Romans 8: 28-30)*

## Segment Three – A Choral Interlude. Verses 13 - 14

As noted in the beginning of our comments on Psalm 135, this psalm was probably written as part of the Temple liturgy, and verses 13 aand 14 were sung by the chorus, adopted from Moses' Song in Deuteronomy 32:36. The Psalmist joyfully claims that the LORD's name will endure forever. *(V.13)* And He will have compassion for his servants. *(V.14)* An important Hebrew word in verse 14 is "servant." In Hebrew it is *("Ebed")* and it means "one who serves Jehovah." Initially, the Jews were to evangelize the world. They were to become God's ambassadors, evangelizing not by force of arms but by service and love. The Prophet Isaiah, in his chapters 54-66, speaks of the Suffering Servant, which applies to Israel; however, Christians have taken this term and seen it as applying to Christ's suffering on the cross for the salvation of the world.

## Segment Four – The Scorn of Idol Worship. Verses 15 - 21

In verses 15-18, the Psalmist is making fun of gods made by humans (idols), and he obviously borrowed word-for-word from Psalm 115:4-6, 8. These idols cannot talk, see, hear, or smell. *(V.17)* The problem of these gods is that they are lifeless and quite impotent. The Prophet Isaiah in chapter 44 is another place where the Psalmist could be quoting. The Psalmist's concluding scathing remarks on idols are that the gods they created are just as foolish as them. *(V.18)*

Psalm 135 closes with words of encouragement to the congregation, to the priests of Israel and Zion. *(V.19-21)* The Psalmist then gives one final instruction to the God-fearers (the converts) – our Yahweh God will hear our praises in Zion, for this is where the LORD lives. *(V.21)* Then as the psalm began, it ends with a lusty praise to the LORD.

# PSALM 136
## God's Loving Kindness Continues Forever

This is a liturgical psalm (a hymn) of thanksgiving to God. It traditionally has been known as The Great Hallel. (It should not be confused with the psalms known as The Egyptian Hallel - Psalms 113-118.) Psalm 136 could be used at any one of the annual festivals. It is also one of the Praise Psalms (Psalms 135-150). The first verse's wording bears a similarity to the following: Psalm 106:1; Psalm 107:1 118:1-4; First Chronicles 16:34:2; Second Chronicles 20:21; and Ezra 3:11. After every one of the 26 verses in Psalm 136 there is a refrain: the faithful love of God is forever. Usually a priest would speak or sing a verse and then the congregation would respond with the chorus (refrain).

### Segment One – Giving Thanks to God. Verses 1 - 3

Psalm 136 is a litany composed for public worship and as such has many quotes from other places in the Old Testament. It really is a dialogue among the Covenant people in the Temple, a call to worship. The first three verses say in turn: (1) God is good; (2) God is the God of gods; and (3) God is the Lord of lords. The refrain, that God's faithful love endures forever, follows after each verse. "Faithful love" is the Hebrew word *("Checed")*, which tells of God's Covenant love for His people. His love also is unending, forever enduring.

### Segment Two – Reasons to Praise God. Verses 4 - 25

In this segment, the Psalmist makes statements about God's attributes and His deeds followed by the refrain that God's faithful love endures forever.

For example, God alone does miracles. *(V.4)* And God made the heavens *(V.5)*, He killed the Egyptians' first born *(V.10)*, He gave Israel the land of wicked kings *(V.21)*, and He provides food for every living being. *(V.25)*

Verses 4-9 = The Psalmist praises God for His miracles of creation. (See Genesis 1:1, 14-18.)

Verses 10-15 = In this section the congregation is asked to give thanks for their liberation from Egypt, the opening of the Red Sea and that God led them safely through it. (See Exodus 12-14.)

Verse 16 = The wilderness wandering. (See Deuteronomy 8:15.)

Verses 17-22 = The conquest of Canaan, and the killing of famous kings. (See Psalm 135:10-12; Numbers 21:21-26, 33-35.)

Verses 23-24 = This may have been a reference to the Babylonian Captivity and their release. (See Judges 3-8; and Nehemiah 9:26-28.)

Verse 25 = Because God is good, He cares not only for Israel, but for all His creatures, including birds and animals.

## Segment Three – Final Call for Giving Thanks. Verse 26

With the congregation singing the refrain that God's faithful love endures forever, the liturgy comes to an end. The Psalmist is telling the world through this composition that no matter what difficulties the Covenant people have to undergo, God's unfailing covenant love will not let go of them or give up on them!

Psalm 135 and 136 are both powerful worship hymns. Both of them ask the worshipers to praise the LORD because He is good and because God has chosen them as God's own special treasure." *(Psalm 135:4)* In Psalm 136, the Covenant people are asked to praise God for what He has done for them in the past, and how He brought them out from slavery in Egypt, fought their battles for them, and gave them the land of Canaan as His personal gift. God does not go back on His promises. Part of His goodness involves being faithful. When He chose the Jews to work out His plan for the world's salvation, they were to become His servant people within the context of His contract with them (His Covenant). God would be faithful to them and would give them certain privileges and advantages. They - on the other hand - were to maintain certain standards of obedience, putting God first in their lives. Unfortunately, from the time of the Second Temple (when many of these psalms were written) until the days of the Roman occupation of

Judea, the religion of the Hebrew people diminished until it became merely a series of legalistic rituals that had very little to do with evangelizing the world – what God, through the Prophet Isaiah, had envisioned them to become. *(Isaiah 49:6)*

Because God is faithful and because His Covenant people were not, God went to Plan B and raised up a Jewish man who was from David's lineage. God chose this man named Jesus to be His Messiah, from Nazareth. God's plan was that Jesus would inspire and lead the Jews in bringing the Good News to the world. In Jesus' three years of public ministry, He worked many miracles of healing people and he chose and trained a small cadre of disciples. The common people followed Him gladly and claimed Him as their leader.

God's plan was working with the exception of one big problem: the Jewish hierarchy. They would not accept Jesus and wanted Him out of the way. Finally, at Passover, they had Him arrested and convicted on trumped up charges. They convinced the Roman authorities to kill Him by hanging Him on a cross – a slow and very painful death. So the mighty Sovereign God went to Plan C – He raised Jesus from death and took Him up to heaven with Him. He set Jesus' Spirit free from the limitations of time and space so He could come back to earth and indwell His followers. God's plan is working.

One of the hierarchy's hit men, a brash young Pharisee named Saul (from Tarsus), was busy intimidating Jesus' disciples and followers, doing his best to stop the movement from spreading. God took care of that, also. When Saul was on his way to Damascus to harass some of Jesus' followers, the Spirit of Christ came to Saul and confronted him. We can read about this miraculous encounter in The Acts of the Apostles, chapter 9. God, through Jesus, turned this talented Jew around to become a flaming apostle for the Christian cause. It was through Saul (now Paul) that the Good News spread to the Gentiles and became a world religion.

# PSALM 137
## Forced Exile in Babylon

Psalm 137 is a psalm written by a person who had just returned from Babylonian exile. It is filled with pathos and sadness. In fact, every line seems to be alive with pain and anguish! The author still has memories of sitting next to one of the rivers of Babylon and being asked by his tormentors to sing a happy song of Zion. It is difficult to understand why this particular psalm was placed in the midst of a grouping of "Praise Psalms" (Psalms 135-150) because praise wasn't possible under the circumstances.

### Segment One – The Situation in Exile. Verses 1 - 4

Homesick and heartsick, the Psalmist and his colleagues sit beside either the Tigris or Euphrates Rivers and weep thinking about what happened to Jerusalem. *(V.1)* They are in no mood to sing so they hang their lyres on a willow tree, too homesick and sad to play them. *(V.2)* The writer doesn't specifically tell us, but this incident may have taken place after they had labored in the field and were sitting exhausted. Then the labor supervisor walks in and demands that they entertain with happy songs of their homeland. *(V.3)* But the Psalmist says how can they sing songs to the LORD away from Jerusalem. *(V.4)*

### Segment Two – Personal Imprecation. Verses 5 - 6

The word "imprecation" means to cause something to happen to self or someone else that isn't good, like a curse. In the writer's case if he can't remember his home and the time when he used to praise God in the Temple, he asks that a curse be put on his right hand and his tongue! *(V.5-6)* The real miracle here is the fact that the Psalmist has kept alive his faith in the face of his anguish and suffering. He probably remembered psalms like the 23rd where David says that even when he walked through death's valley itself, David was not afraid. *(Psalm 23:4)* Or the 46th Psalm that says in time of trouble God is a refuge. *(Psalm 46:1-3)*

## Segment Three – Curses on Zion's Enemies. Verses 7 - 9

The writer couldn't have been present when the Edomites rejoiced over the destruction of Jerusalem, but he probably heard about it. The Edomites were descendants of Esau, the twin brother of Jacob, whom God had renamed Israel. There was great animosity between them because Jacob had taken his brother's birthright (see Genesis 27:41). The people of Edom were present when the armies of Babylon were destroying Jerusalem and its environs and they encouraged the destruction. So the author prays to Jehovah to not forget that the Edomites were joyful when Babylon captured Jerusalem. *(V.7)* Then he turns his fury on Babylon looking forward to the day when Babylon will be destroyed. *(V.8)* The Psalmist concludes this poem by expressing joy when women of Babylon will have their babies smashed against the rocks. *(V.9)* Maybe we can understand how the Psalmist felt when he wrote verse 9, but we cannot countenance it. General Sherman wrote, "War is hell!" That was during the Civil War, and we've had dozens of wars since then, even dropping the atom bomb not once but twice on our enemy, Japan. War is hell!

The moral code of the day called for total devastation of an enemy. The Babylonians' intended policy was to destroy Israel totally so they would never again become a military threat. Consequently, they leveled everything and anyone not killed was taken as slaves into captivity. The Prophet Elisha, in Second Kings, tells Hazael, king of Syria, that he knew that Syria one day would burn Israel's fortified cities and rip open the bellies of her pregnant women. *(2 Kings 8:12)* This didn't happen, but apparently this was the accepted practice in warfare of that day.

During the time when Israel was in captivity, Isaiah had a vision of the doom of the Babylonians. In chapter 12, Isaiah writes that eveyone who is captured will be put to the sword and their childlren will be dashed to death while they watched. *(Isaiah 12:14-16)* This vision never came to fruition (thank goodness), but again it was the going practice. Revenge got

426

out of hand, and there are biblical citations where if you killed a person, his relatives would seek revenge as much as seventy times seven! When Moses came along, he regulated revenge to an eye for an eye. (See Exodus 21:24.)

When Peter asked Jesus how many times he should forgive someone who had hurt him, Jesus went back to the ancient number of revenge and said Peter should forgive he person seventy times seven. *(Matthew 18:21-22)* When Jesus came triumphantly into Jerusalem, He wept over Jerusalem because He knew it would soon be destroyed (again)! Is there no answer to man's in humanity to man? The only answer we Christians have before us, as the Apostle Paul writes, is to be a living sacrifice to God and not copy the customs of this world. *(Romans 12:1-2)* Then he adds that vengeance is God's alone. We should never avenge ourselves. *(Romans 12:19-21).*

# PSALM 138
## A Prayer of Thankfulness

This is the first of what some editors of the Psalter call "A Collection of Eight Davidic Psalms." (Psalms 138-145) Some scholars question whether all of these were actually authored by King David, but there is no question that the language and content echo earlier songs composed by David. It is entirely possible that after the return of the exiles and the rebuilding of the Temple, some of the ancient manuscripts could have been discovered, and, therefore, we will accept David as the writer of Psalm 138. He gives thanks for God's promise that his kingdom would endure forever through the reign of future kings in the Davidic line (the Messiah!), as recorded in 2 Samuel 7. Psalm 139 is also included among the so-called Praise Psalms (Psalms 135-150).

We can examine this magnificent prayer by dividing it into three segments.

### Segment One – David's Personal Gratitude. Verses 1 - 3

In verse 1 of the *New Living Translation*, David thanks the LORD and praises Him before other gods. The Hebrew word for "gods" is *(" Elohiym") (a plural word)*. Verse 2 says David will bow down in the Temple, where the Ark of the Covenant was located. David had learned early that God's "Covenant love" *("Checed")* is always available. When we pray and call upon God, He gives us encouragement to make us bold and stouthearted in our approach to worshiping Him. *(V.3)*

428

## Segment Two – David's Missionary Vision. Verses 4 - 6

This second segment is obviously describing the coming days of Messianic blessings when the promised King will rule from David's throne forever. Back in 2 Samuel 7, the Prophet Nathan had foretold that God was establishing a Davidic dynasty that would be eternally secure. *(2 Samuel 7:16)* Therefore, David is looking forward to a day when all the rulers of earth will bow down before the Messiah, who is King of kings and Lord of lords. He is saying that all the kings of the earth will be thankful to hear words from the LORD. *(V.4)* So how do people get the message of the Good News? He is implying that God's Covenant people need to become missionaries. The Apostle Paul reminds Jewish Christians in Rome that unless they are missionaries to their Gentile neighbors how will their neighbors begin to believe in Jesus Christ as their Lord and Savior. *(Romans 10:14-15)*

Those of us on the victory side of the cross look to the words in Philippians Chapter Two where God gives Jesus a name above all other names, one that would command every knee to bow down on earth and heaven.

*(Philippians 2:9-11)*

David says these eathly kings shall sing praises to the LORD. *(V.5)* Yet, though God is very great, David says He still cares for the humble but distances Himself from the proud. *(V.6)* God has compassion on the lowly, the widow and orphan, but has disdain on those who think they are something when they are not.

## Segment Three – The LORD's Unfailing Love at Work. Verses 7 - 8

This last section is where David comes back to his own needs. He acknowledges that God is great and has compassion for the lowly and disdain for those who vainly want to step into the limelight. In typical Davidic fashion, he tells us trouble surrounds him, but he is confident that God will protect him from his enemies' anger. *(V.7)* In picturesque fashion he asks the LORD to clench His fist against his enemies. *(V.7)*

Verse 8 ends the psalm with David acknowledging that the LORD will work out His plans for David's life. It parallels Philippians 1:6 in the New Testament. The Apostle Paul says he is confident that God who began a good work in his life will continue to do so in the future. It is also similar to Romans 8:28,30 in which Paul reminds the Jewish Christians in Rome that

God causes everything to work together for a good purpose and for God's glory. *(Romans 8:28, 30)* What Paul is saying (reflecting David's words) is that God's purpose is to conform us to be like Jesus and then bring us to glory! We are all sinners who are saved by God's grace. As David says, our confidence is in God's Covenant Love, which tells us we can trust Him for all eternity!

David did not have Jesus and did not know Him (as we do), and so he ends his prayer-song pleading with God not to abandon him.

# PSALM 139

## The Wonderful All-Knowing God

This is a psalm where the author plumbs the depth of the meaning of the omnipotent God! The writer of this composition is a person who strongly feels he is intimately known in all aspects by an All-powerful, All encompassing, and an All knowing Spirit-God. This Deity is aware of the Psalmist's life – past, present, and future– and knows him personally. This Spirit-God exists beyond time and space, and, because He is omnipotent, he is able to invade and influence the course of human life. The Psalmist sees this God as the Covenant God of Israel who chose him and his fellow Jews.

This psalm is listed among the collection of eight Davidic Psalms (138-145) and it is listed among the so-called "Praise Psalms" (135-150).

### Segment One – God's Omniscience. Verses 1 - 6

The writer (probably David) exults in the fact that the All-powerful LORD of the universe has chosen him to be his Savior God. God's saving love has penetrated into his unconscious with an X-ray power that is able to examine his heart (his inner self). *(V.1)* The LORD has penetrated into David's inner being, his "psyche" (using modern terminology). The Hebrew word for this inmaterial part of humans is *("Nephesh")*. David is saying in this segment that God is omnipresent (everywhere present), omnipotent (all powerful), and omniscient (all-knowing). The LORD knows my every thought, and when I stand up and sit down. *(V.2)*

David then says that the LORD plans the paths that David is to take, when he should be active and when he should rest. *(V.3)* The LORD knows what David is going to say even before David speaks. *(V.4)* Because God is a divine Person, and not under the constraints of time and place, He is able

431

to enter the Psalmist's life as He sees fit. *(V.5)* God's awareness of David and God's consideration of him is too wonderful for David. *(V.6)* He feels blessed and is awed at the knowledge (insight) of such a wonderful God.

### Segment Two – An Omnipotent Spirit-God. Verses 7 - 12

Our author continues to reflect on God's ever-presence. He gleefully announces he cannot escape from the LORD's Spirit *(V.7)*, not in heaven or the place of the dead. *(V.8)* In the sky or the farthest oceans *(V.9)*, Your hand is there to guard me. *(V.10)* In the darkness night, I cannot hide from You. *(V.12)* Darkness is the Bible's symbol for evil. Christians know that God is light, there is no darkness in Him. *(1 John 1:5)*

### Segment Three – God the Creator. Verses 13 - 16

In the first two segments, the Psalmist praises the mystery of God's surrounding him with security in the outer world. In this section, he reflects on the awesome complexity of his brain and the inner workings of his body that, in his mother's womb, God had knit together. *(V.13)* He thanks God for making him so wonderfully complex! *(V.14)* He says that God the Creator formed him in utter seclusion in his mother's womb *(V.15)* and actually knew him before he was born. *(V.16)* Amazing!

### Segment Four – Precious Thoughts of the Creator God. Verses 17 - 18

Segment four is like a parentheses. The Psalmist is bowled over by the miraculous fact that God knew him even before he was born. He has trouble controlling his emotions. He literally sings out that God's thoughts about him are precious. *(V.17)* He says he cannot even count the times God has taken care of him. *(V.18)*

We Christians can have the same feelings of overwhelming gratitude when we read the wonderful words of the Apostle Paul in Romans in the New Testament. Paul says he is convinced that nothing can separate us from God's love–not death, life, angels, demons, our worries. God is with us through it all. *(Romans 8:38-39)*

## Segment Five – There Is Sin in the World So Destroy the Wicked. Verses 19 - 22

This could not be a psalm of David's without him complaining about the wicked. After allowing himself to be carried away with loving thoughts, he comes crashing down with the realization that there is human sin in the world! So he cries out and reminds God that He alone can destroy the wicked. *(V.19)* It is these sinners who ruin Your creation! Your perfect plan for our world is that men and women should live together in harmony and peace. The wicked destroy Your perfect plans. *(V.20)* Rhetorically David then asks God shouldn't David hate those who resist You? *(V.21)* David's indignation raises his blood pressure as he shouts that he does hate them, God's enemies are his enemies. *(V.22)*

## Segment Six – See if There Is Any Wickedness in Me. Verses 23 - 24

Suddenly, as he calms down, David is shocked as he realizes that every one is a sinner, and that includes himself, too! I am a sinner. It is my zeal for the LORD that drives and fuels my hatred. LORD God, I have a problem!

Our poet then asks God to test his thoughts and search his heart. *(V.23)* The Hebrew word for "heart" is *("Lebab")* which refers to his inner person, the seat of his will and his innermost feelings. Self chastised David asks God to point out what offends God about him and he will make restitution so he can have everlasting life. *(V.24)* I will change whatever needs to be changed. Humbly I ask for forgiveness for those things that offend You.

Realizing he is a sinner leads our humbled author to bow down to God. I am no better than anybody else. I have an exaggerated ego. In verse 24 the *New Living Translation* translates the Hebrew word *("Olam")* as "everlasting life," which gives the impression of a future life. This is confusing and not accurate. The word *("Olam")* more accurately means "the most distant past," or "from olden times." The prophet Jeremiah uses this same word *("Olam")* (and the NLT translates it as) "the old, gody way." *(Jeremiah 6:16)* The Hebrew word *("Olam")* does not mean "eternal life." The *Revised Standard Version* translants *("Olam")* in verse 24 of Psalm 139 as a "way everlasting or the ancient way."

433

# PSALM 140
## Prayers for Deliverance from Violent People

This is a prayer written by David or in imitiation of how David might write it. It is about people who practice evil for evil's sake, that is to say, they are vicious and incorrigible. It reminds us that we live in a fallen world filled with people who are basically oriented to themselves.

This psalm is listed among the collection of eight Davidic Psalms (138-145) and it is listed among the so-called "Praise Psalms" (135-150).

### Segment One – Preserve Me from Violent People. Verses 1 - 5

It is true that we live in an imperfect world. While we would like everything to be sweetness and light, that is not to be as long as we are sinners who sin to extreme and commit evil deeds. Without any self-control or inner discipline, we commit violent crimes of murder, rape, and robbery. These cruel individuals are the ones who stir up hatred and fear, and by their cruelty and self-centeredness, ultimately lead the world into unthinkable wars.

David was a strong leader able to make courageous and bold decisions, which caused much opposition. Consequently, he had many enemies throughout his life. David begins this psalm by asking the LORD to rescue him from evil people. (V.1) All day long they plot trouble. (V.2) David uses several metaphors to describe his evil enemies in many of his psalms. In Psalm 140 he compares them to a snake with posion dripping from their lips. (V.3) He probably was thinking about the Garden of Eden and how the serpent (the Devil) was able to poison Eve's mind into rebelling against God. (Genesis 3:1-6) David realizes how heinous and subtle these wicked people are, yet how two-faced and vicious – like a snake. He then says they treat him like an animal and would set traps to catch him. Many of his enemies are like hunters waiting in ambush to throw a net over him. *(V.5)*

## Segment Two – Destroy These Evil People. Verses 6 - 11

In this segment, David prays to God in an imprecatory manner asking the Sovereign LORD to protect him *(V.6-7)* and not to allow these self-centered and evil individuals to succeed or prosper. *(V.8-9)* Then he asks God to curse them and cause evil to fall upon them. David can be very vicious when he summons the LORD to deal with his enemies. On their heads burning coals should fall. *(V.10)* He asks God to bring disaster on them. *(V.11)*

This prayer is similar to Psalms 58 and 69. For example, in Psalm 58, the Psalmist, who probably also is David, asks God to break their fangs, and smash their jaws. *(Psalm 58:6-7)* He uses the metaphor of poisonous snakes in verse 5 of Psalm 58, (same as in verse 3 in the current psalm). In Psalm 69, David begs God to blind his enemies, consume them and erase them from the Book of Life. *(Psalm 69:23-28)* These imprecatory prayers implore God to curse and cause evil to fall upon the evil doers. In Psalm 140, David is asking the LORD to let the enemies' schemes boomerang! Turn their wicked plots back on themselves.

## Segment Three – We Can Count on the LORD. Verses 12 - 13

David's faith in God's Covenant Love toward those who love Him motivates David to exclaim that the LORD will help those who are persecuted and especially the poor. *(V.12)* And that includes himself and all those who live in the LORD's presence. *(V.13)*

When we Christians read David's psalms and see his prayers of imprecation, it shocks us. We must understand that David and his compatriots were children of his time. The Law of Moses was an eye-for-an-eye way of dealing with the world. When God sent Jesus to be the Messiah and our Savior, He promulgated a higher law. In His Sermon on the Mount (see Matthew Chapters 5-7), Matthew gives Jesus' teachings about revenge. Under law of Moses, Jesus says an eye lost requires an eye taken. But Jesus teaches us not to resist an evil person. *(Matthew 5:38)* Jesus goes on to teach us to love our enemies and pray for those who persecute us. Then we will be acting like children of God. *(Matthew 5:43)*

Jesus knew the world was filled with violent and arrogant individuals. He suffered at their hands mightily. But before He went to His death on the cross, He spoke to us Christians, saying He loves us like the Father loves Him and He asked his Disciples and us to remain in His love. The greatest love is when people lay down their lives for their friends. He ended His teaching by commanding us to love one another. *(John 15:9-17)*

# PSALM 141
## Help Against Temptation

This psalm is a prayer for deliverance from evil people and their ways of wickedness. The superscription says that David wrote the psalm. It is a lament where the author seeks God's help. This psalm is listed among the collection of eight Davidic Psalms (138-145) and it is listed among the so-called "Praise Psalms" (135-150).

It can be analyzed by dividing the prayer up into four parts: One, A Plea to the LORD, Verses 1-2; Two, A Prayer for Protection, Verses 3-4; Three, Disciplined by the Godly, Verses 5-7; and Four, The LORD is David's Refuge, Verses 8-10.

### Segment One – A Plea to the LORD. Verses 1 - 2

The Psalmist is eager to communicate with the LORD. Hurry up and listen to me. *(V.1)* He is not at the Temple where sweet-smelling "incense" *("Q toreth")* fills the air and the worshipers believe its fragrance goes up to the nostrils of God, making Him receptive to their requests. It's evening and our writer tells God that his inner heart (his inmost being) is using his prayer as a sacrifice. *(V.2)*

### Segment Two – A Prayer for Protection. Verses 3 - 4

It is interesting that David wants the LORD to help him control what he says and to help him keep secrets or perhaps not pass on gossip. *(V.3)* Obviously he is struggling inwardly. He apparently is lusting after some evil or acts of wickedness. *(V.4)* He is asking for purity of heart.

Jesus speaks of us being like trees that are identified by the kind of fruit we produce. He tells us that good people produce good deeds from a good heart. And then He adds that our heart determines what our mouths say. *(Luke 6:45)* This is similar when we Christians pray together in church on Sundays and ask the Lord that we not be led into temptation. *(Matthew 6:9-13)*

## Segment Three – Disciplined by the Godly. Verses 5 - 7

In this section, David is being quite mature when he says he can accept the rebukes of the godly because he knows they mean it benevolently. He considers it soothing medicine. *(V.5)* This is very close to the wisdom of Solomon when he writes that the LORD loves those who He disciplines. *(Proverbs 3:11-12)* The author of Psalm 141 reminds God that he is in constant prayer against the wicked and their evil deeds. *(V.5)* He wants the LORD to neutralize the evil that these people do. But then the more vicious side of David gets the upper hand. He looks forward to the leaders of the wicked being thrown over a cliff *(V.6)* and their bones being scattered without burial. *(V.7)*

## Segment Four – The LORD Is David's Refuge. Verses 8 - 10

As usual in a psalm by David, he looks to the LORD as his refuge and is fearful that he might be killed. *(V.8)* David trusts in the LORD's leadership. The Hebrew word for "trust" is *("Chacah")* and it means "have hope," and "make refuge." He seeks insight from the LORD on traps and snares the wicked are planning for him. *(V.9)* David ends the psalm asking the LORD to have his enemies seccumb to the very evil they plan for him.

Life is full of traps and snares to trip us up. But keeping our eyes on Jesus, the author of the Book of Hebrews writes (probably the Apostle Paul), will enable us to bypass many dangers. *(Hebrews 12:1-2)*

# PSALM 142
## Prayer for Deliverance from Enemies

The title says Psalm 142 is maskil of David involving his experience hidding in a cave. Maskil is a Hebrew word that means the psalm contains certain instruction in godliness. This short lament of seven verses is listed among the collection of eight Davidic Psalms (138-145) and it is listed among the so-called "Praise Psalms" (135-150).

There were two incidents in the Old Testament where David hid in a cave: one was at Adullam (see I Samuel 22); the other was at En Gedi (see 1 Samuel 24). Both times he was escaping from King Saul and his soldiers.

A little background from 1 Samuel 22 would be helpful: After killing Goliath, the Philistine giant, David entered the military service of King Saul. Because of David's God–given natural abilities and his rising fame, Saul's jealousy was provoked and he threatened to kill David. In defense, David fled for his life into the wilderness. He had no provisions and no following. Ahimelech, the priest at Nob, gave him food and a sword that once belonged to Goliath. As a result of this innocent kindness, Saul later had Ahimelech killed.

David then fled to the city of Gath, a Philistine stronghold, but that proved to be dangerous, so David once more goes into the wilderness and hides in a cave. It was in this cave where David wrote Psalm 57 and 142, two very similar poems. The trauma of being hunted and hated produced a tremendous strain on his faith. But as one writer said, his faith stretched but did not break!

### Segment One – David's Plea. Verses 1 - 2

We can understand the pressure David was under – isolated and alone – he pours out his troubles before God, pleading for the LORD's "mercy"

439

*("Checed"),* God's kindness and unfailing love. *(V.1)* But then he goes on to say he has complaints about how the LORD has permitted him to be so poorly treated. *(V.2)*

## Segment Two – David's Plight. Verses 3 - 4

Come on LORD you alone know what I should do and you are not letting me know. *(V.3)* David is pouring out his personal distress before the LORD, seeking God's help. In verse 4 he also is seeking help from friends or family but no one seems to be giving any thought about him at all. Notice the parallelism in these two verses. Essentially they say the same thing. This is a good example of Hebrew poetry.

But in time God did step in and protected David's life! His brothers and about 400 fighting men came to the cave and this formed the nucleus of David's army.

## Segment Three – David's Portion. Verses 5 - 6

This is really a second summit of faith, as David expresses his confidence in God in spite of his outward circumstances. He prays to God, saying that the LORD is really all I want in life. *(V.5)* But right now I need to be rescued! *(V.6)* In Psalm 57 (Psalm 142's companion piece), he says fierce lions with teeth that pierce like spears surround him. *(Psalm 57:4)*

Most of us will not be in a cave surrounded by ferocious enemies. But all of us, at times, will face sickness and/or other crises. In these times of anxiety we need to say with David only God can save me. For Christians God has sent us the Savior, and we need to take refuge in Jesus. He says to us that He will carry our heavy burdens. *(Matthew 11:28)* Jesus is offering us His yoke, where He will put His shoulder in the yoke along with us and will help us pull our load.

All of us are beholden to God. He is our refuge from troubles. But all of us are sinners, and, as such, we are subject to God's wrath. A far greater danger than any human danger. So how are we to escape God's wrath? Psalm 142 informs us that:

1. God is our place of refuge. *(V.5)*
2. God is our rescuer for things too strong for us. *(V.6)*
3. Our LORD will bring us out of our imprisonments. *(V.7)*

## Segment Four — Plea, Plight, Prison (finally) David's Prospect. Verse 7

The last part of this short psalm is where David asks God to help him escape from the cave, which he compares to a prison. *(V.7)* This is really <u>faith in action.</u> That is, David thanks God in advance for what he hopes God will accomplish for him. He knows the Prophet Samuel had anointed him to be king some day and so he anticipates a day when he will not only be king, but will enjoy the love and fellowship of God's people. That is the meaning of the final words of this psalm in which David looks forward to godly people surrounding him and treating him kindly. *(V.7)*

We Christians who read the psalms can find wonderful truths that can help us in our walk with the Lord. However, reading the psalms from a Christian perspective is like the icing on the cake. We all get into certain caves or prison houses at times in our lives – not necessarily of our own making, and when we find ourselves in these situations, we need the resources of the Bible to fortify our souls. A good passage that is very inspirational is from the fourth chapter of the Book of Hebrews in the New Testament. It says our High Priest (Jesus) understands we are weak and subject to temptations. But we should not be afraid but should come boldly before his throne and receive His mercy and find the grace to help us in our needs. *(Hebrews 4:15-16)*

Question: do you feel alone? Are there times when you feel deserted by your friends? The wonderful message of our Christian faith is that when Jesus died on the cross, God loved Him (and us) so much that He raised Him from death, and set His Spirit free from the limitations of time and space. What that means is His Spirit of love and forgiveness can come to us at any time and any place (even caves!). It tells us that Jesus will never desert His own. His Spirit will be with us in our time of need. All it requires is for us to have faith in Him and be receptive to His love and Holy Spirit.

# PSALM 143

## Compared with the LORD, No One Is Perfect

Psalm 143 is the seventh and final "Penitential Psalm." They are Psalms 6, 32, 38, 51, 102, 130 and 143. The Book of Common Prayer lists these psalms as suitable for reading on Ash Wednesday, the beginning of Lent. The title says this is a psalm of David. It is a prayer for deliverance from his enemies and asks God for divine direction in life.

This psalm is listed among the collection of eight Davidic Psalms (138-145) and it is listed among the so-called "Praise Psalms" (135-150).

### Segment One – A Plea for Mercy. Verses 1 - 2

David is staking his whole being on the conviction that the LORD never reneges on His promises. David's faith is centered in God's Covenant that He made with the Hebrew people, where God said He is the LORD, merciful and gracious, slow to anger and rich in faithfulness. *(Exodus 34:6)* In verse 1 of Psalm 143, David reminds the LORD that He must answer him because the LORD is faithful. The Hebrew word *("Emunah")* means "faithful."

David knew the Scriptures *("Torah")* and he probably thought back to Deuteronomy and Moses' words describing God as a rock, perfect in His work, just and fair. *(Deuteronomy 32:3-4)* With these words in mind, David begs God not to bring him to trial (that is, to judge him) because he knows there is no way he can measure up to the sinless and all-powerful God of the Universe! No one is perfect compared with You. *(V.2)* The Hebrew word for "perfect" is *("Ts daqah")* which can also mean "righteous."

For us Christians, we are aware of the Apostle Paul's words in Romans. In chapter three, he says not even one of us is good and without sin. *(Romans 3:10)* and then Paul adds that God shows us a different way to be right or perfect in His sight. Our trust and belief in Jesus Christ makes us right and sinless to the Father. *(Romans 3:21-24)*

## Segment Two – Living in Darkness. Verses 3 - 4

In these two verses (3 and 4), David tells us some of the unpleasant circumstances about which he is pleading for mercy. His enemies force him to live in darkness and paralyze him with fear. David's many psalms are filled with enemies who are attempting to harm or destroy him. For example, Psalm 18 was written at a time when the LORD delivered David from many enemies, including Saul. In Psalm 18, David writes that floods of destruction sweep over him and death itself stares him in the face. *(Psalm 18:4-5)* In Psalm 143, David tells us how his current enemies knocked him to ground, to the very grave. *(V.3)*

## Segment Three – Reaching Out to the LORD. Verses 5 - 6

However, David is alive enough to recall the LORD's mighty miracles. He stops worrying about his own troubles and puts his mind on all the LORD's great works. *(V.5)* He thinks about all God has done, like bringing His people out of slavery from Egypt. In remembering, David feels much better and reaches out to God. He says I am a parched land that thirsts for You. *(V.6)*

## Segment Four – Show Me Where to Walk, LORD. Verses 7 - 12

But things get worse, not better. David cries out come quickly, LORD, I am about to die. *(V.7)* David pleads with the LORD. Show me what to do! *(V.8)* Show me where to hide. *(V.9)* Lead me where to go. *(V.10)* Do this for me for the glory of Your Name. *(V.11)* We know from hindsight that God did bring David out of whatever trouble he was in at the writing of this psalm, and many other difficulties like the rebellion of his son, Absalom. The last verse of this psalm says he is trusting in the LORD's unfailing love because He is the LORD's servant. *(V.12)* The Hebrew word for "servant" is *("Ebed")*.

Also using hindsight, we know God did act for all of us Christians as well. He worked His wonderful plan for the salvation of the world by sending His Son, Jesus, to be born in Bethlehem, in the lineage of David. As the

Apostle's Creed puts it Jesus was born of Mary, crucified, buried, ascended into heaven and sits on the right hand the Father Almighty. As a follower of Jesus, our task is to put aside out selfish ambitions, shoulder our crosses and follow Jesus. As Jesus tells us we will lose our live if we try to keep it for ourselves, Better to lose if for Jesus and find true eternal life. *(Matthew 16:25-26)*

# PSALM 144

## Prayer for the Rescue of a King and a Picture of a Happy Land

Psalm 144 would appear to be two separate prayers. The first, verses 1 – 11, are a request for deliverance from enemies. The second group of verses, 12 – 15, is a description of a peaceful world. The editors have placed the title of David on this psalm. Verses 1 – 11 are quite similar to Psalm 18, an early composition by David, and perhaps this is why Psalm 144 is attributed to him. These verses also seem to be a composite of verses from other psalms, notably from Psalm 8, 18, 33 and 39. The first prayer is characterized as a lament. The second prayer is written in the style of wisdom literature.

This psalm is listed among the collection of eight Davidic Psalms (138-145) and it is listed among the so-called "Praise Psalms" (135-150).

### Segment One – Prayer for Divine Help as a Warrior. Verses 1 - 2

The psalm begins with David (or someone writing as if he were David) thanking the LORD for gving him skill in battle and being a rock of strength to him. (V.1) The writer quotes from 2 Samuel 22:1-3 and Psalm 18:2. In both of these the word "rock" is used. Verse 2 of Psalm 144 uses the words "fortress," tower," and "shield." These are metaphors often used by David in his many writings to describe God's protective care.

### Segment Two – Human Life Is Transitory. Verses 3 - 4

The writer has put together thoughts from Psalm 8:5 and 39:5-6. He is overwhelmed by the sheer majesty and power of God, who nevertheless cares for mere human beings and thinks of them. (V.3) Psalm 8 says that God made humans a little lower than God. (Psalm 5:4-5) Psalm 144 verse

4 says we human beings are as emphemeral as a breath of air. Psalm 39: 5-6 says the Psalmist's life is but a breath, a moving shadow, his efforts are busy but end in nothing.

## Segment Three – Bend Down and Scatter Your Enemies. Verses 5 - 8

The author pleads with the Almighty to bend down from heaven and send lightning bolts against the enemies of God and the Psalmist. *(V.5-6)* It would appear that the writer is borrowing from Psalm 18 (and others) where the Psalmist (probably David) asks God to send fierce flames to consume David's enemies. *(Psalm 18: 7-9)* This obviously is a replay of the LORD coming down at Mount Sinai in the days of Moses amid thunder and lightning with the thought just maybe God would do it again. Also, our writer in Psalm 144 is updating old psalms. He is thinking of the exodus from slavery, and personally he prays for God to deliver him from deep waters. *(Psalm 144:7)* All these verses in this segment are transplants from other psalms (see Psalm 12:5 and 69:1-4).

## Segment Four – Sing to Celebrate Future Victories. Verses 9 - 11

Our Psalmist borrows from other psalms like 33:2-3, 96:1 and others, and invites us readers to join him in singing a New Song to God. *(V.9)* Songs of old are based on what happened to King David, and how he conquered the neighboring countries and made Israel great. But this New Song recognizes that the Psalmist needs to be protected from his enemies. *(V.11)* But this New Song in verses 12 to 15 are also ones more fitting to the changed circumstances of the atomic age in America and the rest of the modern world.

## Segment Five – The Blessings of Peace. Verses 12 - 15

In this segment there doesn't seem to be much connection with what has gone on before, unless the Psalmist is projecting victories of a military nature that will end all future wars. Speaking perhaps as King David, the Psalmist seeks blesses for the nation itself. He asks that the nation's sons flourish, the daughters be graceful, the farms be filled with every crop and flocks, and Jerusalem's walls be unbreachable. *(V.12-14)* The Prophet Isaiah predicted that in the last days many nations will come to Jerusalem to worship and the LORD Himself with settle disputes for all nations. *(Isaiah 2:2-5)*

The Good News is that God has actually made provisions for all who would come to Him in Christ Jesus. This wonderful God who worked out His plan to save us all, loved the world so much that anyone who believes in Jesus will not perish but have eternal life. *(John 3:18)*

This picture of bliss in verses 12 to 15 will indeed be a reality for those of us who have the Spirit of Jesus living in our hearts. We are invited to attend the wedding feast of the Lamb. We can look forward to a time when we can look and see the heavens open and Jesus come down to earth and judge all people of all nations. *(Revelation 19:11-16)*

Those of us Christians who belong to Christ's Church here on earth know a foretaste of heaven. We are Jesus' Covenant people and we love our Christian brothers and sisters. Admittedly our love is imperfect, but we all look forward to going to heaven and being with God and Jesus and all the Saints who are His. For Christians death is not something we fear; no, we look forward to that time when we will be with God and there will be no death, sorrow, crying or pain. *(Revelation 21:4)* The exciting part of knowing that life doesn't end at death is that this takes all the anxiety and fear out of it.

# PSALM 145
## A Hymn of Praise to God Our King

The superscription calls Psalm 145 a psalm of praise of David. A "hymn of praise" in Hebrew is a *("Tehillah")*. This is a hymn used for public worship, both in the Hebrew daily liturgy, and it is also in use with the Common Lectionary in the Christian church. The psalm methodically describes the attributes of the LORD and how He has and continues to take care of his chosen people. This psalm is the last among the collection of eight Davidic Psalms (138-145) and it is listed among the so-called "Praise Psalms" (135-150).

Psalm 145 is another acrostic poem, meaning that each line starts with a word beginning with a consecutive letter of the Hebrew alphabet. You'll notice that there are only 21 lines corresponding with 21 lines of the Hebrew alphabet. The Hebrew alphabet has 22 letters. The letter *"Nun"* is missing. In the *New Living Translation* the last two lines in verse 13 have been added, which might have accounted for the original 22 verses of the psalm. These lines are not found in many of the ancient manuscripts. The *NLT* copied the missing lines from the Masoretic text.

David starts right off praising God as King. *(V.1)* He says he will bless God every day. *(V.2)* In verse 3, he uses the familiar phrase the LORD is great. This phrase also appears in psalm 96:4, which deals with the kingship of God. In verses 4 through 7, David exhorts each generation to teach their children of the LORD's mighty deeds *(V.4)*, says he will meditate on the LORD's miracles *(V.5)*, His awe-inspring deeds will be recounted throughout the world *(V.6)*, and everyone will share stories of the LORD's goodness. *(V.7)* Throughout this hymn are words of inspiration and hope. Like Psalm 103, David goes to Exodus 34:6 as his model and writes the LORD is slow to anger and full of love. *(V.8-9)* The theme of kingship is repeated in verses 10 – 12. David tells us that God's faithful followers *(V.10)* will talk about God's glorious kingdom *(V.11)* and about God's power and mighty deeds. *(V.12)*

The Psalmist points out that the LORD's kingdom is everlasting. *(V.13)* For those carrying heavy loads, the LORD helps lift them. *(V.14)* The LORD opens His omnipotent hand and provides food and water for all living creatures.00 *(V.15-16)* In verses 17 – 20, this kind and righteous king listens to everyone who calls on Him with a sincere heart. *(V.18)* He also rescues and protects those who love Him. *(V.20)* David brings his helpful hymn to a climax with the repetition of his beginning words, proclaiming that he will and everyone on earth will praise the LORD. *(V.21)*

This inspired word of God was placed in its present position in the Psalter by some post-exilic Priest-Editor to be a fitting overture to the five "Hallelujah Psalms" that end Book Five.

# PSALM 146
## Placing One's Hope in the LORD

The Psalter ends with five "Hallelujah Psalms." Psalm 146 is the first of these. This psalm is listed among the so-called "Praise Psalms" (135-150).

This psalm acts as a teaching hymn and, like Psalms 103 and 104, it begins with "praise" *("Hala")* and the author telling "himself" *("Nephesh")* to "praise" *("Hala")* the LORD. He vows to continue praising even with his last breath. *(V.2)* In verses 3 and 4, the Psalmist warns the reader not to put his confidence in people who are powerful *(V.3)* because like everyone else they will die and their plans will die with them. *(V.4)* In contrast those who put their trust in the God of Isreal will be blessed for God will help them. *(V.5)* Then there follows a series of reasons for trusting in the LORD:

1.  God is the powerful Creator. *(V.6)*
2.  He keeps His promises forever. *(V.6)*
3.  God frees the prisoners. *(V.7)*
4.  He causes the blind to see. *(V.8)*
5.  He lifts burdens. *(V.8)*
6.  He loves the righteous. *(V.8)*
7.  Protects the strangers in our midst. *(V.9)*
8.  Cares for widows and orphans. *(V.9)*
9.  Frustrates the plans of the wicked. *(V.9)*

The climax of this teaching comes in verse 10. It says we should put our hope and trust in God not only for the nine reasons stated above, but also because we have confidence in God for salvation and because the LORD is eternal.

This teaching hymn was to be sung by the congregation in the newly constructed Second Temple. As people sang its words and placed their trust in God, they would be learning to follow God's leading, to be like Him and do what God does.

As we Christians read these psalms, we are helped to understand God's character. We are to love God and praise Him, not only with our lips but also with our lives! We believe God inspired the writers of these psalms aided and abated by the Prophets and the Torah. We further believe that God acted supremely by sending His Son, Jesus, to be our Savior. Jesus went to the cross and became a sacrifice for our sins, a sin offering to make us right with God. *(2 Corinthians 5:21)* And we know that those who become Christians are born again, become new persons. And all this newnest of life is brought to us through what Christ did. *(2 Corinthians 5:17-18)* When we bring Jesus' Spirit into our hearts, we become new persons, new creations. And God gives us the task of becoming His Ambassadors, which entails telling others about this Good News.

# PSALM 147
## Singing Praises Is Delightful and Right!

This "Hallelujah Psalm (the second of five) is a hymn written for the Jerusalem congregation in the Second Temple. Obviously it was composed in the period of restoration after the exile. This psalm is listed among the so-called "Praise Psalms" (135-150).

### Segment One – Praise the LORD for Restoring Our Land. Verses 1 - 6

Our author begins Psalm 147 by saying he derives supreme satisfaction and joy from praising God. *(V.1)* He is also thankful that the LORD is bringing back exiles to Israel and rebuilding Jerusalem. *(V.2)* God, who is mighty, has made this return possible. He also is binding up the broken hearts of His people. *(V.3)* Our Psalmist takes a little poetic liberty and sings, God counts and names each star. *(V.4)* The Psalmist sings in superlatives: His power is absolute and His understanding beyond comprehension. *(V.5)* The Psalmist concludes this section by reminding the former exiles and, perhaps God Himself, that God pushes the wicked down into dust. *(V.6)*

### Segment Two – Praise the LORD for All He Does for the World. Verses 7 - 11

In this segment, we are again instructed to sing and give thanks to the LORD. *(V.7)* Our delight is for all the LORD does for our world of nature. He makes grass grow *(V.8)* and feeds wild animals and young ravens. *(V.9)* He delights in those who put their hopes in Him. *(V.11)* In verses 9, our writer says he feeds the young ravens which reminds us Christians of Jesus's words in the New Testament: Jesus instructed us not to worry about everyday life. He says look to the ravens they neither plant nor harvest because God feeds them. Then looking at those listening to Him, Jesus says you are far more valuable to God than birds. (*Luke12: 22-25*)

## Segment Three – Praise the LORD for Giving Us Security. Verses 12 - 18

In Segments three the Psalmist's praises the LORD for Jerusalem (*V.12*) and the security that God gives the beleaguered Israelites who have returned from exile. (*V.13*) He provides inhabitants of Zion with peace and well being. (*V.14*) But He is also the LORD of the world. What God orders with His Word takes place in the world. (*V.15*) He sends snow (*V.16*), He hurls hail like stones (*V.17*), His wind thaws ice. (*V.18*)

We Christians can identify with the power of the Word of God. The Book of Hebrews in the New Testament speaks of two things that Psalm 147 implies: (1) God's Word is mighty. The Book of Hebrews says God's Word is full of living power. It cuts deep into our innermost thoughts and desires. (*Hebrews 4:12-13*) And (2) God is always with those of us who love Him. He will not forsake us.

## Segment Four – The Principles and Laws of God. Verses 19 - 20

Segment four ends with the Psalmist rejoicing in the LORD's taking special interest in Israel and providing its people with principles and laws. (*V.19*) The LORD did this for no other nation. (*V.20*) It was God's decrees and statutes that set the Israelites apart from all other peoples. In Deuteronomy the LORD informs the Hebrews if they obey His decrees and statutes their wisdom and intelligence will be acknowledged by other nations. (*Deuteronomy 4:6*) The Torah became the essence or the most significant form of the Word for Israel. For Christians, we appreciate God's gift of the law (the Ten Commandments), but we in the church see God's' gift of His Son, Jesus, as the epitome of the the Word, the Good News!

# PSALM 148

## An Invitation for all Creatures to Praise God

Psalm 148 is another hymn, the third in a series of "Hallelujah Psalms." *"Hallelu"* = is a summons to praise and *"juh"* = is an abbreviation for Jahweh, the informal name of Jehovah God (the LORD). This composition is a carefully crafted song inviting every spiritual, living creature and inanimate thing to give honor to the Creator God. In between the bookends of the phrase *"Praise the LORD,"* there are two distinct sections. In the first part (verses 1-5), the summons to praise is for those beings and things in the heavenly realm—for angels, sun, moon, stars and clouds. Praise Him from the heavens and skies. *(V.1)* Angels are to praise Him. *(V.2)* Sun, moon, stars and clouds are to praise Him. *(V.3-4)* Finally all created things are to praise Him. *(V.5)*

The second section (verses 7-13), the invitation to praise God is given to the beings and things on earth—creatures in the ocean, weather, mountians, hills, trees, livestock, kings, judges, men, women and children. All are exhorted to lift their voices and praise God. And finally and most importantly for this Psalmist, the people of Israel, His godly ones, are to praise the LORD. *(V.14)*

This psalm is listed among the so-called "Praise Psalms" (135-150).

A well-known hymn by Francis of Assisi says, "All creatures of our God and King, Lift up your voice and with us sing, Alleluia!" This sets the tone for this psalm. Verse 13 especially lets us know that God dwells outside the scope of our being. It says the LORD's glory towers over heaven and earth.

The Psalm ends in verse 14 by bringing the focus back on Israel. The LORD made His people strong, the people of Israel who are most close to Him. Obviously this encouraged the Jewish people to rely on the moral and spiritual strength of their Divine hertiage and to be faithful to their Covenant obligations, so that God can honor them.

All of the five final "Hallelujah Psalms" that close out Book Five of the Psalter were composed during the period of restoration. They all praise God for the miracle of Israel's physical deliverance from bondage in Babylon back to their homeland in Jerusalem. This miracle was on a par, if not greater, than any of the other mighty works of God in the Old Testament.

Reviewing some background: We must remember that God claimed Israel as His own people. In Exodus, the LORD made a covenant with them. Speaking through Moses, God told them how He carried them on Eagles' wings, bringing them back from slavery in Egypt. He said the Hebrews would be His special treasure among all the nations if they kept His Covenant. (Exodus 15:5) In plain language it is clear that God chose the Jews to keep His commandments and to perform priestly functions. What does this mean? To answer this question, we turn to the great Prophet Isaiah, whom God chose to be His spokesman. I, the LORD, Isaiah writes in speaking for the LORD, have selected you to be a light to guide all other nations. How can you do that? By keeping My commandments. (Isaiah 42.6) In gratitude the returnees from Babylon rebuilt Jerusalem and reconstructed the Temple. These were the "godly ones," God's ("Yasha"), His "redeemed," spoken of in Paslm 148:14. He empowered them with His Spirit and gave them a righteousness not of their own. This made them safe and secure.

With this new stance, they were expected to demonstrate God's righteousness and His love to others. When they turned to share God's love with others, their gift of ("Yasha") became ("Ye shuw ah") (Yesh-oo-ah) (the feminine form). God's Spirit was empowering His chosen returnees to feel safe (saved) and to motivate them to take God's love to others, thus fulfilling Isaiah's words.

Unfortunately, by the time of Jesus, much of the motivation to take their faith to others and to becoming a light to the Gentiles had all but died. Sadly, a narrow Legalism claimed Israel.

455

# PSALM 149

## A Hymn of Preparation for a Holy War

This is number four of the five "Hallelujah Psalms." All five begin and end with praising the LORD. This psalm is listed among the so-called "Praise Psalms" (135-150). Following this liturgical cry, the psalm says we are to sing a new song to the LORD. *(V.1)* Each generation has to find new expressions for praising the LORD because God reveals Himself differently with each generation. The new song sung by God's faithful people of the Second Temple was for them to be prepared to execute the LORD's vengeance on all nations. *(V.7)* They are to be ready to fight the battles of the LORD against the evils of the world.

We must remember that Psalm 149 was written following the return of the exiles from two generations of torturous humiliation and slavery in Babylon. Wrath and revenge were not only on the returnees' lips, but these thoughts were in the writings of the Prophets, which spoke of judgment against the LORD's enemies. The great Prophet Isaiah, speaking for God, says that in God's anger He will stump on His enemies as if they were grapes. *(Isaiah 63:3)* (This is the scriptural passage that inspired Harriet Beecher Stowe to write her Civil War hymn "The Battle Hymn of the Republic.") Isaiah adds that it was time for the LORD to avenge His people. *(Isaiah 63: 4)* Nations and their rulers were perceived as the opposition to the reign of God. The faithful in this psalm are being called to praise God with a sharp mouth and a sharp sword in their hands. *(V.6)*

Psalm 149 can be examined by dividing it into two main sections.

## Segment One – Singing Praises by the Faithful. Verses 1 - 5

This psalm along typically with many of the other "Kingship Psalms," like 95 and 96, challenges the chosen people to rejoice in the LORD with singing *(V.1-2)*, and dancing accompanied by harp and tamourine. *(V.3)* The Psalmist then reminds the people that the LORD blesses the humble so don't get too carried away. *(V.5)*

## Segment Two – Praise and Militancy! Verses 6 - 9

In verse 6, our Psalmist tells the world that God's faithful will praise the LORD by preparing for battle against His enemies. Verses 7 and 8 instructs the faithful to punish the people of other nations and put shackles on their kings. This was in keeping with the prophecy of Micah in which he exhorts the Jews to destroy the nations, trample many into small pieces. *(Micah 4:13)* Verse 9 instructs the faithful to execute the "judgment"*("Mishpat")* that the prophets had written against the other nations.

The Prophets expressed much of the accepted thought of Israel's future. They said that a coming anointed messianic King would militarily free Israel from her oppressors and would establish the Kingdom, which would be governed from Zion.

For Christians, we also want to sing a new song to the Lord. But our song is praise to God for sending the world His Son, Jesus Christ. We believe Jesus is the true Messiah! God sent Him to earth to announce the coming of the Kingdom. And by means of His death and resurrection, God bestows on those of us who put our faith and trust in Him, not only inner peace, but also that we will have the promise of life eternal. (See John 3:16.) Our ministry here on earth is to become Christ's ambassadors. For God has given us the task first presented to the Hebrews of reconciling people to God. *(2 Corinthians 5:18-21)* We are also called to be peacemakers. (See Matthew 5:9.)

Just before Judas came to arrest Jesus with a mob armed with swords and clubs, the impetuous Peter pulled a short sword out of his tunic and slashed the ear off the High Priest's servant. With this, Jesus stepped forth and said to Peter to put his sword away for those who use the sword will die by the sword. *(Matthew 16:53)* Jesus' words ring true. Although we live in a fallen world, there are conflicts that arise on a personal level as well as among nations. Jesus knew that violence was a reality. Jesus prophesied that until He return again nations will war against one another. *(Matthew 24:7)* But wars that are started in God's name always end in disaster. Although many metaphors are used utilizing militarism in the New Testament, love, peace and forgiveness are the important ideals by which we are to live. As Christians, we don't wage war with human plans and methods. Rather, as the Apostle Paul tells us, we are to use God's weapons. God's weapons will conquer rebellious ideas. Chief among these weapons is teaching the wicked to obey Christ. *(2 Corinthians 10:3-5)*

# PSALM 150

## All Living Creatures Need to Praise the Lord!

This is the fifth and final "Hallelujah Psalm" in the Jewish Song Book (the Psalter). This psalm is listed among the so-called "Praise Psalms" (135-150). Psalm 150 is the last crescendo of praise for God's mighty works. *(V.2)* The Old Testament started with charismatic characters such as Abraham, Moses and David, and it goes on and finally reaches a climax by inviting every creature that "lives" *("N shamah")* to sing the LORD's praises. *(V.6)*

Like the four preceding "Hallelujah Psalms," Psalm 150's verses are arranged in praise sentences.

1.  Praise the LORD in his heavenly habitation.
2.  Praise His mighty works.
3.  Praise the LORD with musical instruments.
4.  Praise with tambourine, dancing, stringed instruments and flutes!
5.  Praise Him with cymbals.
6.  Let everything that lives praise the LORD.

To help us better examine this wonderful hymn of praise, we need to ask and answer four important defining questions. They are:

1.  WHO is to be praised? Answer: *("El")* the LORD *(Psalm 150:1)* His power is absolute! *(Psalm 147:5)* He is merciful and slow to anger. *(Psalm 145:8)* He is the creator of all things in heaven and earth who gives justice. *(Psalm 146:6-7)*
2.  WHY are we praising Him? Answer: For his mighty works. *(Psalm 150:2)* He will reign forever. *(Psalm 146:10)* He gave us His

principles and laws. *(Psalm 147:19)* He is close to His people Israel. *(Psalm 148:14)*

3. HOW are we to praise God? Answer: With instruments and dancing. *(Psalm 150:3-5)* Singing accompanied by harps. *(Psalm 147:7)* Dancing accompanied with harp and tambourine. *(Psalm 149:3)*

4. WHO is to do the praising? Answer: The assembly of the faithful. *(Psalm 149:1-2)* In particular young men and maidens, old men and old women and children. *(Psalm 148:12-13)* All who live in Jerusalem, Zion. *(Psalm 147:12)*

We Christians can join in with our Jewish brothers and sisters in singing praises to the Living God. This is no mere pious mouthing of words and music. We can wholeheartedly praise the Living God with the perspective that we are aware of the cost of our salvation. At the heart of our worship is A CROSS! It cost the mighty God the suffering and death of His only Son, Jesus. We celebrate and praise Him for His wonderful plan of salvation not only for us, but also for God's amazing plan for the salvation of the whole world!

Praise the LORD!!!

# ABOUT THE AUTHOR

Rev. Dr. George L. Earnshaw was son of legendary baseball pitcher George "Moose" Earnshaw, foot solider in the Pacific during WWII, received an undergraduate degree from Penn State, attended seminary at Colgate Rochester Crozer Divinity School and obtained a PH. D. in psychology. He was chaplain at various universities, minister at various churches, worked with Rev. Dr. Billy Graham.

Printed in the United States
By Bookmasters